Voluntary Regulation of Advertising

Voluntary Regulation of Advertising

A Comparative Analysis of the
United Kingdom and the United States

Gordon E. Miracle
Michigan State University

Terence Nevett
Central Michigan University

Lexington Books
D.C. Heath and Company/Lexington, Massachusetts/Toronto

Library of Congress Cataloging-in-Publication Data

Miracle, Gordon E.
  Voluntary regulation of advertising.

  Includes bibliographies and index.
    1. Advertising—United States—Self-
regulation.   2. Advertising—Great Britain—Self-
regulation.   3. Advertising laws—United
States.   4. Advertising laws—Great
Britain.   I. Nevett, T.R. (Terence R.)   II. Title.
HF5834.M57   1987   338.4′76591′0941   86-45294
ISBN 0-669-13135-0 (alk. paper)

Published simultaneously in Canada
Printed in the United States of America
International Standard Book Number: 0-669-13135-0
Library of Congress Catalog Card Number: 86-45294

The paper used in this publication meets the minimum requirements
of American National Standard for Information Sciences—
Permanence of Paper for Printed Library Materials, ANSI
Z39.48-1984. ♾ ™

87   88   89   90   8   7   6   5   4   3   2   1

Contents

6. An Assessment of Performance: The United States 193

7. An Assessment of Performance: The United Kingdom 235

8. Conclusions and Recommendations 265

Figures and Tables

Figures

Tables

Summary of Recommendations

Abbreviations

AA	Advertising Association
AAAA	American Association of Advertising Agencies
AAF	American Advertising Federation (previously the AFA)
AAW	Advertising Association of the West
ABBB	Association of Better Business Bureaus
AFA	American Federation of Advertisers (now the AAF)
AID	Advertising Investigation Department
AIRC	Association of Independent Radio Contractors
ANA	Association of National Advertisers
ARC	Advertising Review Committee
ARF	Advertising Research Foundation
ASA	Advertising Standards Authority
ASBOF	Advertising Standards Board of Finance
BBB	Better Business Bureau
BCAP	*British Code of Advertising Practice*
BCSPP	*British Code of Sales Promotion Practice*
BTA	British Transport Advertising
CA	Consumers Association
CAA	Cinema Advertising Association
CAP	Code of Advertising Practice
CARU	Children's Advertising Review Unit

CBBB	Council of Better Business Bureaus
CFA	Consumer Federation of America
DGFT	Director General of Fair Trading
EEC	European Economic Community
FCC	Federal Communications Commission
FDA	Food and Drug Administration
FTC	Federal Trade Commission
IBA	Independent Broadcasting Authority
ICAP	*International Code of Advertising Practice*
ICC	International Chamber of Commerce
IPA	Institute of Practitioners in Advertising
IRS	Internal Revenue Service
ISBA	Incorporated Society of British Advertisers
ITA	Independent Television Authority
ITCA	Independent Television Companies Association
LARB	Local Advertising Review Board
LARP	Local Advertising Review Programs
LTA	London Transport Advertising
MOPS	Mail Order Protection Scheme
NAB	National Assocation of Broadcasters
NAD/NARB	National Advertising Division/National Advertising Review Board
NARC	National Advertising Review Council
NBBB	National Better Business Bureaus
NCB	National Consumer Board
NCC	National Consumer Council
NPA	Newspapers Publishers Association
NS	Newspaper Society
OAA	Outdoor Advertising Association

OFT	Office of Fair Trading
OTC	Over the counter
PAGB	Proprietary Association of Great Britain
SCAPA	National Society for Controlling the Abuses of Public Advertising
SEC	Securities and Exchange Commission
SFD	Society of Film Distributors
TRR	Trade Regulation Rules
WFA	World Federation of Advertisers (previously the International Union of Advertisers Associations)

Foreword

This is an important and authoritative book. It compares two of the world's most sophisticated systems of self-regulation of advertising. This is a complex subject relying, as it does, on both the written codes and the interpretation of the spirit of the codes by ever-changing groups of regulators who fortunately work within set-down parameters.

My seven years as an ASA Council member taught me that the most difficult areas are those that call for subjective judgements and are vulnerable to endless debate. However, we have here a comprehensive description of the two systems with detailed comparisons, a historical profile of each, the relationship between advertising law and advertising self-regulation, an appraisal of the industry's codes and standards, and an assessment of their effectiveness. Additionally, the last chapter draws on the lessons learned so far and makes important recommendations for future action.

This book is timely in that both in the United Kingdom and in the United States there is a proliferation of codes in order to meet the needs of the new areas of advertising, such as television via satellite and cable, radio developments, direct response, and so on. Special categories of advertising with special arrangements and codes have been developed in areas where the general provisions of the existing codes need to be supplemented. For example:

Financial services

Tobacco products

Alcoholic drinks

Medicines and treatments

Food products

Special audiences such as children or particular ethnic groups, as well as men and women as stereotypes.

This book, therefore, is a comprehensive guide to the current working of the codes, and it makes a tremendous contribution to current thinking.

—*A.E. Pitcher*
President, Ogilvy & Mather, London
Director General, Periodical Publishers
Association, London

Preface

In recent decades, consumers and governments in many of the most economically developed nations of the world have become increasingly interested in the question of advertising control. Correspondingly, the advertising industries in many of these countries have become increasingly interested in voluntarily regulating themselves. Some of the self-regulatory systems that have been established have now reached what might be termed a fairly mature stage, after fifteen or more years of operation. Two of these, in the United Kingdom and the United States, have been selected for study and comparison because their experience, compared and contrasted, may hold lessons for themselves and others.

Advertising is controversial. Some believe it manipulates and misleads consumers, and causes serious harm to society; others believe advertising can do almost no wrong, and that it is an integral part of business, economic, and social activity. There are many shades of opinion in between—and complex variations and combinations of such viewpoints. Consequently there have long been pressures to regulate perceived advertising abuses, and conversely to protect advertising from such regulation. The diversity of viewpoints and calls for action seem sure to continue.

This book is about restrictions on advertising in the United Kingdom and the United States—primarily industry-imposed restrictions. It includes brief information on conditions under which advertising operates in the two nations, historical perspectives on advertising regulation, the evolution and development of the self-regulatory systems to their current state, the codes and standards that emerged and remain, an evaluation of the performance of each self-regulatory system, and a set of conclusions and recommendations.

The purpose of this study is to compare the advertising self-regulatory systems in the United Kingdom and the United States along the above dimensions. Comparative analysis can be a powerful tool. It is useful not only in helping us understand the differences and similarities between the subjects being studied, but also in enabling us to gain deeper insights into the subjects themselves. This in turn helps us understand the reasons for the differences and similarities, and leads to questions (and answers) as to whether either of the systems might be improved in some way.

Advertisers and advertising agencies that operate in the United Kingdom and the United States need comparative information on advertising self-regulation to operate effectively within each system, and within the law and within the social norms that each regulatory system reflects. And they need such information to make judgments as to what actions they might take to improve each self-regulatory system. Likewise, those in government who make or enforce public policy, or those who apply the rules of each regulatory system, need a deep understanding of their own system to make and enforce such policy effectively, and to know when and how to help the system evolve in accordance with the changing forces in society that shape the system. Additionally the study should interest consumer group leaders, as well as university educators and their students, some of whom will pursue careers in the just mentioned organizations.

Before the similarities and differences and the reasons for them can be specified one must understand each system separately. The deeper understandings from the comparisons emerge later. Therefore this study includes considerable information on each self-regulatory system and the relationships between the self-regulatory system and relevant cultural, economic, legal, political, social, and technological developments in each society.

The relationships between advertising self-regulation and the characteristics of each society are complex. In a broad sense the law reflects such characteristics, with a time lag. For example, a change of government that brings another political party into power or rapid technological changes in mass media, may well lead eventually to changes in advertising regulation. Discussion of such topics is integrated, as appropriate, into the main body of the book. However, the law is such a fundamental determinant of an advertising self-regulatory system that it is necessary to give it special treatment.

Advertising may be controlled or regulated at several levels in a nation: (1) federal, (2) state or county, and (3) local. At each of these levels there may be five main types of interrelated regulatory activities: (1) legislation; (2) administrative law and policies of enforcement agencies; (3) court decisions; (4) industry self-regulation; and (5) combinations of these, sometimes with other organizations, people, or institutions.

The impetus for organizing a centralized voluntary or self-regulatory system can stem from several sources, for example: (1) advertisers, (2) advertising agencies, (3) advertising media, (4) business groups such as Better Business Bureaus or chambers of commerce, (5) consumer organizations, (6) industry trade associations, (7) educators and others who speak and write about consumer protection, and (8) combinations of these.

Interestingly, the type of unacceptable advertising practices that sometimes are controlled in one country by the federal government are controlled by state or local government in another country. Or, what may be covered in legislation and administrative law in one country, may be covered by the self-regulatory system—or by some combination system—in another. Many additional complexities and interactions exist. Therefore, before studying and comparing advertising self-regulation in the two countries, one must have a clear understanding of each of the levels and aspects of the respective regulatory systems.

With this point in mind we shall endeavor in the first three chapters of this book to provide brief background on these topics, so that in the succeeding chapters, which comprise the main body of the study, we may then focus on comparing advertising self-regulation in the two countries.

This study answers specific questions about the essential nature of the advertising self-regulatory system in each of the two countries. What are the most important differences and similarities in the two self-regulatory systems? What are the main reasons for such differences? Are there any characteristics of one system that might suggest useful changes in the other system (that is, should the industry support advertising self-regulation more vigorously, or less vigorously, or differently)? What are the implications of the findings for public policy toward advertising (that is, more or fewer or different laws, or enforcement activities)? What should be the role of consumer groups?

Comparative Research and Analysis

The organization of the research for this book was guided by the diagram of steps in the comparative process shown in figure P–1.

This diagram led us to define the basic problem as the following: What are the relevant alternative means of advertising self-regulation? Which have been employed? What are their advantages and disadvantages? What specific environmental factors are relevant (that is, the cultural, economic, legal, political, social, and technological conditions that explain the answers to the above questions)?

As the next level in the diagram suggests, we then attempt to outline the answers to these questions as they have emerged in the United States and the United Kingdom. Next comes the comparisons of the differences and similarities in the solutions in the two countries. And, along the way we look for environmental variables that help explain the differences and

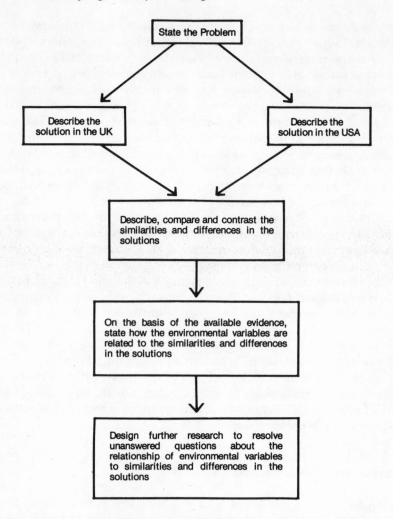

Figure P–1. Diagram of Steps in Comparative Analysis

similarities. Specifically we are concerned as to why the differences and similarities occur, in view of the relevant cultural, economic, legal, political, and social technological factors.

The last step in the diagram is reserved for future research, and therefore is not covered in this book except that we offer guidelines in the final chapter as to what questions remain partly or wholly unanswered, and what research seems likely to be needed to answer them.

With regard to this process, we should note that to understand the relationships between advertising self-regulation and the environment, we need to go beyond a simple description, comparison, and contrast of each system. We need to know how the processes, structures, and functions of each of the two systems are related to the environmental variables (for example, what is the relationship between certain aspects of the *British Code of Advertising Practice (BCAP)* and the British culture; between the British method of financing the Advertising Standards Authority/Code of Advertising Practice (ASA/CAP) Committee and political factors; between certain of the National Advertising Division/National Advertising Review Board (NAD/NARB) or television network standards and the U.S. law?). The environmental factors are the interacting, constraining, and stimulating forces that determine the uniqueness or sameness of the systems of advertising self-regulation in the two countries.

The main research methods that we have employed are (1) a thorough review of the literature; scholarly and professional articles and books, as well as published talks, research reports, pamphlets, and other materials used by each system to advise and work with advertisers, advertising agencies, and advertising media to make the system work, and (2) personal, mail, and telephone contacts with knowledgeable persons from a number of organizations.

Acknowledgments

The authors are indebted to many people who have contributed to this work. First, we thank Marlene Corner and Barbara Story for their patience and endurance in typing and retyping the many drafts through which such a manuscript must go. They always sought perfection and never complained of our difficult handwriting.

We also owe the many people who have given generously of their time and knowledge. A number have helped us off the record; our debt to them is considerable. Though our many sources of information are too numerous to mention here, we must express our gratitude in particular to Professor J.J. Boddewyn, City University of New York; Sir Gordon Borrie, Director General of Fair Trading and others in the Office of Fair Trading; Harvey Dzodin, director, East Coast Broadcast Standards and Practices, American Broadcasting Company; Attorney at Law Frederick Hoffecker, Consumer Protection Division, State of Michigan; Dr. Richard Lawson, consultant in marketing law; Lorraine Reid, senior vice president, Dr. Ronald H. Smithies, vice president and director, Dr. Rita Weisskoff, director of the Children's Advertising Review Unit (CARU) and the many other helpful staff of the National Advertising Division, Council of Better Business Bureaus; Carolyn Cosmos, Arlington Office of the Council of Better Business Bureaus; Rein Rijkens, retired Unilever/SSC&B:Lintas

executive and former president of the European Association of Advertising Agencies; Peter Thomson, director general, Enid Cassin, deputy director general, and Gwenan Williams and David Williamson, deputy directors, the Advertising Standards Authority; Roger Underhill, director general, and Ludwig Berlin and Philip Spink, the Advertising Association; David Wheeler, director, Philip Circus, barrister and legal counsel, and Norma Fryer, chief information officer, Institute of Practitioners in Advertising; Professor Eric Zanot, University of Maryland; and the many other members of the following organizations who have treated our prolonged enquiries with such considerable tact, courtesy, and patience: Association of the British Pharmaceutical Industry, Advertising Standards Board of Finance, British Board of Film Censors, British Transport Advertising, Cinema Advertising Association, Department of Trade, History of Advertising Trust, Independent Broadcasting Authority, Incorporated Society of British Advertisers, London Transport Advertising, Medicines Acts Products Advertising Authority, Newspaper Publishers Association, Newspaper Society, Outdoor Advertising Association, and the Proprietary Association of Great Britain.

We also received significant input from a number of students at Michigan State University who served as research assistants at various stages of the project: Lori Bates, Martha Bergadine, Janice Bukovac, Kathy Dillsworth, Barbara Durham, Katherine Greif, Thomas Hollerback, Amy Lantz, Karen Mell, Mary Mikelonis, Mark Molisani, Bruce Pinkleton, and Ay-Ling Tsien.

While many people have contributed, the authors must take sole responsibility for any errors or misinterpretation of information that may have occurred.

Finally, we owe a huge debt to those with the vision to provide the financial support for this research. We are grateful first to the Michigan State University Foundation, and the anonymous reviewers and officials who saw merit in the proposed research and provided the seed money to initiate the research. Second, we are deeply indebted to one of the giants of the advertising industry, Mr. Richard C. Christian, previously chairman of the board of Marsteller, and the Marsteller Foundation for its generous grant to support the main body of research that made this book possible. Dick Christian is now associate dean of the Medill School of Journalism at Northwestern University. He has long been a friend and supporter of advertising education and research, and his faith in us is but one example of his many contributions.

—*Gordon E. Miracle*
Terence Nevett
September, 1986

1

Introduction

Advertising regulation has a variety of meanings to those responsible for it as well as to those who write about it. Many use the term broadly to include all controls or regulations from all sources, including self-discipline by individuals and by organizations involved in advertising—advertisers, advertising agencies, and media, as well as industry associations, media associations, other types of industry-supported organizations, and government. Some contributors to the literature have argued that defining terms and delineating topics with greater precision will increase clarity of thought.

One scholar offers the following three types of control of advertising behavior:

1. Laissez-faire and self-discipline.
2. Regulation.
3. Self-regulation (Boddewyn 1985, 129–130).

Boddewyn points out that self-discipline is based on moral principles and notions of fair and ethical behavior or on self-interest, because advertising must attract and not repel consumers and because advertisers fear government regulation. He adds that the term *regulation* refers to advertising behavior that is mandated or circumscribed by government rules or penalties, and that *self-regulation* refers to the control of advertising conduct and performance by one's peers (that is, by business associations or organizations) rather than by government or market forces (Boddewyn 1985, 130).

Boddewyn (1985, 135) also provides a detailed classification of six types of advertising controls, including four types of self-regulation. Although such precision may have merit, most authors and people working in advertising do not make these distinctions. Because we wish to include the ideas of those who use these terms in a broad sense, we follow that practice in this book.

An understanding of "advertising regulation" presupposes an understanding of (1) the basic conditions in society under which advertising is practiced, (2) consumer attitudes toward and acceptance of advertising, (3) the nature of advertising media, and (4) the practice of advertising by advertisers and advertising agencies. These matters are far too complex to discuss here in detail. However, the reader who takes the time to read and to think about these matters before reading the rest of this book will subsequently gain a great deal more from it. Most readers are likely to be a product of only one culture: their own. But the reader with an understanding of the general principles of advertising, along with specific details on how advertising works in his or her own society, can then consider the lessons from the standpoint of what he or she knows best and decide which conclusions from this study are relevant for his or her particular nation.

Therefore, in this chapter we only briefly discuss these matters to illustrate their importance and to provide general understanding, rather than to offer exhaustive information.

Comparisons of the United Kingdom and the United States

National Similarities and Differences

Just as many of the idiosyncracies of an advertising self-regulatory system stem from distinctive national characteristics, so the similar characteristics of advertising self-regulatory systems stem from similarities. In this section some of the relevant similarities and differences between the United Kingdom and the United States are highlighted to provide the frame of reference for the later comparison of the two self-regulatory systems.

The United Kingdom comprises England, Northern Ireland, Scotland, and Wales, and is located on islands physically separate from the rest of Europe. It is a large pluralistic nation of 56 million people. Although the standard language is English, minority groups in Scotland, Wales, and Cornwall as well as members of several immigrant communities take great pride in preserving their language and customs.

The United States, in comparison, is a larger nation of more than 240 million people living in a land of diverse physical features and climate. Although the common language is English, there is considerable cultural, ethnic, and racial heterogeneity, especially considering the black and Hispanic communities.

The United Kingdom and the United States are among the major democracies of the world, yet they are considerably different. The United Kingdom evolved over many centuries to achieve a parliamentary democracy. Its unwritten constitution, which in many respects has been reflected in statute form over the years, was the source of many of the features of the U.S. Constitution, ratified in 1789 and subsequenctly amended many times. Today the United Kingdom has a "unitary system," which means that the powers of local government (county, metropolitan, and borough councils) are defined by statutes enacted by Parliament, which is free to expand, reduce, or rearrange these powers.

The United States, in contrast, has a federal system of government, which means that the Constitution delegates certain powers to the national government and the states retain residual powers. However, the courts have ruled fairly consistently in ways that have expanded and confirmed the powers of the federal government, especially since the middle 1930s. Today the fifty states retain numerous powers but, on balance, the federal government remains relatively strong. Administrative law mechanisms in the executive branch of the federal government are highly developed, which serve as a strong source of power at the national level.

Another important feature in a legal system is in the ways in which free speech is protected. In the United States constitutional protection of speech and of the freedom of the press have given a special status to newspapers and other print media. Journalistic materials in the press receive strong, almost absolute, protection. Constitutional protection for the broadcast media is not as strong, because stations must operate under license, and the Federal Communications Commission (FCC) may require standards designed to cause stations to carry or not to carry certain information or materials. However, the situation is changing. Under recent deregulation policies, the FCC has dropped virtually all specific requirements on the broadcast media. The implications for advertising are discussed in chapter 3.

Freedom of the press in the United Kingdom is a matter of historical accident. When the monarchy was restored after the Civil War in the 1640s, the press was brought under tight control. The Printing Act (1662) limited printing to the master printers, the two universities (Oxford and Cambridge), and the Archbishop of York. The number of master printers was reduced from fifty-nine to twenty, and the number of apprentices and presses was strictly limited. A Surveyor of the Press was appointed in 1663 with a patent for the exclusive right of publishing "all narratives or relacons not exceeding two sheets of paper and all advertisements, mercuries, diurnals and books of public intelligence" (Nevett 1982). In spite of

these restrictions many unofficial newsletters were circulated. The freedom to print and publish newspapers, however, may be said to date from
1695. The Printing Act lapsed in that year, and hard though the government tried, it was unable to secure agreement in Parliament as to what
form a new measure should take. Four bills were introduced, and each in
turn were rejected. Finally the government abandoned its efforts, and the
freedom of the press, that most cherished of British liberties, had been
won by default.

The same is not true of television and radio. The British Broadcasting
Corporation (BBC), which does not carry advertising, enjoyed a monopoly in both fields until the passing of the Television Act (1954) signaled the
arrival of independent stations carrying advertising. At that time the
country was divided into fourteen regions and contracts were awarded
on a regional basis, so that opportunities were limited. The BBC retained
its radio monopoly until the Sound Broadcasting Act (1972) provided for
the setting up of sixty independent local stations financed by advertising.

The main constraints on freedom of reporting in both the press and
broadcast media are the law of libel and the government's power to deem
matters as being related to national security. Because no legislation guarantees the freedom to publish, the question of whether these also affect
advertising does not arise.

Both countries are common law nations, with the U.S. system evolving in large part from British traditions. Today much legislation has been
codified in both countries. But the essential features of the common law
heritage remain, especially the precedent-setting tradition in the courts
that results in court-made common law.

Background on Advertising

Before one can understand the nature of an advertising regulatory system, one must understand advertising. Nearly everyone has views on
how advertising works, who it influences, and who gains (or loses) from it.
But not everyone understands fully the nature of the advertising business, the nature of the economic and social system in which advertising
operates, and whether advertising makes a worthwhile contribution to
society. For example, how many consumers or consumerists have a thorough understanding of how advertising operates, and its economic and
social effects?

Both the United Kingdom and the United States are among the
world's most developed pluralistic countries—culturally, economically,
legally, politically, socially, and technologically. Of course, the particular
mix of industries and services that form the economic base of each country differs substantially; and the cultural, political, and social institutions

of each country differ in numerous ways. Nevertheless, on examination we find that in both the United Kingdom and the United States, advertising performs important communication functions and plays a complex role as a business, economic, and social force.

Total advertising expenditures in 1983 in the United States were more than $75 billion, compared with about $6 billion for the United Kingdom. But this difference is due in large part to the relative size of the populations of the two nations. Advertising as a proportion of gross national product (GNP) is about 2.4 percent in the United States and 1.1 percent in the United Kingdom, as shown in table 1-1. Per capita advertising expenditures are more than $320 in the United States and just less than $110 in the United Kingdom. The somewhat higher level of advertising in the United States has held for many years, suggesting that the use of advertising has stabilized at a higher level in the United States than in the United Kingdom.

Another important aspect of advertising is the proportion of advertising expenditures in each economy devoted to different types of advertising. In both the United Kingdom and the United States, only a small proportion of advertising is industrial, or business-to-business, advertising; the bulk of advertising is directed at consumers. Of this consumer advertising, however, roughly half is by retailers and the rest is largely manufacturers' advertising to consumers of specific brands and products, along with some corporate or institutional advertising.

Background on Advertisers and Advertising Agencies

The practice of advertising in the United Kingdom and the United States, although not identical in details, is broadly similar in many respects. Both countries have large, medium, and small advertisers, especially

Table 1-1
Selected Advertising Statistics, 1983
(U.S. dollars)[a]

	United Kingdom	United States
Advertising as percent of GNP	1.1%	2.4%
Per capita advertising	$108	$323
Per capita advertising in print media	$ 52	$115
Per capita television advertising	$ 30	$ 72
Per capita radio advertising	$ 2	$ 22

Source: *World Advertising Expenditures* (New York: Starch INRA Hooper in cooperation with the International Advertising Association, 1985, various pages).

[a]Currency values fluctuate from year to year, and comparisons in any given year are at best only a general indicator of the relative importance of advertising.

manufacturers and retailers. Many advertisers employ an advertising agency or other specialized services, although some use in-house facilities; small retailers often depend on the media for assistance in preparing their advertising.

The levels of marketing and advertising sophistication, as well as technology, are roughly similar in the two nations. Thus the practice of advertising differs not so much in the basic methods to solve problems and to implement compaigns as it does in the use of particular creative appeals, approaches, and executions and in the selection of particular media to reach target audiences.

Background on Advertising Media

In the United States all advertising media are privately owned business enterprises, with broadcast media deriving virtually 100 percent of their revenues from advertising. Newspapers and magazines derive the majority of their revenues from advertising, with a small but significant proportion coming from subscription or newsstand sales. Print media in the United Kingdom are supported in essentially the same way as are print media in the United States: primarily from advertising, but a significant proportion of revenue comes from per copy sales at the cover price.

The situation with regard to television and radio is mentioned earlier in the chapter. Independent stations—that is, those that carry advertising—are financed almost entirely from advertising revenue, unlike the BBC, which carries no advertising and is financed by a license fee paid annually by every owner of a television or radio receiver.

In contrast, the broadcasting industry in the United States is decentralized. It includes several hundred television stations, and several thousand radio stations, each licensed individually by the FCC. There are three major television networks, and more than thirty-five percent of U.S. homes receive network, local, and cable programs. The industry is fragmented and consists mainly of "small businesses," because until recently no single organization or person was permitted by the FCC to own more than five VHF stations or a total of more than seven UFH and VHF stations. Moreover, some stations are affiliated with a network and some are not. Each local television or radio station can, at its option and at the invitation of a network, become a network affiliate. Because of differences in competitive and market conditions, the bargaining power of local stations varies, and so do the provisions of the contracts between networks and local stations.

Table 1–2 shows the relative importance of the media as advertising vehicles. Although newspapers attract the largest proportion of advertising dollars in both countries, print media dominate in the United Kingdom

Table 1–2
Advertising Volume, 1983
(in U.S. dollars)

	United Kingdom		United States	
Medium	Amount Spent (millions of dollars)	Percent of Total	Amount Spent (millions of dollars)	Percent of Total
Newspaper	$2,117.3	35	$20,582.0	27
Consumer and trade magazines	755.6	13	6,386.0	8
Outdoor and transportation	207.0	3	12,589.0	17
Radio	122.4	2	5,210.0	7
Television	1,676.0	28	16,786.0	22
Direct advertising	451.9	8	n.a.	n.a.
Miscellaneous	649.8	11[a]	14,297.0	19[a]
Total	$5,980.0	100	$75,850.0	100

Source: *World Advertising Expenditures* (New York: Starch INRA Hooper in Cooperation with the International Advertising Association, 1985).

[a]Includes cinema, exhibitions, demonstrations, information centers, display and point of sale advertising, and miscellaneous sales promotion, as well as direct advertising for the USA.

to a greater extent than in the United States. Yet, per capita advertising expenditures in British print media are only a little more than $50, substantially lower than the U.S. figure, which is about $115. Importantly, about forty percent of the newspaper advertising revenue in the United Kingdom is from the national press, whereas in the United States few newspapers can claim anything approaching substantial national or even regional circulation, other than *USA Today*, the *Christian Science Monitor*, the *Wall Street Journal* and perhaps the *New York Times*, all of which have relatively small readership compared with the total in the United States.

Television advertising attracts more than twenty-five percent of total advertising expenditures in the United Kingdom, and about twenty-two percent in the United States. On a per capita basis, however, the television advertising in the United States is more than $70, which is more than double the $30 per capita spent in the United Kingdom.

Radio advertising attracts about seven percent of all U.S. advertising expenditures, but only two percent in the United Kingdom. On a per capita basis, radio advertising in the United States is more than ten times as great as in the United Kingdom.

There are also some significant differences and similarities as to the importance of other media. The somewhat greater share of advertising expenditures in British magazines reflects the orientation of the United Kingdom toward print media. And, although statistics are not available from the United Kingdom, direct advertising has become increasingly important there as well as in the United States, and it seems likely to continue to grow in importance in both countries. Miscellaneous expenditures also seem likely to continue to grow in both countries, particularly in view of the importance of sales promotion in modern marketing.

Background on Advertising Messages

The nature and content of advertising messages and their creative execution also vary somewhat between the United Kingdom and the United States. This large subject has not been researched comprehensively, but observation can provide a few examples of how the British advertising accent differs from that of the United States, while many similarities continue to exist.

For example, to the typical British consumer, U.S. advertising often appears to be "hard sell" or even strident, compared with British advertising. Conversely, to the typical U.S. consumer, British advertising often appears to be "soft sell" or entertaining. The reason probably relates to the proliferation of broadcast media in the United States; the U.S. consumer is exposed to relatively more advertising, and commercials must compete for attention. The United Kingdom has far fewer commercial broadcast stations than does the United States.

Some observers believe that British advertisements contain more information than U.S. advertising for comparable products, suggesting perhaps that the target markets or the behavior and information needs of consumers in those targets differ. Among the British, understatement has a special cachet. Moreover, when the British advertisements are not informative, they are likely to be entertaining.

A Concluding Observation

Although there are many similarities between the United Kingdom and the United States, there are also many differences. In this chapter, we discuss these similarities and differences illustratively rather than comprehensively, and the thoughtful reader will no doubt wish to obtain additional information and insights on the topics mentioned. Many possible references provide further information on topics in this chapter, and it is impossible to enumerate them here. The reader is urged to review this chapter to consider whether he or she is broadly knowledgeable about each. If not, we recommend a careful reading of selected parts of several British and U.S. books on advertising, business, culture, economy, legal and political systems, social conditions, and marketing practices. The remaining material in this book assumes that the reader has considerable specialized knowledge of these topics.

References

Boddewyn, J.J. (1985), "Advertising Self-Regulation: Private Government and Agent of Public Policy," *Journal of Public Policy and Marketing* 4:129–141.
Encyclopaedia Britannica Macropaedia, 15th ed. (1974) (New York: Encyclopaedia Britannica).
World Advertising Expenditures (1985) (New York: Starch INRA Hooper Group of Companies and International Advertising Association).

2
Historical Perspectives on Advertising Regulation and Self-Regulation

Introduction

This chapter continues the effort begun in chapter 1 to provide a context for the main body of the analysis of the British and U.S. systems. We now present historical material to explain the environment that led to the formation of the centralized systems of advertising self-regulation in the two countries, and the circumstances that influenced their subsequent evolution and development. We also present brief information on other (noncentralized) self-regulatory activities, because they complement the central systems and provide additional useful context.

Voluntary self-regulation of advertising is a product of many forces, perhaps the most fundamental of which is the long-time acceptance of the market economy by both the British and the U.S. people. This acceptance derives from the classical liberal tradition of British economists of the eighteenth and nineteenth centuries, as it was further developed by U.S. economists, and manifests itself in the prevailing attitudes of the populaces of both nations and their governments.

Although there have been many critics of advertising, it has been generally accepted as a legitimate business activity in a market economy. The criticisms, then, tended to lead to control of advertising rather than to its abolition, although critics have by no means been unified in their opinions and their demands for change.

Under the market system consumers and producers make decisions in response to price and other considerations generated by the interplay of supply and demand forces in more or less freely operating markets. The fundamental assumptions about human behavior are that consumers and producers act individually and rationally in their own best interests, and that the interplay of sufficiently large numbers of buyers and sellers,

---

Much of the material in this chapter is adapted with permission from Miracle (1985a) and Nevett and Miracle (1986).

operating under conditions of effective competition, leads to good performance of the economy. Good performance is a multidimensional attribute that embodies numerous social goals, such as the following:

1. Decisions as to what, how much, and how to produce should be efficient in two respects: scarce resources should not be wasted outright, and production decisions should be responsive qualitatively and quantitatively to consumer demands.

2. The operations of producers should be progressive, taking advantage of opportunities opened up by science and technology for increasing output per unit of input and making available to consumers superior new products, in both ways contributing to the long-run growth of per capita real income.

3. The operations of producers should facilitate stable full employment of resources, especially human resources. Or at the very minimum, they should not make maintenance of full employment through macroeconomic policy instruments excessively difficult.

4. The distribution of income should be equitable. Equity in economics is a notoriously slippery concept, but it implies at least that producers do not secure rewards far in excess of those needed to call forth the amount of services supplied. A sub-facet of this goal is the desire to achieve reasonable price stability, for rampant inflation distorts the distribution of income in widely disapproved ways" (Scherer 1970).

To the extent that advertising contributes to these performance goals, it has continued to be accepted in the United Kingdom and the United States. Conversely, to the extent that advertising inhibits the achievement of these performance goals, it has been to some extent controlled. Control of advertising has evolved from a nonspecific or indirect form (that is, preserving competition and prohibiting the exercise of monopoly power) to specific and direct control (that is, prohibiting specific practices to protect consumers regardless of whether competition is injured). Unfair or deceptive advertising falls primarily in the latter category, because its effects on competition are even more difficult to measure than its effects on consumers. This evolution of controls has occurred in a broad sense in both the United Kingdom and the United States, but the details are different.

In both the United Kingdom and the United States there are numerous laws and court decisions (case law) with respect to advertising offenses, as well as orders, directives, and the administrative law system to enforce them. And because the centralized advertising self-regulatory system in each country begins with the basic idea that advertising must be legal, the activities of the self-regulatory system are influenced directly by the law. However, the law and legal systems of the two countries differ in their approach to advertising regulation, which in turn changes the emphasis of self-regulation.

The *type* of political and government system, and its responsiveness to public attitudes toward advertising, also influence advertising self-regulation. In a democracy, if the public is generally critical of advertising, and if government is responsive to public attitudes, there is a strong incentive for the advertising industry to attempt to regulate itself in its own self-interest. In a market economy, the advertising industry's self-interest requires not only that consumers have confidence in advertising, but also that government regulation should not take the place of legitimate business judgments. Thus, self-regulation of advertising seems to develop as a more or less direct response to the pressure from society for consumer protection and the fear that if the industry does not act then the government will take steps to control advertising. As the popularity of consumer protection waxes and wanes, so does the advertising industry's interest in self-regulation. The impetus, it should be noted, comes not only from the advertisers, agencies, and media and their trade associations, but also from representative organizations in other industries and from broadly based bodies such as chambers of commerce.

The United States

The Economic Setting

Historically, the classical liberal tradition of economic thought has been the intellectual basis for the U.S. economic system. In the United States the emphasis has been on preserving competition as the prime means by which the interests of consumers and sellers, indeed the interests of society, are protected. U.S. policy has relied heavily on preserving competition to allocate resources effectively so that the economy may achieve expected performance goals. U.S. government policy to preserve competition has focused especially on protecting against the monopoly power of private business. Sometimes, though, government policy protected competitors from each other, instead of protecting conditions of competition. It became clear over the years, however, that the intended function of government was to preserve conditions of effective competition, under which inefficient competitors must either become more efficient or perish.

Also, as we discuss, events in the United States in the 1930s, after World War II, and especially in the 1960s, led to the prohibition of certain acts or practices to protect consumers regardless of the impact of such acts on competition.

Early Pressures for Self-Regulation

Although advertising has long been an important business activity in the United States, concern about self-regulation has been almost entirely a twentieth century phenomenon. Still, early in the nation's history, consumers complained about false or misleading advertising, especially about patent medicines. But it was not until the late 1800s that any collective effort was made to protect the buying public from the nostrums and quackery that abounded. Interestingly, the earliest efforts were not instigated by consumers but by farm industry magazines. As early as 1859 Orange Judd began exposing fraudulent sellers in his publication *American Agriculturist*, which, along with others such as the *Farm Journal* and the *Rural New Yorker*, led the first major attack on advertising practices by attempting to "clean up" the advertising they carried (Wood 1958; Kenner 1936).

Before 1900 the most urgent consumer concern was patent medicine advertising. There was a growing awareness of the response to false advertising which spurred popular consumer magazines to begin offering readers "guarantees" of products sold by the advertisements they carried. An early example was the *Good Housekeeping* "Seal of Approval." (White 1939; Kenner 1936).

Interestingly, during the 1880s and 1890s most consumers seemed to have little concern about advertising, although the efforts of the magazines brought about a greater consumer awareness of the possible risks they were facing from false advertising. The reform that was to occur in the first two decades of the 1900s was spearheaded by businessmen who had decided that bad advertising was bad business (White 1939). Until 1900 American business had enjoyed a rapid expansion with few restraints. Resources were abundant and seemed inexhaustible. Few seemed to care who was harmed by whom in the great race to success, as long as everyone started with equal opportunities. About 1900 views changed. Suddenly resources seemed to be finite, and opportunities were no longer equal. Competition became increasingly intense, moral indignation grew, and consumer dissatisfaction increased. Magazines such as *McClure's* became famous for their exposés revealing corruption and fraud in American business. Advertising did not escape the surge of calls for reform, which, since 1800, had grown to enormous proportions. Although advertisers who sold reputable branded products were generally truthful and trustworthy, there were cases in which fraudulent claims not only led to consumer monetary loss but for a few unfortunates even to injury and death (Wood 1958).

In 1892 the *Ladies Home Journal* announced that it would print no more medical advertising. Other popular magazines and newspapers followed.

This fact alone, however, did little to change the patent medicine business, which continued to flourish. The needed sensation occurred in 1902 when the editor of the *Ladies Home Journal,* Edward W. Bok, began publishing chemical analyses of advertised medications and revealed that many medications used regularly by children and adults contained ingredients such as morphine and cocaine. Together the *Ladies Home Journal, Colliers,* and *Good Housekeeping* helped fight the battle that eventually led to the passage of the Food and Drug Act of 1906 (Wood 1958; Kenner 1936).

During these years the publishing business was not the only one to recognize that advertising reform was needed. Business groups as early as 1896 talked about the need for changes. The Sphinx Club of New York was one such group of advertising men who met on a regular basis, mostly for social functions. By the year 1903 the question of advertising reform had become such a concern that the club began to lay aside social activities and address the problems of increasing consumer dissatisfaction. Attacks from various corners led some businessmen to the conclusion that action was needed to ensure the continued success of the advertising business (Wood 1958), as we discuss in a later section. But first we present a brief overview of early advertising regulatory actions of the federal government.

Early Government Regulation

The Criminal Fraud Statute passed in 1872 was the first federal legislation to recognize explicitly the need for consumer protection (Consumerism 1973). However, the main body of law that led to "effective" regulation of advertising, which came to be called antitrust law, developed somewhat later.

In 1890 Congress passed the Sherman Antitrust Act, which prohibited restraint of trade and monopolization of any part of trade or commerce. The many antitrust laws that followed and the executive agencies to enforce them generally provided needed detail to cover continuing problems with specific practices and industries. Although the number of subsequent laws and amendments to them is very large, the two that are of greatest concern to advertising are the Food and Drug Act (FDA) (1906) and amendments and the Federal Trade Commission (FTC) Act (1914) and amendments.

The FTC Act originally was not directed toward deceptive or unfair advertising, but rather toward preventing acts or practices that were considered to be monopolistic or unfair methods of competition. The focus was on preserving competition, which in turn was necessary if the free market system was to function effectively to the benefit of the economy and the participants in it, including both sellers and consumers.

The FTC took the view, however, that accurate and truthful information was essential to preserving fair competition and maintaining the market economy. The FTC's position was that deceptive or misleading claims for an advertiser's product were "unfair competition" and that such claims gave the seller an unfair competitive advantage over those sellers who did not engage in such practices. In *Federal Trade Commission v. Winsted Hosiery Co.*, 258 U.S. 483, 42 S. Ct. 384, 66 L. Ed 729 (1923), the Supreme Court said "that when misleading ads are . . . in competition with truthful ads, potential customers are unfairly diverted from the honest advertiser's products. By 1925 three quarters of the FTC's orders concerned false and misleading advertising" (Zuckman and Gaynes 1983, 308–309).

For many years there was some confusion as to whether the preservation of competitors was synonymous with the preservation of competition. Court decisions ultimately clarified the matter in favor of the latter.

The question remained, however, whether the FTC could prohibit unfair advertising without demonstrating injury to competition. "In *Federal Trade Commission v. Raladam Co.*, 283 U.S. 643, 51 S. Ct. 587, 75 L. Ed. 1324 (1931), the Supreme Court answered that question in the negative" (Zuckman and Gaynes 1983, 309). Thus, in 1938 the U.S. Congress amended the law to prohibit "unfair or deceptive acts or practices in commerce," per se, regardless of the impact on competition.

The Food and Drug Act was intended to protect against unsafe or adulterated food and drug products. The original act brought false advertisements of such products under the jurisdiction of the FDA, especially regarding statements on the safety of food and drug products. Later the FTC and FDA divided jurisdiction regarding advertising, with the FDA responsible for overseeing advertising of prescription drugs and the FTC taking responsibility for advertisements of proprietary medicines.

The Efforts of Advertising Industry Associations

In 1904 The National Federation of Advertising Clubs of America began a campaign for truth in advertising. Although the Federation's objective was to expose fraudulent advertising, there was more talk than action. In 1905 the Club was renamed The Associated Advertising Clubs of America (later renamed "of the World"). In 1906 a reform campaign was once again adopted but with only a score of clubs; it turned out that this "army" was too small to achieve substantial changes. It was not until 1911 that about 100 clubs, meeting in Boston, adopted the "truth in advertising" slogan, and the fire for reform began to burn more brightly with the establishment of local "vigilance committees." These committees heard complaints, reviewed advertisements, and reported to government authorities those deemed fraudulent. These committees were the forerunners of what were soon to become the Better Business Bureaus (BBBs), but unfortunately they had little power to enforce honesty in advertising. They made an effort but increases in false advertising outran their attempts at control (Kenner 1936).

Between 1911 and 1915 *Printers's Ink* took the lead in efforts to clean up advertising; J.I. Romer began the campaign by retaining Harry D. Nims of the New York Bar Association to draw up a "model statute," which *Printers' Ink* published in November 1911, and it was greeted with approval by the advertising clubs (Kenner 1936; Digges 1948; White 1939). The model statute enumerated the following seven practices that were unfair to the public and tended to discredit advertising:

1. False statements or misleading exaggerations.

2. Indirect misrepresentation of a product, or service, through distortion of details, either editorially or pictorially.

3. Statements or suggestions offensive to public decency.

4. Statements which tend to undermine an industry by attributing to its products, generally, faults and weaknesses true only of a few.

5. Price claims that are misleading.

6. Pseudoscientific advertising, including claims insufficiently supported by accepted authority, or that distort the true meaning or application of a statement made by professional or scientific authority.

7. Testimonials which do not reflect the real choice of a competent witness. (Reproduced in *Printers' Ink*, 26 May 1932, 52).

By 1913 the model statute or some parts of it had been enacted into legislation in fifteen states; eventually the total reached forty-three. The statute gave the reform movement something tangible, which it had lacked before. However, most of the state "unfair practices acts" were "watered down" versions of the original. Perhaps the most important departure from the model by most states was that intent to defraud was required before prosecution under the law could occur. Such intent was difficult to prove, and this provision made successful prosecution rare.

Better Business Bureaus

In 1916, at the general convention of the Associated Advertising Clubs of the World, the vigilance committees were replaced by the BBBs (Kenner 1936). Established and backed financially by business and aided by local, state, and national governmental authorities, the BBB's greatest thrust in the fight against false advertising was to show how questionable practices operated against successful business. The BBB's efforts, like many of the earlier reform efforts, represented an attempt to improve business for its own good rather than to protect individual buyers. The BBB hoped that showing the harm that false advertising did to business in general would mobilize advertisers to back and support their efforts. Aloof from any specific connection with individual businesses, the BBBs scrutinized business activities to identify improper practices. To correct such practices they consulted with the offending parties and stressed the wisdom of better methods. In most cases in the early years, moral persuasion prevailed and legal action was rarely taken (French 1926).

By the end of World War I the BBBs had the cooperation of trade associations and publishers who were attempting to improve advertising standards, and by the 1920s BBBs had been established in most major cities. Although BBB energies served primarily to halt predatory price cutting and the selling of defective merchandise by local retailers, they also encouraged the local press to refuse dishonest advertising. As advertising grew rapidly in the early twenties, however, the volume of fraudulent advertising also grew. Although advertising had gained a certain amount of respect through its efforts to regulate itself, the codes were superficial and often ineffective. All too much advertising still contained false or misleading assertions and promises (Kenner 1936).

In the early 1920s the BBBs often were faced with what came to be referred to as "borderline offenses," which were difficult to deal with because of the lack of consensus as to what constituted fraudulent advertising. Especially difficult were seemingly sophisticated advertising messages by large national advertisers, which the small BBBs felt they did not have the resources or the power to handle. Therefore in 1925 the National Better Business Bureau (NBBB) was formed. The NBBB needed and received the cooperation of national advertisers, but the fight against borderline offenses continued to be difficult. Effectively the NBBB did little more than warn offenders of public disapproval, scold them, and if necessary, attempt to enlist the aid of the FTC for exceptional violations. But the FTC did not really have the mission to protect consumers against fraudulent advertising until the 1938 revisions to the FTC Act of 1914. It was still widely believed that advertisers could and should control themselves (Pease 1958).

The American Association of Advertising Agencies

In 1924 the American Association of Advertising Agencies (AAAA) published its *Code of Ethics*. Its main thrust was to ask all member agencies to agree voluntarily not to produce false advertising. Types of deceptive practices were listed in the code in a effort to define false advertising, but because no examples were included it was difficult to pin down violators. The code remained essentially the same until 1956, when it was revised. In 1962, it was revised again to state that violators were vulnerable to expulsion from the AAAA, but there was no mechanism to carry out expulsion for such violations. Because the enforcement of the code included no punitive power, it proved ineffective. Honest advertisers "didn't need it" and dishonest ones "didn't heed it" (McTigue 1974).

Broadcast Advertising

The first radio station was licensed to broadcast in 1922. By 1929 radio had become an important advertising medium. People had by then accepted radio as an integral part of their lives and accepted advertising as the price paid for the entertainment it provided. By 1932, 600 stations had been licensed to broadcast. Two years later the public outcry for the control of radio reached such heights that the Federal Communications Commission (FCC) was established (Wood 1958).

The National Association of Broadcasters (NAB) was organized in 1922, and it has had as one of its several purposes "to do all things necessary and proper to encourage and promote customs and practices which will strengthen and maintain the broadcasting industry to the end that it may best serve the public" (*History of the NAB* 1965). The NAB adopted the Radio Code in 1937, which covered program and advertising standards as well as regulations and procedures to apply to NAB members. The purpose was to establish guidelines and to set forth minimum standards of performance (*NAB Radio Code* 1972). Although the standards were quite strict, they were accepted by most of the stations throughout the country. Whether this easy acceptance was a result of fear of further government intervention or of increasing public pressure is speculative. In any event, radio advertising and programming were definitely improved. In 1952 a separate code was prepared to cover television advertising. As we discuss more fully later, the NAB for more than six decades has had a powerful influence on advertising.

Combined Advertising Industry Efforts

In its continuing effort to control borderline offenses, the NBBB with the support of major magazines attempted to set stricter standards. It adopted specific codes of behavior, which it hoped trade associations and individual companies and media would enforce. Not achieving much success, the NBBB in 1931 teamed with *Printers' Ink* and set up committees in an effort to draw advertisers more closely into policing their business. Representatives from the Association of National Advertisers (ANA), American Association

of Advertising Agencies (AAAA), publishers, and the general public combined to form a review committee that was given responsibility to review
cases of unfair advertising. The review committee had begun its work by
1933. In some respects it represented an effort to appease businessmen who
had originally thought the NBBB was much too powerful because it was
effectively both judge and jury. The copy codes it adopted in 1932 were
generally agreed on by the ANA, the AAAA, and the American Federation
of Advertisers (AFA), but unfortunately they did not survive. Cooperation
was not achieved and the committee without the power of enforcement
could do nothing to save itself. Major objections were that advertisers
would pressure their agencies to violate the code anyway and an agent
could do nothing else if he wished to remain in business and survive (Pease
1958).

Similar codes adopted by trade associations for various industries met
with the same fate. The trade associations were reluctant (or unable) to
enforce rules on their members, especially in the case of borderline practices. Internal discipline was attained only where infractions were such
that all could unite in condemning them (Pease 1958).

These efforts to enforce codes, however unsuccessful, were at least a
declaration of ideals. They were often cited by advertisers as evidence that
they were trying to regulate their business. The inadequacy of the review
committee and organizations like it reflected an unwillingness and perhaps
an inability of business associations to enforce internal sanctions on their
own members. But as far as the business world was concerned these
attempts were considered important (Pease 1958).

Publishers were also pressured by advertising trade associations and
others to aid in the fight against unfair advertising. While they accepted the
argument that they had a public obligation, like the trade associations and
advertising associations they refused to take full responsibility. By the late
1930s publishers generally followed guidelines set up by the NBBB and the
FTC, but refused to take responsibility for advertising regulation when
borderline practices were involved (Pease 1958).

The advertising industry at least attempted to establish control over
the behavior of its members. Nevertheless, these efforts were motivated in
large part by the desire to forestall government regulation of advertising.
During the uncertain economic conditions in the early 1930s many people
criticized business. Advertising as the voice of business caught the attack
full force. Not only was misleading and false advertising under attack, but
the very function of advertising was questioned as an unfortunate partner
in an economic system that was failing the nation (Wood 1958).

The Consumer Movement and Consumerism to 1960

The attacks on advertising in the 1930s came mainly from consumer organizations and government. The consumer movement of that time had its

roots in the formation of the National Consumers' League in 1916. This group's major contribution was the publication of "white lists," lists of manufacturers whose operations were approved and whose products were consequently worthy of consumer purchase (Wood 1958). *Your Money's Worth* (Chase and Schlink 1927) gave the consumer movement a boost. The authors were responsible for organizing the Consumer's Club to protect the consumer from the crafty salesman. In 1929 this group became Consumers Research, Inc. Prior to the depression most consumer groups had been local, consisting mainly of women's groups concerned about high prices and the difficulties of the amateur buyer. But during the depression the movement broadened. An increasing number of publications echoing *Your Money's Worth* were published. They were sensational books for a depressed society. Often they mixed truth with false statements, attacking advertising with unparalleled fanaticism (Wood 1958).

After the depression the consumer movement continued to grow. In the minds of many, rapid proliferation of consumer goods outpaced buyers' skills in judging, making reliance on advertising more important. Resentment against the decline in product quality and the demand for reasonableness of advertising increased. The cry for more objective information from advertising was strong (Pease 1958).

In response to the need for objective information, some consumerists split from Consumer Research, Inc. in 1936 and formed the Consumers Union of the United States. Both groups operated as testing agencies, issuing levels of approval or disapproval of the products tested. Pamphlets, guides, and mailings were used to alert consumers to the pitfalls of product buying and what products they could or could not trust. Both agencies operated on the assumption that most or all advertising was fraudulent in intent and designed to cheat the consumer. Interestingly, the impact of these agencies seemed greater in the academic world than on society in general. Intellectuals who were offended and insulted by advertising claims helped foster a cynicism about advertising that became popular nationwide (Pease 1958; Wood 1958).

During these times the *Nation* and the *New Republic* were two of the most important magazines to champion the consumer movement; they published ariticles to guide buyers, supported testing agencies, and encouraged federal control (Pease 1958).

The furor caused by the consumer movement opened the way for government intervention. When Franklin Delano Roosevelt took office as president in 1933, he brought into government a number of persons who were sympathetic to the critics of advertising. They were the forerunners of those who favored government control of the advertising industry. Advertisers became increasingly alarmed at the very real possibility of government regulation (Pease 1958; Wood 1958).

In subsequent years the strong tension between the public and the advertising industry was clearly evident. A number of government bills supported by public groups were introduced in Congress. They met with strong resistance from advertisers and eventually they died (Pease 1958; Wood 1958).

It was not until 1938 that the Wheeler-Lea Amendment to the FTC Act of 1914 broadened the powers of the FTC over advertising, prohibiting "unfair or deceptive acts or practices," which was interpreted to include false or misleading advertising. In addition to the FTC and the FDA, a number of other federal agencies had some power to control advertising: for example, the FCC, the Securities and Exchange Commission (SEC), the Alcohol and Tobacco Tax Division of the Internal Revenue Service (IRS), and the U.S. Post Office.

Attempts at Self-Regulation in the 1950s and 1960s

The changing conditions of the early 1950s brought the next wave of attempts at self-regulation. Television became a major medium, and by 1951 advertisers were spending nearly one billion dollars annually on television advertising. The NAB television code, which had been established in 1952, was revised several times, and each revision increased the emphasis on eliminating deception in commercials and the need for substantiating claims, while continuing the emphasis on good taste. The three major television networks also joined the effort, and began to pre-screen commercials to adhere to the NAB Code. Although their limited resources forced them to be selective, they were an effective force to help eliminate fraudulent advertising (McTigue 1974).

In the 1960s the NAB control of broadcast advertising became increasingly strict. In the revisions of the code special efforts were made to protect children and to control promotions such as liquor and lotteries. Although not all radio and television stations subscribed to the code, by 1970 it had become an effective force for consumer protection (McTigue 1974).

Other than in the broadcast media, little effort was made during the 1950s to increase self-regulation. Print media seemed reluctant to accept additional responsibility for the truth of the advertisements they carried, and advertising agencies, enjoying another period of growth, acted as if there were no real need to regulate advertising. Puffery and exaggeration were all too often the keys to advertising success, and few advertisers seemed concerned (McTigue 1974). In the late 1950s consumers again became increasingly upset with advertising and again became a significant force for further regulation. Concern also began to redevelop among advertisers. As consumers voiced their dissatisfaction and more pressure was put on Congress to act, advertisers began to seek means of further self-regulation to avoid government intervention (McTigue 1974).

In 1960 several advertising associations gathered together to try to establish a self-regulatory system. The AAAA, the AFA, the Association of

Better Business Bureaus (ABBB), and the NBBB decided to work together. The BBBs set up review boards to police deception by local advertisers, and deceptions in national advertising were reported to the NBBB (McTigue 1974).

The advertising industry was divided on what to do about the growing pressure from both consumers and government. Some advocated further self-regulation to avoid government intervention, and others argued that more controls of any kind would inhibit creativity. In June 1960 the AFA and the AAAA established a four-part self-control program, which included the creation of a rule book called the "Truth Book." Its purpose was to help advertisers and agencies identify deceptive advertisements as well as to establish guidelines for honest advertising. Unfortunately, although the intricate and well-designed program was promising, it failed because it lacked any means of enforcement (McTigue 1974).

In the early 1960s some smaller groups within the industry also tried to regulate advertising. For example, the Advertising Association of the West (AAW) established a code that later became the base for the code adopted by the AFA, AAW, and ABBB in 1965. Although this code was no more enforceable than those that preceded it, it was widely accepted by major advertisers and agencies, and served as an ethical standard for the industry through 1970 (McTigue 1974). The industry was not successful in obtaining the cooperation of the less scrupulous advertisers, however, and demand for honesty in advertising reached a new peak in the 1960s. Because government opinion of self-regulation was negative, increasing attention was focused on government intervention.

A Decade of Consumer Legislation: The 1960s

More than twenty-five major acts affecting advertising directly were passed by the U.S. Congress between 1960 and 1972 (*Consumerism* 1973). They included such well-known legislation as the following:

1. The Kefauver-Harris Drug Amendment of 1962, which provided for labelling of drugs by generic names, and for limiting the advertising of drugs under certain circumstances.

2. The Fair Packaging and Labeling Act of 1966, which provided for uniform packaging standards.

3. The Child Protection Act of 1966, which prohibited certain kinds of advertising of potentially harmful toys and other articles used by children.

4. The Cigarette Labeling Act of 1966, which required the statement on the label and in advertising: "Caution: Cigarette smoking may be hazardous to your health."

5. The Consumer Credit Protection Act of 1968, which required disclosure in advertising of terms and conditions of finance charges.

6. The Child Protection and Toy Safety Act of 1969, which banned advertising of toys which posed hazards to children.

7. The Public Health Smoking Act of 1970, which prohibited cigarette commercials on television and changed the labeling and advertising statement requirement to: "Warning: The Surgeon General has determined that cigarette smoking is dangerous to your health."

Although there were later several relatively minor pieces of legislation influencing advertising in the early 1970s and beyond, there has been no major legislation affecting advertising for some years. The administrations in power in Washington have shown more inclination to consolidate the gains and to eliminate the excesses of the 1960s than to introduce further controls. It may be that major abuses of the present age have been reduced to an acceptable level, not only by government action, but aided by industry reform, not the least of which has been the emergence and steadily increasing influence of the NAD/NARB system.

Consumerism in the 1960s

Consumerism was only one of a number of major changes occurring in U.S. society in the 1960s. The period marked the end of a time of relative calm and prosperity. Major issues such as civil rights, pollution, the war in Vietnam, and the uprisings in cities and at universities created a climate for criticism and change. The period produced a new generation of consumer advocates, including those who focused increasing criticism on advertising.

In earlier decades consumerists, writers, and government acted in response to fairly narrow needs, focusing especially on particular products such as food and drugs. But in the 1960s more than a dozen books appeared that were generally critical of business and especially of advertising, for example:

Schlink and Phillips' book, "Don't You Believe It!" is a vigorous attack on false advertising. "Trade Trickery," by John W. Anderson, examines what the author views as growing retail monopolies, discount house practices and private labels. Fred J. Cook's "The Corrupted Land" describes major political and payola scandals of the day. The subject of "Hidden Assassins," by Booth Mooney, is food additives. "By Prescription Only" (originally "The Therapeutic Nightmare") by Morton Mintz, accuses the drug industry of lax safety standards and, in some cases, of marketing ineffective products.

Fraud, quackery, unsafe products and cigarettes are attacked in Senator Warren G. Magnuson's book "The Dark Side of the Marketplace." The book, coauthored with Jean Carper, recommends both Federal and state legislation to remedy consumer problems and suggests how reputable businesses can clean up the marketplace.

Ralph Nader's book, "Unsafe At Any Speed," published in 1964, criticized U.S. auto manufacturers for failing to remedy safety defects. The book was partly responsible for passage of the National Traffic and Motor Vehicle Safety Act of 1966 and triggered a major consumer movement aimed at Detroit.

"Hot War on the Consumer" is a marketplace exposé edited by David Sanford. Mr. Sanford has collected essays by leading writers in the consumer protection field, including Mr. Nader and staff members of New Republic magazine.

Recent additions to the growing list include: "The Radical Consumer's Handbook," by Goody L. Solomon, which discusses tactics to use when lodging a complaint and tells how consumers can organize to get action; "The Great American Food Hoax," by Sidney Margolius, which discusses convenience foods and warns the consumer of the higher cost he pays for prepared foods; "Eater's Digest," by Michael F. Jacobson, a consumer's fact-book on food additives; "The Great American Auto Repair Robbery," by Donald A. Randall, a report on alleged deficiencies in the industry and what can be done about it; and "The Great American Land Hustle," by Morton C. Paulson, documenting irresponsible land selling (*Consumerism* 1973).

Consumers became increasingly aware of advertising "abuses," and there was widespread sentiment for corrective action.

In April 1966 thirty-three consumer organizations met in Washington, D.C., "to develop closer understanding and unity in lobbying for consumer measures. . . . In 1967 the Consumer Federation of America (CFA) was formed," and soon included as members about "200 national, state and local consumer groups, labor unions, electric cooperatives and . . . other organizations with consumer interests. . . . " And private product testing organizations such as Consumers Union and Consumers' Research, Inc., continued to grow in importance, as did many new consumer publications (*Consumerism* 1973).

Those in government reacted. As early as 15 March 1962, President Kennedy declared that every consumer has four basic rights—the right to be informed, the right to safety, the right to choose, and the right to be heard. He urged strong legislation to protect these rights. In 1962 President Kennedy formed the first Consumer Advisory Council and appointed ten private citizens to serve on it. President Johnson subsequently expanded the council to twelve members and formalized its existence by executive order (*Consumerism* 1973).

In 1964 President Johnson named the first Special Assistant to the President for Consumer Affairs. In 1969 President Nixon asked Congress to pass a Buyer's Bill of Rights, and he called for the establishment of a new Division of Consumer Protection within the Justice Department. When these proposals did not fare well in Congress, President Nixon proposed a Consumer Product Safety Act, a Consumer Fraud Prevention Act, a Fair Warranty Disclosure Act, and a National Business Council for Consumer Affairs within the Commerce Department. At the same time, by executive order, he created the Office of Consumer Affairs in the Executive Office of the President. This office was given responsibility for analyzing and coordinating all federal activities in the field of consumer protection (*Consumerism* 1973).

The Establishment of the NAD/NARB System in 1971

The climate for advertising in the 1960s made it clear to the advertising industry that action was needed to forestall additional government initiatives that seemed likely to restrict greatly the traditional methods of the advertising industry to operate in the market economy. It brought together four major trade associations that were interested in the long-term viability of the advertising industry: the American Advertising Federation (AAF), the AAAA, the ANA, and the Council of Better Business Bureaus (CBBB).[1] One spokesman said: "We think it would be better to wear a self-regulatory hair shirt *now*, than a tight-fitting legislative straight-jacket later on" (Purdon 1972). Interestingly, however, the goals and purposes of the NAD/NARB system were expressed not in terms of self interest, but in terms that conveyed the clear intent to improve advertising and thereby serve consumers and society. The advertising industry seemed to begin with the notion that establishing a self-regulatory system was clearly a matter of enlightened self-interest. A genuine consumer orientation had been for some years a part of the modern approach to marketing employed by at least some firms, and, it was argued, it should be a part of the approach to advertising regulation.

The already existing National Advertising Division (NAD) of the CBBB was designated as the investigatory body and the National Advertising Review Board (NARB) was established as an appeals body. Funding was provided from general funds of the CBBB contributed by member companies.

At the outset some consumerists called the NAD/NARB a tool of big business; and in contrast some conservatives called the system a captive of consumerists. However, because the NAD receives valid as well as invalid complaints it can be argued that the NAD/NARB system serves "as the first line of criticism for the public [for valid complaints and also] as the first line of defense for the advertiser" [for invalid complaints] (Purdon 1972).

Since its inception the NAD functions have been to (1) receive complaints or initiate inquiries, (2) determine the issues, (3) collect and evaluate data, and (4) negotiate agreements. After the investigatory stage and if negotiations between the NAD and the advertiser fail to resolve the complaint or controversy, the NARB can establish a five-member panel to handle an appeal. If the matter is not resolved satisfactorily by the panel, the NARB can refer advertising it believes is unlawful to government enforcement agencies.

The guidelines under which the NAD/NARB system was set up to operate were as follows:

1. To deal with matters of fact, truth, and accuracy.
2. To deal with substantiation.
3. Advertising should provide relevant and adequate disclosure.
4. Advertising should contain no false disparagement.
5. Advertising should contain no deception, intended or otherwise.
6. Advertising should be in accordance with FTC precedents (Purdon 1972).

Because the NAD/NARB system is the major form of advertising self-regulation to be compared with self-regulation in the United Kingdom, further description and analysis of the system are deferred until chapter 3. Other forms of advertising self-regulation, however, comprise the environment for and complement the NAD/NARB system. They are discussed briefly here to provide further context in which to understand the NAD/NARB system.

An Overview of Advertising Self-Regulation
(Except NAD/NARB)

Self-Discipline by Advertisers and Agencies. Little literature discusses advertising preclearance or other self-controls by advertisers and their agencies (Zanot 1985, 51). However, some sort of advertising clearance process is a necessity for virtually all of them. Many advertisers have long had policies in writing, and they publicly express their intent to be "good citizens" and to be responsive to the needs of consumers and the economy in a socially responsible fashion. For example, General Mills, in a statement of corporate responsibility, recognizing that the company and its subsidiaries spent $54 million for media advertising in 1971, said:

> Recognizing the power and importance of such amounts to the corporation and to *society*, the company through the years has endeavored to

produce advertising that is not only truthful, but also informative and educational, that renders a maximum of helpful service and that, insofar as possible, seeks to expand markets rather than merely to take business away from competitors.

Any competitive or comparative statement to be made about any product or service must be supported. Each manager responsible for a product is also responsible for the preparation of claims and the development of adequate substantiation for them where necessary (*Advertising Age*, 27 September 1971, 3).

Certainly the enlightened self-interest as expressed in the consumer orientation of the "marketing concept" in the 1950s was a step in the right direction. In that same view, the response to the consumerism of the 1960s and the development of increased sensitivity to consumer complaints were also steps toward greater social responsibility. Manufacturer programs to improve and police reseller practices are also a part of such self-control. However, the precise degree and nature of ethics as they are applied by advertisers across the broad spectrum of business are not known. Advertiser and agency decisions are "grounded in pragmatics . . . [and] do not seem to incorporate any absolute standard of ethics and honesty but, rather are grounded in the enlightened self-interest of avoiding subsequent regulatory action or suit by competitors" (Zanot 1985, 47). Probably it is fair to say that there is great diversity among companies and industries and over time, as ethical standards reflect changes in managers within each company. The ethical standards that are applied are probably close to the minimum perceived social norms within business, which are reflective primarily of whatever is believed to be within the law at any given time.

Advertising control begins when advertisers and their agencies consider whether their proposed advertising meets legal and ethical standards. "Some would go so far as to say that . . . the routine clearance process that takes place long before the public sees the ads in the media . . . is the most critical and effective of all the different methods of regulating false and deceptive advertising" (Zanot 1985, 44). The recent trend toward deregulation and the 1982 suspension of the NAB Television Code make the advertising clearance process even more important (Zanot 1985, 44).

The legal clearance process for advertising is "routine but complex," and includes both legal and ethical considerations (Zanot 1985, 45). Zanot (1985, 44–45, 59, 68) presented "a model of the clearance process and a chart depicting primary concerns of each entity involved." The process includes the initial and final clearances that normally involve reviews by the agency, the advertiser, their law firms or legal counsel, and the print or broadcast media. These reviews include consideration of "the full gamut from compliance with existing codes and laws through substantiation of claims and potential points of deception through matters of taste and propriety" (Zanot 1985, 51). He concludes that the advertising clearance process is less than perfect, but, "It is difficult to contemplate ways that would make the

the clearance process more effective without making it unduly cumbersome and time consuming" (Zanot 1985, 51).

Self-Regulation by Individual Media. Most newspapers and magazines (Greyser 1967), as well as the three major television networks, have a code or set of standards that they apply to advertising submitted to them. Little literature describes and characterizes such self-regulation, and media standards are not well known except by those who apply or who must live by them. Probably the best known are those of the television networks, which are discussed at some length in chapter 4.

Self-Regulation by Industry Associations. A great deal of advertising self-regulation stems from industry groups comprising advertisers, advertising agencies, and media. At least twenty-two associations have advertising codes, as shown in table 2–1.

Among these twenty-two associations LaBarbera (1980) has identified twenty-six distinct codes: she concluded that "the policy statements and ethical codes range from those which are general to those which are detailed." She has categorized the issues covered in these codes in table 2–2.

Table 2–2 shows the relative importance of the advertising code provisions, with the broad issues of truth and accuracy at the top, followed closely by substantiation of claims. The more specialized categories that follow these broad issues are product or industry specific to a greater extent than the broad issues, and therefore not appropriate for as many of the codes.

It is impossible in this brief overview to examine all of these codes in detail. The selection that follows is designed to cover the codes that have had the greatest influence on advertising self-regulation in the United States, and that permit the most accurate generalizations about advertising self-regulation.

Self-Regulation by Advertising Agency Associations. The AAAA is the most important of the advertising agency associations, counting among its members the advertising agencies that account for a high proportion of national advertising in the United States. The *AAAA Standards of Practice* were first adopted on 16 October 1924, and most recently revised on 28 April 1962. The document that was endorsed by the ANA includes a creative code that states that agency members of the AAAA will not knowingly produce advertising that contains the following:

1. False or misleading statements or exaggerations, visual or verbal.

2. Testimonials which do not reflect the real choice of a competent witness.

Table 2–1
Industry Groups with Advertising Self-Regulation Programs

Group	Year Created	Last Year Code Revised
Advertising associations		
1. American Advertising Federation	1965	1979
2. American Association of Advertising		
Agencies	1924	1962
3. Association of National Advertisers	1972	Transferred code to CARU in 1974
4. Business Professional Advertising		
Association	1975	1980
Industry groups		
5. Council of Better Business Bureaus	1912	1984
Household furniture	1978	—
Automobiles and trucks	1978	—
Carpet and rugs	1978	—
Home improvement	1975	—
Charitable soliciations	1974	1977
6. Children's Advertising Review Unit of the NAD/NARB	1974	1984
7. National Advertising Division/National Advertising Review Board (NAD/NARB)	1971	—
Media associations		
8. American Business Press	1910	1971
9. Direct Mail Marketing Association	1960	1978
10. Direct Selling Association	1970	1979
11. National Association of Broadcasters[a]		
Radio	1937	Disbanded in 1982
Television	1952	Disbanded in 1982
12. Outdoor Advertising Association of America	1950	1972
Trade associations		
13. American Wine Association[b]	1949	1978
14. Wine Institute[b]	1949	1978
15. Distilled Spirits Association	1934	1973
16. United States Brewers Association	1955	Revision in process
17. Pharmaceutical Manufacturers Association	1958	1967
18. Proprietary Association	1934	1975
19. Bank Marketing Association	1976	—
20. Motion Picture Association of America	1930	1979
21. National Swimming Pool Institute	1970	1978
22. Toy Manufacturers Association	1962	1975

Source: LaBarbera 1980b; updated by Miracle 1985, 59–60.

[a]Since the advertising self-regulatory activities of the NAB were disbanded, the three major broadcast networks have individually assumed primary responsibility for self-regulation of commercials.

[b]These groups share the same code.

3. Price claims which are misleading.

4. Comparisons which unfairly disparage a competitive product or service.

5. Claims insufficiently supported, or which distort the true meaning or practicable application of statements made by professional or scientific authority.

Table 2–2
Summary of Subject Matter of Advertising Code Provisions
(*n* = 26 distinct codes of the twenty-two industry groups[a])

	Codes Including Provision	
Subject Matter of Provision	*Number*	*Percentage*
Truth and accuracy	26	100
Substantiation of claims	21	81
Testimonials and endorsements	16	62
Illustrations or television presentations	16	62
Comparative advertising	15	58
Disclosure of complete information	14	54
Price claims	13	50
Puffery	13	50
Taste	12	46
Guarantees and warranties	10	38
Young and immature markets	9	35
Bait advertising	9	35
Use of word *free*	8	31
Layout	8	31
Contests, prizes and other promotions	8	31
Credit	7	27
Health and safety	7	27
Placement and acceptance in media	7	27
Use of professionally significant words such as *bonded, insured*	6	23
Degradation of societal groups	5	19
Asterisks	5	19
Use of words *factory, manufacturer, wholesaler*	5	19
Fear appeals	3	12
Advertising frequency	3	12
Trade-in allowances	3	12
Abbreviations	2	8
Indentification, age, or volume of business	2	8
Advertising space for public causes	1	4

Source: LaBarbera 1980.

[a]The Council of Better Business Bureaus has created five additional industry codes and the National Association of Broadcasters has two different codes. The American Wine Association and Wine Institute share the same code. The Association of National Advertisers transferred implementation of its code to the Children's Advertising Review Unit.

6. Statements, suggestions or pictures offensive to public decency (American Association of Advertising Agencies, undated).

Self-Regulation by Advertiser Associations. Most of the industry associations are product or product–class specific and do not lend themselves well to generalization. The ANA is the largest and most important of these associations, cutting across all major industries. Although the ANA has long professed interest in self-regulation, it was argued (correctly or incorrectly) that the heterogeneous nature of its members made any kind of code difficult for the association to develop. The ANA therefore tended to support codes of other associations, such as the AAAA, and was a major force in establishing the NAD/NARB/CARU. The ANA continues to serve on the National Advertising Review Council (NARC) and urges its members to support the NAD/NARB system and its CARU. The NAD/NARB system and CARU embrace a diversity of industries successfully, as does the *BCAP* in the United Kingdom. Because industry associations and the ANA have not taken the lead role in self-regulation, they are not discussed further here.

Self-Regulation by Media Associations. Although several media associations have a long history of setting advertising standards, the NAB deserves special mention. In 1978 the NAB membership included "over 500 television stations. . . . In 1978 over 65% of all commercial television stations, accounting for an estimated 85% of all television viewers, subscribed to the code" (Cohen 1982).

The NAB codes on radio and television advertising were quite detailed, covering numerous matters with respect to products and acceptable or unacceptable advertising practices for them. The NAB published from time to time numerous interpretations of the codes and a series of detailed policy guidelines on controversial issues such as comparative advertising, advertising to children, personal care products, and lotteries. In the 1970s the NAB also maintained committees on (1) alcohol, beverage, and tobacco advertising; (2) children's advertising; (3) comparative and general advertising; (4) personal products; and (5) health issues advertising (*NAB Code News*, January–February 1978).

Also, in contrast to other advertising self-regulatory programs that deal primarily with complaints about advertising after it is run, the NAB (along with the television networks and the Motion Picture Association of America) prescreened advertising. The NAB required prescreening of "all broadcast commercials in four areas which have received extensive criticism: (1) children's toys, (2) children's premiums, (3) personal care products, and (4) vegetable oil and margarine products involving health claims (LaBarbera 1980).

After many years of NAB activity to regulate advertising so that "it may serve the public interest" (*History of the NAB* 1965), the Justice Department in June 1979

> filed suit against the NAB . . . to prevent the association from writing commercial-time standards. The standards in existence recommended maximum levels of commercials per hour at various times during the day to stations that subscribe to NAB's television code. Justice Department

attorneys believe that time standards represent an illegal attempt to limit the amount of television advertising time available for sale, which [restrains] free competition among broadcasters . . . [thereby] keeping television commercial prices and profits high. . . . The Justice Department also opposes NAB standards which prevent code subscriber stations from airing certain categories of products, such as liquor (LaBarbera 1981).

On 11 March 1982 a federal district court ruled that

the NAB's advertising standards . . . [are] a per se violation of the anti-trust laws, and declared that several other standards will be evaluated at a trial based on a rule-of-reason analysis . . . [also] . . . The multiproduct standard which prohibits advertisements of more than one product in a commercial lasting less than 60 seconds [unless integrated to appear to the viewer as a single commercial] was declared per se illegal (Cohen 1982).

Immediately after this decision the NAB suspended its Television Code. Subsequently in November 1982 the NAB, in a consent decree, agreed not to disseminate or enforce advertising standards that artificially limit the supply of advertising time (Cohen 1983; *Advertising Age*, 29 November 1982).

The United Kingdom[2]

The Economic Setting

Historically, the classical liberal tradition of economic thought has been the intellectual basis for the British economic system. The United Kingdom had a prior history of government's granting monopolies or special privileges to certain interests or companies. Consequently, British competition policy was in large part directed at preserving competition against government-supported monopoly power, as well as against private monopoly power.

From the late 1800s to the twentieth century the British economy was probably the most competitive in the world. But before and during World War I tariffs were erected. In the 1930s manufacturers learned to cooperate and to share available markets. During World War II and for several years thereafter the economy was regulated by rationing and price controls. As markets continued to be protected from foreign competition, there was a tendency to share them in a way that produced a comfortable life for all concerned.

Early Pressures for Self-Regulation

The United Kingdom has a long history of attempts by people working in advertising to exert some measure of control over the style and content of advertisements. Though until the middle of the twentieth century these generally took the form of individual initiatives rather than concerted action, they provide an interesting indication that regulation in some form was recognized as necessary and that in some quarters at least there was an awareness of advertising's ethical and social responsibilities.

As early as 1800 William Cobbett, when issuing a prospectus for his newspaper *The Porcupine,* declared that "the obscene and filthy boastings of quackery will, on no consideration whatsoever, be admitted," and in 1824 the anonymous author of *The Periodical Press of Great Britain and Ireland* commented, "Every day there are advertisements offered to English newspapers that are refused for the personal allusions they make, or the object they wish to accomplish." There was, however, an enormous variation in attitudes, and while some publications—notably *The Times*—were to set high standards throughout the century, there were many others whose proprietors believed that sufficient protection was already afforded by the law, and who argued publicly that readers must look after their own interests because publishers could not act as their guardians. It was also argued that if the public knew that some advertisements were being rejected, they would put undue trust in those which did appear, and it was therefore best to leave them to question everything.

During the nineteenth century the majority of advertisements were acceptable even by present-day standards, and many of those that seem exaggerated or even untruthful may well have been acceptable by the standards of the time. A number of serious abuses occurred in connection with advertising, however, in which action was clearly required. Apart from the dishonest and sometimes dangerous claims made by some of the medical quacks, the lack of care by some publications when accepting copy meant that blackmailers, swindlers, and seducers lurked undetected in their classified columns. More explicit material, such as fraudulent begging letters and pornography, was sent by post.

By the turn of the century some notable progress had been made. Some journals required mail order advertisers to allow a representative to inspect the goods being offered; *London Opinion Magazine* guaranteed a refund if any article advertised in its pages turned out to have been misrepresented; and *The Times* invited readers to write to its manager in the case of a problem arising from an advertisement in its pages and promised to ban the advertiser if the complaint were found to be justified.

There was also considerable disquiet about standards on the part of leading advertisers, not from the point of view of protecting the public but rather because the presence of undesirable advertisements in a publication might have an adverse effect on their own. In 1910 the Advertisers Protection Society, the body representing the leading advertisers, wrote to the Association of Advertisement Managers (that is, those responsible for selling advertising space) proposing a meeting to discuss the problem. The Association replied that "the matter having been thoroughly debated, it was decided that the ills are not so prevalent as was suggested in your letter, and that no good could come from a conference on the subject" (Nevett 1982).

Goodall (1914) found it difficult to describe the operation of contemporary controls on press advertising: "Naturally, all papers of standing draw a more or less hard and fast line with a view of excluding obviously questionable or undesirable advertisements, the point at which the line is drawn varying according to the philosophy of life which the journal adopts."

In the case of posters, the other major medium of the period, there is evidence that control of content was exercised by major site proprietors such as railway companies at least as early as the 1850s. The poster industry also provided the first example of a concerted move to establish self-regulation, when in 1890 the two leading bill-posting bodies combined to set up a Joint Censorship Committee. Although the body was concerned with points of design and aesthetics rather than product claims, and busied itself with such matters as lurid theatrical posters and nude figures, it marks the establishment of an important principle—namely, that a section of the industry could unite in the enforcement of standards.

Early Legal Controls

From the early years of the nineteenth century Parliament was enacting statutes that affected various aspects of advertising activity, although it should be emphasized that these were intended to correct abuses rather than to regulate advertising in general. Among the areas affected by the most important statutes were:

The Metropolitan Paving Act (1817): advertising boardings and projecting signs.

The Vagrancy Acts (1824 and 1832): obscene advertising and fortune tellers.

The Metropolitan Police Act (1839): sandwich-board men, billposters, and writing on walls; the use of horns and other noisemakers to attract attention.

The London Hackney Carriage Act (1853): the display of advertising on and in carriages and carts.

The Metropolitan Streets Act (1867): sandwich-board men and the distribution of handbills.

The Trade Marks Acts (1875, 1883, 1888, 1905): defining trade marks and giving legal protection to users.

The Post Office (Protection) Act (1882): the sending of obscene or indecent material by post.

The Indecent Advertisements Act (1889): advertisements concerned with venereal disease and other sexually related complaints.

The Betting and Loans (Infants) Act (1892): material inciting minors to bet or to borrow money.

The Uniforms Act (1894): the wearing of British military or naval uniforms for advertising purposes by sandwich-board men.

The Advertisements Regulations Act (1907): protecting beauty spots from advertising hoardings.

Public Health Act Amendment Act (1907): sky signs (that is, solid letters forming a silhouette against the sky).

In addition to this major legislation, local authorities could introduce bye-laws that sometimes affected advertising. The London County Council, for instance, was able to ban the use of flashing lights or searchlights in 1900, and had prohibited skysigns sixteen years before Parliament took similar action. Authorities could also promote local acts of Parliament if a particular matter was ultra vires: Dover Corporation, for example, secured the power to rid itself of a much publicized Quaker Oats sign erected on top of the famous white cliffs.

At the same time an important body of case law was growing up as the courts were asked to apply common law rules to new situations that were arising with the increasing use of advertising. Comparative advertising was to prove a problem from the outset. As early as 1731 in *Harman v. Delaney* the judge declared: "The law has always been very tender of the reputation of tradesmen, and therefore words spoken of them in the way of their trade will bear an action, that will not be actionable in the case of another person, and if bare words are so, it will be stronger in the case of a libel in a publick newspaper, which is so diffusive."

In a number of cases in the following century, advertisers who disparaged competitors found themselves defendants in actions for defamation. Provided that the disparagement was confined to the goods rather than the maker, however, it was necessary for the plaintiff to show that damage had resulted. The courts were, in fact, quite prepared to allow comparative advertising as long as the quality of the rival product was not falsely represented. As Lord Lindley, Master of the Rolls, declared in *Hubbuck v. Wilkinson* (1899), "If the only false statement complained of is that the defendant's goods are better than the plaintiff's, such a statement is not actionable, even if the plaintiff is damnified by it."

As branded products became more heavily promoted, the temptation increased for less scrupulous firms to profit from a competitor's advertising by adopting the same or a similar name. Such tactics were condemned by the Master of the Rolls in *Croft v. Day* (1844), "It has been very correctly said that the principle, in these cases, is thus: that no man has the right to sell his own goods as those of another . . . It is perfectly manifest that to do such things is to commit a very gross fraud."

One of the most important cases affecting advertising to come before the courts was *Carlill v. The Carbolic Smoke Ball Company* (1892). The company advertised its Smoke Ball as a rapid cure for a variety of ailments including influenza. In the copy it promised a reward of £100 to anyone who contracted the complaint having used the Ball according to the printed instructions. Mrs. Carlill bought the product, used it as directed, and caught influenza. When she applied to the company for £100 they refused to pay; she then sued in the High Court. The company's defence—that no contract existed and that they clearly had no intention of being bound by the offer—was dismissed by the judge and his decision was upheld on appeal. The Carbolic Smoke Ball case served as a warning to advertisers and agencies about irresponsibility in the use of financial guarantees, and it is an important case in contract law because it established the principle that an offer in advertisement constitutes an offer capable of acceptance and is not simply an offer to receive offers from others. In both respects it probably had a moderating effect on the framing of copy claims.

Early Consumer Reaction

The upper classes of British society have always disliked advertising; they believed that a properly conducted business had no need of it. Macaulay in 1830, for example, wrote that "We expect some reserve, some decent pride in our hatter and bootmaker," and Carlyle declared in similar vein, "There is not a man or hat-maker born into the world but feels, or has felt, that he is degrading himself if he speak of his excellences or prowesses, and supremacy in his craft" (Turner 1965). Those who were influenced by advertisements were also disdained. According to an article in the *Atheneum*, "It could not otherwise happen that Day and Martin, Rowland,

Colborn and Bentley, Eady, Warren and those after their kind could lavish so much money in the praises of their oil, their books, their pills and their polish, if there did not exist a class of human beings who are greedy beyond belief" (Nevett 1982).

The first organized reaction against advertising in the form of the National Society for Controlling the Abuses of Public Advertising, known commonly as SCAPA, arose in the last decade of the nineteenth century. Although its foundation in 1893 was prompted by the need to protect beauty spots against disfigurement by advertising hoardings, its declared aims show it to have represented an attack on advertising in general. These were:

1. To amend existing law to give local authorities power to control advertising visible from throughfares or public places.
2. To insert in every bill giving legislative authority for the acquisition of land or construction of works provisions prohibiting or controlling the use of any part of the fabric for advertising.
3. To undertake to boycott products promoted in an offensive way.
4. To consider a tax on all exposed advertisements.

SCAPA achieved an enormous amount of press coverage and was largely instrumental in securing passage of the Advertisements Regulations Act of 1907, pressure for which received considerable impetus in 1901 from a wave of anti-American feeling resulting from the erection of the Quaker Oats advertising sign on Dover Cliffs. Its achievements, however, were largely those of one man—its indefatigable Honorary Secretary, Irish barrister and journalist Richardson Evans. Even at its peak SCAPA's paid-up membership did not number more than a few hundred, and these were drawn almost exclusively from the upper classes.

The mass of the population was unmoved by Evans' efforts. When he wrote a book on the Society and its work, it sold only thirty copies. Advertising seems not to have been perceived as a threat by the public at large. In fact, it was a subject of humor in contemporary music-hall songs.

> There are fifty cures for every ill, and each one is the best,
> You can drink them down or rub them in, or nail them on your chest,
> You can make hair grow on an ostrich egg if you try the proper stuff,
> You can make toes sprout on a timber leg, if you only use enough (Nevett 1982).

SCAPA lost momentum after the 1907 Act was passed, and it was a spent force when Evans eventually relinquished his post in 1923 at the age of 77. It was still in existence after the Second World War, by which time its title had been changed to the Society for the Prevention of Disfigurement. When in 1948 the Town and Country Planning (Control of Advertisements) Regulations brought outdoor advertising under official control, it was believed that the Society could no longer serve a useful purpose and in 1953 it was finally wound up.

Although particular advertising abuses needed correction, attacks on advertising per se were bound to fail. National expenditure rose dramatically from an estimated £161,960 in 1800 to £5,000,000 by mid-century and £15 million by 1912 (Nevett 1982). Business found that advertising worked—a point illustrated ironically by the way the writer of the *Atheneum* article just quoted is able to recall the names of heavily promoted brands.

The Interwar Years

Although the period from 1919 to 1939 saw increasing public pressure for some form of control, particularly on medical advertising, evidence also suggests that advertising was actually growing more acceptable at all levels of society. During the World War I it had been used on a large scale by the government for recruiting and the sale of War Bonds. In the years following, its case was put persuasively by the two most celebrated agency heads of the day, William Crawford and Charles Higham. Both were involved in public service campaigns, both became nationally known, and both received Knighthoods—the first advertising men to be thus honored. Although Parliament steadfastly refused to allow the British Broadcasting Corporation (BBC) to carry advertising or commercial stations to operate in the United Kingdom, during the 1930s there were audiences of millions for broadcasts in English from Continental stations. The general public seemed to prefer programs with advertising. But perhaps the ultimate accolade (in British eyes) came when King George V and Queen Mary visited the Advertising and Marketing Exhibition in 1933.

There remained a lack of concerted action for self-regulation, though there is ample evidence of high standards being set by individual media. The *Radio Times*, for example, introduced a scheme in 1932 under which all medical advertisements were scrutinized by a panel of doctors, and the *Daily Mail* was stated in 1937 to have rejected 637 advertisements in the previous five years. *John Bull*, a leading weekly magazine, also introduced a notable scheme under which it only accepted advertisements for food products after a sample had been analyzed and compared with the claims made in the copy.

At the same time there was a perceptible movement toward centralized regulation. The Newspaper Society, the body representing the regional and local press, set up its advertising department in the late twenties to give advice to members on undesirable products and claims, and the Newspaper Proprietors Association representing the national papers exercised a measure of control through its Copy Committee. The strongest impetus came, however, from the newly created Advertising Association (AA). Founded in 1925, it had as one of its declared aims, "To promote public confidence in advertising and advertised goods through the correction or suppression of abuses which undermine that confidence." In 1928 it set up its Advertising Investigation Department, which was to remain the official industry body for the investigation of complaints for almost fifty years. Although its efforts were denigrated by critics who pointed out that it could scarcely be called objective when it was organized and financed by those very elements it was supposed to control, it probably did much to move advertisers and agencies further along the road toward collective responsibility. By October 1937 it had collected some 2,860 confidential dossiers, and during the preceding twelve months, had dealt with 1,169 enquiries.

Also notable during this period was the action taken by the pharmaceutical industry to stop some of the more outrageous claims made for certain proprietary medicines. In 1919 fifty of the more reputable manufacturers formed the Proprietary Association of Great Britain (PAGB) to deal with just this kind of problem. Many of these firms were producing tried and trusted family remedies to which no objection could be raised, but their reputation was suffering at the hands of unscrupulous operators making outrageous claims. An example of this occurred in 1924 when the *Daily Mail* launched an attack on Yadil, a heavily advertised preparation that was claimed to cure a wide range of complaints including consumption, cancer, bronchitis, pleurisy, pneumonia, malaria, scarlet fever, measles, diphtheria, and pernicious anemia. The paper printed a condemnation of the product by a Cambridge professor. The manufacturer took legal action to try to prevent the publication of further damaging facts. The action failed, and the product had to be withdrawn from the market (Turner 1965).

During the 1930s, pressure for some form of action on medical advertising grew noticeably stronger. The Royal College of Surgeons produced a report in 1934 stating that claims for patent medicines were "always exaggerated and are, in general purely fraudulent." The following year the Chemistry Society urged the medical profession to educate the public about which substances were good for them and which were not. In 1936 the Medicines and Surgical Appliances (Advertisement) Bill was introduced in Parliament. Drafted in consultation with the Pharmaceutical Society after four years of negotiations, it was aimed at banning advertisements for "cures" for a range of serious complaints including cancer and tuberculosis. When it came before Commons for its second reading, however, insufficient members were present in the Chamber and it was counted out. Advertising for cancer treatments was subsequently banned by the Cancer Act (1939).

The prospect of impending legislation eventually stimulated a firm response from the pharmaceutical manufacturers. In 1936 the Proprietary Association of Great Britain promulgated a code of standards that, although of limited value in the short term because it applied only to members, nevertheless set a notable precedent. For the first time in the United Kingdom there existed a set of rules for the guidance of advertisers and agencies. The principle was subsequently extended to cover all medical advertisers with the appearance of the British Code of Standards Relating to the Advertising of Medicines and Treatments (1948). A quarter of a century after the first initiative, it was extended again to cover all types of commercial advertisement when the Advertising Association introduced the first edition of the *British Code of Advertising Practice (BCAP)*.

Recent Trends in Legislation

As previously discussed, Parliament's concern with advertising tended to focus on correcting what it considered to be specific abuses, rather than regulating advertising in general terms. Consequently pressures on advertisers to tell the truth were commercial rather than legal. A consumer who had been deliberately misled by an advertisement might sue in the civil courts on the basis of misrepresentation, but such cases are few and they tend to relate to sales by private individuals. The main change in recent decades has been to bring advertising within the ambit of the criminal law, so that those found guilty of an offense face possible fines and imprisonment. The threat of action in the civil courts still remains, but there can be little doubt that the possibility of criminal prosecution has had a valuable deterrent effect.

Not all government action involves direct legislation. Because of pressure on parliamentary time, governments are tending increasingly to use a device known as the enabling act, which means in effect that Parliament passes an act granting power to a particular minister to make such regulations as he or she may see fit. These regulations then have statutory force.

The following are some of the most important measures creating criminal offenses with respect to advertising:

The Trade Descriptions Act (1968) makes it an offense to apply a false trade description or to supply or offer to supply goods to which a false trade description has been applied. Penalties on conviction on indictment include imprisonment for up to two years, or an unlimited fine, or both.

The Powers of Criminal Courts Act (1973) empowers courts to order those convicted of offenses under certain statutes such as the Trade Descriptions Act (1968) to pay compensation to those consumers affected. Previously they had been obliged to sue through the Civil Courts, using proof of conviction as evidence.

The Fair Trading Act (1973) provides for the appointment of a Director-General of Fair Trading and staff to keep a watch on consumer interests and to recommend government action when necessary. He or she may recommend that an order be made to regulate or prohibit a particular trade practice. The Secretary of State is empowered to make regulations accordingly. Two such orders affecting advertising are

1. The Mail Order Transactions (Information) Order (1976), which specifies that mail order advertisements must carry the name and actual address of the seller (that is, not just a box number).

2. The Business Advertisements (Disclosure) Order (1977), which makes it an offense for a trader to advertise in the guise of a private individual. This order is of particular importance because the Trade Descriptions Act, as the name suggests, only applied to traders.

The Supply of Goods (Implied Terms) Act (1973) effectively ends the use of bogus "guarantees."

The Control of Pollution Act (1974) includes the concept of noise pollution and prohibits the use of loudspeakers for advertising purposes.

Unsolicited Goods and Services Acts (1971 and 1975) and regulations, as well as making provisions regarding the rights and duties of recipients of unsolicited goods, tightened up the law relating to payment for directory entries (long a field for con men) and prohibited the unsolicited distribution of promotional material for publications on sexual technique.

The Consumer Transactions (Restriction on Statements) Order (1976) prohibits advertisements purporting to apply terms made void under the Unfair Contract-Terms Act (1977), which if permitted would deprive a consumer of his or her legal rights (for example, a statement that goods on sale at a reduced price may not be returned if faulty).

In addition to legislation on a general level, there has been a continuation of measures aimed at correcting abuses that may arise in connection with the advertising of particular types of goods or services. These include, in chronological order, the following:

Customs and Excise Act (1952) as amended prohibits misdescription in advertising for wines and spirits.

Food and Drugs Act (1955) as amended and with subsequent regulations specifies requirements for advertising and labeling food.

Prevention of Fraud (Investments) Act (1958) as amended governs statements that can be made in advertisements seeking to induce persons to make investments of money.

Children Act (1958) prohibits anonymous advertisements offering to take care of children.

Protection of Depositors Act (1963) governs advertisements seeking to attract deposits of money.

London Cab Acts (1968 and 1973) prohibit the use of the words *taxi* or *cab* in advertising for private hire cars. (London taxis are under the control of the Metropolitan Police and are the only vehicles permitted to ply for hire.)

Sex Discrimination Act (1975) prohibits advertisements indicating an intention to discriminate on the grounds of sex or because a person is married.

Adoption Act (1976) restricts advertisements relating to the adoption of children. In particular, it prohibits advertising by couples wishing to adopt a child.

Race Relations Act (1976) prohibits advertisements indicating an intention to discriminate on the grounds of race.

One further piece of legislation that should be mentioned reflects Parliament's continued desire to hold advertising at bay in the sixties. A number of "pirate" radio stations had been set up on disused forts off the British coast and on ships moored just outside British territorial waters. They gave British youth a diet of pop music dispensed with an informality totally different from the staid BBC. The government's response was twofold. First, in 1964 it made border adjustments to bring the ships within British territorial waters. Then, in 1967 Parliament passed the Marine Broadcasting Offences Act, which prohibits off-shore stations, advertisements for them, and their use for advertising.

No legislation of note has affected advertising for some years. There are several possible reasons for this. The Thatcher government, in power since 1979, had shown little interest in consumer protection and was accused of being too sympathetic to the interests of business. Thatcher is even alleged to have removed a minister because he was seeking to introduce tighter controls on cigarette advertising. It may be, too, that the major abuses of the present age may have been prohibited or reduced to an acceptable level, and that we must wait for serious new abuses to arise (as they certainly will) or for the climate of opinion to change. Without doubt, as we discuss later in detail, the voluntary control system has worked effectively, both in terms of the operation of ASA and of the speed with which media react to new problems such as advertisements for fallout shelters. In addition, the policy of the Office of Fair Trading is to encourage trades and industries to regulate their affairs by means of voluntary codes of practice whenever possible, thus obviating the need for legislation. Yet although the advertising industry seems relatively free from the prospect of further legislative controls at the moment, the Labour Party's recently adopted *Charter for Consumers* promises to replace self-regulation with a statutory code.

The Emergence of Centralized Self-Regulation

During the Second World War (1938–1945) the standard of advertising unquestionably improved. The reason probably had more to do with the shortage of newsprint than with patriotism or the public interest. News-papers were small, the national dailies for example being rationed to four pages, so that the demand for advertising space exceeded supply to the extent that publishers could pick and choose, and so could exclude less desirable advertisements without being in any danger of losing revenue.

Perhaps it was this vision of what was possible that led to a more concentrated attack on advertising in the ensuing decades. Changes in the climate of public and political opinion brought advertisements under close scrutiny. There may well have been an increased level of general awareness of advertising after 1955, when the intrusive new medium of television began bringing it directly into people's homes, but there was no united opposition. Some telling criticisms were made on ethical grounds by Charles Medawar and Social Audit, but failed to attract widespread attention. Teachers complained that advertising prostituted the English language and promoted bad manners. The activities of Ralph Nader in the United States aroused a certain interest in consumerist circles, but nobody raised the banner in the United Kingdom. Uncertain how to respond, the government adopted the time-honored expedient of British administrations in such circumstances and appointed a commission. The Malony Committee, as it was known, produced a report that was to lead eventually to the passing of the Trade Descriptions Act (1968).

An important source of consumer discontent was the difficulty likely to be experienced in making a complaint related to an advertisement, especially because the AA and its AID were little known. This point was seized by the BBC, which had always been ideologically opposed to advertising, and which was losing its radio audience to commercial stations broadcast-ing from outside the United Kingdom. It introduced consumer advice programs on both television and radio, inviting complaints from members of the public and exposing the activities of shady operators. Program researchers were shown being abused and sometimes physically assaulted by advertisers. That these were disreputable tricksters rather than blue-chip companies was a distinction probably not apparent to the average viewer. The need for some mechanism for handling complaints probably was.

If the advertising industry's image was becoming a little tarnished, it suffered still further as considerable publicity was given to evidence linking smoking with lung cancer. Though research world-wide had demonstrated this link beyond reasonable doubt, the Advertising Association, the Institute of Practitioners in Advertising, and the Incorporated Society of British Advertisers joined in an ill-judged and unsuccessful atttempt to stop cigarette advertising being banned from television. The poster industry's joint censorship committee went even further, rejecting a Ministry of Health poster with the words "Cigarettes cause lung cancer" on the grounds that this is not the same as saying "Cigarette smoking is a cause of lung cancer." Lord Hailsham, a Conservative minister and one of the country's leading lawyers, described this as "absolutely indefensible and indeed irresponsible, illogical quibbling." And the advertising industry stood accused of putting revenue before lives.

Cigarettes apart, criticism of advertising was tending to operate on a far more general level, rather than being directed against specific abuses as in earlier decades. To some extent it was also becoming politically based, and sections of the Labour Party were particularly outspoken. Novelist C.P. Snow, who had been a critic of advertising in the 1930s, became a minister in the Wilson administration. And as the fluctuating fortunes of the press saw the demise of a number of newspapers favorably inclined toward the party, The Labour Party became convinced that this was brought about by pro-Conservative advertisers starving the left-wing press of advertising revenue. In 1959 a public meeting called by Francis Noel-Baker, a prominent Labour member of Parliament, set up the Advertising Inquiry Committee, intended to function as an independent watchdog with the job of identifying "all kinds of socially harmful advertisement." Two years later the party set up a commission under the chairmanship of Lord Reith, which in 1966 produced a report that recommended the establishment of a body called the National Consumer Board, finance for which was to be provided by a levy on advertising. Six years later, in 1972, the Labour Party produced its *Green Paper* on Advertising, which led to the taxation of advertising being adopted as official party policy, though it was not implemented when the party returned to power two years later.

In the meantime, as pressure began to mount, the advertising industry's initial response was to draft *BCAP*, which was first published in 1961 at the Advertising Association Conference. At the same time it set up the Code of Advertising Practice (CAP) Committee to supervise the operation of the Code and ensure that it was kept up to date. Critics expressed doubts as to whether it could really operate in the public interest, including as it did representatives of virtually every advertising organization of note. The industry accordingly responded in the following year by setting up the ASA under the chairmanship of Professor Sir Arnold Plant, a distinguished academic whose impartiality was beyond question. The objects of the Authority were defined as "The promotion and enforcement through the United Kingdom of the highest standards of advertising in all media, so as to ensure co-operation with all concerned that no advertising contravenes or offends against these standards." As originally constituted the Authority was not involved in investigating complaints or resolving disputes. Its function was to supervise the operation of the Code, making additions or modifications as necessary, which critics argued was when the weight of public opinion left no other option. Control within the industry was still in the hands of the CAP Committee, which consisted of representatives of each of the eighteen organizations subscribing to the Code. Consumer complaints were still investigated by the Advertising Association's Advertising Investigation Department, which would also provide guidance to advertisers or agencies if required.

Meanwhile, the first commercial television transmissions had begun in the London area in 1955, and regional stations were added until full national coverage was achieved in 1962. The controlling body, the Independent Television Authority, had been charged under the terms of the Independent Television Act of 1954 with responsibility for program content, which included advertising. It discharged this statutory duty by means of a code of practice, observance of which was enforced by ensuring that all commercials were examined prior to broadcasting.

Even at this time, with the trends clear for all to see, it must be open to question how seriously the matter of control was taken by the majority of those working in the advertising industry. A good indicator would seem to be the extent to which students of advertising were taught about the need for control and how the system operated. The standard textbook, *Lane's Advertising Administration* (1951), did not mention the subject. By the time the fourth edition appeared in 1968 control was deemed worthy of two paragraphs.

Reform and Strengthening the ASA/CAP Committee

It was political pressure that finally forced the industry to take decisive action. The Advertising Association conference in 1974 was addressed by Shirley Williams, at that time Minister for Prices and Consumer Protection in the Labour government. She told delegates in no uncertain terms that existing measures used for the self-regulation of advertising were not sufficiently effective, and that unless the industry put its house in order, the government would intervene with a statutory code of practice and would establish machinery to see that it was properly observed. The conference also heard Sir John Methven, the greatly respected Director General of Fair Trading, ask:

Is the voluntary system being operated on a shoestring? Was this the reason why so few staff were employed to vet the 25 million advertisements produced every year? Why has the industry been reluctant for so long to publish the details of complaints concerned? After all, the Advertising Standards Authority was set up in 1962 and not until 1973 were the decisions on individual public complaints published (Jefkins 1976).

Critics had constantly derided the efforts of the ASA, claiming it was a "toothless watchdog" biased in favor of advertising and that its operation could be likened to the police investigating complaints against themselves. Business had turned a deaf ear to such complaints. Now, however, it was forced to act, and the ensuing reorganization of the self-regulatory system comprehensively answered Methven's criticisms. The result was the structure that exists today, which effectively marks the beginning of the modern phase of advertising control. But although the structure is impressive, there still remains the question of whether the industry has the general will to make it operate.

As set up in 1961 and reformed in 1974, the centralized system is based on rules set out in *BCAP* and enforced by two bodies, the ASA and the CAP Committee. The Code sets out the rules to be followed by all concerned in commissioning, creating, and publishing advertisements, and makes consumers aware of the kind of standard they have a right to expect in the advertisements to which they are exposed. It does not apply to television or radio commercials, which are the responsibility of the Independent Broadcasting Authority, and also specifically excludes certain other types of advertisements that the ASA and CAP Committee would not wish or could not reasonably expect to control. The operation of the enforcement bodies is considered in chapter 4, and the Code is examined in detail in chapter 5.

Industry Codes of Practice

Under the Fair Trading Act (1973), the Director General of Fair Trading has a duty to encourage trade associations to draw up codes of practice—rules for their members to follow that should provide a better deal and improved standards of service for customers (*Fair Deal* 1981).

Following are the codes that have been negotiated in conjunction with the OFT:

1. Code of Practice for the Motor Industry
2. Vehicle Builders and Repairers Association Code
3. Direct Sales and Services Association Code
4. Code of the Association of Manufacturers of Domestic Electrical Appliances

5. Code of the Electrical and Television Retailers' Association
6. Code of Practice for Footwear
7. Code of Practice for Shoe Repair
8. National Association of Funeral Directors Code
9. The Furniture Code of Practice
10. Code of the Association of British Launderers and Cleaners
11. Mail Order Traders Association Code
12. Code of the Association of Mail Order Publishers
13. Code of Practice for the Photographic Industry
14. Postal Service Code
15. Telecommunications Services Code
16. Code of the Association of British Travel Agents

Those who adhere to these codes include retailers and manufacturers, depending on the industry. The codes may or may not refer directly to advertising practices; but even so the general requirements of good practice would cover advertising. Because the ASA/CAP Committee system is quite thorough, however, those who administer these industry codes have relatively few advertising control matters to handle.

Comparisons

This brief outline of the history of self-regulation in the United States and the United Kingdom enables us to identify several general factors that affected the course of its evolution in each country. The first factor is the size and character of the countries themselves, which provided differing conditions in which advertising has had to operate. In particular, the population of the United States is more than four times that of the United Kingdom, and its area is almost forty times greater. The relative compactness of the United Kingdom has been accentuated by the status of London as both the legislative and commerical center of the country, enjoying a greater dominance in relation to the main regional centers than New York possessed in relation to other major U.S. metropolitan areas. As the British transport system developed, it therefore tended to spread out radially from London. National newspapers grew up there because they could be distributed by rail overnight. Manufacturing firms often had their headquarters there, even if their manufacturing units were elsewhere. This in turn obliged local newspapers to keep representatives in London if they wanted to attract other than small local advertisers. Advertising agencies also set up business in London because that was where the clients and media were located. In contrast, the large industrial and commercial centers in Chicago, Detroit, Los Angeles, Philadelphia, and elsewhere led to greater decentralization of the media and of advertising in the United States. It is therefore hardly surprising that while the U.S. advertising industry initiatives towards control tended to be somewhat fragmented, the concentration of British advertising in London enabled advertisers, agencies, and the various media to form organizations effectively representing their interests. These organizations were able to speak with an authoritative voice when self-regulation was under discussion, and formed a natural channel for the dissemination of information and decisions. The eventual success of the current self-regulatory system owes a great deal to their support.

A second factor to affect the evolution of self-regulation in both countries was the growing importance of repeat-purchase consumer goods since the last quarter of the nineteenth century. By 1900, although the marketing concept had not been explicitly enunciated, awareness was increasing among certain industry leaders of the importance of ensuring consumer satisfaction to ensure continuing sales. Advertising claims were of particular relevance in this respect because the product that failed to satisfy consumer expectations would not be bought a second time. To this extent the growing understanding of the processes of marketing produced their own constraints on the activities of advertisers.

A third factor has been the different degree of reliance by the two countries on preserving competition as a means by which consumer interests are protected. Since the late 1800s the main emphasis of U.S. antitrust legislation and policies was to protect against concentration of economic power in the hands of a few oligopolists. This environment to preserve effective competition fostered relatively aggressive competitive activity in the United States, and its limited collusion or cooperation among competitors, because such activities were of questionable legality. Thus advertisers, agencies, and media were relatively constrained from meeting to secure agreements among themselves about standards for advertising and the machinery for their enforcement.

In the United Kingdom, on the other hand, so long as markets were protected from foreign competition, firms tended to share them in a way that produced a comfortable life for all concerned. Sharing was particularly apparent during the Second World War when many firms helped competitors who had lost supplies or stocks through enemy bombing. When a full-scale system of advertising control was set up, it would seem that this inherent spirit of cooperation made it comparatively easy to secure acceptance and compliance.

Our historical outline suggests that it is possible to see pressure for advertising reform as falling into three main periods, though events in the two countries by no means followed a similar pattern. The first lasted roughly from the 1880s to the early years of the twentieth century, and was

characterized by a growing awareness in business circles that to be effective, advertising had to be truthful. The main impetus on both sides of the
Atlantic seems to have come mainly from publishers, with the poster
industry in the United Kingdom also assuming an important role though
its concern was more with matters of taste and decorum. There was at this
time in the United Kingdom little evidence of a general public concern
about advertising. Indeed, if British music-hall songs are any indication,
they seem to have found it rather amusing (Nevett 1982, 119). It may be,
however, that what was lacking was not the concern but the means to
articulate it, because critical articles certainly appeared in publications with
an upper class and upper-middle-class readership, and persons in those
classes formed the membership of the SCAPA Society. In the United States,
in contrast, public opinion and antitrust activity led the Sphinx Club to be
seriously concerned about advertising reform as early as 1903.

By the early years of the twentieth century, there was no cohesive
action on the part of the industry as a whole in either country, probably
because the threat of government intervention was not sufficiently strong.
In both countries numerous pieces of legislation affected advertising. In the
United States such legislation dealt broadly with preserving competition,
with only a few features to protect consumers directly—for example,
regarding food and drugs. But early United Kingdom legislation dealt more
specifically with certain practices or even a particular example of advertising considered undesirable. Such legislation was not always strictly
enforced; the Indecent Advertisements Act in 1889, for example, was described in 1907 as "a dead letter" (Nevett 1982, 137). The British courts also
went further in placing contractual obligations on advertisers than did
their U.S. counterparts.

Business in the United States took an earlier and more active role than
did business in the United Kingdom in promoting centralized advertising
self-regulatory codes. Early in the 1900s advertising clubs formed "vigilance committees," and later they formed the BBBs at local and national
levels to deal with advertising control, among other matters. The *Printers'
Ink* model statute of 1911, subsequent BBB activities in the first half of the
twentieth century, and efforts of the advertising industry associations and
media associations (especially the NAB) amounted to a regular flow of
information, ideas, and attempts to bring about self-regulation of advertising. By and large these attempts had a positive general impact, but
enforcement difficulties precluded the development of an effective system
of self-control of advertising abuses. Simultaneously the consumer movement, with varying degrees of intensity from time to time, was an important force in the United States. Nevertheless, the main stream of U.S.
advertising industry sentiment over the years continued to favor self-
regulation or no regulation. For example, the industry believed that the

Printers' Ink model statute should serve as a guideline not only for possible government legislation but, more importantly, as a guide for advertisers to follow if they were to forestall government regulation. Although the *Printers' Ink* model statute had little impact at the federal level, it had considerable impact in many state governments, and it served as a guide for trade associations and the BBBs. Nevertheless, many advertisers, agencies, and media continued to produce advertising that did not conform to the model statute.

In the United Kingdom, in contrast, there were no counterparts to the BBBs, and little sentiment existed for industry-wide or cross-industry codes for advertising self-regulation. Nor were there comparable consumer movement and consumer organizations to spur public consciousness of advertising abuses.

The second main period of advertising reform occurred between the two world wars and was at its height in the middle to late twenties. Advertising in the United States achieved ever-greater influence as an important business activity. Yet the influence of the consumer movement also grew, creating a kind of polarization that encouraged business to continue its efforts at self-regulation. The number of BBBs increased, to include virtually all major metropolitan areas, and the NBBB was formed in 1925. Codes were introduced by organizations such as the AAAA. However, attempts at self-control were generally ineffective. In the past the impetus for reform within the industry had come largely from the media side. But now the advent of radio led to greatly increased competition for advertising revenue, and both broadcasters and publishers sometimes lowered their standards to accept copy they might otherwise have rejected, which in turn produced additional attacks from consumer groups and from within government. Broadcast advertising in the United States grew rapidly in the 1920s, sometimes leading to excesses that in turn stimulated strong criticisms of advertising. During these interwar years the United Kingdom did not permit broadcast advertising, possibly the reason for the relatively more respectable reputation of advertising in the United Kingdom.

The United Kingdom took the first step towards self-regulation when the newly formed AA set up its Advertising Investigation Department in 1926. Because claims made in British advertisements seem not to have been as outrageous as they had been half a century earlier, and because there was no commercial radio, the vociferous outcry that occurred against advertising in the United States did not occur in the United Kingdom where, as we have seen, advertising became if anything more respectable. Criticism of advertising on a general level was limited to a few intellectuals such as C.P. Snow (Nevett 1982, 161). Otherwise it was concentrated on the old problem of patent medicines, with a major step forward coming in 1936 when the PAGB introduced its *Code of Standards*. The attitude of Parliament on the question may be judged by the fate of the bill introduced in the same year aimed at curing the advertising of medical products including "cures" for tuberculosis and cancer. It failed because too few members were present.

Pressure for controls on advertising in both countries declined noticeably during the Second World War and the years immediately following. In the United Kingdom the shortage of newsprint meant that press space was rationed and, as there was as yet no advertising on radio or television, publishers could exclude advertisements that they considered undesirable. In the United States the NAB in 1952 added its Television Advertising Code, but in general there was no strong movement for comprehensive advertising self-regulation. In the United Kingdom, recovery for advertising was slow after World War II, but by the mid-1950s advertising was coming under closer public scrutiny, especially with the coming of "intrusive" commercial television. It was only when the climate of business in the United Kingdom began to return to something like normal in the early fifties that pressure for control began to build up once again. Criticisms gradually built to the point that in 1961 the *BCAP* was established for print media, and broadcast media came under the quasi-government control of the IBA.

By the 1960s there was a quite different approach to advertising regulation by the government of each country. Both introduced a number of acts aimed at combatting specific abuses, the United Kingdom perhaps going furthest in general terms with the Trade Descriptions Act (1968), which, among other things, made it a criminal offense to publish a false or misleading trade description. Beyond this their paths diverged.

The United States had a much more vocal and highly organized consumerist lobby, and administrations had little faith in the industry's ability to discipline itself—hardly surprising given that such efforts were usually plagued by disagreements on what standards to introduce and what sanctions were needed to enforce them. In the United Kingdom, however, both political parties were inclined to work in partnership with the industry as much as possible. Television advertising was made the responsibility of a statutory authority, which discharged this duty by means of cooperation with the program companies; the Code of Advertising Practice was regarded as complementing the existing legal controls; and the threat of legislation was used to force the industry to overhaul its own self-regulatory system, which has since satisfied two searching government investigations. In the United Kingdom there was little feeling that advertising was not fit to control itself, only that it was not doing the job as well as it might.

In a sense there is something typically British about such a compromise that lets each side claim what it will. Politicians can claim either to have acted to curb advertising or to have preserved the freedom of business from government interference, depending on their political allegiance, while the advertising industry can claim that it has taken voluntary action to curb its own excesses, conveniently overlooking that it did so under threat. Honor is thus satisfied on all sides.

In contrast, the United States had long ago developed relatively strong federal government agencies to enforce antitrust law. These agencies dealt with unfair or deceptive acts, including advertising, in a much fuller fashion than occurred in the United Kingdom (as is discussed in chapter 3). Therefore, there was a less apparent void for self-regulatory controls to fill. Moreover, U.S. advertising industry efforts at self-regulation were deterred by the realistic fear of antitrust actions against cooperation, a factor that continues to be of great importance, as we discuss more fully in the next chapter.

The self-regulatory system in the United States came somewhat later in 1971, because the advertising industry was incapable of unifying its efforts earlier, not only because criticisms of advertising were of insufficient strength to create a genuine sense of urgency, but also because federal agencies were available to deal with advertising control. In the 1960s, however, intense consumerist activity and numerous pieces of new legislation finally aroused the U.S. advertising industry to establish the NAD/NARB system, as well as the beginnings of local controls through LARBs. At the same time the NAB continued to make changes to strengthen the system of broadcast self-regulation.

In the United Kingdom, meanwhile, the early years of the ASA/CAP Committee were fairly quiet. But criticism of advertising gradually mounted from consumer organizations, which had recently become influential, and especially from government and from the Labour Party. In 1974 the system was reconstituted and refinanced, as we describe in more detail later.

Also, during these years, in both countries numerous other forms of self-control of advertising continued to function, especially codes and standards of individual media and of particular industries in which advertising played an important role in the marketing mix of firms. In the United States some of these industry codes that had been in existence for many years were modernized. In the United Kingdom the OFT, which had as one of its missions to foster industry codes whenever possible, exerted a strong positive force for such codes in the mid-1970s.

Notes

1. These associations *unsuccessfully* explored antitrust exclusion when setting up the system so that the media could be included (Zanot, Eric, discussion with one of the authors, 22 March 1986). See chapter 3 for further discussion of this issue.

2. Much of this section is adapted from material in Nevett 1982.

References

Advertising Age, various editions.

American Association of Advertising Agencies (undated), "Good Advertising is your Bread and Butter," New York: The ANA–AAAA Committee for the Improvement of Advertising Content (brochure).

American Association of Advertising Agencies (1962), "Standards of Practice," Washington: AAAA, 28 April 1962.

Annual Reports of the Director General of Fair Trading, various years.

Boddewyn, J.J. (1982), "Advertising Regulation in the 1980s: The Underlying Global Forces," *Journal of Marketing* 46(Winter 1982):27–35.

Boddewyn, J.J. (1983), "Outside Participation in Advertising Self-Regulation: The Case of the Advertising Standards Authority (UK)," *Journal of Consumer Policy* 6:77–93.

Brandmair, Lothar (1977), *Die Freiwillige Selbstkontrolle der Werbung* (Munich: Carl Heymanns Verlag, KG).

The British Code of Advertising Practice (1979 and 1985), London: CAP Committee (6th ed., April 1979, and 7th ed., October 1985).

Buell, Victor (1977), *The British Approach to Improving Advertising Standards and Practice* (Amherst, Mass.: Business Publication Services, School of Business Administration, University of Massachusetts).

Chase, Stuart, and Schlink, Frederick J. (1927) *Your Money's Worth* (New York: The Macmillan Company).

Cohen, Dorothy (1982), "Legal Developments in Marketing," *Journal of Marketing* 46 (4), Fall.

Cohen, Dorothy (1983), "Legal Developments in Marketing," *Journal of Marketing* 47 (2), Spring.

Consumerism: A Growing Force in the Market Place, 4th ed. (1973) (New York: Burson-Marsteller Public Relations).

Digges, I.W. (1948), *The Modern Law of Advertising and Marketing* (New York: Funk and Wagnalls Company).

Dzodin, Harvey, C. (1984), "Some Thoughts on the Commercial Clearance Process from an ABC Perspective," unpublished presentation at Michigan State University, East Lansing, April 23).

Fair Deal (1981) (London: Office of Fair Trading, Her Majesty's Stationery Office, September).

French, George (1926) *20th Century Advertising* (New York: D. Van Nostrand).

Goodall, G.W. (1914), *Advertising: A Study of Modern Business Power* (London: Constable & Co.)

Greyser, Stephen A. (1967) "Advertising Acceptability—Practices and Problems" (Boston: Harvard Business School, ICH 13M43, M256).

Hall, Roland (1921), *The Advertising Handbook* (New York: McGraw-Hill).

History of the NAB (booklet) (1965) (Washington, D.C.: National Association of Broadcasters, August 1965).

Jefkins, Frank (1976), *Advertising Today* (London: Intertext).

Kallet, Arthur, and Schlink, Frederick John (1933), *100,000 Guinea Pigs* (New York: The Vanguard Press).

Kenner, H.J. (1936), *The Fight for Truth in Advertising* (New York: Round Table Press).

LaBarbera, Priscilla (1980), "Analyzing and Advancing the State of the Art of Advertising Self-Regulation," *Journal of Advertising* 9 (4):27–38.

LaBarbera, Priscilla (1981), "The Antitrust Shadow over Advertising Self-Regulation," *Current Issues and Research in Advertising*, 57–70.

Lane's Advertising Administration (London: Butterworth, 1951 [2nd ed.], and 1968 [4th ed.]).

Lawson, R.G. (1978), *Advertising Law* (Estover, Plymouth: Macdonald and Evans).

McTigue, John (1974), "Self-Regulation Efforts of Advertisers, Their Agents, and the Media," in Fredric Stuart (ed.), *Consumer Protection from Deceptive Advertising* (Hempstead, N.Y.: Hofstra University). Chap. B-1, pp. 83–121.

Miracle, Gordon E. (1985a), "A Brief History of US Advertising Self-Regulation to 1970," in Nancy Stephens (ed.), *The Proceedings of the 1985 Conference of the American Academy of Advertising* (Tempe, Ariz.: Arizona State University), R2–R7.

Miracle, Gordon E. (1985b), "Advertising Regulation in Japan and the USA: An Introductory Comparison," *Waseda Business and Economic Studies*, No. 21, 35–69.

NAB Radio Code, 1937, and as amended.

NAB Television Code, 1952, and as amended.

NAB Code News, various issues.

Neelankavil, James P., and Stridsberg, Albert B. (1980), *Advertising Self-Regulation* (New York: Hastings House Publishers).

Nevett, T.R. (1982), *Advertising in Britain—A History* (London: Heinemann).

Nevett, T.R. (1981), "The Scapa Society: The First Organized Reaction Against Advertising," *Media, Culture and Society* 3:179–187.

Nevett, Terence (1985), "The Ethics of Advertising," *International Journal of Advertising* 4 (4):297–304.

Nevett, Terence R., and Miracle, Gordon E. (1986), "The British System of Advertising Regulation: An Historical Perspective," in Ernest F. Larkin (ed.) *Proceedings of the 1986 Conference of the American Academy of Advertising* (Norman, OK: Oklahoma State University), R2–R6.

Pease, Otis (1958), *The Responsibilities of American Advertising* (New Haven: Yale University Press).

Pickering, J.F., and Cousins, D.C. (1980), *The Economic Implications of Codes of Practice* (Manchester, Engl.: University of Manchester Institute of Science and Technology, Department of Management Sciences).

Pickering, J.F., and Cousins, D.C. (1983), "Corporate Reactions to Voluntary Codes of Practice: Results of a Survey," *Journal of Consumer Policy* 6:37–54.

Presbrey, Frank (1929), *The History nd Development of Advertising* (Garden City, N.J.: Doubleday).

Purdon, Roger (1972), "Advertising Self-Regulation—A New Reality," presented to the 1972 Annual Meeting of the American Association of Advertising Agencies, Boca Raton, Fla., 16 March 1972.

The Radio Code (Washington, D.C.: National Association of Broadcasters, various issues).

Review of the UK Self-Regulatory System of Advertising Control: A Report by the Director General of Fair Trading (1978) (London: Office of Fair Trading, November 1978).

Scherer, F.M. (1970), *Industrial Market Structure and Economic Performance* (Chicago: Rand McNally and Company).

The Self-Regulatory System of Advertising Control—Report of the Working Party (1980), (London: Department of Trade).

The Television Code, (Washington, D.C.: National Association of Broadcasters, various issues).

Thomson, Peter (1979), "The Future for Self-Regulation," presented to the conference "Advertising Law in the 1980s," Cavendish Conference Centre, London, 25 September 1979.

Turner, E.S. (1965), *The Shocking History of Advertising* (Isleworth: Penguin Books).

White, Roderick (1980), *Advertising: What It Is and How To Do It* (London: McGraw-Hill).

White, William A. (1939), "The Ethics of Advertising," *Atlantic Monthly* (November 1939), 665 ff.

Wood, James P. (1958), *The Story of Advertising* (New York: Ronald Press).

Zanot, Eric J. (1985), "Unseen but Effective Advertising Regulation: The Clearance Process," *Journal of Advertising* 14 (4):44–51, 59, 68.

Zuckman, Harvey L., and Gaynes, Martin J. (1983), *Mass Communications Law* (St. Paul, Minn.: West Publishing Co.), 308–309.

3
The Relationship Between Advertising Law and Advertising Self-Regulation

Introduction

One reason for differences in the nature of the self-regulatory systems in the United Kingdom and the United States is their relationship with their respective legal systems in terms of lines of demarcation and of cooperation between them. This largely determines the area over which the advertising industry is able to exercise some measure of authority, and also the nature of this authority. In this chapter, we examine briefly some of the salient features of the British and U.S. legal systems that have a direct bearing on advertising self-regulation.

The Basic Legal System

We note earlier that both the United Kingdom and the United States historically are common law countries, although they differ in the degree to which certain aspects of the law have been codified. The United States has a written constitution, for example, but the United Kingdom does not. In both countries much commercial law has been codified. Several of the most important laws and concomitant regulatory programs are described in the following sections and then compared and contrasted.

It should also be remembered that the United Kingdom has a unitary system of government and the United States has a federal system, which affects directly the relative powers of central regional and local governments.

Antitrust Law

The differences and similarities between the United Kingdom and the United States regarding the relative emphasis on preservation of competition are mentioned briefly earlier in the book. Antitrust policy and laws have been pursued more vigorously in the United States than in the

United Kingdom. The spirit of cooperation continues to be stronger in the United Kingdom than in the United States, and currently the difference seems to be increasing during this era of deregulation in the United States. Although, in some respects, there seems also to be a trend toward deregulation in parts of the British economy, this trend has as yet had no apparent influence on advertising regulation or self-regulation, as it has had in the United States.

Central Government versus State and Local Government Powers

The U.S. Constitution requires that the powers not exclusively given to the federal government are reserved for the states; one of the powers granted at the federal level is to regulate interstate commerce. Because the states retain the power to regulate intrastate commerce, most of them have some sort of legislation and enforcement mechanisms to police unfair or deceptive acts or practices. In view of their lack of uniformity they cannot be described adequately here. Many examples of retail and local advertising, however, clearly are in the jurisdiction of each state. In Michigan, for example, the Consumer Protection Division in the State Attorney General's Office enforces: (1) the Michigan Consumer Protection Act, which prohibits specified unfair or deceptive methods, and (2) an act to regulate the advertising of consumer goods and services. Because the television networks and the NAD/NARB deal only with national advertising, they are concerned primarily with federal law. But the television networks do indeed have some problems with state laws; for example, two states prohibit advertising of alcoholic beverages on television and, until a recent federal court ruling, such network commercials had to be blacked out in those states. This situation is mentioned here because it also illustrates the inexorable trend in the shift of power from the states to the federal government.

When considering legal control in the United Kingdom, it should be remembered that the relationship of central to local governments is quite different from the federal-state relationship in the United States. In the United Kingdom the London boroughs, metropolitan districts, nonmetropolitan districts, and county councils are essentially administrative bodies, whereas in the United States the states and municipal governments have legislative, administrative, and judicial functions. These differences stem from the previously mentioned differences in the forms of government—the unitary system in the United Kingdom compared with the federal system in the United States—and the residual powers of the states. With the exception of the City of London, the origins of which go back to the Norman Conquest, British local councils are all statutory corporations and so have only those powers expressly conferred on them by statute. Under the Local Government Act (1972) they are empowered to make bye-laws (that is, laws enforceable within their own areas) exclusively for "good rule and government" and "the prevention and suppression of nuisances," but even these are subject to central government approval.

London boroughs, metropolitan districts, and the county councils also control trading standards. Originally known as Inspectors of Weights and Measures, Trading Standards Officers now have a wider brief that includes initiating criminal proceedings in cases of false or misleading advertising coming within the scope of the Trade Descriptions Acts. Apart from this, local authority concern with advertising is mainly limited to granting permission for erecting advertising hoardings (billboards).

Freedom of Speech and Freedom of the Press

With respect to the constitutions of the United Kingdom and the United States, there are some differences in the degree of protection that advertising receives against government regulation. The First Amendment to the U.S. Constitution, among other features, guarantees freedom of speech from government interference except for slander or libel, both of which are difficult to prove, and cases are infrequent. In 1942 a Supreme Court case on the issue of whether commercial speech was protected by the First Amendment was decided negatively. Therefore, until the mid-1970s commercial speech had no protection, and government at all levels were free to regulate advertising essentially as they felt was appropriate. In the 1970s several Supreme Court decisions gave advertising partial protection, especially when advertising concerned matters of public interest, such as the public's right to know, or the basic need for the free flow of information to protect the effective operation of the market system and conditions of competition. This limited protection, however, does not cover commercial speech that is false or misleading or advertising that, for some other reason, is in the interest of the state to prohibit. On this latter point, however, the prohibition of commercial speech must directly advance the government's legitimate interests, and the regulation may be only as broad as is necessary to serve the state's substantial interest (Zuckman and Gaynes 1983, 297).

Finally, it should be noted that the First Amendment protection of U.S. commercial speech is not identical in the broadcast and nonbroadcast media. This topic has many uncertainties, but basically the print media are in a stronger position than the broadcast media. Newspapers and magazines have a long history of virtually complete freedom from government regulation, but the public airwaves used by the broadcast media are regulated by the FCC "in the public interest." Therefore, there are instances in which freedom of speech in the broadcast media is abridged; for example, the "fairness doctrine." Under this doctrine the media must grant time to opponents of those who purchase advertising time to broadcast controversial public issue messages. This doctrine has had only one major application to advertising: free time for anticigarette commercials to counteract cigarette advertising (before it was prohibited from television in 1971).

Freedom of speech in the United Kingdom is a more nebulous concept than it is in the United States. Although there is no written constitution, every Briton regards it as a fundamental democratic right, and every child at school learns about Speakers' Corner in London's Hyde Park, where anyone can stand and harangue passersby on any subject he or she chooses.

Generally, the British government's only rights in terms of restricting this freedom relate to the disclosure of information that might prejudice national security, which is hardly relevant to advertising. Apart from this, both the advertising and editorial sections of a newspaper are subject to the constraints imposed by law. A libel action, for example, might arise from a statement covered in either, and in both cases the editor could be personally responsible. A major difference arises, however, in that advertising constitutes commercial communication and is therefore subject to a battery of additional constraints. Most of the British statutes in appendix 3A would not be relevant in the case of editorial material—a point well illustrated by the Trade Descriptions Acts. The publication of an advertisement that contains a false trade description constitutes an offence that, depending on circumstances, may involve the advertiser, the agency, the publishers, or a combination. If, however, that same description is carried in the editorial columns, no liability attaches. The reason for this apparent anomaly is that the advertisement represents a description issued in the course of trade or business, whereas editorial comment does not, although it may be taken verbatim from an advertiser's news release.

> It is important to realize that an offence can be committed even in the absence of *mens rea*, a guilty mind. The accused will be able to use the defences provided in SS24 and 25, but if he cannot bring himself within those sections he will be guilty of an offence however "innocent" his intentions may have been (Lawson 1978, 205).

The position of broadcast media differs somewhat from that of the press in that the BBC (incorporated by Royal Charter) and the IBA (established by Parliament) are charged to provide the nation with unbiased and objective reporting. Advertising on independent television and radio is limited by statute in certain important respects, and a number of types of product and creative appeals are excluded from broadcast media that other media can carry quite legitimately.

The concept of free speech in the United Kingdom has never been a major issue in debates about the regulation of advertising. Legislation has been written in general terms, and because it has usually been directed at correcting specific abuses, it has tended to meet with approval.

The United States

The Basic Interface

The legal system of advertising control in interstate business in the United States is characterized by federal legislation that is enforced by agencies in the executive branch of government; disputes are resolved in the courts with precedents affirming "administrative law" or adding to "common law." Additionally, many of the states have a long history of regulating intrastate business; forty-three states enacted legislation based on at least part of the *Printers' Ink* Model Statute proposed many years ago; and many states in recent years have added a much more complete set of consumer protection laws that deal also with advertising control.

It is unknown how many inquiries and complaints state governments receive about advertising. But in Michigan, a state with less than four percent of the nation's population, the Consumer Protection Division within the state government receives approximately 10,000 per year, a majority of which deal at least in part with advertising. Most of these do not lead to serious investigations. The assistant attorney general in charge of this division also works with the FTC, the BBBs, and with other organizations, depending on the type of inquiry or complaint and the jurisdiction of each organization. Other states may have similar divisions and functions, although there appears to be no published information on this matter.

The activities of the NAD/NARB system, the BBBs, and the LARPs are concentrated primarily in the areas of advertising substantiation and truth and accuracy, as discussed in chapters 4 and 5; the point is that such activities serve not only to support the legal base, but also to extend it somewhat, as we discuss later in detail. The television networks, in applying the preclearance standards as well as in handling complaints, not only consider the law in making decisions, but they go far beyond the law—in matters of taste and decency, for example. They tend to mirror the prevailing standards of society, and they are able to adapt to changes in mores fairly rapidly.

At the local and state levels there are numerous contacts and referrals between the BBBs and state government consumer protection divisions (or similar bodies) when they exist in the executive branch of state governments, and between BBBs, state government, and certain federal agencies such as the FTC or FDA.

At the national level, the NAD/NARB will not accept complaints for investigation if it seems clear that unlawful business practices are involved, but will instead refer them to the appropriate government agency. The NAD also will not initiate an inquiry when a complaint deals with a matter that is already the subject of an investigation or litigation by the FTC or other government agency. If, however, the NAD undertakes an investigation that, after NARB review, indicates the advertising has the potential to mislead or is not substantiated adequately, and if the advertiser refuses to cooperate, the complaint would also be referred to the appropriate government agency. This sequence of actions, however, has not yet occurred because advertisers have up to this point always accepted the NAD/NARB decision. Thus, the self-regulatory system represents both reinforcement and extension of the law more vigorously and comprehensively than is possible by government agency enforcement alone.

Numerous federal laws and amendments in one way or another regulate or control advertising. A list of some of the major pieces of legislation is included in appendix 3A, and a list of some of the major enforcement agencies in appendix 3B. The most important major laws (and corresponding enforcement agencies) that relate to advertising are (1) the FTC Act (1914), as amended many times, most recently in 1975, 1980, and 1982; and (2) the FDA Act (1906), also amended many times.

Administrative law and enforcement in the executive branch of the U.S. government is well developed. The FTC bears primary responsibility for advertising regulation, and other specialized agencies play a major role for certain product groups or certain types of advertising. One important division of authority and responsibility is with regard to medicines. The FTC handles unfair or deceptive advertising relating to nonprescription drugs, but the FDA has jurisdiction over the promotion and advertising of prescription drugs.

When the NAD/NARB system was established, and still today, it was viewed by government agencies as a useful step in the system of advertising control, to act speedily and to take care of matters that might not otherwise receive the attention of the relatively small staffs of those agencies.

There have also been a substantial number of court cases, and such common law covers numerous issues. Much of U.S. legislation states only a broad principle, and establishes the administrative agency to serve as the accepted authority and to administer the law, checked by the judicial system that resolves disputes. Thus, for example, Section 5 of the FTC Act, as amended, makes "unfair or deceptive acts or practices" unlawful without defining them. Then, after FTC definition of a deceptive practice (such as certain kinds of markups or inadequate substantiation of a claim) disputed cases are finally resolved by litigation in the courts (Turk 1977). For example, in *American Home Products Corporation v. Federal Trade Commission* (1982) the court reviewed existing criteria that the FTC may use in "Interpreting an Advertisement for a Finding of Deception" (thirteen criteria) and "Remedial action for Deceptive Advertising" (five criteria), and added a new one when it upheld an FTC cease and desist order (Cohen 1983b, 119–121).

The FTC currently administers a number of advertising regulatory programs. The "Advertising Substantiation Program" has evolved to the point that FTC standards at any time are widely understood by industry, and the Commission handles "violations." Leaders in the AAAA, among others, believe that this program has had a deterrent or preventative influence, which in turn has enhanced the credibility of advertising in the marketplace (AAAA 1983, 100, 107). In cases in which there is no clear-cut violation of the law, the NAD may accept a complaint for investigation to determine if indeed the claim is substantiated adequately. As described in chapter 4, substantiation cases comprise a major part of the NAD's activities, along with determinations as to whether a particular claim or advertisement has the potential to mislead. Another major activity of the FTC is to issue Trade Regulation Rules (TRRs). There are more than thirty such rules dealing primarily with particular practices and products.

In the 1970s the FTC and the courts on occasion mandated corrective advertising. Because the last such case was in 1979, it appears as if this program is no longer being actively pursued.

The line between legal and voluntary control of advertising is quite clear. Federal and state governments play the central role in regulating advertising; they not only provide the basic minimum standards for substantiation, for example, but also engage in programs that a self-regulatory body does not have the authority to exercise effectively, such as issuing TRRs that have the force of law or mandating corrective advertising. The federal and state governments handle complaints about individual cases of allegedly unlawful advertising, and the federal government has numerous mechanisms to compel performance such as affirmative disclosure requirements, along with consent orders, cease and desist orders, and similar types of mechanisms at the state level. Thus, self-regulation of advertising supports and complements the law, depending on how vigorously government agencies enforce the law, as well as going considerably beyond the law on some issues, particularly preclearance activities of the television networks.

Broadcast Media

The control of broadcast media advertising deserves special mention in this interface chapter for a number of reasons. It is an example of a jurisdiction that in the United Kingdom comes under a statutory body, the IBA. But in the United States the preclearance standards are applied in the self-regulatory process. The networks and the NAD handle complaints that arise after airing, and the appropriate government agency, usually the FTC, handles complaints that occur after the self-regulatory process has been completed or that, for some reason, it has not dealt with.

In the 1950s, during the early years of commercial television, the FTC assigned a small staff to review advertising scripts, first monthly, then quarterly. Although the job quickly became too big for the small FTC staff, they continued selective monitoring for some years. Importantly, the FTC pursued a limited number of cases in the courts to establish guidelines for a number of deceptive practices. The FTC used these cases to establish precedent on important issues (such as markups, endorsements, camera trickery, and competitive claims), leaving the advertising industry to adhere to them. In preclearance as well as handling complaints, the FTC came to work closely and to depend heavily on the ill-fated NAB self-regulatory system (Turk 1977). The FCC, until it recently deregulated the broadcast media in important ways, mandated certain standards that influence advertising. For example, no longer do FCC rules regulate the maximum number of radio or television commercial minutes. But, as a practical matter, the three networks have for some time remained below previous FCC standards of 16 minutes per hour; ABC and CBS have limited their commercial time to 6½ minutes per prime time hour and 11 minutes per daytime or late-night hour; NBC has had a ceiling of 10 "nonprograming" minutes per prime time hour and 16 minutes per daytime or late-night hour (NBC's minutes presumably include program promotions and noncommercial announcements as well as commercials).

After the court decision and consent decree that put the NAB out of business regarding advertising regulation, the three networks

> revised their clearance procedures and incorporated many of the NAB standards, almost verbatim, into their own standards. . . . Armed with first amendment protection and no fear of violating antitrust laws as long as they do not act collusively, the three networks are well prepared to enforce their own advertising acceptance policies (Maddox and Zanot 1984).

But although many of the standards remained intact, a review of the written documents of each network reveals substantial differences in standards. Advertisers complain that not only do standards regarding content of commercials differ from network to network and from product to product, but their interpretation varies within a network over short periods of time. Network procedures and standards are discussed more fully in later chapters.

For comparison with the IBA it should be noted that the networks in their preclearance function probably reviewed more than 100,000 story boards in 1983. ABC reviewed a reported 32,500, NBC about 55,000 (Farhi 1983), and CBS probably a similar number. In view of this extensive preclearance activity, the networks receive only a very small number of complaints about commercials that have been aired; ABC, for example, received only 180 such challenges in 1983 (Dzodin 1984).

Antitrust Law

In 1972 the advertising industry, under the leadership of the AAF and the CBBB, formed a number of LARBs to function in local communities much as the NARB functioned at the national level. The LARBs were cooperative efforts of the local AAF club and the BBBs.

In 1974, a Denver franchisee of a Los Angeles–based weight-reduction business filed suit against the Denver LARB. The suit "alleged that the review board process had taken over a governmental function and that self-regulation violated the antitrust laws. In April, 1976 a judge dismissed the . . . contention of antitrust violations and allegation of a conspiracy among the defendants to restrain trade in the weight loss business in the Denver area" (LaBarbera 1981). The court costs, however, were large, and the CBBB, which had covered most of them, was nearly bankrupt and lost its insurance policy in the process. Its new insurance had a substantially increased premium and specifically excluded protection against antitrust actions. Furthermore, the case generated considerable publicity, some of which was adverse to the advertising industry. In short, the effect was to stop or reduce greatly the activities of other LARBs and to stop new ones from forming. In effect the self-regulatory system won the battle but lost the war.

In 1981 a new system of self-regulation was established by the AAF and the CBBB: Local Advertising Review Programs (LARPs). The program was carefully drafted to retain insurance coverage and to reduce the likelihood of antitrust action by establishing local Advertising Review Committees (ARCs), which are strictly advisory to the BBB. Also, the ARCs comprise only members of local advertisers, advertising agencies, and the public; media personnel are specifically excluded. The legality of this new system has not been tested in the courts, but because it was planned carefully with tne law in mind, it seems no more likely to be the subject of litigation than the NAD/NARB system at the national level, which has endured without serious challenge since 1971.

Summary Viewpoint on the Legality of Advertising
Self-Regulation in the United States

Considerable uncertainty remains. The FTC's official position is that a code is not in violation of federal law if adherence to a code or set of practices is entirely voluntary (LaBarbera 1981). Thus, the strongest clearly legal self-regulatory sanction for violation by a trade association or an organization such as the CBBB (which is not a trade association) is a recommendation to change the advertising.

Some believe, however, that expulsion from membership for an unacceptable practice such as deceptive advertising is permissible. Some trade associations, with great caution, invoke one or more penalties such as fines, suspension, expulsion, public disclosure, or referral to the proper government agency. Such enforcement, however, must be nondiscriminatory and it must afford due process. Additionally, from the standpoint of the Department of Justice, if the motivation for self-regulation is determined to be in the economic self-interest of a trade association's members, it is in violation of the law. Thus, the government looks to the substance of the code standards rather than to the enforcement mechanism. If a code is purely proconsumer (that is, if a trade association expels members for clear cases of deception), it is unlikely to be an antitrust violation (LaBarbera 1981).

In 1979 the Justice Department filed suit alleging that certain NAB code provisions violated the Sherman Act (1890). In *United States vs. National Association of Broadcasters,* CCH 50823 DC July, 1982, the federal district court ruled that the NAB code had anticompetitive effects and was subject to antitrust provisions. The NAB in a consent decree agreed not to adopt or enforce a code or guideline limiting certain member actions. It did not, however, prohibit individual broadcasters or networks from adopting rules independently (Cohen 1983b, 127)

The NAB case also indicates that attempts by media or media associations to regulate advertising that in any way reduce competition among the media, limit the supply of time, or artificially increase the prices and profits of the media seem to be a clear violation of antitrust laws. Additionally, boycotts of media, or even "sending a letter recommending that an advertising medium require certain advertisers to amend their copy is not permitted under the antitrust laws" (LaBarbera 1981).

The United Kingdom

The Basic Interface

A notable feature of advertising control in the United Kingdom is the way in which the legal and self-regulatory systems work closely together.

Although measures introduced by the industry may well have been prompted by a desire to avoid having its activities curbed by legislation, this does not mean that there was any intention to subvert or supplant the rule of law or to restrict in any way the jurisdiction of the courts. Indeed, government ministers and the Director General of Fair Trading have made it clear on a number of occasions that they see voluntary codes of practice in general as performing a valuable function in helping protect the consumer by complementing existing legal controls.

Sir Gordon Borrie, the present Director General, is also aware of the shortcomings of voluntary codes. He pointed out in his Annual Report for 1982 that self-regulation is not the answer in every case, and that it may actually bring problems of its own such as constraints on competition. He was nevertheless able to write that "there is no doubt that self-regulation can provide a good or even better safeguard to the public than legal sanctions or, as with the advertising industry, be complementary to a measure of legal regulation that would need to be extended if self-regulation was absent" (Borrie 1982).

A further token of official acceptance of the self-regulatory system may be seen in the fact that the Department of Trade and Industry is consulted during the selection of the chairman of the ASA.

The line between legal and voluntary control is not an easy one to draw. Some of the United Kingdom's laws are codified, and constraints on advertising can appear in many different forms, usually as a minor feature of legislation concerned primarily with some other matter. The most important statutes are listed in appendix 3A. A few other laws are also mentioned in chapter 2 and, as previously noted, a body of common law has grown up over the centuries and this too has some bearing on advertising, as in the areas of comparative advertising and unauthorized endorsements.

Unlike the United States, the United Kingdom has relatively few government agencies that have responsibility for regulating advertising, and they have less responsibility than do the similar agencies in the United States. In addition to the OFT, the main British control of advertising is by the local trading standards officers. These officers have the responsibility to enforce the Trade Descriptions Act (1968) and a considerable range of other statutes (see appendix 3B) and statutory instruments.

A further complication is that constraints may be the concern of either civil or criminal law. A member of the public considering himself to have been defamed in an advertisement, for instance, would need to sue those responsible in the civil courts with the object of obtaining damages. The publication of an advertisement containing a false or misleading trade description, on the other hand, would result in a criminal prosecution and a fine or imprisonment if found guilty.

A clear distinction also exists between broadcast and nonbroadcast media with regard to advertising control. These are considered in turn.

Broadcast Media

The control of advertising in broadcast media deserves some explanation, although it does not form part of the self-regulatory system as such. No advertising is allowed on any transmission of the BBC, but it is permitted in connection with programs transmitted by local radio stations and regional television companies coming under the jurisdiction of the IBA. Under the terms of the Independent Broadcasting Authority Act (1973) as amended and supplemented by the Broadcasting Act (1981), the Authority is responsible for "programmes broadcast," which includes advertisements. Neither the Authority nor any program contractor is allowed to act as an advertising agent (S.8(2)) defined in the 1973 Act as "a business involving the selection and purchase of advertising space or time for persons wishing to advertise" (S.37(3)).

Advertising is permitted at the beginning and end of programs and in what are termed "natural breaks." There is no statutory limit to the amount of time that may be devoted to advertising, but in practice the Authority allows a maximum of 10 percent of broadcast time (that is, 6 minutes per hour) averaged over the day, with a maximum of 7 minutes in any single clock hour for television and 9 minutes for radio. The sponsorship of programs is specifically prohibited, and nothing may be included in any program that might be supposed to have been paid for by an advertiser.

It is the duty of the Authority to consult with the appropriate government minister, the Home Secretary, regarding types and classes of advertisements that must not be broadcast and methods of advertising that are not allowed. The Authority must also carry out any directions on such matters that may be given to it by the Minister (S.8(5)). It has the duty to draw up a code to regulate advertising standards and practice, which should include those advertisements and methods that are prohibited, and to secure observance of the code's provisions (S.9(1)). In addition it is empowered to give directions to program contractors regarding times when advertisements may be transmitted, the maximum amount of time to be allowed for advertising in any given period, the minimum interval to elapse between two periods of advertising, and the exclusion of advertisements from particular programs (S.9(2–5)).

The Code is drawn up in consultation with the Authority's Advertising Advisory Committee and the Medical Advisory Panel. The Authority's Advertising Advisory Committee is constituted to represent both advertising and consumer interests, and sits under a chairman who must be free of any financial or business involvement in advertising. This committee is also concerned with the periodic review of the Code, and may recommend to the Authority any alterations it believes to be desirable in the light of new legislation, changing public attitudes, or advances in knowledge.

The Medical Advisory Panel advises the Authority on advertisements for medicines, treatments, and appliances; certain categories of toilet products; and veterinary products. The Authority may also ask it to consider any other type of product. Members of the panel are appointed after consultation with various medical and related bodies and represent the views of general medicine; pharmacology; chemistry; dentistry; veterinary science; nutrition; pediatrics; gynecology; dermatology; and conditions of the ear, nose, and throat. In addition to being involved in drafting the Code, members may be consulted individually with regard to specific advertisments submitted for broadcasting.

Although the Code does not have statutory force, the Authority discharges its responsibility to Parliament by ensuring that all television and radio advertisements are scrutinized before being accepted for broadcasting, both in terms of their presentation and of the claims on which they are based. To this extent, therefore, the provisions of the Code are mandatory and binding on all advertisers. Television scripts have to be cleared at the preproduction stage by the Authority's Advertising Control Division working with the copy clearance group set up by the Independent Television Companies Association, the body representing the program contractors. Any amendments specified have to be incorporated into the script before final approval is given. During the year ending 31 March 1985, they scrutinized 9,668 original preproduction scripts of which almost eighty-two percent were approved as submitted.

Completed commercials have to correspond with the approved script. When submitted they are viewed by the specialist staff of the Authority and the program companies in a daily closed-circuit session. In the year 1984–1985 6,317 commercials were seen, of which 172 required changes. Approval when given is for showing in any region, so avoiding the possibility that a commercial might be accepted by some contractors and not others. Should an advertiser wish to advertise in one region only, however, responsibility for clearance rests with the contractor (licensed station) concerned, without recourse to the central machinery.

The situation with regard to radio advertising is somewhat different because so much of it is purely local. In these cases it is cleared by individual local stations, which review many thousands of scripts each year. To help ensure that standards are being applied similarly throughout the country, the Authority holds one-day seminars in advertising control for the station staff most closely involved. Scripts intended for a wider audience are cleared centrally, as are those for certain classes of advertisement that the Authority has specified for compulsory preclearance: medicines and treatments, veterinary products, alcohol, claims relating to guarantees, financial advertising, and anything requiring the advice of a specialist consultant.

The actual clearance procedure is handled by a central copy clearance office operated by the Association of Independent Radio Contractors (AIRC), the body representing the local stations, and the ITCA in cooperation with the IBA's specialist staff and the Medical Advisory Panel and independent advisers as necessary. In the year 1984–1985 8,608 scripts were examined centrally of which about 12 percent required some form of change.

In 1984 the Authority established a regional clearance system under which a regional clearance officer can approve a script on behalf of a group of stations. The intention was to simplify copy clearance arrangements, but in fact the system is not often used because the pattern of radio commercials tends to be either single station or national, and they are therefore cleared by the local station or centrally by the AIRC.

The control of advertising in broadcast media provides a good example of cooperation between the legal and self-regulatory systems. Although the IBA is a statutory body carrying out its duties by means of a code setting out provisions that advertisers cannot escape, the preclearance procedures involved in enforcing that code are left largely in the hands of the television and radio contractors who, however, work closely with the Authority at all times.

Nonbroadcast Media

Advertising in media other than television and radio is subject to the provisions of *BCAP* and the *British Code of Sales Promotion Practice* (*BCSPP*), which are drawn up and enforced by the advertising industry. The Code itself and the machinery of enforcement are considered in detail in chapter 5. For the moment it should be noted that the Code lays considerable emphasis on the importance of observing the rule of law in the creation of advertisements.

> All advertisements should be legal, decent, honest, and truthful. Advertisements should contain nothing which is in breach of the law, nor omit anything which the law requires.
> Advertisements should contain nothing which is likely to bring the law into disrepute (*BCAP* 1985, B.2).

But the British self-regulatory system is not intended in any way to usurp the power of the courts in enforcing the law. It is up to the courts to judge whether the law has been broken, and the ASA has no wish to exercise such a function. The reversal of the burden of proof, quite reasonable in the context of voluntarily accepted rules, would run counter to a basic principle of English law: That an accused person is innocent until proved guilty beyond reasonable doubt. Furthermore, the ASA lacks the resources and powers necessary for law enforcement. If, therefore, a complaint to the Authority appears to relate to a breach of the law, the Authority will only pursue that complaint if a contravention of *BCAP* is also involved. Otherwise it will inform the media that an advertisement they are carrying appears to be illegal, advise the complainant to contact what it considers to be the relevant enforcement body, and tell the advertiser what action has been taken.

Self-regulation helps buttress the law in another important respect: it can sometimes act when the law cannot. For example, it would often be difficult to take legal action against an advertisement appearing to encourage illegal behavior, but because *BCAP* prohibits anything likely to bring the law into disrepute, sanctions would be available within the self-regulatory system (*ASA Case Report* 136).

The statements contained in the Code should not be regarded as mere declarations of intent. They are given practical effect by the ASA, the organization that oversees the operation of the self-regulatory system, and that cooperates closely with the two main bodies involved with legal aspects of advertising: the Trading Standards Inspectorate and the OFT. The Trading Standards Inspectorate is composed of local authority employees whose responsibilities include enforcement of the Trade Descriptions Acts (1968 and 1972)—probably the most important legislation affecting advertising. The Director General of the OFT is responsible, among other things, for investigating trade practices that may adversely affect the interests of consumers, and recommending government action when appropriate. He must also be notified by the relevant trading standards officer in the case of an impending trade descriptions prosecution. In 1978 he published a *Review of the U.K. Self-Regulatory System of Advertising Control*, which is considered in chapter 7.

A Special Case: Medicines

A further instance of cooperation is to be found in the area of pharmaceutical products, advertising for which is governed by the Medicines Act (1968) and ensuing regulations. Advertisements for all medicines must conform to the terms of a product license issued by the Medicines Commission, and responsibility for ensuring compliance rests with the Department of Health and Social Security. Several trade bodies, however, screen advertisements before they are submitted for publication, and the department has long had the policy that should a precleared advertisement be found subsequently to be in breach of the law, it will be dealt with by self-regulatory rather than by legal processes (PAGB 1979, 7–8).

Prescription medicines can only be advertised to the medical profession. Under terms of the Medicines (Advertising to Medical and Dental Practitioners) Regulations (1978), every such advertisement must contain certain specific information, and the advertiser must have available a datasheet for the medical profession. The relevant trade body, the Association of the British Pharmaceutical Industry, has its own code, which has been negotiated with the Department of Health and Social Security.

The industry does not accept preclearance as being workable for prescription products, because a company's own experts would have a much better idea of what could be claimed than the people doing the clearing. It therefore relies on two disciplinary forces: complaints (which emanate from doctors, competitors, health lobbies, and the Department of Health and Social Security); and a system of monitoring to ensure that advertisements actually carry the required information.

The United Kingdom and the European Community

As a member of the European Community, the United Kingdom is subject not only to its own laws but also to European Community "Council Directives." The Community's attitude to the United Kingdom's self-regulatory system was initially unsympathetic, possibly because the systems in operation in other member countries are so different from the British version. Some determined lobbying, particularly on the part of the AA, succeeded in gaining recognition for self-regulation in the *Directive on Misleading Advertising,* in which it was stated: "This Directive does not exclude the voluntary control of misleading advertising by self-regulatory bodies and recourse to such bodies by persons or organizations . . . if proceedings before such bodies are in addition to the court or administrative proceedings . . . " (*Council Directive* 1984, Article 5). At the time of writing it seems likely that the British government will introduce legislation to give the ASA statutory backup from the OFT, probably the power for the OFT to intervene when the ASA cannot act swiftly enough or when its power is ineffective—for example, when an offending firm does not belong to one of the recognized advertising organizations. In effect, this power would parallel that of the IBA, which is able to prevent misleading advertising from being transmitted.

It must be emphasized that the British government remains firmly committed to the principle of self-regulation. In a speech to the National Consumer Council in April 1986, the Parliamentary Under-Secretary for Corporate and Consumer Affairs declared: "There is talk of ditching the well-tried self-regulatory system and putting everything into statutory codes enforced through the courts. I have no doubt that this would be a grave mistake. It would lead neither to swifter nor better decisions and would be a great deal more expensive to the tax-payer."

Another matter of continuing potential conflict is harmonization of broadcasting in the European Community. The Commission's green paper, *Television Without Frontiers,* proposed the creation of a common market for this important branch of the European economy—to facilitate cross-frontier broadcasting and to exploit its integrative effects. These matters affect advertising in important ways, which are currently being reviewed and debated by interested parties in preparation for a proposed Council Directive. The IBA is disputing the need for broadcast advertising regulation to be harmonized as proposed.

Comparisons

The first requirement under *BCAP* is that advertising must be legal. The same is true for self-regulation in the United States. Neither the ASA or the CAP Committee, nor the NAB/NARB or the U.S. television networks, can act officially on the basis of a complaint against advertising that appears to breach the law.

Because of the federal system in the United States and the unitary system in the United Kingdom, the two countries differ in the division of power between the central government and the states, boroughs, and counties with regard to the regulation of advertising. In the United Kingdom, the OFT or other appropriate statutory body and the local trading standards officers enforce the law as enacted by Parliament. In the United States, local governments enforce local law and federal agencies enforce federal law.

In the United Kingdom a breach of a law such as the Trade Descriptions Act is a criminal offense with criminal penalties. In the United States, in contrast, civil law is the norm, although a few offenses can be prosecuted under criminal law. In recent years it has become increasingly common regarding possible advertising violations for one U.S. advertiser to sue another under provisions of the Lanham Trade Mark Act (1946). Instances of one British advertiser suing another are relatively rare.

Both nations enjoy freedom of speech, particularly in press reporting; yet there are some differences in perspective regarding protection afforded to commercial speech. In particular there are substantial differences between the United Kingdom and the United States with regard to the way in which broadcast advertising is regulated: in the United Kingdom by a quasi-governmental agency (IBA), but in the United States by both the government (especially the FDA, FCC, and FTC) and by the individual television networks. However, the IBA has quasi-legal powers to pre-screen and exclude advertising that does not adhere to the IBA Code. No government agency in the United States exercises such powers. Rather, the television networks in the United States, as private firms, exercise their right to accept or reject advertising, each acting individually to avoid an antitrust violation.

Numerous agencies of the U.S. federal government, as well as departments in state governments and even municipal authorities, have responsibilities to regulate advertising in accordance with the laws at their respective levels. However, there are relatively few government enforcement agencies in the United Kingdom beyond the OFT and the local Trading Standards Officers, and they are not as active as their U.S. counterparts. For example, local authorities in the United States often regulate outdoor advertising according to strict standards.

In the United Kingdom the legal and self-regulatory systems work closely together, and the main burden of control is carried by the ASA and by the IBA. Advertising control in the United States rests on a base of law enforced by government agencies at both the federal and state levels, and advertising self-regulation by the NAD/NARB system and the networks plays primarily a supporting and complementary role.

Both the United Kingdom and the United States give special attention in law (and in enforcement agencies) to medical advertising, and in the United States to food advertising as well when health issues are involved.

Antitrust law limits greatly the role of self-regulation in the United States, and especially makes media participation with advertisers and agencies virtually impossible. The division of powers between the federal and state governments also corresponds to the choice of the centralized NAD/NARB self-regulatory system to limit its cases to national advertising, whereas the LARP local counterparts of that system help the BBBs control local advertising, as appropriate under state and local conditions. The situation in the United Kingdom is different. The ASA has the cooperation of the media to administer *BCAP* nationally and locally, covering matters over which the law does not and would not wish to claim jurisdiction, while the IBA regulates advertising on television and radio within guidelines set by Parliament. The IBA limitation on the amount of time allowed for advertising (and setting that limit lower than in the United States) should not be confused with similar action taken by the NAB, for which it was held in 1982 to be violating antitrust laws by limiting competition. The IBA restricts advertising time because it has a statutory duty to do so under the terms of the Independent Broadcasting Authority Act 1973 S.9(4). Parliament still seems to take a nineteenth century paternalistic view of advertising as something against which the masses need protection.

The current trend in the United States is toward deregulation of broadcast advertising. In the United Kingdom there is no sign of such an attitude developing. The number of television channels carrying advertising has recently been raised from one to two, but commercials are still limited to the beginning and end of programs and to natural breaks. The number of radio stations is also controlled by statute, and all are local. Could it perhaps be significant that there has been no demand from the general public for these constraints to be lifted?

References

AAAA (1983), "Response to the FTC's Inquiry on the Advertising Substantiation Program," 13 July 1983 (unpublished).

ASA Case Reports (London: Advertising Standards Authority), various issues.

BCAP (1979, 1985), *The British Code of Advertising Practice,* 6th and 7th eds. (London: CAP Committee).

Borrie, Sir Gordon (1982), *Annual Report of the Director General of Fair Trading 1982* (London: Her Majesty's Stationery Office).

Borrie, Gordon, and Diamond, Aubrey L. (1973), *The Consumer, Society and the Law* (Harmondsworth, Middlesex: Penquin Books).

Cohen, Dorothy (1983a), Report in "Legal Developments in Marketing," *Journal of Marketing* (Spring 1983), 127.

Cohen, Dorothy (1983b), Report in "Legal Developments in Marketing," *Journal of Marketing* (Summer 1983), 119–121.

Commission of the EC, *Television Without Frontiers* (84) 300/5 (Brussels: 23 May 1984).

Council Directive Relating to the Approximation of the Laws, Regulations and Administrative Provisions of the Member States Concerning Misleading Advertising (Brussels: The Council of the European Communities, 10 September 1984).

Dzodin, Harvey C. (1984), "Some Thoughts on the Commercial Clearance Process from an ABC Perspective," unpublished presentation at Michigan State University, 23 April 1984.

Farhi, Paul (1983), "Agencies, Networks Battle Over Censors' Role," *Adweek* (14 November 1983), 50, 52.

IBA (1981), *The IBA Code of Advertising Standards and Practice,* (London: Independent Broadcasting Authority, May 1981).

IBA Annual Reports, various years.

LaBarbera, Priscilla A. (1981), "The Antitrust Shadow over Advertising Self-Regulation," *Current Issues and Research in Advertising,* 57–70.

Labour Party (1966), *Report of a Commission of Enquiry into Advertising* (known as the Reith Report) (London: Labour Party).

LARP (1981), *Local Advertising Review Program* (New York: Council of Better Business Bureaus).

"LARBs Founded to Promote Self-Regulation" (1972), *Exchange* 4 (2): 1–4.

Lawson, R.G. (1978), *Advertising Law* (Estover, Plymouth: Macdonald and Evans).

Local Advertising Review Program (undated 22-page booklet) (New York: Council of Better Business Bureaus, and Washington: American Advertising Federation).

Maddox, Lynda M., and Zanot, Eric J. (1984), "Suspension of the NAB Code and Its Effect on Regulation of Advertising," *Journalism Quarterly* 61 (1, Spring 1984): 125–130, 156.

NAD Case Reports, various issues (New York: Council of Better Business Bureaus).

PAGB (1979), *Annual Report* (London: Proprietary Association of Great Britain, 1978–1979).

Rijkens, Rein, and Miracle, Gordon E. (1986), *European Regulation of Advertising* (Amsterdam: North Holland [Elsevier Science Publishers]).

Turk, Peter (1977), "The Genesis of Television Advertising Regulation (FTC: 1948–1969)," in Gordon E. Miracle (ed.), *Proceedings of the Annual Conference of the American Academy of Advertising,* (East Lansing, Mich.: Department of Advertising, Michigan State University), 110–116.

Zuckman, Harvey L., and Gaynes, Martin J. (1983), *Mass Communications Law,* 2nd ed. (St. Paul, Minn.: West Publishing Company).

Appendix 3A
Legislation Affecting Advertising in the United States and the United Kingdom

United States

Following is a partial list of major U.S. federal laws that apply directly to advertising in important ways:

1. Sherman Antitrust Act (1890)
2. Food and Drug Act (1906; many amendments)
3. Clayton Act (1914; many amendments)
4. FTC Act (1914; many amendments)
5. Communications Act (1934)
6. Federal Alcohol Administration Act (1935)
7. Robinson-Patman Act (1936; amendment to the Clayton Act of 1914)
8. Food, Drug and Cosmetic Act (1938)
9. Wheeler Lea Act (1938; amendment to the FTC Act of 1914)
10. Lanham Trade Mark Act (1946)
11. Federal Aid Highway Act (1936; many amendments)
12. Delaney Amendment to the FDCA (1958)
13. Federal Hazardous Substance Act (1960)
14. Kefauver-Harris Amendment to the FDCA (1962)
15. Fair Packaging and Labeling Act (1966)
16. Child Protection Act (1960 and 1966)
17. Cigarette Labeling Act (1966)
18. Consumer Credit Protection Act (1968)
19. Child Protection and Toy Safety Act (1969)
20. Postal Reorganization Act (1970)
21. Public Health Smoking Act (1970)

22. FTC Improvement Act (1975; amendment to FTC Act of 1914)
23. Medical Device Amendments (1976; amendment to FDA Act)
24. FTC Improvements Act (1980)

United Kingdom

Following is a partial list of major British laws that apply directly to advertising in important ways:

1. Trade Marks Act (1938)
2. Defamation Act (1952)
3. Post Office Act (1953)
4. Food and Drug Act (1955); Food Act (1984)
5. Copyright Act (1956)
6. Weights and Measures Act (1963)
7. Trading Stamps Act (1964)
8. Misrepresentation Act (1967)
9. Advertisements (Hire Purchase) Act (1967)
10. Theft Act (1968)
11. Gaming Act (1968)
12. Medicines Act (1968)
13. Indecent Advertisements Act (1970)
14. Unsolicited Goods and Services Acts (1971 to 1975)
15. Trade Descriptions Act (1968; 1972)
16. Independent Broadcasting Act (1973; 1981)
17. Fair Trading Act (1973)
18. Consumer Credit Act (1974)
19. Sex Discrimination Act (1975)
20. Race Relations Act (1976)
21. Resale Prices Act (1976)
22. Price Act (1977; 1974)
23. Sale of Goods Act (1979)
24. Competition Act (1980)
25. Cable and Broadcasting Act (1984)

It is important to keep in mind that numerous statutory instruments under these acts are just as important as these Acts of Parliament (Circus, letter to the author, 13 August 1986).

Appendix 3B
Federal Agencies that Regulate Advertising in the United States

Following is a partial list of the major U.S. federal agencies with major responsibilities for the regulation of advertising. Administrative law and regulations applied by these and other agencies in the executive branch of government often are just as important as Acts of Congress.

1. Bureau of Alcohol, Tobacco and Firearms
2. Civil Aeronautics Board
3. Consumer Product Safety Commission
4. Customs Bureau
5. Department of Agriculture
6. Department of Commerce, Bureau of Standards
7. Department of Transportation
8. Farm Credit Association
9. Federal Communications Commission
10. Federal Deposit Insurance Corporation
11. Federal Home Loan Bank Board
12. Federal Power Commission
13. Federal Trade Commission
14. Food and Drug Administration
15. Housing and Urban Development
16. Interstate Commerce Commission
17. Patent Office
18. Post Office Department
19. Securities and Exchange Commission
20. Treasury Department

4
The Current System of Centralized Self-Regulatory Bodies

Introduction

The centralized systems of advertising self-regulation in the United Kingdom and the United States are distinguished by several important facts that dictate the content of this chapter. First, in the United Kingdom, most of those engaged in self-regulatory activities with regard to print advertising adhere to a single code, the *BCAP*, but no such single code exists in the United States.

The *BCAP* guides not only the formal centralized system of self-control in the United Kingdom—the CAP Committee and the ASA—but also the associated regulatory activities of the media; the media associations; and a number of industry, trade, and professional associations. Because the *BCAP* provides a common set of standards and all these organizations adhere to the code, they are, in a sense, part of the centralized system. Therefore they are included in this chapter.

The centralized control of advertising in the broadcast media is the responsibility of the IBA. Strictly speaking, the IBA is not a part of the self-regulatory system; it was established by statute and it is subject to direction from the Home Secretary, a senior government minister. Nevertheless, it is included in this chapter for comparison purposes, because television advertising in the United States is "self-regulated" by the networks. The reader should be careful, however, not to think of the IBA in the same terms as the ASA. In publishing a code, ensuring its enforcement, and in regulating the amount and type of advertising that may be transmitted, the IBA is carrying out the wishes of Parliament.

There is no common advertising self-regulatory code in the United States at the national level. The great diversity in advertising standards among the individual media and their associations, as well as among industry and trade associations, makes it difficult to summarize them any more completely than is done in chapter 2, and they are not included in this chapter. The U.S. institutions covered in this chapter include the

NAD/NARB/CARU system, the emerging LARPs, and the individual self-disciplinary systems of the three television networks. With regard to the three television networks, it is important to keep in mind that they each are independent business enterprises, they each have their own set of advertising standards, and they exercise control over national advertising that is carried by hundreds of network stations across the country.

The closest thing to a published national set of standards in the United States is contained in *Do's and Don'ts in Advertising Copy,* a loose-leaf service for advertisers, advertising agencies, broadcasters, and printed media. This CBBB compilation of government laws and regulations and industry and product guidelines is hundreds of pages long. It is useful primarily as a reference document for details on the probable acceptability of many advertising practices for many products and services.

Finally, it should be noted that there is a common set of standards for local, primarily retail, advertising: The *BBB Code of Advertising,* published in 1973 by the CBBB and most recently updated in 1985. But the BBBs, with offices and branches in approximately 173 cities in 45 of the 50 states, do not have a common system of enforcement, except for the few that are part of the emerging system of LARPs. The BBBs attempt to have both members and nonmembers comply with the code; and if a complaint is received about a BBB member or nonmember, the local BBB usually will attempt to find a solution through mediation. However, adherence to the BBB code is essentially voluntary because the BBBs have no real sanctions at their disposal.

Another distinguishing feature of the two systems is that the ASA and the IBA codes are applied to local as well as to national advertising. In the United States, except for the emerging LARP system and the local BBB activities with greatly limited resources and powers, the only substantial advertising controls at the local level are by state governments. The NAD/NARB system and television networks do not concern themselves with local advertising.

U.S. Enforcement Bodies

The NAD/NARB System

Founding and Supporting Organizations. As previously discussed, the forces of consumerism in the 1960s mounted well-publicized attacks on the business community. Advertising came under particularly strong attack. Fearing further deterioration in the reputation of advertising, and concerned particularly about new laws and enforcement agencies that would limit advertising's ability to perform effectively in the U.S. market economy, the industry responded. Leaders in advertising from the AAAA, AAF, ANA and CBBB combined forces to form the NARC and the NARB and to designate the NAD of the CBBB as its investigative arm. The system began to function in July 1971.

To understand the NAD/NARB system, it is helpful to keep in mind the nature and purposes of the founding and supporting organizations. Therefore, we describe each briefly.

1. The AAAA is a national body representing advertising agencies. Its fundamental purpose "is to improve, strengthen and interpret the advertising agency business . . . and to provide counsel and expertise . . . [and to work with others] to improve performance, efficiency and conduct of the agency business" (*NAD/NARB,* 1978, 23).

2. The AAF brings together all elements of advertising. Membership includes advertisers, advertising agencies, media and advertising service companies, advertising clubs and federations, and college chapters. Its primary objectives are generally to promote the best interests of advertising in a number of ways, including: "To promote higher standards of advertising practice through a program of industry self-regulation" (*NAD/NARB* 1978, 23).

3. The ANA is "devoted exclusively to serving the needs of advertisers. . . . [Its objectives] include the preservation of free and responsible advertising; and [generating and assuring] sound policies and practices in the advertising community" (*NAD/NARB* 1978, 23).

4. The CBBB serves major national businesses in a number of ways, especially by working to maintain "consumer confidence in the marketplace, . . . to protect business against illegal and unethical practices of competitors, to serve as an interface between business and the consumer, and between business and government." One of its major goals is to advance the system of advertising self-regulation (*NAD/NARB* 1978, 23).

The NAD/NARB system has received strong support from advertisers who have participated in the system. In the first ten years of operation, ninety-six of the top one hundred U.S. advertisers voluntarily took part in the process as advertisers or challengers. Thus, the NAD/NARB system receives support from national advertisers and advertising agencies and their trade associations as well as from the CBBB, which represents business broadly. It should be noted, however, that advertising media associations do not participate in the NAD/NARB system because such cooperation might constitute a violation of U.S. antitrust law.

Table 4–1
NAD/NARB/CARU Operating Budgets, 1978–1985
(in U.S. Dollars)

	1978	1979	1980	1981	1982	1983	1984	1985
NAD	$246,939	$264,129	$279,904	$356,061	$384,477	$375,118	$352,215	$390,032
NARB	151,079	144,762	136,723	142,869	142,066	145,082	142,721	152,238
CARU	139,897	131,206	172,148	175,869	192,212	189,524	205,308	225,217
Total	$537,915	$540,097	$588,775	$674,799	$718,755	$709,724	$700,244	$767,487

Source: CBBB *Annual Reports* and letters to the authors from NAD/NARB officials.

Financing and Staff. The NAD/NARB/CARU budgets for 1978 through 1985 are shown in table 4–1. The CBBB allocates to the NAD and the NARB a percentage received from its dues contributions from advertisers (which use other CBBB services, as well as supporting the NAD/NARB). The CARU has a separate budget contributed by children's advertisers, and funds are specifically earmarked for the CARU. One hundred percent of council membership dues paid by advertising agencies go directly into the NAD/NARB budgets. In addition to the budget, the NAD/NARB/-CARU receives administrative services from the CBBB in the areas of law, personnel, accounting, and so on.

> The current staffing in the New York NAD/CARU offices includes the Senior Vice President and Vice President/NAD, a Director/CARU, four advertising review specialists covering general advertising and one concerned with children's advertising, an administrative assistant plus office manager and supporting secretarial staff (Smithies, letter to the author, 7 June 1986).

The NARB is headed by a chairman and executive director, with fifty board members from which are selected five-member panels to hear cases appealed after NAD investigation or consultative panels.

Structure and Organization of the NAD/NARB. Although the NAD is a division of the CBBB, the NARB is autonomous. The founders decided that a sponsoring corporation, the NARC, should be formed to nurture and oversee the development of the NARB.

The NAD/NARB/CARU system is supported broadly by U.S. advertisers and agencies. As of December 1984, seventy-five of the top one hundred U.S. advertisers, as well as ninety-five advertising agencies, supported the system through their membership dues to the CBBB (*CBBB Annual Report* 1984, 4).

The principal roles of the NARC are (1) to create and monitor the application of the basic policies of the NARB and (2) to select the NARB chairman and board members. The NARC does not interfere with nor take any part in the workings of the NARB panels. The eight board members of this sponsoring corporation include the full-time presidents and chairmen (or designees) of the AAAA, AAF, ANA, and CBBB.

The NARB body of fifty members consists of thirty from advertisers, ten from advertising agencies, and ten from the "public"; most of the public members are prominent educators, top executives of consumer organizations or foundations, senior attorneys who specialize in this field, or former government officials.

A NARB panel consists of three advertisers, one agency member, and one public member. Advertiser members are not qualified to serve if their employing companies manufacture or sell a product or service that directly competes with a product or service sold by the advertiser involved in the proceeding. Likewise, an advertising agency member is not qualified if his or her employing agency represents a client that sells a product or service that directly competes with a product or service involved in the proceeding. A public member is not qualified to serve on a particular panel if his or her past or present employment or affiliation is not likely to permit him or her to reach an unbiased decision.

The NARB is intended to be completely autonomous and independent of any and all persons and organizations. It is to conduct its business and issue its reports with full regard for the public interest. The individual members of the NARB are answerable to no one for the decisions reached and actions taken by the NARB or any panel thereof.

The Role of Public Members. Even before the NAD/NARB system was launched, critics voiced strong support for substantial public participation. Robert Choate, a prominent advocate of consumer interests, advocated that at least 40 percent of NARB members and panels should be from outside the advertising industry; and he contended that public members should be selected by a nominating committee of five leading citizens (*Advertising Age*, 14 June 1971, 16).

> A former member of the Code Staff of the NAB "said he did not understand how men who have reached high positions by being masters of half truths, exaggeration, puffery, distortion and oversimplification can be called upon to rebel against this expertise when serving on the NARB. . . . With one consumer and four admen on each panel, the admen will find it impossible to vote against a peer who has committed the same violation that they themselves will go back to their offices to commit in slightly different form and with a different product" (*Advertising Age*, 14 June 1971, 16).

As a practical matter, however, the two-tiered system of the NAD and the NARB is structured to provide needed expertise and information, as well as checks and balances to ensure responsible use of that information to arrive at responsible decisions, as is discussed in the next section. The NAD staff, outside consultants, and representatives of the advertising business provide needed expertise on the technical aspects of advertising or legal opinions, and the "public members" of NARB panels serve as "sensors, interpreters and expressers of public opinion . . . [on] the 'soft' matters of taste, decency and morality." (Boddewyn 1985, 8–9).

Additionally the CARU has had an Academic Advisory Panel since its inception in 1974. The panel is composed of six academic members who are well known as leaders in research relevant to children's advertising. They specialize in fields such as education, mass communication, nutrition, and psychology. Their main function is to keep the CARU staff up-to-date on research findings relevant to children's advertising. The panel also meets once a year with CARU and other NAD/NARB personnel to review current issues in advertising directed at children and to provide information on current developments in children's programming, because the programming provides the environment in which advertising is run (*Better Business News and Views*, September 1986, 4; Rita Weisskoff letter to and discussions with one of the authors, 1986).

NAD/NARB Complaint Handling. Since 1971 the NAD/NARB system has handled many thousands of inquiries and complaints about national advertising, more than 2,000 of which have led to formal investigations and resolution and were reported in *NAD Case Reports*. (See chapter 6 for additional details.)

The step-by-step procedure for handling complaints is shown in figure 4–1. The NAD process is shown on the left side of the figure, beginning with the receipt of a complaint or question.

When inquiries or complaints are received, they are evaluated to determine if they are trivial, obviously not within the NAD mission, or not of sufficient public interest to warrant opening a case. Some serious but relatively simple cases are handled quickly by a telephone call or letter to the "offender," who has already stopped the practice or who has agreed immediately to stop the practice. Trivial cases are handled by a polite letter of explanation to the complainant; those not within the NAD mission are either refused, with a polite letter of explanation to the complainant, or they are referred to the appropriate forum or government agency. Only a small number lead to an active case involving an investigation, negotiation, and a decision by the NAD, as we discuss in detail in chapter 6.

In accordance with the procedures shown in figure 4–1, if the NAD determines that the advertising is substantiated, it dismisses the case. If the complaint is upheld, the advertiser is asked to modify or withdraw the advertising. A few cases are suspended or terminated for other reasons, such as a concurrent action by another agency, and a few are appealed to the NARB—only forty-one cases have been appealed in the fifteen-year history of the system (see chapter 6). Finally, the last box on the right in

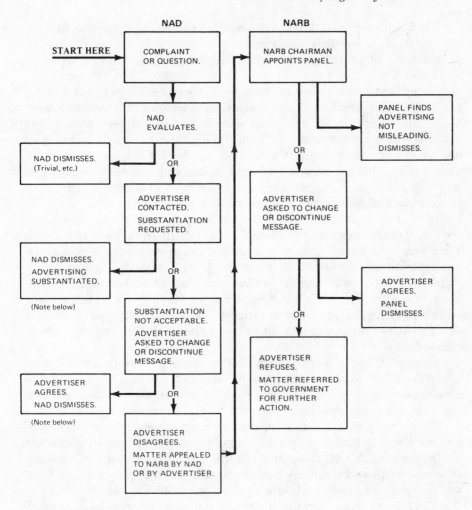

Source: *A Review and Perspective on Advertising Industry Self-Regulation* (New York: NARB, 1978), p. 12.

Note: If the original complaint originated outside the system, the outside complainant at this point can appeal to the chairman of NARB for a panel adjudication. Granting of such appeal is at the chairman's discretion.

Figure 4–1. Advertising Self-Regulatory Procedures Step-by-Step

figure 4–1 shows a step that has not yet been necessary. If the advertiser should refuse to comply after a negative NARB decision, the matter could be referred to a government agency for further action. Although this outcome has not yet occurred in the forty-one cases adjudicated by the NARB, the possibility of it probably is an important incentive for advertisers to cooperate with the system.

The basic responsibilities of the NAD are to receive, evaluate, investigate, analyze, or handle complaints or questions from any source involving the truth or accuracy of national advertising and to hold negotiations with advertisers.

Complaints and questions arise from a number of external sources such as competitors, consumers, consumer groups, and referrals from local BBBs. Additionally, the NAD maintains and operates a recording system, which takes commercials off the air from hundreds of hours of television and radio broadcasts, for later review by NAD staff. The staff also checks national print advertising in several hundred weekly and monthly magazines. No detailed information is available on sampling procedures and methods of operating this monitoring activity.

In the rare instances in which an advertiser refuses to cooperate with the NAD, the matter may be referred to the chairman of the NARB for his agreement that the advertiser was offered full opportunity to cooperate. With the chairman's approval, if the case warrants, the NAD files a complaint with an appropriate law enforcement agency. These referrals are not reported in the *NAD Case Report* because there has been insufficient opportunity for the NAD to investigate the matter fully and to make a decision. Any future action is left to the agency to which the matter was referred.

The NAD tries to be flexible in dealing with advertisers. Some advertisers prefer an informal approach whereas others restrict contacts to formal meetings and reports. The NAD finds that one-on-one contacts encourage the easy transfer of information and opinion that helps resolve controversies. The NAD staff approaches each advertisement on a case-by-case basis, although they rely for guidance on previously published NAD decisions, NARB cases and reports, FTC guides and FTC consent orders and litigation, various industry codes when appropriate, and the seventy-year tradition of advertising review by BBBs.

NAD cases take varying times to complete. Some inquiries are resolved by a simple exchange of correspondence whereas others may require several meetings and the retention of consultancy services. The Advertising Research Foundation (ARF), for example, is available to provide advice to evaluate research findings. Some competitor challenges tend to be complex, especially when each party provides technical data to support its position. Normally more than one-half of cases are resolved within six months.

It is sometimes appropriate for an advertiser to go directly into the court system, especially when a severe grievance requires quick action such as an injunction. "Also, when competitive cases go to court, both parties are entitled to the process of discovery, through which they obtain information from each other; the NAD, however, affords no such exchange" (Belsky 1984).

The NAD follows a strict rule that draft copies of a case report are shared with an advertiser and its agency prior to publication, with a request for suggested corrections on matters of fact. Additionally, an advertiser has the opportunity to add a brief statement if it is factual and nonpromotional. These rules help make the *NAD Case Reports* an accurate and authoritative record of the advertiser's agreement to any necessary modifications as well serve as a guide to other advertisers.

In addition to its initiating and investigatory functions, the NAD assists advertisers in avoiding future problems by consulting on advertising messages prior to their production and use. The NAD will not approve advertising in advance, but it will give expert opinion on questions of truth and accuracy.

At the outset the NAD worked without public disclosure (Purdon 1972), but it subsequently began to publish each month a *NAD Case Report* covering all cases decided the previous month. After complaints that such reports contained too little information, the NAD began in 1974 to issue reports that were sufficiently detailed to explain the reasons for decisions so that the reports would be useful to (1) complainants, to decide whether to appeal a decision; and (2) advertisers and agencies to benefit in planning future advertising. Each case reported names the company and the product, describes the nature of the alleged "abuse," and reports the findings of the NAD and the agreement reached with the advertiser. NARB panel decisions are published in somewhat expanded form with several pages of description and explanation.

The NAD has a separate unit that deals with children's advertising. Guidelines for children's advertising were published originally by the ANA in 1972 to encourage truthful and accurate advertising, sensitive to the special nature of children; they were revised for use by CARU when it was established in 1974 (and most recently in 1983) to promote responsible children's advertising and to respond to public concerns.

> The basic activity of CARU is the review and evaluation of child-directed advertising in all media. When children's advertising is found to be misleading, inaccurate or inconsistent with the Guidelines, CARU seeks changes through the voluntary cooperation of advertisers.
>
> CARU provides a general advisory service for advertisers and agencies and also is a source of informational material for children, parents and educators. In addition, CARU maintains a clearinghouse for research on children's advertising and has published an annotated bibliography.
>
> CARU's Academic Advisory Panel helps evaluate advertising and information provided by advertisers in support of their advertising claims. The Panel also advises on general issues concerning children's advertising and assists in revisions of the Guidelines (*Self-Regulatory Guidelines for Children's Advertising* 1983).

In 1978, the Clearinghouse for Research on Children's Advertising, which was established by the NAD's CARU in December 1977, published *Children and Advertising: A Bibliography*. The work contained references from books, articles, speeches, statements, and testimony relating to the effects of advertising on children (*News from NAD*, 15 August 1978). In 1980 an updated bibliography was distributed "to 1,400 leaders in the advertising and research communities as well as government, media, consumerists and educators" (*CBBB Annual Report* 1980, 2).

In December 1978, the "NAD's CARU announced that it had sent a letter to more than one-hundred children's advertisers, asking their cooperation in simplifying the language of commonly used disclosures in their child-directed advertising," so that such advertising would be in accordance with a new guideline as revised in September 1977. The new guideline read as follows:

> In general, information which requires disclosure for legal or other reasons should be in language understandable by the child audience to which the advertisement is addressed. In television advertising, audio as well as video disclosure is encouraged. In all media, disclaimers, when used, should be clearly worded, legible and prominent (*News from NAD*, 15 December 1984).

"During 1981, the CARU expanded its advisory services available to advertisers and agencies to include workshops for creative people" (*Better Business News and Views* 7 (4):1).

NAD Selection of Complaints to Investigate. An *NAD Case Report* (15 July 1983) describes the kinds of complaints the NAD will investigate:

> The essential requirement is that a complaint raise an issue of public interest [as opposed to the interest of a particular company or industry]. Only a minority of complaints is accepted for formal inquiries because NAD has limited resources but, more to the point, because there are often more expeditious ways of resolving the complaint, for example, by an informal query to the advertiser. Every effort is made to be consistent in the review of cases selected for formal inquiries. The following are some of the reasons why NAD would decline a complaint or refer it to another organization:
>
> 1. If it concerns local advertising or business practice such as prompt delivery of goods, the most appropriate self-regulatory organization to handle the problem is the Better Business Bureau located in the same area as the advertiser's head office. Ninety percent of the complaints received from individual members of the public belong in this category. They are handled by referral and are therefore not counted as NAD cases. . . .

2. Questions related to the basic performance of products and services, label claims and directions, matters of taste, and political and issue advertising are not within NAD's mandate.

3. Advertising addressed to a business, professional or select audience with specialized knowledge of the subject matter is inappropriate for review by NAD.

4. Where possibly unlawful business practices are involved or the advertiser belongs to the very small minority unresponsive to self-regulation, NAD refers complaints to the appropriate government agency.

5. NAD will not initiate an inquiry involving advertising which is the subject of litigation by the FTC or another government agency (*NAD Case Report,* 15 July 1983, 21).

The NAD does not define the public interest precisely, but attempts to act in the interests of consumers—without attempting to quantify the potential degree of harm of misleading or unsubstantiated advertising to consumers or to competition. Presumably it is in the public interest of both consumers and business to maintain fair and open competition so that the free flow of accurate and truthful information between sellers and buyers facilitates the efficiency of the market system.

Although the NAD focuses on truth and accuracy and will not deal with matters of taste, the NARB has been sensitive to such matters, as evidenced by special studies it has commissioned to identify and evaluate issues relating to advertising and women and advertising to the elderly.

Advertising Substantiation Policies. A fundamental question is how to determine what data are relevant and sufficient to substantiate a claim. Frequently a high level of technical expertise is required. Thus the NAD staff includes specialists in areas such as food, nutrition, and psychology. However, because the NAD staff is small it necessarily must have access to outside consultants from time to time. One such source is ARF, which volunteered to act as marketing research consultant to the NAD in 1980. The press announcement pointed out:

"A major key to the substantiation of many advertising claims is marketing research data, particularly in the area of consumer perception," said Mrs. Lorraine Reid, CBBB Vice President. "The NAD has often sought outside expert opinion regarding the methodology of studies and interpretation of results. This relationship with ARF will give us access to a wide range of research expertise to help assure equitable resolution of NAD cases," she added.

Mr. Roll representing the ARF stated that the foundation was in full support of industry's self-regulatory mechanism. "ARF has been committed to setting and maintaining the highest standards of research for advertising substantiation," he said, "and acting as NAD's consultant is a natural extension of that role."

In dealing with substantiation questions, the NAD does not depend only on specialized knowledge or expert opinion. The staff also exercises "common sense judgements" in interpreting available evidence.

NAD staff are required to put themselves in the position of the advertiser and ask the question: "On the available facts could we make these claims in this language or form?" To answer this question, NAD requires undigested data so that it can repeat the reasoning by which the advertiser concluded its claims were truthful (*NAD Press Release*, 6 August 1980).

In 1983, an NAD staff member collected a number of substantiation cases dealing with treatment cosmetics that the NAD had resolved between 1981 and 1983. These cases illustrated the basis on which such decisions were made, especially regarding the use of experimental studies, clinical tests, and the views of technical experts to support advertising claims. This selection of cases demonstrated the possible outcomes with respect to the claims: (1) fully substantiated, in which the advertiser continued to use the claims; (2) not substantiated, in which the advertiser withdrew the claims; and (3) partly substantiated, in which the claims were modified by clarification, or partly withdrawn and partly modified (*NAD Case Reports*, various issues).

The same as with *BCAP* in the United Kingdom, the NAD's substantiation policy "reverses the burden of proof"; that is, the advertiser must demonstrate adequate substantiation or the NAD will rule against the advertiser. The NAD will, however, accept additional substantiation compiled after the advertisement has been questioned, provided that such evidence is accurate and relevant. It also is clear from *ASA Case Reports* that there are instances in which the Authority has accepted additional substantiation submitted retrospectively.

Local Advertising Review Program: Organizations and Functions. As described in the previous chapter, in the early 1970s the CBBB worked with local BBBs and other local advertising groups to establish LARBs. In 1974 an advertiser filed suit in Denver against the LARB alleging a violation of antitrust laws. Although unsuccessful, the suit led to the demise of LARBs, as described in chapter 3. In 1981 a new system of LARPs was initiated and as of 1 June 1986, thirty-three such LARPs had been formed. Under the LARP system, ARCs hear the few cases that are not resolved by the BBBs and the advertiser. Because ARCs hear so few cases, perhaps less than a dozen or so per year nationwide, it is tempting to conclude that the system is ineffective. However, the system is similar in a sense to the NAD/NARB; the BBBs and advertisers resolve most cases and therefore find it unnecessary to appeal very often to the ARCs. Moreover, those who administer the program point out that its main purpose is to be preventive rather than remedial; the fact that they exist and are prepared to act is believed to be an important deterrent because few local businesses desire to be called before their peers and to receive the attendant bad publicity, as a CBBB vice president put it (Reid, discussions with one of the authors, 1986).

If a complaint requires action, the process begins with the local BBB, which is

> responsible for receiving or initiating, evaluating, investigating, analyzing, and holding initial negotiations with an advertiser on complaints or questions from any source involving the truth or accuracy of local advertising. . . . When an advertising matter cannot be satisfactorily resolved by the BBB, the advertiser or the complainant may request the BBB to submit the issue to the ARC (*LARP* 1981, 8).

The new system for establishing local ARCs "composed of members whose principal affiliation is in the following categories and ratio: local advertisers (1/3), local advertising agencies (1/3), local public members (1/3)." (*LARP* 1981, 4).

When an advertising matter cannot be satisfactorily resolved informally by the local BBB, the advertiser or the complainant may request the BBB to review and submit the issue to the ARC. The ARC chairman then appoints a panel of ARC members to confer and to decide and fix the procedure and time schedule; the panel aims for informality and speed, consistent with due process considerations.

If the panel determines that an advertising claim is misleading or not substantiated, it recommends to the BBB that the advertiser be asked to modify or withdraw the advertising. In the case of noncompliance the BBB may make known the facts of the case to the media or to the general public, and may also refer the matter to a government agency. A key fact in this process is that the decision to act is made by the BBB, which is not a trade association, nor does it represent any particular industry or advertising media. The chances of an antitrust action are reduced greatly because there is no clear economic gain to the members of any industry; moreover, the decision is limited to requesting changes in or withdrawal of misleading advertising, an action that is proconsumer rather than anticompetitive.

A local ARC can also issue white papers on common or widespread problems, without naming individual companies.

The local advertising self-regulatory process is summarized in figure 4–2.

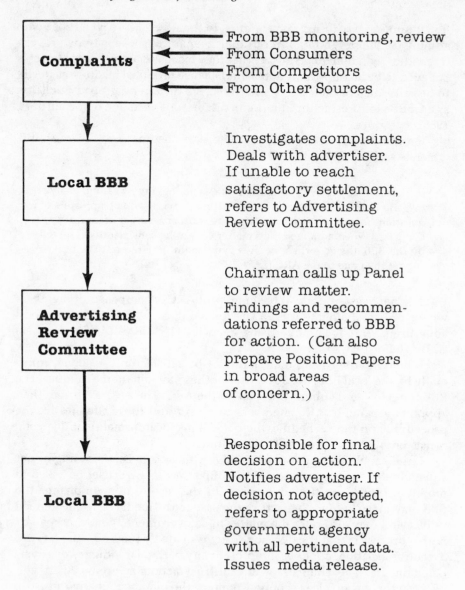

Complaints ← From BBB monitoring, review
← From Consumers
← From Competitors
← From Other Sources

Local BBB

Investigates complaints.
Deals with advertiser.
If unable to reach
satisfactory settlement,
refers to Advertising
Review Committee.

Advertising Review Committee

Chairman calls up Panel
to review matter.
Findings and recommen-
dations referred to BBB
for action. (Can also
prepare Position Papers
in broad areas
of concern.)

Local BBB

Responsible for final
decision on action.
Notifies advertiser. If
decision not accepted,
refers to appropriate
government agency
with all pertinent data.
Issues media release.

Source: *Local Advertising Review Program* (New York: CBBB, June 1981), p. 20.

Figure 4–2. The Local Advertising Self-Regulatory Process

Most cases are resolved in the early stages shown in figure 4–2. For example, between fifty and sixty advertisements are challenged daily in the Denver, Colorado, area, and less than 5 percent are referred to the

ARC. Apparently most advertisers cooperate immediately rather than appear before their peers and others on an ARC.

It appears as if the LARPs have great potential importance. It is unknown how many consumer complaints are made every year across the nation to BBBs, but the number is undoubtedly very large. In recent years the local BBBs probably have handled approximately 10,000 advertising complaints per year (authors' estimate based on statistics and conversations with CBBB personnel).

State governments also handle intrastate complaints. In Michigan alone, as mentioned in chapter 3, many of the nearly 10,000 advertising complaints per year handled by the Consumer Protection Division in the State Office of the Attorney General are trivial or not actionable. But the total number, along with the occasional serious complaints, suggests strongly that an effective self-regulatory program is needed at the local and state level.

The Television Networks

Commercials are precleared and complaints against them are handled as a self-regulatory activity by each television network. Because television advertising is controversial, and because the network preclearance and complaint-handling processes are so important (especially in view of the demise of the NAB Code), we give special attention to this part of the U.S. system.

Because there is no longer any other major self-regulatory mechanism for broadcast advertising in the United States, the three major television networks—ABC, CBS, and NBC—have developed and enforced their own individual network standards to a much fuller extent than was the case in 1979 and earlier when the NAB Codes were still applied industry-wide.

Parenthetically it should also be noted that there are no broadcast industry codes and control procedures for nonnetwork radio and television advertising. In the future, local stations and cable operations may be influenced by the activities of LARPs. But because there are LARPs in only thirty-three communities, control of local advertising, including print, is largely in the hands of the BBBs and whatever laws and enforcement mechanisms exist in each state or municipality.

Preclearance and Complaint Handling. Dzodin (1986, 5) characterizes the nature of television network control of advertising, speaking for ABC: "We take great pride to ensure that each and every commercial that we air is truthful, accurate and in good taste. The commercial clearance process is very much an exercise in self-regulation."

Most of the preclearance work is done on the basis of original story boards submitted by the advertising agency. Networks initially ask for additional information or substantiation for approximately twenty-five percent of the submitted commercials, with some variation between the networks, of course. In approximately another 10 percent of cases, the networks in their initial contact with the advertising agency immediately ask for changes. Many of these changes are relatively minor, such as altering a few words of copy or a camera angle. Initially, about three percent of the commercials are rejected outright. Occasionally, after tentative clearance of the story board, a finished commercial still may be rejected or major modification may be requested, which can be very costly to the advertiser.

There are several common complaints about networks' clearance procedures.

1. Standards regarding content of commercials are inconsistent from network to network and from product to product. Furthermore, standards within a network vary over short periods.

2. Guidelines are often not clearly spelled out or are not stated at all [although each network has a standards guidebook].

3. In the absence of binding arbitration, an agency's ability to appeal a network decision is limited. . . . Network executives maintain that their internal appeals mechanisms, as well as such nonbinding arbitrators as the National Advertising Division of the Better Business Bureau, are sufficient to handle claims. "Self-regulation works if everyone lets it," says Alice Henderson, vp/program practices for the CBS Broadcast Group.

4. Commercials are held to far stricter standards than network programs, especially regarding the depiction of children in dramatic situations, the consumption of alcoholic beverages and the use of dramatic or violent stunts. One creative director tells the story of a motorcycle manufacturer whose ad depicted a motorcycle rider driving through a flock of scattering chickens. The commercial, he said, was rejected as "too violent."

5. Large advertisers and their agencies, in the judgment of the president of a small shop, are given the benefit of the doubt in borderline cases and generally receive more favorable treatment because of their clout. That charge is vigorously disputed by program practices representatives at the three networks and the 4As in New York. If discrepancies exist, these sources agree, it is because small agencies are less familiar with established procedure than are major advertisers (Farhi 1983).

Network Policies and Practices. Examining the policies and practices of one of the networks will lead to an understanding of the nature of network advertising control. The following material deals with ABC policies and practices:

The commercial clearance process begins with the review of proposed advertising by in-house and outside counsel and other professionals at advertising agencies and their advertiser-clients.

Many, though not all, agencies and companies have independent commercial clearance departments, whose chief responsibility is to ensure that advertising is lawful and compliant with applicable industry standards.

All commercials submitted for broadcast on the American Broadcasting Company's television and radio networks are reviewed for compliance with federal, state, and local laws and regulations, and ABC policy. At ABC this clearance function is performed by the Department of Broadcast Standards and Practices, which has a counterpart at all television and radio broadcasting networks and stations.

Broadcast Standards and Practices is an independent department of ABC. As such it reports directly to corporate management and operates objectively, free of any allegiance to a sales or programming department. It reviews all commercials submitted to ABC to ensure that they are truthful, substantiated, in good taste, and in harmony with applicable legal requirements.

When affirmative claims are made for a product or service, we require that the advertiser submit substantiation or documentation providing a reasonable basis for the claims. This requirement arises from several sources. *First*, the courts have ruled that it is an unfair and deceptive practice in violation of the Federal Trade Commission Act to make an affirmative product claim without a reasonable basis for making that claim. *Second*, the Federal Communications Commission has stated that broadcast licensees have an obligation to avoid the presentation of deceptive advertising on radio and television. (According to the FCC, broadcasters must "take all reasonable measures to eliminate any false, misleading or deceptive matter.") *Third*, it is ABC's corporate policy that our broadcasting facilities may not be used for commercial announcements which are deceptive. This policy is based on our responsibilities as a licensee for our owned and operated stations, and as a surrogate for our affiliated stations.

Under our procedures, advertising agencies should submit a storyboard or script for each commercial sufficiently in advance to permit careful review by the department. Occasionally, agencies and advertisers have submitted finished tapes to us without going through the script or storyboard stage. If the commercial is determined to be misleading, unsubstantiated, or otherwise unacceptable, this can be an expensive mistake. It is much less costly to revise a storyboard or to go back to the drawing board and begin again before an ad has been shot, than to have a cunning but unusable commercial.

We also ask agencies to endeavor to submit adequate substantiation with the initial submission of a proposed commercial. Costly and nerve-wracking delays can ensue when substantiation arrives piecemeal.

Each commercial is reviewed by Broadcast Standards editors. They are experienced and highly competent professionals trained in the disciplines of law, education, social sciences, psychology, child development, and other educational and scientific disciplines. All editors receive an extended period of on-the-job training prior to exercising their review functions. Editors are assigned specific product categories so that each may develop expertise in particular areas. When necessary, commercials are also reviewed by our research specialists, the ABC Research Department, or the Legal Department. After reviewing a proposed commercial, an editor may accept it, reject it, request revisions or request additional substantiation for claims. An agency may appeal an adverse decision to [the director] or to the Vice President of the Department. We will, of course, consider any substantive arguments and will review the staff's decision. If we determine that the commercial is in fact compliant with law and policy, we will accept it.

One argument, which we frequently hear in appeals but disregard, is that other networks or stations have approved the advertising in question. We make independent judgments, and apply *our* individual judgment as best we can. As U.S. Courts of Appeal sometimes arrive at different decisions on the same issues, so do we. That we reach a different result than other networks on occasion reflects the fact that many of the decisions are, by nature, subjective and complex. Frequently there are no hard and fast lines; there are many gray areas.

During the course of the year, our Department reviews approximately *50,000* commercials submitted from several hundred advertisers and agencies. About *30,000* are new commercials. The rest are revisions of ads already submitted. Of the new commercials submitted, about *3 percent* are rejected outright, some *63 percent* are accepted without modification, and for the remaining *35 percent*, modifications are requested. Over the past few years the percentage of comparative commercials has grown steadily. Today, *20 percent (one-fifth)* of all commercials are comparative.

Our editors find certain problems tend to occur more frequently during the commercial review process than others. Some problems relate to the substantiation of claims to meet the reasonable basis requirements, documentation of the authenticity of product's performance during a demonstration, and validity of endorsements and testimonials. Ethnic and sexual stereotyping also create difficulties during commercial review. Another problem involves the false or misleading disparagement of competitors in comparative ads.

Other areas of special scrutiny, include the application of guidelines relating to children's advertising, over-the-counter drugs, personal products advertising, comparative advertising, weight reduction, and other categories.

In the last year or so a lot of attention has been given to some well publicized court battles over advertising. In 1982 there was the celebrated "Battle of the Burgers" begun by Burger King Advertising against McDonald's and Wendy's. Just recently *Vaseline Intensive Care* and *Wondra* sued each other over advertising claims. Not so well known, however, is that these kinds of battles are fought daily at ABC and the other networks.

Any commercial aired on ABC may be challenged by another advertiser or any responsible party. A challenge must be made in writing in a form which permits it, along with any supporting data, to be transmitted to the challenged advertiser for a response. Upon reviewing the challenge, if we determine that it appears to have merit, we will send it to the advertiser and allow 14 days for a response. After receiving the response, it may be necessary to require one or both sides to respond to the arguments and data presented. Oftentimes, highly technical testing is submitted by both sides, and we are called upon to resolve a battle of experts. At the conclusion of this process we reach a decision, and either allow the advertising to continue airing, order modifications to be made, or order it to be withdrawn. Occasionally, the advertiser will voluntarily withdraw a challenged commercial during the course of the proceeding.

Last year [1983] at ABC we received 180 challenges. 60% were dismissed and 40% were upheld in whole or in part. 93% of the commercials involved were comparative (Dzodin 1984).

This material was substantially the same in 1986. A few trends are worth noting; for example, the number of commercials submitted for review is now well over 50,000 per year, of which about 37,000 are new. Substantiation requirements have become increasingly strict and sophisticated, often requiring "highly technical testing . . . the percentage of comparative commercials has grown so that today one-fourth of all commercials are comparative" (Dzodin 1986, 18–19). Additionally, the number of challenges from competitors or other responsible parties declined to 127 in 1984 and to 91 in 1985, virtually all involving comparisons. In 1985 modification or withdrawal was required of more than 40 percent of those challenged (Dzodin 1986, 21).

British Enforcement Bodies

The ASA/CAP System

The ASA/CAP Founding, Structure, and Organization. Although the ASA was established in 1962, it was not until the mid-1970s that changes in financing permitted the development of its current structure and organization. As previously noted, in the 1960s and early 1970s consumer groups, political parties, and government bodies developed an increasingly intense interest in regulating advertising. The "Reith Report" (Labour Party, 1966), for example, based on extensive study by a Labour Party Commission, made a number of recommendations reflecting the climate of opinion that stimulated the industry to action. The Commission recommended that a National Consumer Board (NCB) should be established, with government financing or perhaps a tax on advertising. The NCB was to have broad powers to control any undesirable advertising or advertising practice, and the existing self-regulatory code was to be made statutory. Special considerations and control would be exercised over advertising of medicines, cigarettes, outdoor advertising, and press supplements.

The advertising industry reacted decisively to the numerous criticisms of the times, however, by strengthening the existing self-regulatory system. The main effect of the reforms to the British self-regulatory system carried out in 1974 was the strengthening of the ASA. The advertising industry at last accepted that if government intervention was to be avoided, then justice not only had to be done but had to be seen to be done. The ASA had assumed direct responsibility for the investigation of complaints when it took over the work of the AA's AID in 1972. Now the number of permanent staff was considerably increased, and its freedom from industry influence was ensured because it had a source of finance quite independent of the AA.

The ASA is controlled by a Council that meets under an independent chairman. The chairman is appointed by the Advertising Standards Board of Finance in consultation with the Council, and informally with the Department of Trade and Industry. The chairman in turn appoints the members of the council, two-thirds of whom are independent of any connection with the advertising industry. Those members with advertising experience are able to provide the technical advice that is sometimes needed. For example, if an advertisement is to be withdrawn, members need to know how long it might reasonably be expected to continue appearing, given the copy dates of publications being used by the advertiser.

Each member of the council is appointed initially for a period of three years, but may be invited by the chairman to serve for a further period. An important feature of the ASA is that all members serve as individuals— that is, they do not report to any other organization or represent any sectional interest, although they might belong to bodies holding strong views about advertising and related matters.

As the members meet only monthly, the day-to-day running of the ASA's affairs is in the hands of a permanent secretariat headed by the director general. The secretariat also acts for the CAP Committee, but though some functions are handled jointly, a separate group works exclusively on the Committee's affairs. The ASA, in fact, makes an effort to point out that the activities of the two bodies are treated quite distinctly and their separate identities carefully preserved.

According to the *ASA Annual Report, 1984–1985,* the numbers employed in the secretariat were as follows:

Director general	1
Deputy director general	1
Deputy directors	2
Administrator	1
Central services	8
ASA public complaints	12
CAP	12
External relations	3
Monitoring	3
Student (temporary)	1
Total	44

The Code of Advertising Practice Committee. As the ASA represents the public face of advertising self-regulation, so the CAP Committee represents the industry face, including among its members nominees of each of those trade and professional organizations that agree that their members will uphold and enforce the Code. According to the 1985 edition of *BCAP,* these are as follows:

Advertising Association

Association of Free Newspapers

Association of Independent Radio Contractors[1]

Association of Mail Order Publishers

Bus Advertising Council

Cinema Advertising Association

Direct Mail Producers Association

Direct Mail Services Standards Board

Incorporated Society of British Advertisers

Independent Television Companies Association

Institute of Practitioners in Advertising

Institute of Sales Promotion

Newspaper Publishers Association

Newspaper Society

Periodical Publishers Association

Proprietary Association of Great Britain

Scottish Daily Newspaper Society

Scottish Newspaper Proprietors Association

Videotex Industry Association

In addition, the Code has the support of the following organizations:

British Direct Marketing Association

British Sign Association

Outdoor Advertising Association

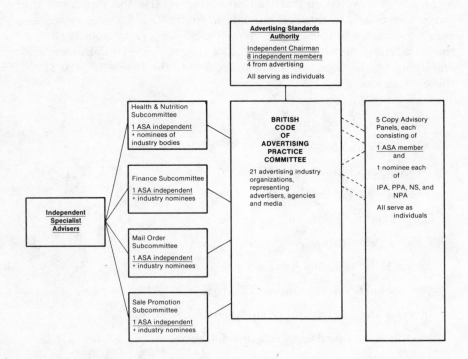

Source: Advertising Standards Authority.

Note: Underlined words and figures indicate that the people referred to are entirely independent of the advertising business.

Figure 4–3. The Relationship Between the ASA and the CAP Committee

The functions of the Committee, which include overseeing the implementation of the Code within the advertising industry, arbitrating disputes, and giving prepublication advice, are discussed in detail later in this chapter.

Supporting Bodies. In addition to the work of the ASA and the CAP Committee, considerable work in enforcing standards is carried out on a day-to-day basis by the various supporting organizations and by other organizations with an interest in seeing that a high standard of advertising is maintained in a particular field of activity. In the case of those organizations represented on the CAP Committee, this means that observance of the Code is integrated firmly into the process of creating and placing advertisements, being enforced at three levels.

The Advertisers. The body that speaks for the advertiser in the United Kingdom is ISBA. Although small in terms of number of members, it includes some of the biggest spenders and is therefore a highly influential body. Among its main aims is "To promote high standards of advertising practice by the observance of and adherence to the Codes governing advertising and sales promotion practice agreed to and promoted by the Society." By virtue of the Society's membership of the CAP Committee, its own members agree in effect to uphold and apply the provisions of the Code in respect of advertising that they commission and pay for.

ISBA also plays an important role representing the interests of British advertisers as a member of the AA, and internationally through the World Federation of Advertisers (WFA; formerly the International Union of Advertisers Associations) and the International Chamber of Commerce (ICC), each of these organizations being strongly in favor of the principle of self-regulation. To emphasize the importance it attaches to the need for action within the industry, ISBA publishes a booklet entitled *Self-Regulation and the Advertiser,* which is available not only to members but also to any interested persons and organizations.

The Agencies. Advertising agencies are normally employed by advertisers to create advertisements and to book space and time in the appropriate media. The organization that represents agency interests in the United Kingdom is the IPA, and though fewer than half the country's 600 or so agencies belong to it, those in membership account for some 90 percent of total British agency billings.

Agencies are pressured from two sources to try and ensure that they observe the provisions of the Code. First, the Institute is represented on the CAP Committee, so that member agencies are in effect accepting that they will uphold the Code in respect of all the work they create and place.

To remind them of this responsibility the Institute publishes its *Advertising Controls Checklist,* which is available to members. It also recommends that they protect their own position vis-à-vis clients by including the following clauses in client contracts:

15. ADVERTISING STANDARDS

A. We abide by rulings of the Advertising Standards Authority and the Code of Advertising Practice Committee and we comply with the *British Code of Advertising Practice,* the British Code of Sales Promotion Practice, the IBA Code of Advertising Standards and Practice for radio and television and other codes of advertising standards laid down on a self-regulatory basis within the advertising industry to ensure that all advertising placed by us is legal, decent, honest and truthful.

B. In order to satisfy the requirements of these codes or any statutory requirements and in the interests of yourselves, ourselves and the public you agree to supply us immediately with objective factual evidence, if so required, in support of any product claims you wish us to make.

C. You agree to inform us without delay if you consider that any claim or trade description in any advertisements submitted to you by us for approval is false or misleading in relation to your product or service.

D. You agree that if we prepare an advertisement for pre-packaged food omitting the statements required by the Food Labelling Regulations 1984, these requirements will be contained in the label which appears on the container of such food (IPA 1986, 10–11).

The Institute also retains a full-time legal officer who can be consulted by members on problems of interpretation.

The second constraint is imposed on agencies by the media, and applies not only to IPA members but to agencies in general. To be able to buy space or time on credit an agency has to be "recognized," which effectively means that its financial status is investigated by the various media organizations on behalf of their members. An agency that satisfies their requirements then signs agreements with the organizations concerned. The NPA and the NS operate a joint recognition system, and under their agreement the agency agrees to the following:

> That all advertising placed by it shall be legal, decent, honest and truthful and that it is aware of, will conform to and support the requirements of the *British Code of Advertising Practice* and any other codes under the general supervision of the Advertising Standards Authority.
>
> That it will conform to and support the provisions laid down by the Advertising Standards Board of Finance Limited which govern the surcharging of the gross media rate on display advertisements at the rate for

the time being promulgated and which require advertisers who are clients of the agency to pay the agency and the agency to collect and to pay to the Advertising Standards Board of Finance Limited those sums required for the maintenance of the Advertising Standards Authority Limited and the code of Advertising Practice Committee (NPA/NS, undated).

Media. The media have always been very much involved in the processes of regulation, partly because of their responsibilities to their readers and viewers, and partly also because of their exposed position in law should the question of criminal proceedings arise concerning an advertisement they carry.

A number of organizations in the United Kingdom represent the interests of various media groups including national and local newspapers, magazines, outdoor, transportation, and cinema. Before the ASA was strengthened in 1974, these and other organizations such as ISBA had their own copy committees. Today, however, most emphasis is put on urging members to obey the provisions of the Code, though the NPA and the NS still have a Joint Copy Committee that can deal with members' queries. It should be emphasized that these bodies are concerned with the whole spectrum of matters relating to their particular areas of activity, and that advertising is only one among many aspects of their work.

Financing the Self-Regulatory System. We are not concerned here with the supporting bodies whose advertising activities are financed out of membership fees, but with the central machinery—the ASA, the CAP Committee, and the supporting secretariat.

The work of the central machinery was originally financed by the AA, a fact that gave rise to considerable criticism among critics of the system both because of the meager scale of the funding provided (particularly when compared with the level of expenditure that the system was being asked to regulate), and because the Authority was being asked in effect to police its own paymaster.

As part of the 1974 reforms the main representative organizations concerned with advertising set up a new independent body, the Advertising Standards Board of Finance Limited, a company limited by guarantee, known in the industry as ASBOF. Its purpose was to finance the strengthened ASA.

As currently constituted, ASBOF has a twelve-member board of directors consisting of two representatives each from the IPA, ISBA, the NPA, the NS, and the Periodical Publishers Association, and one each from the Scottish Daily Newspaper Society and the Scottish Newspaper Proprietors Association. There is also a fifteen-member council consisting of one representative of each of these organizations together with those of the

British Direct Marketing Association, the Association of British Directory Publishers, the Association of Free Newspapers, the Association of Media Independents, the Advertising Association, the Cinema Advertising Association, the Direct Mail Producers Association, and the Outdoor Advertising Council.

Finance is raised by a surcharge of 0.1 percent (that is, £1 per £1,000) on press display, outdoor, cinema, and direct mail advertising, levied on gross media rates. It is collected from advertisers either by agencies and media independents, or by the media when a booking is made directly. They in turn make quarterly payments to ASBOF, and have to provide annual certificates signed by their accountants confirming that the correct amount has been remitted. Since January 1975, media rate cards and standard conditions of acceptance have included statements to the effect that invoices would be subject to the ASBOF surcharge. At the same time the obligation of collection was written into agency recognition agreements (ASBOF 1982). In 1985 approximately 1,280 advertising agencies and media companies made payments to ASBOF. Surcharge revenue for 1985 was more than £1.7 million (*ASBOF Annual Report* 1985–1986). Annual expenditures by the Authority between 1979 and 1984 are shown in table 4–2.

Apart from responsibility for financing the work of the ASA, ASBOF is also responsible for appointing the Authority's chairman.

ASA Complaint Handling.[2] The Authority's aim is to ensure as far as possible that all advertising that comes within its jurisdiction is legal, decent, honest, and truthful. Unlike the IBA, the ASA is unable to examine every advertisement before it reaches the public, so it has to rely broadly

Table 4–2
ASA/CAP Committee Resources

	Budget (£)				
Year	Operating Costs[a]	Advertising and Promotion[b]	Total	Percent Increase Over Previous Year	Number of Personnel Employed by Secretariat[c]
1979	465,058	277,148	742,206	n.a.	n.a.
1980	550,844	331,733	882,577	18.9	40
1981	654,249	350,769	1,005,018	13.9	38
1982	820,085	397,742	1,217,827	21.2	44
1983	898,785	374,593	1,273,378	4.6	42
1984	973,398	455,669	1,429,067	12.2	43

Source: *ASA Annual Reports.*
[a]Operating costs include staff, facilities, and miscellaneous expenses.
[b]Does not include donated media space.
[c]Does not include temporary student help attached to the Secretariat.

on urging compliance within the advertising industry, and investigating complaints from the public about advertisements that fail to observe the provisions of the Code.

Since 1961, and especially since 1974, the ASA/CAP system has handled many thousands of inquiries and complaints about national and local advertising throughout the United Kingdom. Currently the number of complaints runs at a rate of approximately 8,000 per year, leading to about 2,000 ASA investigations per year, of which nearly 1,500 relate to advertising copy investigations (see chapter 7 for additional details).

Complaints from members of the public may relate either to the content of the advertisement or to their treatment by the advertiser. They may, for example, consider the advertisement to be in some respect misleading, untruthful, or indecent, or may be unable to obtain the goods they ordered or their money back from a mail order company. Every complaint must be in writing, and must be accompanied either by a copy of the advertisement or, if that is not possible (as in the case of a poster or a cinema film) by sufficient evidence to allow it to be identified. The actual handling of complaints is in the hands of the Authority's secretariat. If there appears to be a case, a letter is sent to the advertiser and agency concerned setting out the nature of the complaint and asking for their comments and substantiation for any claims made if appropriate. If the secretariat believes that the case in question is particularly serious, the advertiser is asked to stop further publication until it has been resolved. He may also be asked to withdraw the advertisement together with any others making similar claims if it appears that he has been unduly slow in responding.

When replies have been received, they are evaluated by the secretariat, who may ask for further information from the advertiser or, if necessary, call on the assistance of the Copy Panel (see figure 4-4) or of independent consultants. Having completed its investigation, the secretariat then submits a recommendation to the Authority's council, with copies going to the advertiser, the agency, and the complainant. Every council member receives these recommendations weekly. The secretariat attaches a form on which the member can list the advertisements he or she wishes the council to discuss and the reasons for doing so. All complaints concerned with matters of taste and decency are discussed in the council because the values involved are recognized to be so subjective.

Once the council has ruled for or against the secretariat's recommendation, the parties concerned are informed of the decision. If an advertiser is judged to have contravened the Code, he is asked to withdraw the advertisement concerned and to not repeat the breach in the future. If he refuses to comply, the Authority informs those media organizations in membership of the CAP Committee, all of whose members in turn have

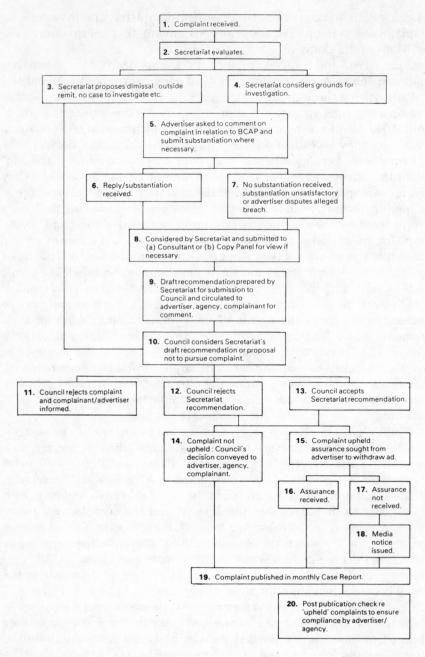

Source: Advertising Standards Authority.

Figure 4–4. Summary of ASA Complaints Procedure

undertaken not to publish any advertisement that is in breach of the Code. Should an advertiser refuse to answer communications from the Authority, media organizations may be asked not to accept any further advertisements from the company concerned. Such action may be rescinded in the future if the advertiser indicates a willingness to comply with the Authority's original ruling.

The notice that the Authority sends to trade associations is technically a request that action should be taken. Those associations then inform their members in whatever form is suited to the circumstances. The Periodical Publishers Association, for example, whose members produce mainly weekly and monthly magazines, includes any notices in a regular circular that it mails to its membership, and the NPA, whose members publish the national dailies, informs its members by telephone. If a publication appears to be ignoring the notice, the chairman of the ASA writes to the association concerned drawing its attention to the matter, and so far this step appears to have been sufficient to secure compliance. It is possible for an association to expel a member for ignoring a notice, but this has never been necessary.

The Authority also has a sanction against advertising agencies that persistently flout the Code by creating and placing advertisements that contravene its provisions. In such cases media organizations can be asked to tell their members to withdraw recognition, which would mean in effect that the agency concerned could no longer buy advertising space for its clients on credit. Because agencies generally rely on being paid by their clients before they have to pay their media bills, the withdrawal of recognition and its effect on cash flow would effectively put an agency out of business.

The outcome of every case investigated is published in the Authority's monthly *Case Reports*. These show in each instance the number of complainants (but not their identity), their home towns, the name of the advertiser, the agency (if any), the substance of the complaint, and the Authority's finding. Since April 1978 they have also included an editorial commenting on trends and discussing current issues and problems. These reports are circulated free of charge to the media, government departments and agencies, and consumer organizations. They are also available to the advertising industry and to interested members of the public.

The Authority has the power to specify particular classes of advertisements for compulsory preclearance, as it has done in the case of cigarettes. Whenever possible, copy is cleared by the secretariat; borderline cases are submitted to the Copy Panel. To protect the confidentiality of advertisers' plans, panels considering new cigarette advertisements are composed only of media and Authority representatives.

Advertisers may appeal to a Copy Panel if they do not accept a secretariat decision, and may appeal to the council of the Authority against a Copy Panel decision, provided that the chairman of the Authority and the CAP Committee both certify that an important point of principle is involved.

Every cigarette advertisement that has been cleared is issued a numbered clearance certificate by the CAP Committee, a copy of which must be sent by the advertiser to each publication the first time the advertisement is submitted. The issue of this certificate, however, is no guarantee that an advertisement may not subsequently be rejected by the ASA Council should it receive a complaint from a member of the public. In such an event the advertiser and agency are notified, the certificate is withdrawn, and its number notified to media organizations.

ASA Monitoring. This activity constitutes a further important aspect of the Authority's work and is undertaken with three main objectives: (1) to ensure that any undertakings given by advertisers in the past are in fact being honored; (2) to identify areas in which advertisers may be going beyond the bounds of what the Authority considers to be substantiable in terms of copy claims; and (3) to ascertain that the provisions of the Code are being generally observed (see chapter 7 for additional information).

The Authority believes that the use of appropriate statistical techniques, particularly random sampling, can provide an accurate measure of the incidence of breaches, and thus of the success or failure of the control system. In this way it compensates for the misleading impression that can be given by figures showing variations in the number of complaints over time. For example, press criticism of a particular product group can produce a sharp increase in the number of complaints, though the number of actual breaches of the Code may in fact have fallen (*ASA Case Report 87* April, 1984).

Publicity. In spite of the extent of its monitoring activities, the success of the ASA in regulating advertising depends to a large degree on the vigilance of members of the public. This in turn presupposes a general awareness and understanding of the Code and how it is enforced. It is for this reason that the Authority devotes considerable effort to publicizing its work. Members of the public are reached by advertisements in virtually all the media that are the Authority's concerns, and the value of the Authority's advertising budget is virtually quadrupled by space donated free by the media themselves.

A long-term campaign directed at the general public aims to achieve greater understanding of the Authority's work and of the effective contribution made by self-regulation to the control of advertising in nonbroadcast media. From 1981 to 1983 public awareness of the Authority increased from 11 percent to 23 percent (*ASA Case Report 103*). Another campaign in the trade press explains the role of the Authority to the advertising industry. Publicity of a more general nature is obtained in national and local media including television and radio in the form of news and feature coverage of the Authority and its work. In addition, it participates in relevant exhibitions, conferences, and seminars; makes presentations to trading standards officers, Citizens' Advice Bureaux, and consumer groups; has two films on its work available for hire; arranges for members of the secretariat to address advertising students; and has a wide range of leaflets available explaining various aspects of its work and the operation of the Code.

The Authority works closely with those bodies concerned with the legal enforcement of standards in advertising, in particular the Office of Fair Trading (OFT) and trading standards officers.

The Functions of the Code of Advertising Practice Committee. The work of the committee falls under three main headings. First, it is responsible for seeing that the Code is kept up to date and ensuring that it is enforced throughout the industry. To this end it issues occasional *Notes of Guidance* on areas of particular difficulty, and also acts as a clearinghouse for decisions reached on advertisements by constituent members.

Second, it arbitrates in disputes between advertisers on points relating to the content of advertisements, and especially on the admissibility of particular claims.

Third, it gives prepublication advice regarding specific copy points to advertisers and agencies, with the intention of helping them conform to the provisions of the Code and avoid giving cause for complaint to the public or competitors. From January through November 1983 the CAP secretariat gave written advice in 839 cases and dealt with approximately 5,000 queries by telephone (*ASA Case Report 105*). It is important to note that clearance by the CAP Committee is no guarantee of acceptability. Members of the public may still complain to the ASA, whose decision would override the views of the CAP Committee.

The Committee normally refers consideration of copy points to its Copy Advisory Panel, which is divided into five sections, one of which meets each week. Each section consists of one member of the ASA independent of any advertising interest together with one nominee each from the ISBA, the IPA, The Periodical Publishers Association, the NPA, and the NS. Members serve in an individual rather than a representative capacity. When a conflict of interest may occur, however, members are required to declare such interests, and it is then left to the discretion of the chairman as to whether the member should be asked to withdraw during discussion of that particular case, or whether he or she should remain but not participate.

An advertiser has the right of appeal from Copy Panel decisions through the CAP Committee to the ASA. If the panel itself considers that a point of substance has arisen, it may refer the case to the ASA Council for a definitive ruling. However, approval by the CAP Committee or the Authority is no guarantee that an advertisement will in fact be accepted by the publication to which it is submitted, because it may still run contrary to a publisher's own "house rules" or be considered undesirable or unsuitable by the editor.

In addition to the Copy Panel, the CAP Committee has four specialist subcommittees to deal with the areas of health and nutrition, finance, mail order, and sales promotion respectively. Each consists of one member of the ASA independent of any advertising interest, together with industry nominees. A member of the Committee also sits as an adviser on the Society of Film Distributors' Advertisement Viewing Committee, which scrutinizes all press advertisements, posters, and front-of-house photographs for films carrying the "18" certificate, and gives advice if requested on material relating to the "15" certificate. (These certificates are issued by the British Board of Film Censors and indicate the minimum age at which a person should be admitted to a performance).

Since December 1980 the Committee has published case reports in a similar way to the ASA. Many in the industry previously argued that if the kind of disputes dealt with by the committee were made public, the complaints procedure might be used as a commercial weapon. The Committee took the view, however, that it was important for the system to be seen to be working fairly and that such openness was essential to reinforce public confidence.

Media Functions and Procedures. The most active body in terms of advertising regulation is the NS, which represents the interests of the regional and local press. This function is the responsibility of its Advertising Control Department, under the supervision of the head of the Parliamentary and Legal Department. Advertising Control operates in four main areas. First, it gives advice to members, which represents the bulk of the department's work. Any member of the society is entitled to ask for guidance as to whether a particular advertisement conforms to the requirements of the law or the Code. Such advice can frequently be given over the telephone, and in the nature of the business often has to be, because dubious copy is often deliberately submitted right on the deadline. The department is fortunate in being able to draw on its comprehensive advertising index, first set up in the 1920s and now comprising some 33,000 entries covering such varied matters as legislation, advice from committees, information on advertisers or products queried in the past, restrictions on advertising imposed by trade or professional organizations, and miscellaneous problems that have previously occurred (for example, what exactly is a Dorset black hen?).

Sometimes the society is faced with a glut of queries about a particular product or type of advertisement, the short-lived boom in personal fallout shelters being a case in point. Under these circumstances it issues a note of guidance to members on the subject. As with all its regulatory activities, however, the society emphasizes that its function is to advise and that it has no power to prohibit. The decision whether to publish a particular advertisement must be taken by each individual newspaper.

Second, the department provides information for members on advertising matters. It publishes *Advertisement Points to Watch* and also produces a monthly newsletter that contains information on matters such as advice and reports from various committees, names of organizations or products that the society believes to be suspect, guidelines on the interpretation of new legislation, and answers to queries of general interest. The *Newsletter* is intended to be circulated to staff in advertisement departments to keep them up to date with current developments.

The society also constantly impresses on members the importance of observing and enforcing *BCAP*. For example:

> Many newly recruited staff lack knowledge of the reason why the self-regulatory system was set up in the first place and they resent the feeling of restriction which it creates. . . . The Society will appreciate it if NS members will impress on their staffs the undisputed fact that the system of self-regulation, as an alternative to legislation, will benefit the industry as a whole in the long term. Its success is crucially dependent on the commitment and involvement of individuals, whether in agencies or in media or as advertisers (*NS Newsletter* No. 602, 29 October 1981).

Third, the department represents the NS on the CAP Committee and its various subcommittees, and on the joint committees of the NS and the NPA, in particular the Joint Recognition Committee. Fourth, it operates its own recognition system for advertising agencies that will be using regional and local rather than national press, acting as permanent secretariat for the Recognition Committee which meets four times a year, and keeping a running check on the financial performance of agencies.

The Joint Copy Committee of the NS and the NPA deals with copy problems in advertisements. Procedures differ between the two organizations, because whereas the NS will only refer cases in which there is a query, the NPA automatically refers all cases submitted by members. A Joint Committee ruling has the same force as that of the CAP Committee;

members are bound to uphold it because they are bound to uphold the Code, and risk expulsion if they do not.

There are three standing subcommittees of the Joint Copy Committee, dealing with franchising, holidays, and mail order. In addition, ad hoc subcommittees are set up from time to time to deal with particular problem areas, fitted kitchens and garden products being two recent examples.

The major publishers' organizations all have some form of Mail Order Protection Scheme (MOPS) to protect readers from loss in the case of default by a mail order advertiser. Advertisers, agencies, and publications have each contributed to a central fund that will recompense readers who send money in response to mail order advertisements placed by mail order traders who fail to supply goods or refund money and who become the subject of liquidation or bankruptcy proceedings. The NPA has a mail order officer who visits the premises of prospective mail order advertisers to investigate both product stocks and the financial status of the company. The scale of the NS's members' operations would make this impossible in their case, so the investigation is carried out by the nearest local newspaper. The advertiser has to sign a special mail order agreement that binds him, among other things, to acknowledge orders and payments promptly, to have staff at the address given in the advertisement and ensure the company's name is displayed there prominently, and to allow the newspaper to refund money if appropriate and recover it from the advertiser on demand.

In addition many publishers, both local and national, have their own house rules to deal with categories of advertising and types of illustration or appeal that they believe would prove unacceptable or offensive to their particular readers. Many local papers, for instance, exclude nude illustrations and advertisements for contraceptives, both permissible under *BCAP*, and may take liberties with clients' artworks such as concealing a pair of naked breasts discreetly behind a bra.

The local press also claims to enforce the provisions of the Code more carefully than its national counterparts, and there are differences between them in terms of operating conditions that seem to add weight to this argument. Although the majority of national press advertisements are prepared by agencies, the reverse is true in the case of the local press, many of whose advertisers are small retailers whose expenditure is too low for even the smallest agency to handle at a profit. In such a situation the advertisement representative, as space salesmen are usually called in the United Kingdom, not only has to sell advertising space but must also act as creative consultant, advising clients on the admissibility of claims, producing rough layouts, commissioning artwork from the paper's own studio, and writing copy. The individual representative therefore has a much closer contact with the advertiser than is the case if an agency is involved, and even more importantly he is directly responsible for any problems arising with regard to an advertisement with which he has had a creative involvement.

Under such circumstances, a criminal liability may exist under the Trade Descriptions Act of 1968. The defence available to a publisher who publishes an advertisement containing a false or misleading trade description only applies if that advertisement is received in the course of trade or business. Therefore, if a member of the publisher's staff has been involved in creating the advertisement or offering creative advice, as distinct from simply selling space, that defence cannot be raised.

Some specialist magazine publishers also offer creative services to small clients. Figure 4–5 shows a flow diagram produced by EMAP National Magazines of Peterborough to guide its representatives when making judgments on the admissibility of particular copy points. In 1983 a step was taken to try and control advertising by post, which had been for many years the resort of tricksters anxious to avoid public scrutiny of their announcements. A new body, the Direct Mail Services Standards Board, was set up with financial backing from the Post Office in an effort to improve standards. The board operates a recognition scheme for direct mail advertising agencies that receive a one percent refund from the Post Office on their annual bill for direct mail shots, provided they can satisfy the board that they comply with *BCAP*, and work only for clients who observe it and who pay the ASBOF levy. The board also has a symbol that recognized agencies are able to use on their literature.

Poster and cinema advertising, unlike that carried by the press, is precleared centrally in a manner similar to television. The poster industry, it will be remembered, was the first to introduce a form of self-regulation at the turn of the century and has always remained sensitive to public opinion. The Outdoor Advertising Association (OAA), the relevant trade body, has a poster-viewing committee that examines designs submitted by agencies and assesses their suitability for general display. Individual poster contractors may also refer queries to the committee, though this is a rare occurrence because the contractor receives the poster in printed form and advertisers obviously do not wish to risk incurring the cost of reprinting and paying rental charges on empty sites while they do so.

The committee deals only with posters that are four sheet or bigger, which effectively excludes advertising for cinemas and theaters. However, it liaises with the trade associations concerned if the need arises, and also maintains links with London Transport Advertising (LTA) and British Transport Advertising (BTA). The criterion used by the committee is whether a given design complies with the provisions of the *BCAP*, although in addition it will consider factors such as the proposed siting so that a poster that advertises contraceptives, for example, would not be permitted opposite a school.

Advertising for cinemas is the responsibility of the Society of Film Distributors (SFD), whose Advertising Viewing Committee includes representatives of the British Board of Film Censors and the ASA. The committee, which meets every two weeks, examines material for all "18" category

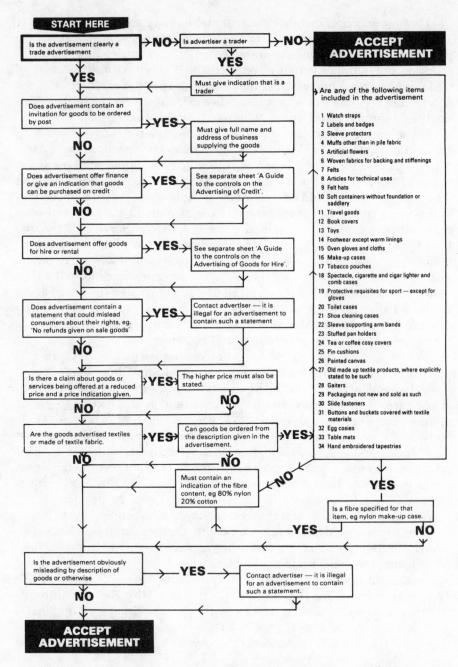

Source: ©Cambridge County Council and EMAP National Publications, Peterborough, United Kingdom. Reproduced by permission.

Figure 4–5. EMAP National Magazines "Acceptance of Advertising" Flow Chart

films (films that may be seen only by persons aged 18 or more) together with any other material that may be referred to it.

The position with regard to commercials shown in cinemas is somewhat more complicated. In general terms, any film of whatever type that is 30 seconds or longer must carry a certificate issued by the British Board of Film Censors certifying that it has been passed as suitable for public exhibition. Such certificates are classified according to whether the board believes the film is suitable for unaccompanied children, children at the discretion of (that is, accompanied by) their parents, and so on. The Cinema Advertising Association (CAA), the trade body concerned, insists that all commercials in this length category must carry a "U" certificate, which means that they can be shown to all types of audience without restriction.

Commercials shorter than 30 seconds do not require a certificate and are precleared by the association itself. The test applied is whether, in the opinion of the Association, the film would have qualified for the award of a "U" certificate had one been necessary. Unlike the IBA dealing with television commercials, the CAA is involved mainly with finished films even though it is preclearing them. The reason for this is that original advertising films shot especially for the cinema are very much in the minority. Advertisers today often use the cinema to complement television campaigns and so make use of material shot at the same time as the television commercial. Because the television storyboard is cleared in advance by the IBA and the film itself is approved prior to transmission, the advertiser can feel reasonably confident in submitting a similar treatment for exhibition in the cinema.

The lack of publicity given to the activities of the trade associations concerned with poster and cinema advertising certainly does not mean that they represent a soft option for the advertiser intent on bending the rules. They operate behind the scenes and at the preclearance stage. Because those submitting material for approval agree to accept their findings, the trade associations represent self-regulation in the true sense of the word. Their sanction is nonappearance. Nothing further is necessary because they do not deal with complaints, which is a function of the ASA and the CAP Committee that the trade associations do not wish to usurp. They aim instead to prevent problems occurring by ensuring that the provisions of the Code are observed and implemented with respect to particular media and conditions.

At the time of writing, the government has taken steps to remove certain types of financial advertising from the area of self-regulation, apparently taking the view that the public interest would be better served by considering such advertising in the context of the activities to which they relate. Accordingly it has given the Takeover Panel control of advertising related to one company's bid to take control of another, and has made the Securities and Investment Board responsible for overseeing the promotion of unit trusts and investments. The understandable reaction of the advertising industry has been to regard this as a dilution of the self-regulatory system, likely to confuse consumers as to how and where to complain. The AA views the situation so seriously that it has set up an inquiry (August 1986) under the chairmanship of Sir Kenneth Clucas, former Permanent Secretary of the Department of Trade, its terms of reference being to "consider the various methods by which advertising standards are set and maintained in the UK; establish whether the proliferation of such methods influences their accessibility or effectiveness; review the respective roles of statutory and self-regulatory control; and consider what balance between them is likely to conduce most fully to the public interest" (Advertising Association News Release, 1 August 1986; Tylee 1986).

Broadcast Media

Although, as previously discussed, advertising carried by broadcast media in the United Kingdom does not strictly speaking fall within the self-regulatory system, outlines of the IBA preclearance and the complaints procedure are included here for purposes of comparison.

All scripts for television advertisements, other than local advertisements, are required to be cleared through the control staffs of the ITCA and the IBA. Local advertisements that are for one television station only are cleared by the local program company staffs. In 1984 and 1985, 9,668 original preproduction scripts for television advertisements were submitted to the IBA through ITCA for clearance. About 81.6 percent were acceptable as submitted, with the remainder requiring changes. Of the 6,317 finished commercials viewed, 172 (2.7 percent) required amendment. Of the 8,606 radio commercials (including resubmissions) submitted for clearance, about twelve percent required revisions (*IBA Annual Report 1984–85*).

Complaints relating to advertisements on television or radio are handled not by the ASA but by the IBA. In the twelve-month period ending 31 March 1985, the IBA received 2,223 complaints, which is double the normal total. However, more than 1,200 of these were the direct result of an IBA promotional campaign inviting comments from viewers and listeners.

Complaints received by the IBA are handled by its Advertising Control Division—that is, the same people who approved the advertisement concerned in the first instance. Indeed, it may well be argued that this is hardly the way to obtain an objective treatment of the complaint because the division already has a view as to the advertisement's acceptability, and there is no outside involvement at this stage that might persuade them to see things differently. Not surprisingly perhaps, only thirteen advertisements were withdrawn during the year, seven of these being from television and six from radio. The television complaints concerned (1) a premium offer by a chain of gas stations, which did not make it clear that redemption had to take place at the station where the purchase was made; (2) a twenty-four-hour film-developing service that could not always deliver in that time; (3) a claim made by a motor insurance company that was challenged by a competitor; (4) the claim made in a hair colorant commercial that "most other colorants faded," which was changed to "many"; (5) an airline that omitted to mention that one of the routes it was advertising involved an overnight stay; (6) a dry cleaning offer of three garments for £5 that omitted to state that there was an extra charge for pleated garments; and (7) a regional airport that omitted to state that an advertised service to Paris had not yet started. Complaints about radio commercials were related to (1) an airline advertisement that did not make it clear that an advertised fare required a fourteen-day notice; (2) a hi-fi commercial that referred to the Japanese as "Nips"; (3) a slimming tablet that made a cost-per-day claim that did not equate with the dosage recommended; (4) a restaurant advertisement that featured an impersonation of Martin Luther King; (5) a motor dealer whose exclusive dealership claim was challenged by a competitor; and (6) a London shopping mall whose commercial included traffic noise of such volume that it was felt likely to distract listening motorists.

It should be emphasized nevertheless that the IBA is extremely sensitive to the pressure of public opinion. Among the advertisements banned during 1982 and 1983 was a government announcement issued by the Central Office of Information and a radio commercial concerned with advertising control that was broadcast on behalf of the Authority itself by a local station. Complaints may also be about product classes rather than individual brands or advertisements. For example, when advertising for women's sanitary products was allowed on television for a trial period, it produced so many complaints that the experiment was discontinued. Although commercials for these products are allowed on radio, a number of stations will not accept them for fear of upsetting listeners.

Comparisons

The first difference to be noted between the self-regulatory systems of the two countries is in the organizations that participate. Both countries' systems include organizations representing advertisers, agencies, and the business generally. The United Kingdom has no equivalent of the BBBs, although arguably they would have little relevance in the British advertising context because the ASA/CAP system operates at both national and local levels. The U.S. system, for its part, cannot include media organizations, which would seem to be a far more significant distinction. The presence of representatives of thirteen media bodies among the twenty-one members of the CAP Committee does much to account for the strength and effectiveness of the British system.

The NAD/NARB system also operates at both consumer and trade levels, investigating complaints from the public and competitors (if there is a question of public interest) and giving prepublication guidance to advertisers. In the United Kingdom the two areas of activity are divided, with the ASA watching over consumer interests, and the CAP Committee dealing with problems arising within the industry itself.

The systems also differ in terms of the degree of outside involvement. Any complaint from a member of the public to the ASA is ruled on by its council, in which independent members outnumber those with advertising interests by two to one. In the United States, however, complaints are investigated first by the NAD, which, like the ASA secretariat, has no public involvement. If an advertiser disagrees with the outcome, the matter is referred to the NARB. But although there is outside involvement on NARB panels, members of the public are outnumbered four to one by industry representatives. Not surprisingly this imbalance has given rise to doubts about the fairness and objectivity of the U.S. system, whereas the independent majority on the ASA Council has helped promote public confidence in its operation.

The two systems are also financed in different ways. The United Kingdom's ASA was originally funded by the AA. This led to criticisms that it was unlikely to act decisively against its own paymaster. In 1974 the system was changed so that it receives the proceeds of a levy on display advertising that, apart from guaranteeing the ASA's freedom from industry influence, has allowed it to expand the number and nature of its activities. The levy principle also means that the ASA's budget grows in proportion to the increase in advertising expenditure.

The NAD/NARB/CARU system has been financed from the beginning in 1971 by way of the CBBB, a broadly based organization representing virtually all industries. Advertising agencies and advertisers support the NAD/NARB indirectly through their CBBB membership dues. Agencies expect their dues to be applied mainly to the NAD/NARB, although they use other CBBB services. Children's advertisers support the CARU directly (Reid, letters to the author, 1986). Budgets have grown regularly but not spectacularly over the years, with gradual evolution and growth in the scope, volume, and nature of the system's activities, albeit with the only substantial change being in the regulation of children's advertising since 1974.

In general, the budget for the ASA/CAP Committee is about double that of the NAD/NARB/CARU. Additionally, the ASA/CAP deals only with nonbroadcast advertising, so that if one were to add the advertising regulatory budget of the IBA, the difference would be even larger. On the other hand, the U.S. television networks handle a much larger volume of preclearance work than does the IBA, and each network maintains a substantial staff at substantial cost. It should also be remembered that the 170 BBBs in the United States handle perhaps 10,000 "local" complaints per year. Because most of these budgets are not readily estimable, we cannot make direct comparisons. Even if the dollar or sterling equivalents were available, the regulatory activities are applied to different volumes of advertising, and comparisons are difficult. Budget differences also reflect a major difference in the objectives of the two systems, because the ASA operates on the assumption that the system should be *seen* as effective, which requires publicity. The NAD/NARB system, on the other hand, has never had the goals of widespread public awareness and the public's use of the complaint handling system, and is not funded to achieve it.

A further difference is in the spheres of operation of the two systems. In the United States, participation by advertisers in the NAD/NARB process is voluntary. In the United Kingdom, although the scheme is technically voluntary because all the major advertising organizations are involved and agree to uphold and enforce the Code, its provisions are ipso facto binding on individual advertisers, agencies, and media. The inclusion of media within the system adds considerably to its strength compared with the United States, because it enables the ASA to order the exclusion of particular advertisements and to ensure that this is done.

In the United States, the NAD/NARB confine themselves to national advertising, local advertising generally being the concern of the BBBs or LARPs. Even then the NAD does not have the resources to tackle every complaint it receives, and so limits itself to matters of public interest. The ASA, on the other hand, is bound to investigate all the complaints it receives from members of the public and to act upon them provided it is the competent authority. (Complaints about television commercials, for example, are referred to the IBA.) No distinction is made between national and local advertising, or between a point of general principle and the indignation or misfortunes of particular individuals.

The British system, though sometimes criticized for lacking "teeth," nevertheless operates on the basis of sanctions that can be applied against advertisers and agencies alike. These include adverse publicity, the non-appearance of advertisements, and withdrawal of agency recognition. In a sense the ASA Council sits like a court, and its decisions represent judgments based on the facts put before it.

The U.S. system is based much more on the principle of negotiation, with emphasis on persuading the advertiser to accept the NAD's point of view. If such efforts are unsuccessful there are (beyond adverse publicity) no direct sanctions to fall back on because the exclusion of media from the machinery of regulation means effectively that there is no means of ensuring that advertisements do not appear. The only option then open is for the NAD, after consultation with the chairman of the NARB or after review by an NARB panel, to refer the matter to the appropriate law enforcement agency. This difference reflects the fact that government agencies, at the state as well as the federal levels, have a long history and relatively well-developed mechanisms to handle advertising control. And, the U.S. system seems to work, because the NARB has achieved the "offending advertiser's" cooperation in every adverse case, and has not yet had to resort to referral of a case to a government agency.

The British system appears to operate more quickly. This is largely due to the requirement that a substantiation statement must be prepared before work begins on a campaign. If a doubt arises over the validity of a claim, the ASA can request to see the statement and, if it is not forthcoming, the advertisement can be banned until the statement is produced, which avoids the use of delaying tactics by the advertiser until the campaign has run its course.

The ASA does not quote figures for the time taken to investigate complaints, but in general it is usually about two months. In contrast, some one-third of cases investigated by NAD in 1982 took longer than six months. When U.S. competitors require quick action to avoid injury to themselves, they must seek an injunction through the courts under the Lanham Act rather than use the self-regulatory system.

Although general concern exists in both countries about the effects of advertising on children, the United Kingdom has no equivalent of the United States' CARU. The ASA has undertaken research on this subject but because a relevant section in the Code guides advertisers, children's advertising is treated for practical purposes in the same way as any other category of advertising. The Authority's *Annual Report* for 1982–1983 contained the following brief mention: "The [CAP] Committee noted the publication by the ICC of International Guidelines for Advertising to Children. These reflected the underlying principles of Appendix B of *BCAP.*"

The IBA Code, in addition to containing broadly similar provisions, also specifies product groups that may not be advertised during children's programs (for example, alcoholic drinks, matches) and those that may only be advertised after 9:00 P.M., by which time it is assumed that children will be in bed (for example, medicines).

Broadcast advertising provides further contrasts. In the United States, the television networks are unable to cooperate in the enforcement of standards because of antitrust legislation, and each therefore has its own set of standards. For nonnetwork stations control is in the hands of state or municipality laws and enforcement mechanisms.

The United Kingdom, on the other hand, has the IBA, a body set up by Parliament to oversee the entire independent broadcasting operation. The regulation of advertising is included among its responsibilities, and to this end it publishes a Code of Practice and arranges for its enforcement.

In neither country do the broadcast media have the kind of complaints procedures operated by the ASA under a council dominated by nonindustry appointees.

Notes

1. This body observes the IBA Code rather than *BCAP*, but is represented on the CAP Committee for purposes of liaison.
2. This section draws on the ASA publications listed at the end of the chapter.

References

Advertising Age, various issues.

Advertising Association News Release, 1 August 1986.

Advertising Self-Regulation and its Interaction with Consumers (undated) (New York: National Advertising Review Board [prepared by an NARB Consultative Panel appointed in 1978]).

The Advertising Standards Authority: What it Does and How it Works (undated) (London: Advertising Standards Authority).

Advertising and Women (1975) (New York: National Advertising Review Board, March 1975 [prepared by a NARB Consultative Panel]).

ASA Annual Reports, various years.

ASA Case Reports, various issues.

ASBOF (1982), *The Advertising Standards Board of Finance* (London: Advertising Standards Board of Finance).

ASBOF Annual Reports (various years) (London: Advertising Standards Board of Finance).

BBB Code of Advertising (1978, 1983 and 1985) (Washington: Council of Better Business Bureaus).

Better Business News and Views, various dates.

Belsky, Gail (1984), "Playing the Short Suit Against 'False' Ad Claims," *Adweek,* 13 February 1984, 26.

Boddewyn, J.J. (1983), "Outside Participation in Advertising Self Regulation: The Case of the Advertising Standards Authority (UK)," *Journal of Consumer Policy* 6(1):77–93.

Boddewyn, J.J. (1985), "U.S. Advertising Self-Regulation: The FTC as Outside Partner of the NAD/NARB" (New York: Baruch College, CUNY, mimeographed March 1985).

CBBB Annual Reports, various years.

Children and Advertising: A Bibliography (1978) (New York: Council of Better Business Bureaus).

Do's and Don'ts in Advertising Copy (undated) (Washington: Council of Better Business Bureaus, various dates [a looseleaf service for advertisers, advertising agencies, broadcasters, and printed media]).

Dzodin, Harvey C. (1984), "Some Thoughts on the Commercial Clearance Process from an ABC Perspective," unpublished presentation at Michigan State University, 23 April 1984.

Dzodin, Harvey C. (1986), "The ABC's of American Television Advertising Review and Clearance," Remarks before the International Bar Association, New York, 19 September 1986 (mimeographed).

Ewen, William H. (1975), *The National Advertising Review Board 1971–1975,* New York: National Advertising Review Board.

Farhi, Paul (1983), "Agencies, Networks Battle Over Censors' Role," *Adweek,* 14 November 1983, 50, 52.

IBA Annual Reports, various years.

Identifying Competitors in Advertising (1977) (New York: National Advertising Review Board, July 1977 [prepared by an NARB Consultative Panel]).

IPA (1980), *Advertising Controls Checklist* (London: Institute of Practitioners in Advertising).

IPA (1986), *Some Suggested Provisions for Use in Agency/Client Agreements* (London: Institute of Practitioners in Advertising).

ISBA (1983), *Self-Regulation and the Advertiser* (London: ISBA).

The Labour Party (1966), *Report of a Commission of Enquiry into Advertising,* (London: The Labour Party).

LARP (1981), *Local Advertising Review Program* (New York: Council of Better Business Bureaus, June 1981).

NAD Case Reports, various dates.

NAD/NARB: A Review and Perspective on Advertising Industry Self-Regulation, 1971–1977 (1978) (New York: National Advertising Review Board, May 1978).

Neelankavil, James P., and Stridsberg, Albert B. (1980), *Advertising Self-Regulation: A Global Perspective* (New York: Hastings House).

News from NAD, various dates (the forerunner of *NAD Case Reports*).

NPA/NS (undated), Form of Application by an Advertising Agency for Recognition by the Newspapers Publishers Association and the Newspaper Society.

NS Newsletter, various issues.

Purdon, Roger (1972), "Advertising Self-Regulation—A New Reality," presented to the 1972 Annual Meeting of the American Association of Advertising Agencies, Boca Raton, Florida, March 16, 1972.

Self-Regulatory Guidelines for Children's Advertising, 3rd ed. (1983) (New York: Council of Better Business Bureaus).

Statement of Organization and Procedures of the NARB (1980) (New York: National Advertising Review Board, as amended, 19 June 1980).

Theobalds, Harry (1983), "The Rules Governing Advertising on Television and Independent Local Radio," in J.J.D. Bullmore and M.J. Waterson (eds.), *The Advertising Handbook* (London: Holt, Rinehart & Winston).

Thomson, Peter (1983), "Advertising Control: Advertisements in Media other than Television and Radio," in J.J.D. Bullmore and M.J. Waterson (eds.), *The Advertising Association Handbook,* London: Holt, Rinehart & Winston.

Thomson, Peter (1979), "The Future for Self-Regulation," presented at Cavendish Conference Centre, London, 25 September 1979.

Tylee, John (1986), "AA in Probe for Single Watchdog," *Campaign,* 8 August 1986.

What Makes Avertising Tick (undated) (London: Advertising Standards Authority).

5
Advertising Industry Codes and Standards

Introduction

This chapter focuses on the roughly comparable "centrally accepted or applied" codes and standards in the United Kingdom and the United States. These are the *BCAP* and IBA codes in the United Kingdom and the NAD/NARB standards, as well as the individual standards of the three national television networks in the United States.

Chapter 2 contains brief mention of the diverse standards of practice of U.S. advertisers, advertising agencies, advertising media, and certain industries and their associations. Because the standards of such U.S. companies and organizations are difficult to summarize succinctly in terms of common features, we do not attempt to do so. But in the United Kingdom many diverse companies and organizations adhere to *BCAP* and therefore are included here, as part of our comparison of the central systems of the two countries.

Another condition that influences our organization and coverage of topics is the nature of changes over the years since inception of each system. Although *BCAP* and the IBA Code have certainly undergone revision, the changes have been relatively minor: particular sections of the codes have been changed, not the fundamental nature of the codes. Also, the U.S. television network standards were so recently adopted that we do not need to review the relatively minor changes in particular sections that have occurred since the demise of the NAB system a few years ago, and the adoption by the networks of many of the features of the NAB code. But, in contrast, the NAD/NARB system began with only a very brief set of principles and guidelines in 1971, and it has only been with the passage of time that the application of these standards has given us an understanding of the specifics that the NAD/NARB system applies. In this chapter we therefore must first devote our attention to bringing up to the present our understanding of the NAD/NARB standards. We trace the evolution and development of NAD/NARB standards so that we may understand their current status. This discussion occupies the first part of the next section on the United States, after which we discuss the written codes and standards of the CARU, the television networks, and the BBBs in the United States. Then, in the section on the United Kingdom, we describe the standards of the major British bodies—the Code of the IBA, and the *BCAP*, as the latter is applied not only by the ASA, but also by other organizations. The last section of the chapter is devoted to comparing the systems of the United States and the United Kingdom.

The United States

The NAD/NARB System in the Early Years

Except for children's advertising, which is covered in a separate section later in the chapter, the NAD/NARB system has no formal code of its own; however, it adheres to relevant parts of the *BBB Code of Advertising* (appendix 5C) as well as to a general set of guidelines contained in an early NARB policy statement that reads, in part:

> The National Advertising Review Board is charged by business primarily to achieve and sustain high standards of truth and accuracy in national and regional advertising.
>
> In the evaluation process advertising will be reviewed in terms of its technical and literal accuracy, and thorough consideration will be given to the question of whether it has the capacity to deceive, by commission or by material omission, the potential customer who would be exposed to the advertising in question.
>
> The issues which come before NARB panels may take a variety of forms:
>
> The adequacy of substantiation, including research data, to support an objective claim for a product or service.
>
> A testimonial involving the competency of the testifier as a regular user reflecting average experience.
>
> A claim with respect to bargain or price savings for a product or service.
>
> The matter of fair and honest reference to a competitor or of a comparison of products.
>
> Substantiation for guarantees and warranties and whether there is adequate disclosure of pertinent information about these.
>
> Advertising directed to children where representation not misleading to the adult mind could have the capacity to confuse or mislead the immature and impressionable mind.

These are cited here for illustrative purposes only, and each case will be decided on its own merit.

The Review Board recognized the existence of various codes and guidelines in advertising which may be currently in use by segments of industry, and which are based on their past experience in evaluating advertising acceptability. The Council of Better Business Bureaus has developed an extensive body of precedents in this area which is available to its National Advertising Division in carrying out its staff role of initial evaluation and review.

In cases submitted to panels of the Review Board, detailed standards within industry, or government decisions may be used as precedents for an NAD decision in a given case. The panels will consider the applicability of the standards or decisions to these cases, but in no cases are bound by them.

Further, the executive director shall make available to NARB panels decisions rendered by previous panels for the assistance and guidance that these previous decisions may provide (NARB 1972).

The Emergence of an NAD/NARB Code

From a subsequent speech by a former vice president of the CBBB in charge of the NAD we find additional refinement, indicating that the guidelines under which the NAD/NARB system operates require that advertising claims should (1) be truthful and accurate; (2) be substantiated; (3) disclose relevant and adequate information; (4) contain no false disparagement; (5) contain no deception, intended or otherwise; and (6) be in accordance with FTC precedents (Purdon 1972).

Although the NAD/NARB did not establish a formal code of advertising practice for national advertising, the CBBB in 1973 established the Better Business Bureau *Code of Advertising,* designed primarily for local advertising. This code was amended in 1973, 1978, 1981, and 1985 (Cosmos, telephone conversation with one of the authors 11 March 1985). The basic principles are as follows:

1. The primary responsibility for truthful and nondeceptive advertising rests with the advertiser. Advertisers should be prepared to substantiate any claims or offers made before publication or broadcast and, upon request, present such substantiation promptly to the advertising medium or the Better Business Bureau.

2. Advertisements which are untrue, misleading, deceptive, fraudulent, falsely disparaging of competitors, or insincere offers to sell, shall not be used.

3. An advertisement as a whole may be misleading although every sentence separately considered is literally true. Misrepresentation may

result not only from direct statements but by omitting or obscuring a material fact (BBB *Code of Advertising* 1985, 1).

The BBB *Code of Advertising* contains twenty sections and deals extensively with various problems such as the following: advertisements using claims relating to price, value, savings, free offers, cents off, trade-in allowances, credit, extra charges, bait and switch, and warranties; layout and illustrations; abbreviations; use or condition disclosures; superiority; comparatives or disparagement; superlatives; testimonials and endorsements; rebates; company name or trade style; contests and games; claimed results; and unassembled merchandise (BBB *Code of Advertising* 1985).

The CBBB has also developed a series of formal standards for specific industries, products, and services. They require adherence not only to the previously mentioned basic principles, but also to standards particularly appropriate for these specific industries, products, and services: for example, automobiles and trucks, automobile rentals, carpets and rugs, home improvements, home insulation materials, household furniture, and residential swimming pools (*CBBB Annual Report* 1984–85).

The NAD/NARB has the policy of basing its decisions not only on BBB codes, but on all available relevant information and reasonable perspectives including the standards of various industries and their trade associations as well as those of government agencies and the courts.

After several years of experience, it became clear that the "NARB judges advertising from what it believes to be the view of the consumer— that is, judgement of the impression left on the receiver [rather] than the judgement of the intent of the communicator" (Zanot and Maddox 1977). Thus, the NARB employs a broad standard in ascertaining whether an advertisement is misleading, which is consistent with the Advertising Evaluation Policy Statement issued before the NARB convened its first panel (NARB 1972). Although the NARB examines the technical and literal accuracy of claims, it also will give "thorough consideration . . . to the question of whether it has the capacity to deceive . . . the potential consumer (Zanot and Maddox 1977; NARB 1972). The NAD in its activities acts in accordance with such NARB policies.

The NAD/NARB Code after Eight Years

Zanot and Maddox (1977) pointed out that the NARB is not especially interested in establishing precedents. The NARB operates on a case-by-case approach, and Zanot (1980) made a significant contribution by analyzing the first eight years of NARB decisions to isolate the detailed standards to which the NAD/NARB has adhered. He identified nine issues of importance, and summarized the NARB standards as follows:

1. Truth and accuracy go beyond the literal. Advertising must not be misleading in any way, including overall impression, even though the advertisement is literally true in every respect. Further, the intent of the advertiser is "irrelevant in judging whether or not deception has occurred."

2. There are "no clear precedents as to the proportion of the audience that might be deceived before the advertising is judged misleading."

3. "Open ended comparisons should be avoided . . . However, the cases . . . reveal no clear guidelines" as to when they are permitted, and when not. The judgment was made in each case as to whether or not "the majority of consumers would . . . be deceived by it."

4. There are no "clear parameters regarding problems of semantics because of the particular nature of each case . . . the misuse and imprecise use of words can be a problem . . . [however, in the cases cited] the defendants were asked to modify or discontinue advertisements." Again, the decision rested on the judgment as to whether or not the language was misleading.

5. When exaggerations are not commonly accepted as statements of fact, and when the claims in those statements are incapable of being measured by objective criteria or in quantitative terms, they are viewed as "harmless puffs." But when such "puffs" are used with claims that are subject to measurement and objectively verifiable, puffery is unacceptable.

6. Regarding omission of relevant information, the relevant test is whether there is "a misconception as to overall superiority," or a "misleading impression" as to the content of a product. "Deception can occur through omission as well as through commission."

7. "It is proper to use celebrities as spokesmen [and] . . . endorsers need not use the product if the ad does not say or imply they do. This attitude toward testimonials is congruent with FTC guides on the use of testimonials and endorsements. And although "there have been no NARB cases involving a celebrity claiming personal use," the FTC "guides also state that endorsers must use the product if the ads say or imply they do." It is NARB policy to follow FTC precedent.

8. Research data must "fully support the [advertising] claims." There must not be methodological weaknesses in research, such as deficiencies in sampling. Interpretation of data in a misleading way, including out of context, is unacceptable.

9. Comparative advertising claims must be supported by adequate substantiating materials. Claims must "be provable under conditions of general use . . . consumer benefits must not be exaggerated and

comparable grades of competitors' products must be used" (Zanot 1980, 20–24).

LaBarbera (1980, 57–58) also reported on her review of the content of the first thirty-five NARB decisions, from which she derived the following list of guidelines for advertisers; it appears as if NARB will rule against an advertisement if it:

1. Misuses research data; research material must be accurately presented.

2. Does not make clear the difference between a testimonial and a presentation. The NARB says that anyone making a testimonial must be a present or past consumer of the product.

3. Misleads the average consumer.

4. Makes use of fantasy or satire in a misleading way.

5. Encourages use of drugs that could be harmful if used excessively.

6. Encourages consumption of pills by people who do not need them (for example, iron consumption should be directed at young women who need iron, not at all women).

7. Makes controversial claims.

8. Uses a trademark that is inaccurate and unfair.

9. Fails to encourage the public's attention to future health.

10. Does not pay special attention to the problems of directing ads at children, who are more vulnerable and, therefore, more easily misled.

11. Presents a competitor's product in a poor manner or misrepresents the facts concerning the competitor's product.

12. Employs competitive product comparisons that are inaccurate and unfair.

13. Does not conclusively substantiate all claims made in a comparative advertisement.

14. Makes a superiority claim, mentions names, and does not inform the consumer that the claim refers only to a few of the leading rival models and brands.

15. Does not make extremely clear the nature and limits of the test performed to acquire the comparative results (LaBarbera 1980, 57–58).

FTC Guidelines: A Base for Self-Regulation

At a number of points in this book, and especially in chapter 3, we make the point that government regulation forms a base for self-regulatory activities. A first requirement is that advertising must be legal. We have discussed broadly the legal/self-regulatory interfaces for the United Kingdom and the United States, including references to legislation, administrative law, and court decisions that serve as precedents. The *American Home Products v. FTC* court case summarizes important features of federal government general rules and criteria established in earlier cases for a finding of deception and appropriate remedial action. We present these points to specify the regulatory base underlying the NAD/NARB standards, which we need to develop our understanding of them in the following section. The court divided its summary of FTS general rule into two components:

1. Interpreting an advertisement for a finding of deception:

    a. A finding that advertisements are deceptive or tend to mislead is "obviously an impressionistic determination more closely akin to a finding of fact than a conclusion of law."

    b. The findings of the Commission as to facts, if supported by evidence, shall be conclusive.

    c. Statements susceptible of both a misleading and a truthful interpretation will be construed against the advertiser.

    d. Omission of a material fact is a deceptive practice.

    e. Failure to possess a reasonable basis for an advertising claim is a deceptive practice.

    f. The tendency of the advertising to deceive "must be judged by viewing it as a whole without emphasizing isolated words or phrases apart from their context."

    g. In interpreting a television ad the Commission may analyze not only the words used but the messages conveyed through the "aural-visual" pattern.

    h. The Commission's familiarity with the expectations and beliefs of the public, acquired by long experience, is especially crucial when "the alleged deception results from an omission of information instead of a statement."

    i. The Commission is not required to conduct a survey of the viewing public before it can be determined that advertisements have a tendency to deceive.

    j. Even though an advertiser has conducted a test "which he honestly believes will prove a product claim, he may not convey to television viewers the false impression that they are seeing the test, when actually they are not because of the undisclosed use of mock-ups."

    k. "In the last analysis the words 'deceptive practices' set forth a legal standard and they must get their final meaning from judicial construction."

    l. The Commission's judgement is to be given great weight by reviewing courts "—since a finding of deceptive advertising—rests so heavily on inference and pragmatic judgement."

m. A reviewing court may determine that there is in the record "such relevant evidence as a reasonable mind might accept as adequate to support a conclusion." However, the court may not "weigh the evidence."

2. Remedial action for deceptive advertising

    a. Regulatory commissions may prohibit business people from making statements which, though literally true, are potentially deceptive.

    b. When advertisements are misleading, it is not necessary to ban particular words or phrases. Qualifying explanatory language is generally a preferable remedy.

    c. Disclosure requirements are acceptable, particularly when they are triggered by claims appearing in the ad. Triggered disclosures are not the same as corrective requirements. Under certain circumstances advertisers may be required to make affirmative disclosure of unfavorable facts.

    d. Substantiation requirements have been supported by the courts. High standards for substantiation for comparative effectiveness and safety claims for drugs may be necessary for several reasons:

        (1) Government regulation of drugs gives rise to consumer expectations that superiority claims are supported by scientific proof.

        (2) The average consumer will have difficulty evaluating such claims through personal experiences.

        (3) There are health risks associated with such products.

        (4) A manufacturer may have a past record of violations.

    e. Multiproduct orders (covering products not included in the complaint) are acceptable as a means of fencing in potentially misleading advertising by a proven violator. In fashioning such orders, the following considerations should apply:

        (1) The deliberateness and seriousness of the violation.

        (2) The manufacturer's past record of violation.

        (3) The transferability of violations to other products.

        (4) The endangerment of public health by the conduct to be proscribed (Cohen 1983).

Because the law and its administration are constantly evolving, one should remember that there have been changes since 1982, for example, in FTC policies on advertising substantiation; but this is not the place for the extensive analysis that is required to present a comprehensive perspective on such changes. The previous summary is sufficiently current for our purposes.

It also must be remembered, of course, that in a clear case of unlawful advertising, the NAD will refer the matter to the appropriate government agency, and the U.S. television networks will not approve unlawful advertising in their preclearance processes. However, many cases are borderline, and others exist in which the advertising does not violate the law but nevertheless contravenes self-regulatory standards. Some of the "refinements" described in the next section fall into this latter category.

Refinements in the NAD/NARB "Code" since 1979

From time to time the NAD/NARB "position" on specific issues has been stated in published reports of cases resolved and in some *NAD Case Reports*. One finds, however, only occasional material designed to clarify the NAD's position or policy so as to assist advertisers and agencies to anticipate the probable NAD reaction to advertising they may have in mind. A review of such materials adds the following discussion to what Zanot (1980) has provided.

One of the key functions of a code is to delineate the scope of regulation, identifying which issues are of concern. Thus, we can begin a discussion of scope by asking: How are the claims at issue selected?

Although there is a procedural answer to this question, which is answered in chapter 4, there are also several types of advertising that will *not* be handled, namely

1. Local advertising. Complaints about local advertising are referred to a local "BBB in the same area as the advertiser's head office. Ninety percent of the complaints received by individual members of the public belong in this category."

2. Questions related to ". . . label claims and directions, matters of taste, and political and issue advertising."

3. "Advertising addressed to a business, professional or select audience with specialized knowledge of the subject matter" (*NAD Case Report*, 15 July 1983).

Furthermore, although the NAD accepts complaints about comparisons of brands, the focus tends to be on *non*comparison claims. The NAD points out that

> competitor challenges, usually, though not always involve comparative claims. However, the majority of . . . complaints [handled, from other sources] involve objective but non-comparative claims. . . . NAD recognized the special importance of cases involving non-comparative advertising claims to the overall program. It may be assumed that non-comparative

misrepresentations are less likely to be subject to self-correcting influences in the marketplace or to be reviewed by other self-regulatory bodies (*NAD Case Report,* 15 July 1983).

Implied Claims. The NAD recognizes that "an advertisement as a whole may be misleading although every sentence separately considered is literally true. Misrepresentation may result not only from direct statements but by omitting or obscuring a material fact. NAD staff put themselves in the position of the consumer and consider the net impression of an advertisement as well as all its individual components" (*NAD Case Report,* 15 July 1983).

Comparison Advertising. The basic position since 1977 has been that "comparisons should be of significant difference and be truthfully stated . . . comparative advertising which misleads or deceives is not acceptable." It is important that the advertiser be "able to substantiate the comparisons made" (Press release 1977).

The NAD's position is refined somewhat by the statement, "In advertising which [compares] grades within a product category, the comparison should be to a truly comparable grade in the competitor's product line" (*News from NAD,* 16 October 1978). The basic criterion remains, however, that to be unacceptable, the comparison must be misleading.

When put together with the NAD's position on implied claims (see the preceding section) it seems likely that comparison advertising might be unacceptable if it focuses on one relatively insignificant fact while it ignores other signficant facts.

The Use of *Up To* in Price Savings Claims. The NAD is concerned about the words *up to* as used with reference to price savings claims.

> Unless a lower savings figure is added, the consumer has no practical way of determining what the range of savings will be on items purchased. For example, the greatest savings may be 45% on some purchases, but there may be a larger number of items on which the savings are only 25%, 15% or less (*News from NAD,* 15 May 1981).

The NAD adheres to the *BBB Code of Advertising* on this issue, which reads as follows:

> Savings or price reduction claims covering a group of items with a range of savings shall state both the minimum and maximum savings without undue or misleading display of the maximum. The number of items available at the maximum savings shall comprise at least 10% of all the items in the offering, unless local or state law requires otherwise (BBB *Code of Advertising* 1983, 5).

NAD urges all advertisers to provide complete information when using an "up to" claim, in order to help the consumer make better informed buying decisions. If it is not possible from a practical standpoint to provide a range of savings, then "up to" claims should not be made. NAD respectfully reiterates its intention, within the framework of self-regulation, to pursue and correct misuse of such claims (*News from NAD,* 15 May 1981).

The Use of Superlatives; the Word *Best.* Whether stated directly or implied, overall superiority of a product must be demonstrated in accordance with NAD standards of substantiation. It is not permissible to state directly or to imply that government approval or endorsement of a product means that a product is "best," when in fact any product meeting "specific government standards of product quality and sanitary conditions" can qualify for such approval. If not adequately substantiated, an advertisement has the capacity to mislead, and is therefore unacceptable. However, the NARB objects to the use of the word *best* only when the claim is measurable. The NARB does not "object to the use of *best* as a statement of subjective opinion of their product" (Report of NARB Panel #35, 30 January 1980).

The Issue of "Taste." On matters of taste or decency, for example the use of profanity, the denigration of women, or violence, the NAD/NARB has no firm guidelines by which it would declare advertising unacceptable. In a word, decisions on taste fall outside the NAD's "area of expertise" (letter to one of the authors from NAD staff, 16 December 1981). However, the NARB was sufficiently concerned about advertising portraying or directed to women, to convene a consultative panel to prepare a report on the subject. The six-member panel examined the issues in considerable detail and offered a lengthy set of recommendations in the form of a checklist of questions under each of the following headings: (1) destructive portrayals, (2) negative appeals, (3) constructive portrayals, and (4) positive appeals. The panel also recommended that with regard to the use of humor involving women, the advertiser should exercise "extraordinary care to insure that the cut is not made at the expense of women's self-esteem." The report concluded that:

> The principal reason the advertising industry wants to do what is right is that its people—men and women—are decent and fair . . . it is also good business to be decent and fair. You don't sell to people by insulting them . . . the panel hopes that its report will encourage advertisers and advertising agencies with new eyes . . . to ask themselves . . . How would I like to be depicted in this way? (*Advertising and Women* 1975, 21)

In sum, the report offered no hard and fast rules, only questions to consider when creating or approving an advertisement (*Advertising Age,* 21 April

1975). This conclusion is in harmony with the NAD/NARB system at the outset in 1972, that they will not "make decisions concerning taste on specific ads . . . [and] will not consider questions of taste and social responsibility" (*Advertising Age,* 24 January 1972).

Requirements for Advertising Substantiation

On questions of substantiation, the NAD offers the following:

> NAD staff are required to put themselves in the position of the advertiser and ask the question: "On the available facts could we make these claims in this language or form?" To answer this question, NAD requires undigested data so that it can repeat the reasoning by which the advertiser concluded its claims were truthful.
>
> For laboratory studies, this means access to the details of the experimental method and measurements. For consumer studies, NAD seeks to review the detailed proposal, instructions to interviewers, questionnaires, responses, work sheets and detailed conclusions.
>
> Technical consultants can be helpful contributors of knowledge and experience but NAD cannot delegate its responsibilities as fact-finder and decision-maker. User testimonials based on casual experience and certification by an advertiser or third party are no substitute for factual support.
>
> An advertiser needing guidance can request a copy of previous NAD decisions in a product category or addressing a particular type of claim. . . .
>
> The organizations that created the NAD/NARB self-regulatory mechanism are committed to the prinicple of prior substantiation. NAD maintains the principle unreservedly, recognizing that it is essential for truthful and accurate advertising.
>
> However, NAD does not, on these grounds, decline to take account of substantiating data developed after a claim is first used. There can be no consumer benefit in discouraging truthful and accurate advertising claims solely on procedural grounds. This is specially relevant when the need for additional data only becomes evident to the parties in the course of the dialog (*NAD Case Report,* 15 July 1983, 22)

A Comprehensive Guidebook

The CBBB publishes a monthly looseleaf service for advertisers, advertising agencies, broadcasters, and printed media entitled *Do's and Don'ts in Advertising Copy.* This service is a successor to *A Guide to National Advertising,* which the NBBB first published in 1939 and supplemented until the war forced abandonment of operations in 1942. Thus, the CBBB has for many years provided a means by which advertising planners could obtain the best available information to ascertain whether their proposed advertising would be in harmony with prevailing standards of legal and social acceptability.

Although it is not, strictly speaking, a code, *Do's and Don'ts* is useful to guide advertising practice. *Do's and Don'ts* contains

1. Copies of relevant federal legislation and some coverage of state law.
2. "Guides," Trade Regulation Rules, programs of action, and other expressions of administrative law by federal agencies in the executive branch of government.
3. Court cases that provide guidance on various issues.
4. The BBB *Code of Advertising* (the general code as well as numerous product-specific codes).
5. Rules and standards of various industry trade associations, especially broadcasting.
6. Lengthy sections on advertising standards drawn from all available sources as they relate to many specific product classes such as, food, alcoholic beverages, cleansing agents, schools, jewelry, fabrics, wearing apparel, appliances, house furnishings, and automotive.

This resource is organized to make it as useful as possible, completely indexed and cross-indexed alphabetically, not only by section, chapter, and page, but also by marginal reference.

Children's Advertising Guidelines

The NAD/NARB believes that children's advertising regulation is special and requires somewhat more specific standards than the rest of advertising.

In 1972 a set of *Children's Advertising Guidelines* was published by the ANA "to encourage truthful and accurate advertising sensitive to the special nature of children" (CARU 1983). Subsequently the NAD/NARB system established CARU, which republished the *Children's Advertising Guidelines* in 1975 and revised them in 1977 and 1983 (CARU 1983; see appendix 5A).

The function of the CARU guidelines is

to delineate those areas that need particular attention to help to avoid deceptive advertising messages to children. . . . The Guidelines have been kept general in the belief that responsible advertising comes in many forms and that diversity should be encouraged. The goal in all cases should be to fulfill the spirit as well as the letter of the Guidelines and the

Principles on which they are based . . . The Guidelines apply to all advertising addressed to children under 12 years of age, including print, broadcast and cable television advertising (CARU 1983, 3–4).

The statement contains basic principles, including reference to the characteristics of children such as their credibility and imagination and the influences that advertising can have on children. The statement then covers the need to avoid (1) misleading or misinforming product presentations and claims and (2) extreme sales pressure and some specific indications as to what is meant by such pressure. The statement also stresses the need for (1) appropriate disclosures and disclaimers, (2) real and understandable comparative claims, (3) careful use of endorsements and promotion by program or editorial characters, (4) focus on the product rather than on premiums, and (5) presentations that keep in mind the safe use of products.

The Code also emphasizes the positive value of advertising in shaping behavior and urges advertisers to use it "by developing advertising that, whenever possible, addresses itself to social standards generally regarded as positive and beneficial, such as friendship, kindness, honesty, justice, generosity and respect for others" (CARU 1983, 4).

In recent years three issues have led the list of complaints about children's advertising.

1. *Product presentations:* Restraint is required so as not to exploit children's imagination through misleading copy, sound and visual effects.

2. *Adequacy of disclosure:* Necessary information and disclaimers need to be conveyed in ways that are understandable to children, taking into account their limited vocabulary and less developed consumer skills.

3. *Safety:* Awareness that imitation and experimentation are important activities to children is essential. They may imitate product demonstrations and other actions without regard to risk" (*NAD Case Report*, 15 July 1983, 21).

The CARU has also published useful reference materials to guide advertisers, such as the following:

1. *An Eye on Children's Advertising Self-Regulation: A Five Year Report, June, 1974–June, 1979,* which contained summaries of all publicly reported children's advertising cases.

2. *An Eye on Children's Advertising,* a pamphlet prepared in 1979 and updated in 1986 that describes the activities of the CARU and tells consumers how to file a complaint about child-directed advertising (*News from NAD,* 17 September 1979; Reid, letters to the author, 1986).

3. *Children and Advertising, An Annotated Bibliography* (*News from NAD,* 14 November 1980).

4. *Advertising to Children: CARU Cases 1983–1985,* Special Issue *NAD Case Report,* March 1986, 12 pages.

The importance of the NAD's children's advertising review program increased greatly in 1982, following the demise of the NAB Code Authority. "The void created by the collapse of the broadcast children's code has . . . considerably heightened NAD's responsibility over children's advertising . . . [as] advertisers have turned to NAD for help, advice and leadership. Requests . . . [in 1982] more than doubled over [1981]" (CBBB, May 1983).

Television and Radio Network Standards: ABC, CBS, and NBC

The networks had adhered to the *NAB Television Code,* and the *NAB Radio Code* since their inception. After their demise each network, independently of the others, adopted many features of the NAB codes. The networks also of necessity assumed responsiblity for many of the administrative policies and procedures previously handled by the NAB, especially preclearance activities. At the same time they continued to refine their standards in accordance with changing conditions and mores. The networks also continued to make those standards as easy as possible for advertisers to interpret and to use as a guide in preparing acceptable commercials.

In view of U.S. antitrust considerations the networks had to fill the void left by the NAB without coordinating or consulting directly with each other. Thus the individual network standards, though similar in character, developed with differences in breadth, depth, and application. They all deal with a large number of specific product and service categories as well as with specific advertising practices. All three networks seem to incorporate the basic guideline of staying within the law, as enacted and enforced by regulatory agencies in the executive branch of government, and as applied in court decisions. In addition, the networks go beyond the law to apply what they perceive to be reasonable ethical, taste, and decency standards to some products, according to their interpretation of what is considered "proper" by large numbers of people in U.S. society; because social norms change slowly over time, the application of the standards continues to evolve to adapt to such changes. "Representatives of ABC, CBS and NBC . . . [refer to their commercial content rules] as a living document subject to revision and interpretation according to the prevailing social norms" (Farhi 1983).

ABC Advertising Standards and Guidelines is a fifty-one-page document that begins with the statement that all advertising must conform to governmental laws and regulations and to the standards and policies of

ABC. The network also notes the broad standard that the acceptability of advertising depends on the "advertiser and the accuracy of all statements and claims made in commercial copy. When affirmative claims are made for the product or service, the advertiser must submit substantiation or documentation providing a reasonable basis for the claims." The network goes on to specify that "All advertising messages should be prepared with proper consideration for the type of product being advertised, the time of broadcast, and the audience to whom the advertising is directed. Good taste must always govern the content, placement, and presentation of announcements" (*ABC Advertising Standards and Guidelines 1983*).

Selected categories of advertising practices, product standards, and audiences covered by ABC are excerpted from the *ABC Advertising Standards and Guidelines* and presented in detail in appendix 5D.

CBS advertising guidelines begin with a statement of the network's responsibility—namely, to review all advertising submitted for truth, taste, and legal requirements. False, misleading, or deceptive claims are not acceptable. In all appropriate instances, claims must be fully substantiated, including those in demonstrations and testimonials. Research results, surveys, or tests relating to advertised products must be used in a truthful and nonmisleading manner. Sponsors must be identified in accordance with FCC requirements.

Selected categories of advertising practices, product standards, and audiences covered by CBS are excerpted from the CBS advertising guidelines and presented in detail in appendix 5E.

NBC's document does not have a general introduction with the kinds of perspectives included in the ABC and CBS documents. NBC's eighteen-page set of guidelines incorporates such principles in each of the seven separate sections, as appropriate. The titles of these seven sections are listed in appendix 5F.

ABC, on the basis of its printed material, seems to have the most complex and detailed standards and guidelines and covers the largest number of products. ABC is not necessarily the strictest, however, because strictness depends on interpretation and application of the written standards by network personnel. ABC states specifically in the beginning that all material broadcast must conform to governmental laws and regulations. CBS and NBC are not quite as explicit in this regard, but it is clear in various places in their "standards" that all advertising must be legal.

ABC and CBS in their introductory sections make a point of mentioning not only truth and legal requirements, but also taste. All three networks have specific requirements in the details of their standards that fit into the category of taste. Additionally, ABC and CBS, in their introduction, make special mention of the need for substantiation of claims. CBS makes special mention of demonstrations and testimonials, as well as noting general requirements for the use of research, and the other two networks discuss the use of research results in connection with claims for certain specific products.

The United Kingdom

In chapter 4 a distinction is drawn in terms of advertising control between broadcast and nonbroadcast media in the United Kingdom, and it is pointed out that the advertisements they carry are subject to two quite separate codes of practice. The situation becomes more complicated, however, when it is realized that the wide variety of media under the heading "nonbroadcast" and the special problems involved in advertising particular categories of products have led to the appearance of a number of specialized codes that supplement the general provisions of *BCAP*. This section first discusses the situation in broadcast media, which is relatively straightforward, and then the more involved position that exists in relation to advertisements carried elsewhere.

For ready reference, the full range of topics covered in the two codes— *The IBA Code of Advertising Standards and Practice* and *BCAP*—are presented in appendixes 5G and 5H; categories of advertising practices, product standards, and audiences covered in the two codes are excerpted from the indexes of the two codes.

Broadcast Media

The principles embodied in the *IBA Code of Advertising Standards and Practice* are generally similar to those in *BCAP*, but tend also to reflect the belief, widely held at the time, that when commercial television was first permitted in the United Kingdom (1955) it constituted a far more powerful and potent medium than anything previously experienced, and therefore it should be subject to special constraints. There seems in particular to have been a fear that it might be used for some kind of idealogical brainwashing. Hence there is a total ban on political and religious advertising and on any advertisements relating to any matter of industrial or public controversy. Subliminal advertising is also specifically prohibited.

The main body of the Code is concerned primarily with matters of presentation—stridency, appeals to fear, good taste, comparisons, denigration, and production techniques—and with excluding particular types of products or services. Advertising for charities, for example, is generally not permitted, and paragraph 18 prohibits advertisements for:

> Breath-testing devices and products purporting to mask the effects of alcohol

Matrimonial agencies and correspondence clubs

Fortune tellers and the like

Undertakers or others associated with death or burial

Betting tipsters

Betting

Cigarettes and cigarette tobacco

Private investigation agencies

Privately owned advisory services dealing with personal or consumer problems

This section also makes it clear that an advertisement for an otherwise acceptable product would be considered unacceptable if its main purpose was considered to be to publicize a product or service that is not itself allowed to be advertised.

Advertising in areas such as homework schemes, instructional courses, mail order, and direct sale are strictly controlled, and that for alcoholic drinks is severely limited in terms of the appeals that can be employed.

Three appendices to the Code concern advertising and children, financial advertising, and medicines and treatments respectively. It is recognized that television can play a highly influential role in forming children's attitudes and opinions, and nothing is permitted that might result in physical, mental, or moral harm, or that would take advantage of their natural credulity and sense of loyalty. A fourth appendix lists the main statutes that relate to broadcast advertising.

Nonbroadcast Media

Advertisements in all media other than radio and television are subject to the provisions of *BCAP*, now in its seventh edition, which adapts for British use the rules of the ICC's *International Code of Advertising Practice* (ICAP). Recent revisions of the Code have tended to represent less a dramatic extension of its scope as a tightening and toughening of existing provisions. Certainly in the past decade, public debate has focused on sanctions and methods of enforcement rather than the content of the Code as such.

Restrictions are placed on the Code's applicability, because it specifically excludes certain categories of advertising that the organizations responsible for enforcement—the ASA and the CAP Committee—either would not wish or could not reasonably expect to control. These are:

Advertisements in media circulating mainly outside the United Kingdom.

Advertisements directed to the medical and allied professions, most of which are subject to the Medicines (Advertising to Medical and Dental Practitioners) Regulations (1978) and to a separate code administered by the Association of the British Pharmaceutical Industry.

Political advertisements so long as they are readily identifiable as such, and are putting forward a point of view as distinct from appealing for funds.

The scope of the Code is further limited because of the narrow definition accorded to the term *advertisement*. According to CAP Guidance Note No. 1 (April 1979), a distinction may be drawn between, on the one hand, "advertisements such as direct mail letters which exist in the same form in each case although personally addressed to individual recipients; and on the other, individually written private letters, even though their intention may be to influence or persuade." The Note also specifies that to be subject to the Code, advertisements have to be addressed *directly* to the public, so that a news release sent out by a public relations consultant would be excluded. They must also be persuasive, which thus excludes any material such as instruction leaflets reaching the consumer after the act of purchase has taken place, and company and official notices that only intend to convey information.

The Note also gives the reasons why the Code is limited in its scope to advertisements that are paid for. A commercial advertising transaction is usually characterized by the presence of a third party, the media owner, who in return for payment communicates the advertisment to a mass audience. The truthfulness or otherwise of that advertisement can only be assessed in relation to the totality of the products with which it is concerned, so that it is in a quite different situation from the label on a pack that relates solely to the goods it contains. A distinction must therefore be drawn between regulations suitable for controlling advertising and those needed for labeling and packaging. The Code applies only to advertising, though it would also apply in the case of a pack that promotes a different product from the one it contains, advertising sent by mail (where the post office is a common carrier rather than a media owner), and brochures and catalogues. No distinction is made between consumer and business advertising.

The seventh edition of *BCAP* came into force on 1 January 1986. It consists of an introduction, three main sections designated Parts A, B, and C, two appendices and an index. The introduction presents the origins and scope of the Code and explains the machinery by which its provisions are enforced. It also tells the reader how to make a complaint. Part A goes into greater detail on the scope of the Code. It sets out how conformity with the Code's provisions will be assessed and how the Code is interpreted.

Part B contains general rules that apply to all advertisements. They must be legal, decent, honest, and truthful, and should contain nothing that is in breach of the law, nor omit anything that the law requires. Responsibility for observance is placed firmly on the advertiser and remains his, even when he is using an advertising agency or other intermediary. The concept of truth is examined in particular detail as it applies to matters of fact and opinion, political advertisements, prices, the word *free,* the expressions *up to* and *from,* testimonials and other indications of approval such as the royal warrant, the recognizability of advertisements, the identity of advertisers, guarantees, and the availability of advertised products.

Another section of Part B states that "All advertisements should be prepared with a sense of responsibility to the consumer and to society," and deals with such issues as fear, violence and antisocial behavior, privacy, unsolicited home visits, and advertising to children. The last section is concerned with fair competition and covers comparisons, denigration, exploitation of goodwill, and imitation.

Part C sets out rules to be followed, in addition to those in the remainder of the Code, when preparing particular classes of advertisement.

Advertisements containing health claims

Advertisements for hair and scalp products

Advertising claims for vitamins and minerals

Advertisements for slimming

Advertisements for cosmetics

Mail order and direct response advertising

Advertising for financial services and products

Advertisements offering employment and business opportunities

Advertising of "limited editions"

Advertising directed to children

A final section sets out the requirements normally enforced by media in respect to particular categories of advertising.

The first of the two appendices deals with the advertising of cigarettes and hand-rolling tobacco, and the second with advertising for alcoholic drinks.

The Code therefore provides a broad framework to guide those involved in commissioning, preparing, and publishing advertisements, supplemented by detailed guidance on specific areas in which problems are likely to occur. The apparent readiness of the CAP Committee to respond to pressures from outside the advertising industry, whether consumer or political, and to make adjustments to the Code as the need arises, seems to have put *BCAP* effectively outside the arena of critical debate. As we note previously, the focus of attention is now concentrated on the effectiveness with which the provisions can be enforced.

The Code can claim with some justification to supplement the provisions that exist in English law. Besides extending into areas such as taste, which the law is scarcely equipped to deal with, it appears in certain respects to be more rigorous in its operation. First, it is applied in the spirit as well as the letter. As the introduction states, "The way in which they [the rules] are interpreted deliberately gives weight to the intentions of those who wrote the Code and not only—as would be the case in the courts—to the words in which those intentions happen to be expressed" (*BCAP* paragraph 1985, 14).

Second, the Code effectively reverses the burden of proof. In English Criminal Law the general position is that a person is innocent until proved guilty, the onus being on the prosecution to show that an offence has been committed. When a disputed advertising claim falls within the terms of the Code, however, the onus is on the advertiser to provide substantiation rather than on the ASA, the CAP, or some competitor to disprove it. In fact, B 1.2 states: "Before offering an advertisement for publication, the advertiser should have in his hands all documentary and other evidence necessary to demonstrate the advertisement's conformity to the Code. This material, together, when necessary, with a statement outlining its relevance, should be made available without delay if requested by either the ASA or the CAP Committee." Although no time limit is set in the Code, the ASA now gives advertisers ten days to provide substantiation for a claim (*IAA Intelligence Summary*, October–November 1982).

Third, the Code extends to members of the public a right to privacy that they do not enjoy under English law. Although an advertiser is well advised not to use an identifiable person in an advertisement without permission because of the risk of an action for defamation, no specific legal provision stops him from doing so. Under the terms of B.17, however, "advertisements should not portray or refer to any living persons, in whatever form or by whatever means, unless their express prior permission has been obtained. This requirement applies to all persons including public figures and foreign nationals."

Although the present work is concerned specifically with media advertising, it is worth noting that the British system of self-regulation also covers sales promotion, and that the ASA and the CAP Committee administer a Code of Sales Promotion Practice that is quite separate from the advertising code.

Its scope is defined in Section 2.1 as embracing "those marketing techniques which are used, usually on a temporary basis, to make goods and services more attractive to the consumer by providing some additional benefit whether in cash or kind." It conforms to the principles of the *International Code of Sales Promotion Practice* drawn up by the ICC, relating those principles to conditions pertaining in the United Kingdom, and is supported by those organizations represented on the CAP Committee as well as by the British Retailer's Association, the Food Manufacturers' Federation, and the Institute of Marketing. Sections of the Code deal with its scope, definitions, and basic principles. Section (5) explains general guidelines that apply to all forms of sales promotion, and section (6) sets out how they apply to particular cases. Another section sets out the various legislative controls that affect sales promotion in the United Kingdom.

In addition to the two Codes that come directly under the control of the two central regulatory bodies, a number of media organizations have their own codes that operate according to the same principles and promote adherence to *BCAP*; however, media organizations introduce supplementary constraints normally related to the particular conditions in which they operate. The poster industry, as mentioned previously, has a long history of self-regulation and continues to be especially active in such matters. British Transport Advertising (BTA), which is responsible for commercial advertising on most of the United Kingdom's nationalized transport undertakings, is the biggest transport advertising company in the world. In addition to stressing the importance of observing *BCAP*, it has its own *Code of Acceptance,* which prohibits posters depicting murder, terror, or violence, or depicting or referring to indecency, obscenity, nudity, or striptease. Posters advertising contraceptives or films that have been refused a permit for public exhibition are also not acceptable. In more general terms the company prohibits anything calculated to demoralize, extenuate crime, break the law, or incite anyone else to do so. Apparently sensitive to the power of public opinion, the company will not accept any poster likely to offend the traveling public or "coloured" or foreign people, or that refers to religious or other sensitive subjects in a manner that might give offence. More difficult to understand is the exclusion of anything that might foment social unrest, that attacks a member or the policies of the government, or that is of a political nature apart from straightforward notices of meetings. Here the company is extending its powers far beyond the limits carefully drawn for itself by the ASA. In addition, paragraph 14 is worthy of particular note, because it prohibits anything that "might adversely affect in any way the Undertaking or Undertakings on whose sites a display is required." Examples given include the advertising of competitive services and offers of employment with a competitor.

The *British Transport Code* also introduces an extra dimension for poster designers when it makes it clear that it will consider not only the design of the poster itself but also any way it is likely to be defaced.

LTA, which controls displays in and on buses, underground trains, and stations in the London area, has conditions of acceptance couched in more general terms, relying mainly on a general prohibition against advertisements likely to offend "the general traveling public" or "*gravely* offend ethnic, religious or other *major* groups" (italics ours). It would appear therefore that whereas the general public need only be offended, particular groups of the type mentioned have to be gravely offended before a poster would be excluded, and minority groups do not appear to merit consideration at all. As with British Transport, advertising for films that have not been granted permission for public exhibition is banned, and the exclusion of political and antigovernment advertisements is extended to include "any legislative, central or local government authority." London Transport protects itself against possible competition with a clause excluding anything that "might adversely affect in any way the interest of the London Transport Executive," and against a possible libel action by specifying that when a poster contains quotations from or references to any living person, the advertiser concerned must have obtained that person's written consent, must produce it to the Executive, and must indemnify the Executive against legal action.

The OAA, the trade body representing the poster industry, has no code or conditions of the kind employed by the two major transportation advertising contractors. The reason for this appears to be one of practice rather than principle. The situation in which a transportation poster is seen is generally one in which the member of the public is waiting—either for the train or bus to arrive, or once inside, waiting for it to reach its destination. Under such circumstances the poster is more likely to be read thoroughly than if, for example, someone is driving past it in a car. The transportation poster, therefore, tends to carry far more copy than the outdoor poster, which in turn carries very little in the way of claims that need to be substantiated. The OAA's Posterviewing Committee is concerned mainly with matters of taste, and because this is an area in which it is virtually impossible to be specific and to cover all eventualities, the organization prefers to rely on the more general provisions of *BCAP*.

In the case of cinema advertising, the CAA also relies on *BCAP*, although here additional factors must be taken into account that would probably render a separate code superfluous (see below).

Newspapers and magazines generally rely on *BCAP*, although individual publishers often have their own house rules that may exclude particular types of appeal or illustration or advertisements for certain types of product. Many local newspapers, for example, will not accept

illustrations of nude persons or advertising for contraceptives, considering them unsuitable in what is essentially family reading. It should also be
remembered that the editor, who has legal responsibility for what is
printed, has the final say in what a publication will or will not carry. The
NS, representing the regional and local press, makes recommendations to
its members about categories of advertising and specific advertisements,
but is always at pains to point out that the ultimate decision lies with the
members themselves. The Society produces *Advertisement Points to Watch*,
which is a quick reference guide for advertisement managers rather than a
code as such. It is arranged alphabetically by subject and combines information on legal constraints with the provisions of *BCAP* and the Society's
own recommendations. Regular newsletters ensure it is kept up to date.

Voluntary codes also play an important role with respect to medical
advertising, both for products that can be bought over the counter by
members of the public (and that are therefore generally known as OTCs),
and for those available only by prescription, which are advertised exclusively to the medical profession. Most important in relation to OTCs is the
Code operated by the PGAB which, as the reader will remember, was the
first organization in the United Kingdom to introduce written guidelines
specifically for use in the framing of advertisements. Today the Association has to work within a legislative framework consisting of the Medicines Act of 1968, the Medicines (Advertising of Medicinal Products)
Regulations 1975 S.I.1975 No. 298, the Medicines (Advertising of Medical
Products) (No. 2) Regulations 1975 S.I. No. 1326, and the Medicines (Labeling and Advertising to the Public) Regulations S.I.1978 No. 41, so the Code
covers not just media advertising but includes provisions relating to
packaging, labeling, and all forms of promotion to the public. It provides
guidance on matters such as sampling, competitions, and vouchers, and
has introduced standard requirements for labeling such as warnings to
keep medicines out of the reach of children, and to consult a doctor if
symptoms being treated by self-medication persist.

The situation with regard to proprietary medicines is particularly
complex because they constitute both licensed medical products closely
controlled by statute, and branded merchandise covered by more general
provisions of commercial and consumer law. The PAGB Code therefore
has an extremely difficult job, and it is interesting to note that the concept
of self-regulation in this area has been totally accepted by the government. In a speech at the Association's Annual Dinner in 1979 Sir George
Young, at that time Minister of Health and Social Security, declared:

> Codes of Practice are in our view much to be preferred to regulations
> because they provide greater flexibility in dealing with the many varied
> circumstances to be found in advertising. Furthermore those concerned
> have a direct hand in drawing up and implementing the arrangements

and are then, I believe, much more prepared to work within the framework and spirit of a Code.

Not surprisingly, the example of the PAGB has been followed by two other trade associations active in this field, the British Herbal Medicine Association and the Health Food Manufacturers Association, both of whom have introduced Codes drawn up in consultation with the Department of Health and Social Security. In 1981 the Medicines Acts Products Advertising Authority was established with its own Code of Practice, the Code's administrator acting in the same general capacity as the director general of the ASA.

The situation with regard to prescription medicines is quite different from that of OTCs. Prescription medicines can only be advertised to the medical profession, and those advertisements must include specific categories of information as set out in the Medicines (Advertising to Medical and Dental Practitioners) Regulations 1978 S.I. 1020. Advertising in this context is under the surveillance of the Association of the British Pharmaceutical Industry, which has its own Code, introduced originally in 1958. Because of the way the relevant legislation is framed, the Association is obliged to operate over a far wider area than that delimited for itself by the ASA. It deals with promotion, defined in the Code as "those informational and marketing activities, undertaken by a pharmaceutical company or with its authority, the purpose of which is to induce the prescribing, supply or administration of its medical products." Included under this heading are the use of sales representatives, audio and video recordings, viewdata systems and data storage devices, gifts, samples, and even hospitality. Whatever method is employed, it must never be such as to bring discredit on or reduce confidence in the pharmaceutical industry.

With regard specifically to advertisements, the information they contain must be accurate and balanced, must not mislead either directly or by implication, and must be capable of substantiation. Exaggeration, the use of superlatives, and disparagement are prohibited, while statements about side effects, the use of the word *new,* and comparison advertising are all strictly controlled. Because medical products may only be offered for sale or supply after a product licence has been granted, they may not be promoted before a licence is granted.

Comparisons

The Interface Between Self-Regulation Standards and the Legal-Social Milieu

From the standpoint of the self-regulatory systems in both the United States and the United Kingdom, advertising must first be legal. However, the legal standards, the nature and mission of government enforcement agencies, and the vigor with which government involves itself with advertising regulation, differ between the two countries. In the United States, the government at various levels concerns itself with advertising to a much greater degree than in the United Kingdom. Thus the missions of the NAD/NARB/CARU/BBB/LARP are not as comprehensive as the mission of the ASA, because "government does more" in the United States, but "government expects industry to do more" in the United Kingdom. However, the U.S. self-regulatory systems go well beyond the law regarding the ethical base for claims—for example, in rulings on the use of the word *natural* and especially regarding children's advertising. With regard to broadcast advertising, the government base of standards under the U.S. networks not only leads them to adhere to legal standards, but other forces lead the networks to adhere to additional standards. The networks, even more than print media, are vulnerable to government pressures or prosecution if they were to maintain unacceptable standards; additionally they are highly visible to the public and highly sensitive to public criticism. They must therefore maintain a balance that ensures broad public acceptance if they are to be able to "deliver" large audiences to advertisers. After all, the continued existence of the networks depends on their ability to sell audiences to advertisers because that is the source of their revenues. Thus the U.S. networks go quite far beyond the base of what is legal, particularly into matters of taste and decency, much like the IBA and the ASA.

This line of thought raises the question as to what specific standards are acceptable and who should make the acceptability decision. The IBA may be described as somewhat more source oriented than the U.S. television networks, or conversely, the U.S. networks are somewhat more receiver oriented than the IBA. We do not explore the many advantages and disadvantages of these orientations in this text. It is sufficient to note here that both systems in fact arrive at standards and their application that seem fairly widely accepted in each of the two countries. Thus, broadly speaking, dissimilar means have led to similar results.

A similar conclusion may be drawn by comparing the NAD/NARB/CARU/BBB/LARP system with the ASA and industry–media application of the *BCAP*. The government–self-regulatory interface and "division of powers/responsibility" is different, and thus the self-regulatory standards are necessarily different. Broadly speaking, both the U.S. and the British systems have reached a point at which they have achieved results that are more or less acceptable in their respective economies and societies. In any event, there is at this time little likelihood of "revolutionary change," although evolutionary changes continue to be made in both countries.

These broad conclusions do not teach us much, however. We must now look at some of the significant differences and similarities in specific ways, keeping in mind the cultural, economic, legal, political, and social milieu in each nation.

Centralized versus Decentralized Application of Codes and Standards

A distinction must be drawn between the United States and the United Kingdom in terms of the status and scope of the various codes in operation. In the United Kingdom the two major codes—one covering broadcast and the other nonbroadcast media—are enforced by centralized machinery, apply to both national and local advertising, and cover virtually every commercial product or service except prescription medicines. The general provisions of these two major codes are supplemented by codes operated by some media owners, which sometimes go beyond protecting the consumer and protect the media owner against possible competition.

In the United States the BBB *Code of Advertising* is oriented primarily toward local advertising. The CARU administers a specialized set of *Self-Regulatory Guidelines for Children*. The three television networks each have their own set of guidelines, primarily for preclearance of commercials, but also to handle complaints. But there is no generally accepted written code of advertising practice, widely accepted by the entire advertising industry, and centrally enforced, as the *BCAP* is accepted in the United Kingdom. It should be kept in mind, however, that years of experience with the NAD/NARB decisions have led the industry to a fairly good understanding of how the NAD/NARB will rule on particular issues.

In the United States, the nearest approximation to a generally accepted written code is *Do's and Don'ts in Advertising Copy* issued by CBBB; this is, however, only a voluminous general guide to what is legal, good practice, and so forth, rather than a code as such.

Coverage of Consumer, Business, and Professional Advertising

In terms of scope, *BCAP* defines *advertisement* in a narrow sense, but its provisions apply to business as well as to consumer advertising. The NAD/NARB system, on the other hand, specifically excludes business and professional advertising as well as appeals to a select audience having a professional or specialized knowledge of the subject concerned.

Public Knowledge of Codes and Standards

The audiences for which the British and U.S. codes are produced also differ in one important respect. In the United Kingdom, as well as being intended to guide those employed in the advertising business, the two major codes are not only freely available to interested members of the public, but their availability is widely publicized. *BCAP* in fact states quite specifically in the introduction that "It indicates to those outside the advertising business the steps that are taken to ensure, through self-imposed regulations, that advertisements can be trusted." In a sense, therefore, the Code represents an extension of the ASA's publicity campaign.

In contrast, the codes and standards of the U.S. self-regulatory system are publicized primarily to members of the advertising industry. And, although industry spokespersons sometimes refer to the desirability of having a reputation for policing themselves, relatively little has been done to develop such a public reputation.

Prior Substantiation of Claims

The principle of substantiation prior to the use of a claim is well established in both countries. In the United States, FTC policies form the base for NAD/NARB policy, although the NAD accepts subsequently acquired substantiation under some conditions. Likewise, the U.S. television networks expect substantiation before a commercial will be cleared to run. The BBB Code contains an explicit statement on prior substantiation, but it is an "unwritten" rule for the NAD and LARPs. In contrast, *BCAP* states specifically: "Before offering an advertisement for publication, the advertiser should have in his hands all documentary and other evidence necessary to demonstrate the advertisement's conformity to the Code. This material . . . should be made available without delay if requested." (*BCAP* 1985: B1.2). An advertisement can be stopped quickly if such substantiation is not provided immediately. In the United States, on the other hand, there tends to be more "slack in the system," and advertisers and agencies still take risks more frequently, it seems, by sometimes using unsubstantiated claims; the system is just not as clearly understood or accepted by advertisers, nor as tightly administered by the regulatory mechanisms. The problem relates in large part to the lack of enforcement or sanctions in the self-regulatory system, and to the lack of staff in regulatory agencies such as the FTC and the FDA to pursue all potential infractions of the substantiation policy. Moreover, in recent times as a part of the trend toward deregulation, the FTC has cut back on its enforcement activities and modified somewhat the conditions under which substantiation is required.

Taste and Decency

The two countries differ somewhat as to whether self-regulation should involve matters of taste and decency. In the United States the NAD and the LARPs specifically exclude these issues but the U.S. television networks are quite similar to the IBA and the ASA with regard to handling such matters. In the United Kingdom, *BCAP* (B3.2) states that "Advertisements should contain nothing which, because of its failure to respect the standards of decency and propriety that are generally accepted in the UK, is likely to cause either grave or widespread offence," so that the ASA is inevitably drawn into making judgments on matters of taste and decency. The *IBA Code* includes a similar provison: "No advertisement should offend against good taste or decency or be offensive to public feeling" (*IBA Code* 1983, paragraph 12).

Setting Precedents

In both countries, those organizations responsible for interpreting and applying the codes judge each individual advertisement on its merits, rather than working according to precedent. This policy has attracted some adverse comment from the legal profession, but because social and marketing conditions can change considerably in a relatively short time, and drawing analogies in advertising situations can in any case be misleading, we do not believe that this criticism is justified. A strict legalistic approach to evaluating advertising might also hinder the policy employed in both countries of taking into account the overall impression or impact of an advertisement rather than its individual parts, and would surely find it difficult to cope with British Transport's interesting concept of excluding material that might be defaced in an offensive way.

Children's Advertising

Advertising to children is a cause of concern in both countries, but although the philosophies are broadly similar, regulation is given different emphasis. In the United States the CARU publishes *Children's Advertising Guidelines* and other reference works for advertisers. In the United Kingdom both major codes have a section concerned with children that is believed to provide sufficient protection when taken together with more general provisions. A 1979 investigation commissioned by the ASA tended to confirm that children are more sophisticated consumers of advertising than critics often believe, but nevertheless, children's advertising requires special standards (*ASA Annual Report* 1980, 8). The IBA's Advertising Advisory Committee reviews a reel of commercials for toys each year after Christmas. After viewing the 1985 selection, "They informed the Authority that in their opinion the Code regulations appeared to be working in the public interest" (IBA 1985).

Philosophy between the two countries is also noticeably different. Both sets of regulations are restrictive in the sense that they are intended to prevent advertising causing any kind of harm to children, directly or indirectly. But the CARU Code also adopts a positive stance, urging advertisers to capitalize on the potential of advertising for influencing social behavior and setting high social standards.

Noncommercial Advertising

In the United States, First Amendment protection of speech requires that government may not restrict speech that advocates particular causes or issues, and, in particular, speech in religious or political advertising; however, freedom of the press also ensures that reporters may print or broadcast what they wish, subject only to infrequently applied law on libel or slander. And the press cannot be forced to accept commercials or to print or broadcast material if they choose not to do so. Some differences exist in the way the law is applied to print and broadcast media, in view of the "public interest" features of FCC regulation of the broadcast industry, but by and large, free speech and a free press are protected. Correspondingly, advertising self-regulatory systems do not attempt to abridge the freedom of the press in any way whatsoever.

But in the United Kingdom, as noted previously, religious and political advertising are restricted. Broadcast commercials of a political nature are not permitted by the IBA, but the ASA specifically excludes political advertisements from its terms of reference (although at the time of writing it is reported that this situation may be changing). It may therefore come as a surprise to the visitor to the United Kingdom to see what are apparently commercials for the main political parties carried not only by the independent television channels but also by the BBC.

The reason for this apparent paradox is that Parliament allocates time for "party political broadcasts," as it prefers to call them, to keep the electorate well informed. The programs are produced by the parties (or their advertising agents) but the time is free. The number of spots is agreed between the parties and is allocated in proportion to the number of Parliamentary seats held by each—an arrangement that, as the smaller parties point out, has the effect of reinforcing the positions of the Conservative and Labour parties.

These broadcasts deal with broad issues and matters of party policy. They must not refer to a particular candidate standing in a specific constituency. The electoral expenses of candidates (including publicity) are severely limited by law, and in practice are only sufficient for leaflets and a few modest posters. Political advertising on the scale of that in the United States is therefore quite unknown in the United Kingdom.

Detailed Comparisons of Topic Coverage

To this point, the comparisons we have made have consisted of generalizations about the codes or standards, and their application. But, one might ask: What specific topics are covered in these codes and standards, and what topics are not covered? And how does such topic coverage compare among the several sets of codes and standards?

We have answered these questions in the body of this chapter in broad form. We also include in the appendices to this chapter the CARU *Self-Regulatory Guidelines for Children's Advertising* (appendix 5A) and the BBB *Code of Advertising* (appendix 5C). Because the NAD/NARB does not have a written code, topics known to be covered in NAD/NARB decisions are identified from several sources and presented in list form (appendix 5B). The U.S. television network standards, as well as the *IBA Code of Advertising Standards and Practice* and *BCAP*, are too long to reproduce in the appendices. Therefore a list of topics that they cover is identified from the indexes of each, which is adequate for our purposes, because we are more concerned with topics covered than with the detailed content of such coverage for each part of the code or standards (appendices 5D through 5H).

The last sentence of the previous paragraph requires explanation. A major limitation of a chapter such as this is that we can prepare a comprehensive list of topics covered in the codes and standards, but we cannot prepare a detailed description of the standards applied to each topic. For example, we can indicate that testimonials, nutrition, pet foods, and children are covered (or not covered), but we cannot go into detail on every such topic to indicate the comparative standards applied regarding advertising controls on these matters by NAD/NARB, BBB, CARU, the television networks, IBA, and *BCAP*. Such an endeavor would require many, many volumes.

Nevertheless, the appendices to this chapter provide the interested reader with a means to identify the topics covered by each set of regulatory standards. Then, if the reader has an interest in the specific content of each topic, he or she can refer to the original source documents from which these lists of topics were extracted.

A perusal of these appendices indicates a great deal of overlap in topics among these codes and sets of standards. However, it would be virtually impossible to document such overlap; the reason is that each system is sufficiently flexible to deal with issues that for one reason or another might not be in written form in a particular code or set of standards. Thus each system has the potential for greater breadth of topic coverage.

It does seem instructive, however, to compare the *topics that are not covered*, because their specific exclusion may give us some insights into the past priorities and current gaps in each system, or possible ways in which each system may evolve (or be improved?) in the future to cover such topics. Therefore, we have briefly analyzed the topics excluded, and grouped them to make relevant comparisons, namely, with regard to (1) children's advertising, (2) broadcast advertising, and (3) the NAD/NARB/BBB/LARP system and the ASA/CAP system.

Our first set of comparisons is with regard to children's advertising, as covered by the IBA, *BCAP*, and CARU. The CARU standards are somewhat more comprehensive than those of the IBA and *BCAP*, although the CARU guidelines and reported cases do not mention employment practices for children and the use of children as presenters, both of which are covered by the IBA Code and *BCAP*. However, the generality of the CARU guidelines permits their interpretation to include these and other practices not specifically mentioned therein when appropriate cases arise.

On the other side, significant matters *covered by the CARU but not by the IBA or BCAP* include

1. Perceived product benefits, status, and popularity appeals.
2. Social stereotyping and appeals to prejudice.
3. Exploitation of imagination and confusion of reality with fantasy.
4. What is included or excluded in the purchase price.
5. Amount of product shown.
6. Prices, price minimization[1] (for example, use of the words *only* and *just*).
7. Items not included with the product[1] (for example, batteries).
8. Items purchased separately.

Additionally, the CARU guidelines are more specific about certain practices such as standards for food products, violence, substantiation of claims, disclosure in understandable language, and comparative claims), whereas *BCAP* is quite brief and refers the advertiser to other sections of the code with the observation that they "also apply" to children.

Another set of comparisons[2] that seems useful is between topic coverage of the IBA Code and ABC standards. The IBA includes certain controls on advertising topics that are not covered by ABC, for example:

1. Treatment of alcoholism.
2. Collecting schemes.
3. Colleges.
4. Contact lenses.
5. Contraceptives.
6. Credit.
7. Death.
8. Drinking and driving.
9. Employment services.
10. Fear appeals.
11. Funerals and undertakers.
12. Hire purchase and installment buying.
13. Imitation.
14. Industrial disputes.

15. Inertia and negative option selling.
16. Instructional courses.
17. Local government advertisements.
18. Matrimonial agencies.
19. Money back orders.
20. Nurses.
21. Photography.
22. Floor and furniture polishes.
23. Politics.
24. Private investigation services.
25. Psychology, psychiatry, and psychoanalysis.
26. Reproduction techniques.
27. Program independence.
28. Scientific terms and statistics.
29. Smoking cures.
30. Stridency.
31. Use of substitute materials.
32. Superstition.
33. Veterinary medicine services.

On the other hand, coverage of topics by ABC that are not covered by the IBA include

1. Ammunition.
2. Billboards.
3. Criminal activities.
4. Currency and coins.
5. Dramatizations, reenactments, and simulations.
6. Firearms.
7. Fireworks.
8. Homework schemes.
9. Indirect advertising.
10. Insurance.
11. Motion picture footage.
12. Multiple product announcements.
13. Perception testing.
14. Personal care products.
15. Pet foods.
16. Premiums.
17. Privacy and publicity rights.
18. Professional advertising.
19. Public symbols.
20. Research.

21. Sponsor identification.
22. Talent commercials.

Moreover, these categories of topics are not always defined in the same way and therefore they are not always directly comparable. Thus, this listing could easily be misinterpreted. Nevertheless, it seems useful to identify the priorities of each organization and the matters that probably need (or do not need) future attention in the two countries.

Another set of comparisons of interest are those between the NAD/NARB/BBB/LARP and the ASA/*BCAP*. The overlap is very great indeed, and only a few differences are worth noting—but some of these are indeed major differences.

The NAD/NARB/BBB standards include the following, which are not covered specifically in *BCAP*:

1. Trade-ins.
2. Extra charges.
3. Use of asterisks.
4. Use of abbreviations.
5. Portrayal of women.
6. Fantasy and satire.
7. Implied claims.
8. Disclosure of relevant information.

On the other hand, *BCAP* includes the following, which are not covered specifically by NAD/NARB/BBB standards:

1. Unsolicited home visits.
2. Inertia and negative option selling.
3. Mail order.
4. Cigarettes.
5. Vitamins and minerals.
6. Medical quackery.
7. Slimming.
8. Credit and investment.
9. Matters of taste and decency.

The codes, guidelines, and standards on which these comparisons are based are presented in this chapter's appendices.

Notes

1. These practices are subject to legal control rather than to the IBA Code and *BCAP*.

2. These listings are intended to be illustrative rather than complete. Both the ABC and the IBA systems have provisions to cover topics not listed in their standards.

References

ABC Advertising Standards and Guidelines (1983) (New York: American Broadcasting Company, as revised December 1983).

Advertising Age, various issues.

Advertising and Women (1975) (New York: National Advertising Review Board).

Adweek, various issues.

ASA Annual Reports, various years.

Association of the British Pharmaceutical Industry, *Code of Practice Committee Case Reports,* Vol. 1 (1979–1980), and Vol. 2 (1981–1982).

Association of the British Pharmaceutical Industry (1984), *Code of Practice for the Pharmaceutical Industry,* 6th ed. January 1984.

BBB *Code of Advertising* (1978, 1983 and 1985) (Washington: Council of Better Business Bureaus).

Boddewyn, J.J. (1979), *Advertising to Children: An International Survey* (New York: International Advertising Association, September 1979).

Boddewyn, J.J. (1984), *Advertising to Children: Regulation and Self-Regulation in 40 Countries* (New York: International Advertising Association).

Boddewyn, J.J. (1982), "Advertising Regulation in the 1980's: The Underlying Global Forces," *Journal of Marketing* 46(Winter 1982):27–35.

Boddewyn, J.J. (1983), *Comparison Advertising: Regulation and Self-Regulation in 55 Countries* (New York: International Advertising Association, January 1983).

Boddewyn, J.J. (1982), *Consumer Credit and Investment Advertising* (New York: International Advertising Association, September 1982).

Boddewyn, J.J. (1979), *Decency and Sexism in Advertising: An International Survey of their Regulation and Self-Regulation* (New York: International Advertising Association, December 1979).

Boddewyn, J.J. (1981), *Direct Mail/Direct Response* (New York: International Advertising Association).

Boddewyn, J.J. (1981), *Endorsements/Testimonials: A 36-Country Survey* (New York: International Advertising Association, August 1981).

Boddewyn, J.J. (1980), *Energy and Advertising* (New York: International Advertising Association).

Boddewyn, J.J. (1982), *Food Advertising Regulation and Self-Regulation, An International Survey* (New York: International Advertising Association, March 1982).

Boddewyn, J.J. (1981), "The Global Spread of Advertising Regulation," *MSU Business Topics* (Spring 1981):6–13.

Boddewyn, J.J. (1979), *Governmental Preclearance of Advertisements: An International Survey* (New York: International Advertising Association, January 1979).

Boddewyn, J.J. (1980), *New Regulatory Developments* (New York: International Advertising Association).

Boddewyn, J.J. (1979), *Outdoor/Billboard Advertising Regulation: An International Survey* (New York: International Advertising Association, April 1979).

Boddewyn, J.J. (1983), "Outside Participation in Advertising Self-Regulation: The Case of the Advertising Standards Authority (UK)," *Journal of Consumer Policy* 6:77–93.

Boddewyn, J.J. (1978), *Premiums, Gifts and Competitions: An International Survey* (New York: International Advertising Association, September 1978).

Boddewyn, J.J. (1978), *The Use of Foreign Language Materials in Advertising* (New York: International Advertising Association, October 1978).

Boddewyn, J.J., and Marton, Katherin, "Comparison Advertising: A Worldwide Study," *Proceedings of the Annual Conference of the American Academy of Advertising 1978,* Steven E. Permut (ed.), 150–154.

Boddewyn, J.J., and Marton, Katherin, (1978), *Comparison Advertising: A Worldwide Study* (New York: Hastings House).

BCAP 6th ed. and 7th ed. (1979 and 1985).

British Transport Advertising, *Code of Acceptance,* contained in British Rail *Code of Acceptance* (undated).

CAP Guidance Note No. 1 (April 1979).

CARU (1980), *Children and Advertising, An Annotated Bibliography* (New York: Children's Advertising Review Unit, National Advertising Division, Council of Better Business Bureaus).

CARU (1980), *An Eye on Children's Advertising Self-Regulation: A Five Year Report,* June 1974–June 1979, New York.

CARU (1983), *Self-Regulatory Guidelines for Children's Advertising,* 3rd ed. (New York: CBBB).

CARU (undated pamphlet), *An Eye on Children's Advertising,* updated in 1986.

CBBB Annual Report, various years.

CBBB, *Better Business News and Views* (Arlington, Va.: Council of Better Business Bureaus, various issues).

CBS Advertising Guidelines (undated) (New York: CBS Television Network).

Cohen, Dorothy (1983), "Legal Developments in Marketing, 5.0 Regulation of Unfair Competition, 5.1 Advertising," *Journal of Marketing* 47(3; Summer 1983): 119–121.

Do's and Don'ts in Advertising Copy (Washington: Council of Better Business Bureaus, various dates [a looseleaf service for advertisers, advertising agencies, broadcasters, and printed media]).

Farhi, Paul (1983), "Agencies, Networks Battle Over Censors' Role," *Ad Week,* 14 November 1983, 50, 52.

IAA Intelligence Summary (New York: International Advertising Association, various issues).

IBA Annual Reports, various years.

The IBA Code of Advertising Standards and Practice (1983).

LaBarbera, Priscilla (1980), "Advertising Self-Regulation: An Evaluation," *MSU Business Topics,* Summer 1980.

London Transport Advertising, *Conditions Governing the Acceptance of Advertisements,* contained in Rate Card 15, effective 1 January 1984.

"Medical Ad Code Revised Again," *Marketing,* 26 January 1984.

NAD Case Reports, various issues.

NARB (1972), *Advertising Evaluation and Policy Statement* (New York: NARB, 20 January 1972).

NBC Broadcast Standards for Television: Advertising Guidelines (1983) (New York: National Broadcasting Company).

News from NAD, various issues.

Press release (1977), "NARB Consultative Panel Finds Comparative Advertising, if Used, Should Serve Consumer Interest," *NAD Case Report*, 22 August 1977.

Proprietary Association of Great Britain Code of Advertising Standards and Practice (editions 1943, 1950, 1967, 1973, 1979).

Purdon, Roger A. (1972), "Advertising Self-Regulation—A New Reality," presented to the 1972 Annual Meeting of the American Association of Advertising Agencies, Boca Raton, Florida, 16 March 1972.

Reports of NARB Panels, various dates.

Theobalds, Harry (1983), "The Rules Governing Advertising on Television and Independent Local Radio," in J.J.D. Bullmore and M.J. Waterson (eds.), *The Advertising Association Handbook* (London: Holt, Rinehart & Winston).

Thomson, Peter (1983), "Advertising Control: Advertisements in Media other than Television and Radio," in J.J.D. Bullmore and M.J. Waterson (eds.), *The Advertising Association Handbook* (London: Holt, Rinehart & Winston).

Young, Sir George, speech delivered to the Annual Dinner of the Proprietary Association of Great Britain, 21 June 1979.

Zanot, Eric J. "The National Advertising Review Board, 1971–1976," *Journalism Monographs* No. 59, February 1979.

Zanot, Eric (1980), "A Review of Eight Years of NARB Casework: Guidelines and Parameters of Deceptive Advertising," *Journal of Advertising* 9(4):20–26.

Zanot, Eric, and Maddox, Lynda (1977), "National Advertising Review Board Decisions Involving Common 'Problem' Areas of Deception in Advertising," *Proceedings of the Annual Conference of the American Academy of Advertising*, Gordon E. Miracle, (ed.)., (East Lansing: Michigan State University), 117–121.

Appendix 5A
Self-Regulatory Guidelines
for Children's Advertising

The following material is reproduced from *Self-Regulatory Guidelines for Children's Advertising,* 3rd edition, 1983, issued by the Children's Advertising Review Unit of the Council of Better Business Bureaus.

The Children's Advertising Guidelines have been in existence since 1972 when they were published by the Association of National Advertisers to encourage truthful and accurate advertising sensitive to the special nature of children. Subsequently, the advertising community established the Children's Advertising Review Unit to serve as an independent manager of the industry's self-regulatory programs. The Unit edited and republished the Children's Advertising Guidelines in 1975 and revised them in 1977.

This third edition has been edited by the Children's Advertising Review Unit to be sure the Guidelines are responsive to current conditions. The assistance of children's advertisers and their agencies has been invaluable, resulting in a clarification of individual Guidelines and an improved format.

INTERPRETATION OF THE GUIDELINES

Because children's knowledge of the physical and social world is in the process of development, they are more limited than adults in the experience and skills required to evaluate advertising and to make purchase decisions. For these reasons, certain presentations and techniques which may be appropriate for adult-directed advertising may mislead children if used in child-directed advertising.

The function of the Guidelines is to delineate those areas that need particular attention to help avoid deceptive advertising messages to children. The intent is to help advertisers deal sensitively and honestly with children and is not

meant to deprive them, or children, of the benefits of innovative advertising approaches.

The Guidelines have been kept general in the belief that responsible advertising comes in many forms and that diversity should be encouraged. The goal in all cases should be to fulfill the spirit as well as the letter of the Guidelines and the Principles on which they are based.

SCOPE OF THE GUIDELINES

The Guidelines apply to all advertising addressed to children under twelve years of age, including print, broadcast and cable television advertising. One section applies to adult-directed advertising only when a potential child-safety concern exists (see page 9, **Safety**).

PRINCIPLES

Five basic Principles underlie these Guidelines for advertising directed to children:

1. Advertisers should always take into account the level of knowledge, sophistication and maturity of the audience to which their message is primarily directed. Younger children have a limited capability for evaluating the credibility of what they watch. Advertisers, therefore, have a special responsibility to protect children from their own susceptibilities.

2. Realizing that children are imaginative and that make-believe play constitutes an important part of the growing up process, advertisers should exercise care not to exploit that imaginative quality of children. Unreasonable expectations of product quality or performance should not be stimulated either directly or indirectly by advertising.

3. Recognizing that advertising may play an important part in educating the child, information should be communicated in a truthful and accurate manner with full recognition by the advertiser that the child may learn practices from advertising which can affect his or her health and well-being.

4. Advertisers are urged to capitalize on the potential of advertising to influence social behavior by developing advertising that, wherever possible, addresses itself to social standards generally regarded as positive and beneficial, such as friendship, kindness, honesty, justice, generosity and respect for others.

5. Although many influences affect a child's personal and social development, it remains the prime responsibility of the parents to provide guidance for children. Advertisers should contribute to this parent-child relationship in a constructive manner.

4. The performance and use of a product should be demonstrated in a way that can be duplicated by the child for whom the product is intended.

5. Products should be shown used in safe environments and situations.

6. What is included and excluded in the initial purchase should be clearly established.

7. The amount of product featured should be within reasonable levels for the situation depicted.

8. Representation of food products should be made so as to encourage sound usage of the product with a view toward healthy development of the child and development of good nutritional practices. Advertisements representing mealtime in the home should clearly and adequately depict the role of the product within the framework of a balanced diet.

9. Portrayals of violence and presentations that could unduly frighten or provoke anxiety in children should be avoided.

10. Objective claims about product or performance characteristics should be supported by appropriate and adequate substantiation.

Product Presentations and Claims

Children look at, listen to and remember many different elements in advertising. Therefore, advertisers need to examine the total advertising message to be certain that the net communication will not mislead or misinform children.

1. Copy, sound and visual presentations should not mislead children about product or performance characteristics. Such characteristics may include, but are not limited to, size, speed, method of operation, color, sound, durability and nutritional benefits.

2. The advertising presentation should not mislead children about perceived benefits from use of the product. Such benefits may include, but are not limited to, the acquisition of strength, status, popularity, growth, proficiency and intelligence. Social stereotyping and appeals to prejudice should be avoided.

3. Care should be taken not to exploit a child's imagination. Fantasy, including animation, is appropriate for younger as well as older children. However, it should not create unattainable performance expectations nor exploit the younger child's difficulty in distinguishing between the real and the fanciful.

Sales Pressure

Children are not as prepared as adults to make judicious, independent purchase decisions. Therefore, advertisers should avoid using extreme sales pressure in advertising presentations to children.

1. Children should not be urged to ask parents or others to buy products. Advertisements should not suggest that a parent or adult who purchases a product or service for a child is better, more intelligent or more generous than one who does not.

2. Advertisements should not convey the impression that possession of a product will result in more acceptance of a child by his or her peers. Conversely, lacking a product should not convey the impression that the child will be less accepted by his or her peers. Advertisements should not imply that purchase and use of a product will confer upon the user the prestige, skills or other special qualities of characters appearing in advertising. Benefits attributed to the product or service should be inherent in its use.

3. All price representations should be clearly and concisely set forth. Price minimizations such as "only" or "just" should not be used.

Disclosures and Disclaimers

Children have a more limited vocabulary and less developed language skills than adolescents and adults. They read less well, if at all, and rely more on information presented pictorially than verbally. Studies have shown that simplified wording, such as "You have to put it together" instead of "Assembly required," significantly increases comprehension.

1. **All information which requires disclosure for legal or other reasons should be in language understandable by the child audience.** Disclaimers and disclosures should be clearly worded, legible and prominent. In television advertising, both audio and video disclosures are encouraged.

2. **Advertising for unassembled products should clearly indicate that they need to be put together to be used properly.**

3. **If any item essential to use of the product is not included, such as batteries, this fact must be disclosed clearly.**

4. **Information about products purchased separately, such as accessories or individual items in a collection, should be disclosed clearly to the child audience.**

Comparative Claims

Advertising which compares the advertised product to another product may be difficult for young children to understand and evaluate. Comparative claims should be based on real product advantages that are understandable to the child audience.

1. **Comparative advertising should provide factual information.** Comparisons should not falsely represent other products or previous versions of the same product.

2. **Comparative claims should be presented in ways that children understand clearly.**

3. **Comparative claims should be supported by appropriate and adequate substantiation.**

Endorsements and Promotion by Program or Editorial Characters

Studies have shown that the mere appearance of a character with a product can significantly alter a child's perception of the product depending on the child's opinion of the presenter. Advertising presentations by program/editorial characters may hamper a young child's ability to distinguish between program/editorial content and advertising.

1. **All personal endorsements should reflect the actual experiences and beliefs of the endorser.**

2. **An endorser represented, either directly or indirectly, as an expert must possess qualifications appropriate to the particular expertise depicted in the endorsement.**

3. **Program personalities, live or animated, should not promote products, premiums or services in or adjacent to programs primarily directed to children in which the same personality or character appears.**

4. **In print media primarily designed for children, a character or personality associated with the editorial content of a publication should not be used to promote products, premiums or services in the same publication.**

Premiums

The use of premiums in advertising has the potential to enhance the appeal of a product to a child. Therefore, special attention should be paid to the advertising of premiums to guard against exploiting children's immaturity.

1. **If product advertising contains a premium message, care should be taken that the child's attention is focused primarily on the product.** The premium message should be clearly secondary.

2. **Conditions of a premium offer should be stated simply and clearly.** "Mandatory" statements and disclosures should be stated in terms that can be understood by the child audience.

Safety

Imitation, exploration and experimentation are important activities to children. They are attracted to commercials in general and may imitate product demonstrations and other actions without regard to risk. Many childhood accidents and injuries occur in the home, often involving abuse or misuse of common household products.

1. **Products inappropriate for use by children should not be advertised directly to children.** This is especially true for products labeled, "Keep out of the reach of children." Additionally, such products should not be promoted directly to children by premiums or other means. Medications, drugs and supplemental vitamins should not be advertised to children.

2. **Advertisements for children's products should show them being used by children in the appropriate age range.** For instance, young children should not be shown playing with toys safe only for older children.

3. **Adults should be shown supervising children when products or activities could involve an obvious safety risk.** For example, using an electrical appliance or playing in or near a swimming pool.

4. **Advertisements should not portray adults or children in unsafe acts, situations or conditions or in acts harmful to others.** When athletic activities (such as skateboarding) are shown, proper safety equipment should be depicted.

5. **Advertisements should avoid demonstrations that encourage dangerous or inappropriate use or misuse of the product.** This is particularly important when the demonstration can be easily reproduced by children and features products accessible to them.

THE CHILDREN'S ADVERTISING REVIEW UNIT

The Children's Advertising Review Unit of the Council of Better Business Bureaus was established in 1974 by the advertising industry to promote responsible children's advertising and to respond to public concerns.

The basic activity of CARU is the review and evaluation of child-directed advertising in all media. When children's advertising is found to be misleading, inaccurate or inconsistent with the Guidelines, CARU seeks changes through the voluntary cooperation of advertisers.

CARU provides a general advisory service for advertisers and agencies and also is a source of informational material for children, parents and educators. In addition, CARU maintains a clearinghouse for research on children's advertising and has published an annotated bibliography.

CARU's Academic Advisory Panel helps evaluate advertising and information provided by advertisers in support of their advertising claims. The Panel also advises on general issues concerning children's advertising and assists in revisions of the Guidelines.

Appendix 5B
NAD/NARB Advertising Standards

Prefatory Comment

The NAD/NARB system is devoted primarily to truth and accuracy in advertising, understood broadly to mean advertising that is not misleading. Because the standards are broadly stated and no single written document includes a comprehensive list of the NAD/NARB coverage of advertising practices, products, and audiences, the following list was constructed from various sources and limited primarily to the topics mentioned in the text of this chapter. Thus we mention the main issues, but it is clear that this flexible system could choose to cover other possible topics, many of which are mentioned in *Do's and Don'ts in Advertising Copy*, a major source used by the NAD/NARB as well as recommended to advertisers, agencies, and media.

Topic Coverage: Advertising Practices, Specific Products, Special Audiences, or Markets

Alcoholic beverages

Appliances

Automotive products

Celebrity spokesmen

Children

Cleaning agents

Comparative advertising

Comparisons of products, open
   end

Competitor comparisons and
   references

Constructive portrayals

Controversy advertising

Deception
   Intentional
   Unintentional

Destructive portrayals

Disclosure of information
   Full

Adequate

Disparagement, false

Drug usage

Endorsements

Exaggerations

Fabrics

Fair advertising

Fantasy

Food

Health claims

Honesty

House furnishings

Humor

Implied claims

Jewelry

Negative appeals

Omission of material facts

Omission of relevant information

Portrayal of women

Positive appeals

Precedents

Price claims
  Bargains
  Price savings
  The use of the words *up to*

Puffery

Research data, use and misuse of

Satire

Schools

Semantics

Sex

Substantiation requirements

Superiority claims

Superlatives

Testimonials

Trademarks

Truth and accuracy
  Literal
  Nonliteral

Wearing apparel

Women, use of sexual appeals

Appendix 5C
Better Business Bureau
Code of Advertising

FOREWORD

These basic advertising standards are issued for the guidance of advertisers, advertising agencies and advertising media.

It is not possible to cover fully the wide variety of advertising practices by specific standards in a code of this type which is designed to apply to the offering of all goods and services. Where the Better Business Bureau has developed specific industry advertising codes, it is recommended that industry members adhere to them. If specific questions arise which are not covered or involve advertising directed to children, it is recommended that *Do's and Don'ts in Advertising Copy* (a comprehensive loose-leaf volume published by the Council of Better Business Bureaus) be consulted. Advertisers, agencies and media should also be sure that they are in compliance with local, state and federal laws and regulations governing advertising.

Adherence to the provisions of this Code will be a significant contribution toward effective self-regulation in the public interest.

BASIC PRINCIPLES

1. The primary responsibility for truthful and non-deceptive advertising rests with the advertiser. Advertisers should be prepared to substantiate any claims or offers made before publication or broadcast and, upon request, present such substantiation promptly to the advertising medium or the Better Business Bureau.

2. Advertisements which are untrue, misleading, deceptive, fraudulent, falsely disparaging of competitors, or insincere offers to sell, shall not be used.

3. An advertisement as a whole may be misleading although every sentence separately considered is literally true. Misrepresentation may result not only from direct statements but by omitting or obscuring a material fact.

1. Comparative Price, Value and Savings Claims

Advertisers may offer a price reduction or saving by comparing their selling price with:

(a) their own former selling price,

(b) the current selling price of identical merchandise sold by others in the market area, or

(c) the current selling price of comparable merchandise sold by the advertiser or by others in the market area.

When any one of these comparisons is made in advertising, the claim should be based on the following criteria *and* the advertising should make clear to which of the above the comparative price or savings claim relates.

a. Comparison with own former selling price

(1) The former price should be the actual price at which the advertiser has been currently offering (see below (2)) the merchandise immediately preceding the sale, on a regular basis, and for a reasonably substantial period of time.

(2) Offering prices, as distinguished from actual former selling prices, have frequently been used as a comparative to deceptively imply a saving. In the event few or no sales were made at the advertised comparative price, the advertiser should make sure that the higher price does not exceed the advertiser's usual and customary retail markup for similar merchandise, not an inflated or exaggerated price, and is one at which the merchandise was openly and actively offered for sale, for a reasonably substantial period of time, in the recent, regular course of business, honestly and in good faith.

(3) Descriptive terminology often used by advertisers includes: "regularly," "was," "you save $_____," and "originally." If the word "originally" is used and the original price is not the last previous price, that fact should be disclosed by stating the last previous price, or that intermediate markdowns have been taken, e.g., "originally $400, formerly $300, now $250"; "originally $400, intermediate markdowns taken, now $250."

b. Comparison with current price of identical merchandise sold by others

(1) The comparative price should not exceed the price at which representative principal retail outlets in the market area have been selling the identical merchandise immediately preceding the advertiser's offer, on a regular basis and for a reasonably substantial period

of time. Such comparisons should be substantiated by the advertiser immediately prior to making any advertised comparisons.

(2) Descriptive terminology often used by advertisers includes: "selling elsewhere at $_____." (Refers to market area cited in (1) above.)

c. Comparison with current price of comparable merchandise sold by the advertiser or by others

(1) The comparative price should not exceed the price at which the advertiser or representative principal retail outlets in the market area have been selling the comparable merchandise immediately preceding the advertiser's sale, on a regular basis and for a reasonably substantial period of time. Such comparisons should be substantiated by the advertiser immediately prior to making any advertised comparisons.

(2) In all such cases, the advertiser should make certain that comparable merchandise is similar in all respects and of at least like grade and quality.

(3) Descriptive terminology often used by advertisers includes: "comparable value," "compares with merchandise selling at $_____," "equal to merchandise selling for $_____."

d. List prices

"List price," "manufacturer's list price," "reference price," "suggested retail price," and similar terms have been used deceptively to state or imply a saving which was not, in fact, the case. A list price may be advertised as a comparative to the advertised sales price only to the extent that it is the actual selling price currently charged by the advertiser or by representative principal retailers in the market area where the claim is made.

Such a comparison should be substantiated by the advertiser immediately prior to making any advertised comparison.

e. "Imperfects," "irregulars," "seconds"

No comparative price should be used in connection with an imperfect, irregular or second article unless it is accompanied by a clear and conspicuous disclosure that such comparative price applies to the price of the article, if perfect. The comparative price advertised should be based on (1) the price currently charged by the advertiser for the article without defects, or (2) the price currently charged by representative principal retailers in the trade area for the article without defects, and the advertisement should disclose which basis of comparison is being used.

f. "Factory to you," "factory direct," "wholesaler," "wholesale prices"

The terms "factory to you," "factory direct," "wholesaler," "wholesale prices" and others of similar import have been the subject of great abuse in advertising. They imply a significant saving from the actual price at which identical merchandise is currently being offered by representative principal retailers in the market area, or where identical merchandise is not being offered, from comparable values in the market area. Such terms should not be used unless the implied savings can be substantiated and the terms meet all of the requirements below.

(1) The terms "factory to you," "direct from maker," "factory outlet" and the like should not be used unless all advertised merchandise is actually manufactured by the advertiser or in factories owned or controlled by the advertiser.

(2) The terms "wholesaler," "wholesale outlet," "distributor" and the like should not be used unless the advertiser actually owns and operates or directly and absolutely controls a wholesale or distribution facility which primarily sells products to retailers for resale.

(3) The terms "wholesale price," "at cost" and the like should not be used unless they are the current prices which retailers usually and customarily pay when they buy such merchandise for resale.

g. Sales

(1) The unqualified term "sale" may be used in advertising only if there is a significant reduction from the advertiser's usual and customary price of the merchandise offered and the sale is for a limited period of time. If the sale exceeds thirty days advertisers should be prepared to substantiate that the offering is indeed a valid reduction and has not become their regular price.

(2) Time limit sales should be rigidly observed. For example, merchandise offered in a "one-day sale," "three-day sale," "this week only," sale should be taken off "sale" and revert to the regular price immediately following expiration of the stated time.

(3) Introductory sales should be limited to a stated time period, and the selling price should be increased to the advertised regular price immediately following termination of the stated period.

(4) Price predictions—advertisers may currently advertise future increases in their own prices on a subsequent date provided that they do, in fact, increase the price to the stated amount on that date and maintain it for a reasonably substantial period of time thereafter.

h. "Emergency" or "distress" sales

Emergency or distress sales, including but not limited to bankruptcy, liquidation and going out of business sales, should not be advertised unless the stated or implied reason is a fact, should be limited to a stated period of time, and should offer only such merchandise as is affected by the emergency. "Selling out," "closing out sale," and similar terms should not be used unless the concern so advertising is actually going out of business. A "liquidation sale" means that the advertiser's entire business is in the process of actually being liquidated prior to actual closing. Advertisers should conform with the requirements of applicable local, state and federal laws.

i. "Up to" savings claims

Savings or price reduction claims covering a group of items with a range of savings should state both the minimum and maximum savings without undue or misleading display of the maximum. The number of items available at the maximum savings should comprise a significant percentage, typically 10%, of all the items in the offering, unless local or state law requires otherwise.

j. Lowest price, underselling claims

Despite an advertiser's best efforts to ascertain competitive prices, the rapidity with which prices fluctuate and the difficulty of determining prices of all sellers at all times preclude an absolute knowledge of the truth of generalized underselling/lowest price claims.

Advertisers should have proper substantiation for all claims prior to dissemination; unverifiable underselling claims should be avoided.

k. Price equaling, meeting competitors' prices

Advertisements which set out company policy of matching or bettering competitors' prices may be used, provided the terms of the offer are specific and in good faith and provided the terms of the offer are not unrealistic or unreasonable. Advertisers should be aware that such claims can create an implicit obligation to adjust prices generally for specific merchandise upon a showing that the advertiser's price for that merchandise is not as low as or lower than a competitor's, in order to preserve the accuracy of the advertised claims.

An advertisement which expresses a policy of matching or bettering competitors' prices should conspicuously and fully disclose any material and significant conditions which apply and specify what evidence a consumer must present to take advantage of the offer. Such evidence should not place an unrealistic or unreasonable burden on the consumer.

2. "Free"

a. The word "free" may be used in advertising whenever the advertiser is offering an unconditional gift. If receipt of the "free" merchandise or service is conditional on a purchase:

—the advertiser must disclose this condition clearly and conspicuously together with the "free" offer (not by placing an asterisk or symbol next to "free" and referring to the condition(s) in a footnote);
—the normal price of the merchandise or service to be purchased must not have been increased nor its quantity or quality reduced; and
—the "free" offer must be temporary; otherwise, it would become a continuous combination offer, no part of which is free.

b. In a negotiated sale no "free" offer of another product or service should be made where:

(1) the product or service to be purchased usually is sold at a price arrived at through bargaining, rather than at a regular price; or
(2) there may be a regular price but other material factors such as quantity, quality or size are arrived at through bargaining.

3. "Cents-off" Sales

The principles stated in the standard dealing with "free" should be followed in the advertising of "cents-off" sales.

4. Trade-in Allowances

Any advertised trade-in allowance should be an amount deducted from the advertiser's current selling price without a trade-in. That selling price must be clearly disclosed in the advertisement. It is misleading to offer a fixed and arbitrary allowance regardless of the size, type, age, condition, or value of the article traded in, for the purpose of disguising the true retail price or creating the false impression that a reduced price or a special price is obtainable only by such trade-in.

5. Credit

Whenever a specific credit term is advertised, it should be available to all respondents unless qualified as to respondents' credit acceptability. All credit terms must be clearly and conspicuously disclosed in the advertisement, as required by the federal Truth in Lending Act and applicable state laws.

The Truth in Lending Act and Regulation Z which implements the Act, as well as Regulation M which covers consumer leasing, contain important provisions that affect any advertising to aid or promote the extension of consumer credit and should be carefully reviewed by every advertiser.

a. Open-end credit

The requirements for advertising open-end credit under Regulation Z are complex. Therefore, advertisers are advised to consult Section 226.16 of the Regulation for details on terms triggering disclosure, prescribed terminology and information that must be disclosed.

b. Closed-end credit

Advertisers are advised to consult Section 226.24 of Regulation Z for details of closed-end credit advertising.

If an advertisement of closed-end credit contains any of the following triggering terms, three specific disclosures must also be stated, clearly and conspicuously. The *triggering* terms are:

(1) the amount or percentage of any downpayment;
(2) the number of payments or period of repayment;
(3) the amount of any payment, expressed either as a percentage or as a dollar amount; or
(4) the amount of any finance charge.

The three *disclosures* are:

(1) the amount or percentage of the downpayment;
(2) the terms of repayment; and
(3) the "annual percentage rate," using that term spelled out in full. If the rate may be increased after consummation of the credit transaction, that fact must be disclosed.

c. "Easy credit," "liberal terms"

The terms "easy credit," "easy credit terms," "liberal terms," "easy pay plan" and other similar phrases relate to credit worthiness as well as to the terms of sale and credit repayment, and should be used only when:

(1) consumer credit is extended to persons whose ability to pay or credit rating is below typical standards of credit worthiness;

(2) the finance charges and annual percentage rate do not exceed those charged to persons whose credit rating has been determined and who meet generally accepted standards of credit worthiness;

(3) the down payment is as low and the period of repayment of the same duration as in consumer credit extensions to those of previously determined credit worthiness; and

(4) the debtor is dealt with fairly on all conditions of the transaction including the consequences of a delayed or missed payment.

d. "No credit rejected"

The words "no credit rejected" or words of similar import should not be used unless true, since they imply that consumer credit will be extended to anyone regardless of the person's credit worthiness or financial ability to pay.

6. Extra Charges

Whenever a price is mentioned in advertising, any extra charges should also be disclosed in immediate conjunction with the price (e.g., delivery, installation, assembly, excise tax, postage and handling).

7. Bait Advertising and Selling

A "bait" offer is an alluring but insincere offer to sell a product or service which the advertiser does not intend to sell. Its purpose is to switch consumers from buying the advertised merchandise or service, in order to sell something else, usually at a higher price or on a basis more advantageous to the advertiser.

a. No advertisement should be published unless it is a bona fide offer to sell the advertised merchandise or service.

b. The advertising should not create a false impression about the product or service being offered in order to lay the foundation for a later "switch" to other, more expensive products or services, or products of a lesser quality at the same price.

c. Subsequent full disclosure by the advertiser of all other facts about the advertised article does not preclude the existence of a bait scheme.

d. An advertiser should not use nor permit the use of the following bait scheme practices:

—refusing to show or demonstrate the advertised merchandise or service;

—disparaging the advertised merchandise or service, its warranty, availability, services and parts, credit terms, etc.;

—selling the advertised merchandise or service and thereafter "unselling" the customer to make a switch to other merchandise or service;

—refusing to take orders for the advertised merchandise or service or to deliver it within a reasonable time;

—demonstrating or showing a defective sample of the advertised merchandise; or,

—having a sales compensation plan designed to penalize salespersons who sell the advertised merchandise or service.

e. An advertiser should have on hand a sufficient quantity of advertised merchandise to meet reasonably anticipated demands, unless the advertisement discloses the number of items available or states "while supplies last." If items are available only at certain branches, their specific locations should be disclosed. The use of "rainchecks" is no justification for inadequate estimates of reasonably anticipated demand.

f. Actual sales of the advertised merchandise or service may not preclude the existence of a bait scheme since this may be merely an attempt to create an aura of legitimacy. A key factor in determining the existence of "bait" is the number of times the merchandise or service was advertised compared to the number of actual sales of the merchandise or service.

8. Warranties (or Guarantees)

a. When the term "warranty" (or "guarantee") is used in product advertising, the following disclosure should be made clearly and prominently:

a statement that the complete details of the warranty can be seen at the advertiser's store prior to sale, or in the case of mail or telephone order sales, are available free on written request.

b. (1) "satisfaction guarantee," "money back guarantee," "free trial offer," or similar representations should be used in advertising only if the seller or manufacturer refunds the full purchase price of the advertised product at the purchaser's request.

(2) When "satisfaction guarantee" or similar representations are used in advertising, any material limitations or conditions that apply to the guarantee should be clearly and prominently disclosed.

c. When the term "lifetime," "life" or similar representations are used in advertising to describe the duration of the warranty or guarantee, the advertisement should clearly and prominently disclose the life to which the representation refers.

d. Sellers or manufacturers should advertise that a product is warranted or guaranteed only if the seller or manufacturer promptly and fully performs its obligations under the warranty or guarantee.

e. Advertisers should make certain that any advertising of warranties complies with the Consumer Products Warranty Act, effective July 4, 1975, relevant Federal Trade Commission requirements and any applicable state and local laws.

9. Layout and Illustrations

The composition and layout of advertisements should be such as to minimize the possibility of misunderstanding by the reader. For example, prices, illustrations, or descriptions should not be so placed in an advertisement as to give the impression that the price or terms of featured merchandise apply to other merchandise in the advertisement when such is not the fact. An advertisement should not be used which features merchandise at a price or terms boldly displayed, together with illustrations of higher-priced merchandise, so arranged as to give the impression that the lower price or more favorable terms apply to the other merchandise, when such is not the fact.

10. Asterisks

An asterisk may be used to impart additional information about a word or term which is not in itself inherently deceptive. The asterisk or other reference symbol should not be used as a means of contradicting or substantially changing the meaning of any advertising statement. Information referenced by asterisks should be clearly and prominently disclosed.

11. Abbreviations

Commonly known abbreviations may be used in advertising. However, abbreviations not generally known to or understood by the general public should be avoided.

For example, "deliv. extra" is understood to mean that there is an extra charge for delivery of the merchandise. "New Battery, $25 W.T.," is not generally understood to mean "with trade-in."

12. Use or Condition Disclosures

a. Used, secondhand, etc.

A product previously used by a consumer should be clearly and conspicuously described as such, e.g., "used," "secondhand," "pre-owned," "repossessed," "rebuilt," "reconditioned."

b. Rebuilt, reconditioned

(1) The term "rebuilt" should be used only to describe products that have been completely disassembled, reconstructed, repaired and refinished, including replacement of parts.
(2) The term "reconditioned" should be used only to describe products that have received such repairs, adjustments or finishing as were necessary to put the product in satisfactory condition without rebuilding.

c. "As is"

When merchandise is offered on an "as is" basis, i.e., in the condition in which it is displayed at the place of sale, the words "as is" should be indicated in any advertising and on the bill of sale. An advertiser also may describe the condition of the merchandise if so desired.

d. Second, irregular, imperfect

If merchandise is defective or rejected by the manufacturer because it falls below specifications, it should be advertised by terms such as "second," "irregular," or "imperfect."

e. "Discontinued"

Merchandise should not be described as "discontinued," "discontinued model," or by words of similar import unless the manufacturer has, in fact, discontinued its manufacture, or the retail advertiser will discontinue offering it entirely after clearance of existing inventories. If discontinuance is only by the retailer, the advertising should indicate that fact, e.g., "we are discontinuing stocking these items."

13. Superiority Claims-Comparatives-Disparagement

a. Truthful comparisons using factual information may help consumers make informed buying decisions, provided:

(1) all representations are consistent with the general rules and prohibitions against false and deceptive advertising;
(2) all comparisons that claim or imply, unqualifiedly, superiority to competitive products or services are not based on a selected or limited list of characteristics in which the advertiser excels while ignoring those in which the competitors excel;
(3) the advertisement clearly discloses any material or significant limitations of the comparison; and
(4) the advertiser can substantiate all claims made.

b. Advertising which deceptively or falsely disparages a competitor or competing products or services should not be used.

14. Superlative Claims-Puffery

Superlative statements, like other advertising claims, are objective (factual) or subjective (puffery):

—objective claims relate to tangible qualities and performance values of a product or service which can be measured against accepted standards or tests. As statements of fact, such claims can be proved or disproved and the advertiser should possess substantiation.
—subjective claims are expressions of opinion or personal evaluation of the intangible qualities of a product or service. Individual opinions, statements of corporate pride and promises may sometimes be considered puffery and not subject to test of their truth and accuracy. Subjective superlatives which tend to mislead should be avoided.

15. Testimonials and Endorsements

In general, advertising which uses testimonials or endorsements is likely to mislead or confuse if:

—it is not genuine and does not actually represent the current opinion of the endorser;
—it is not quoted in its entirety, thereby altering its overall meaning and impact;
—it contains representations or statements which would be misleading if otherwise used in advertising;
—while literally true, it creates deceptive implications;
—the endorser is not competent or sufficiently qualified to express an opinion concerning the quality of the product or service being advertised or the results likely to be achieved by its use;
—it is not clearly stated that the endorser, associated with some well-known and highly-regarded institution, is speaking only in a personal capacity, and not on behalf of such an institution, if such be the fact;
—broad claims are made as to endorsements or approval by indefinitely large or vague groups, e.g., "the homeowners of America," "the doctors of America";
—an endorser has a pecuniary interest in the company whose product or service is endorsed and this is not made known in the advertisement.

Advertisers should consult Federal Trade Commission Guides on Testimonials and Endorsements for detailed guidance.

16. Rebate

"The terms "rebate," "cash rebate," or similar terms may be used only when payment of money will be made by the retailer or manufacturer to a purchaser after the sale, and the advertising should make clear who is making the payment.

17. Company Name or Trade Style

No words should be used in a company name or trade style which would mislead the public either directly or by implication. For example, the words "factory" or "manufacturer" should not be used in a company name unless the advertiser actually owns and operates or directly and absolutely controls the manufacturing facility that produces the advertised products. Similarly, the term "wholesale" or "wholesaler" should not be used in a company name unless the advertiser actually owns and operates or directly and absolutely controls a wholesale or distribution facility which primarily sells products to retailers for resale.

18. Contests and Games of Chance

a. If contests are used, the advertiser should publish clear, complete and concise rules and provide competent impartial judges to determine the winners.

b. No contest, drawing or other game of chance that involves the three elements of prize, chance and consideration should be conducted since it constitutes a lottery and is in violation of federal statutes.

c. The Federal Trade Commission has rendered various decisions on contests and games of chance relating to disclosure of the number of prizes to be awarded and the odds of winning each prize, and issued a trade regulation rule for games of chance in the food retailing and gasoline industries. Advertisers should make certain any contest conforms to FTC requirements as well as any applicable local and state laws.

19. Claimed Results

Claims as to energy savings, performance, safety, efficacy, results, etc. which will be obtained by or realized from a particular product or service should be based on recent and competent scientific, engineering or other objective data.

20. Unassembled Merchandise

When advertised merchandise requires partial or complete assembly by the purchaser, the advertising should disclose that fact, e.g., "unassembled," "partial assembly required."

Appendix 5D
Excerpts from *ABC Advertising Standards and Guidelines*

Topic Coverage: Advertising Practices, Specific Products, Special Audiences, or Markets

Advocacy advertising

Alcoholic beverages

Animals

Arthritis and rheumatism

Astrology

Bait-switch advertising

Banking services

Bartender guides

Bathroom tissue

Beer and wine

Betting

Billboards

Body and foot odor products

Bonds

Cable programming

Calmatives

Candidates for public office

Candy, snacks, gums, soft drinks

Casinos

Catamenial devices

Character reading

Charity

Children's advertising

Cholesterol

Claim substantiation

Clinical studies

Coins

Comparative advertising

Comparative claims based on testing

Consecutive announcements

Consideration

Contests

Controversial issues

Taken from *ABC Advertising Standards and Guidelines*, New York: American Broadcasting Company, December 1983 (excerpted from index).

Criminal activities

Currency and coins

Diet foods and regimen

Distillers and distributors of hard liquor

Documentation

Douche products

Dramatizations and recreations

Drugs

Emergency techniques, simulation of

Endorsements

Endorsement questionnaire

Energy

Exhortative language

Feature films

Feminine hygiene

Financial advertising

Firearms

Fireworks

Flag

Food

Food supplements

Fortune-telling

"Free"

Gambling

Games of chance

Genital odor products

Government action

Guarantees

Hard liquor

Heads of state and other officials

Health-related professionals

Hemorrhoidal products

Hypnotism

Incontinence products

Indirect advertising

Insurance

Laboratory testing

Laxatives and binders

Liquor advertising

Liquor, use of

Lotteries

Mail order (medical products)

Market research

Medical products

Menses-related products

Military uniforms or vehicles

Mind reading

Mixer products

Monadic testing

Money, use of

Motion picture footage

Mouth or denture odor

Multiple product announcements

National buildings and monuments

News, simulation of

Numerology

Nutrition

Occultism

Offers

Off-track betting

On-camera ingestion of pills

Palm reading

Patriotic music

Perception testing

Personal products

Personal nonprescription
    medications

"Persons in white"

Pet foods

Phrenology

Pregnancy test kits

Premiums

Prescription products

Price and value claims

Price comparisons

Privacy and publicity rights

Product availability

Professional advertising, medical

Professional advertising, legal

Public symbols

Racetracks

Real estate

Reenactments

Religious time

Research

"Safe"

Safety

Sample size

Separator devices

Simulation

Sleeping aids

Solicitation of funds

Sponsor identification

Stimulants

Stocks

Subliminal perception

Superiority claims

Surveys

Sweepstakes

Tags

Talent commercials

Test designs

Tobacco

Toys

Trade name identification

Undergarments

Visual supers

Vitamins

Warranties

Weight reduction and control

Wine

Appendix 5E
Excerpts from *CBS Radio and Television Network Advertising Guidelines*

Topic Coverage: Advertising Practices, Specific Products, Special Audiences, or Markets

All of these categories include details similar to those listed for ABC, but the CBS document does not provide such a comprehensive index.

Advertising claims

Advocacy and political advertising

Alcoholic beverages

Betting and gambling

Billboards

Child-directed advertising

Health-related advertising

Comparative advertising

Contests and sweepstakes

Mail orders

Motion pictures

News simulation

Over-the-counter medical products

Taken from CBS Radio and Television Network Advertising Guidelines, New York: CBS Television Network, undated. (Excerpted from the table of contents. These excerpts are condensed and are not direct quotations of the entire Table of Contents of CBS documents). The CBS Radio and Television Guidelines are subject to CBS's sole interpretation and may be subject to change from time to time. Thus the CBS Radio and Television Guidelines may not reflect current CBS practices, interpretation, or policy.

Personal products

Premiums and offers

Prescription drugs

Price information

Professional advertising

Public service announcements

Resubmission of previously approved commercial after hiatus of six months or more

Sound effects

Testimonials

Time standards

Unacceptable products and services

Weight reduction

Appendix 5F
Excerpts from *NBC Broadcast Standards for Television: Advertising Guidelines*

Topic Coverage: Advertising Practices for Product Categories and Special Audiences or Markets

Alcohol products

Betting

Children's advertising (including general standards and specifically toys, premiums and offers, food, feature film "trailers," sweepstakes and adult-oriented commercials

Control of serum cholesterol

Gambling

Games of chance

Health care products

Lotteries

Personal products

Weight reduction and control

Appendix 5G
Excerpts from *IBA Code of Advertising Standards and Practice*

Topic Coverage: Advertising Practices, Specific Products, Special Audiences, or Markets

Actors

Advertising and children

Advertising of medicines and treatments

Advisory services

Alcohol, products to mask the effect of

Alcoholic drinks

Alcoholism, products for the treatment of

Analgesics

"Bait" advertising

Banks and licensed institutions

Behavior, good manners and

Betting and betting tips

Breath-testing devices

Burial

Cartoon characters and puppets

Caustic substances

Celebrities, advertisements by

Charities

Child audience, The

Child in advertisements, The

Children, advertising and

Children as presenters

Children, safety of

Cigarette advertising

Claims, descriptions and

Claims, exaggerated or misleading

Clubs, children's

Clubs, correspondence

Collecting schemes

Colleges

Commodity investment

Comparisons

Taken from *The IBA Code of Advertising Standards and Practice,* London: Independent Broadcasting Authority, May 1981 (excerpted from index).

Competitions

Contact lenses

Contraceptives

Credit

Cure, claims to

Death

Debentures, shares and

Denigration

Dental hygiene

Dentists

Diagnosis by correspondence

Direct sale advertising

Disinfectants, antiseptics

Doctors

Drinking and driving

Employment, conditions of

Employment services, registers or bureaus (unlicensed)

Exaggerated claims

Excessive use of products

Family planning services

Fear, appeals to

Fétes

Financial advertising

Financial information

Fires, open

Flag days

Fortune tellers

"Free," use of the word

Free gifts

Friendly Societies

Gas

Gifts or prizes

Good manners and behavior

Good taste

Government stocks, British

Government stocks, local

Guarantees

Hemorrhoids, products for the treatment of

Hire purchase

Homework schemes

House Purchase and Housing Act

Hypnosis

Identification of advertisements

Illustrations

Imitation

Industrial disputes

Inertia selling

Instructional courses

Insurance

Insurance companies

Interest

Investment, commodity

Investment and savings

Lending and credit

Local government advertisements

Lotteries and amusements

Mail order advertising

Mains-powered appliances

Manners

Matches

Matrimonial agencies

Mechanical appliances

Medical attention

Medical conditions

Medical statements, trials and tests

Medicines and treatments, advertising of

Midwives

Misleading claims

Money-back offers

Nationalized industries

"News Flash"

Nurses

Paraffin

Petrol

Pharmaceutical chemists

Photography

Polishes, floor and furniture

Politics

Political end

Pools

Prescriptions or treatment by correspondence

Pregnancy testing services

Premium bonds

Price claims

Prices

Private investigation agencies

Prizes or gifts

Professional advice, avoidance of impression

Professional recommendation

Prospectuses

Psychology, psychoanalysis, or psychiatry

Religion

Religious end

Reproduction techniques

Safety, contributions to

Savings and investments

Savings certificates

Scientific terms and statistics

Shares and debentures

Slimming treatments

Smoking cures

Special claims

Special techniques, the use of

Statistics, scientific terms and

Stock exchanges

Street scenes

Stridency

Subliminal advertising

Substitute materials, the use of

Superstition

"Switch selling"

Tax benefits

Appendix 5H
Excerpts from *British Code of Advertising Practice*

Topic Coverage: Advertising Practices, Specific Products, Special Audiences, or Markets

Abortion counseling

Actors

Addictions

Adolescents

Aerial advertisements

Ageing

Agricultural machines

Alcohol

Anesthesia

Anthroposophic remedies

Antiseptics

Antisocial behavior

Appeals for funds

Appetite depressants

Appliances for self-treatment

Approval, goods on

Arthritis

Athletes

Availability of products

Baldness

Bath additives

Bath essences

Bespoke goods

Betting tipsters

Biochemic remedies

Breath test products

Brochures

Business opportunities

Calories in balanced diet

Cancer

Cataract

Caustic substances

Cellulite

Charitable appeals

Taken from the *British Code of Advertising Practice*, seventh edition. London: October 1985 (excerpted from index).

Sportsmen

Statutory notices

Sterilization

Substantiation of claims

Sunburn: preventing

Suntan: promoting

Sweeteners, nonsugar

Switch selling

Telephone calls

Testimonials

Tiredness, chronic

Tobacco

Toiletries

Tranquilizing

Truthful presentation

Tuberculosis

Turkish baths

Unit trusts

Unsolicited home visits

Vasectomy

Venereal disease

Vibrator machines

Videocassette commercials

Viewdata services

Violence, condoning or inciting

Vitamins

Vocational training

Weight control and loss

Wrappers

Young people

6
An Assessment of Performance: The United States

Introduction

This chapter is the first of two that are devoted to assessing the performance of the U.S. and British systems of advertising self-regulation. This chapter provides the framework for assessing performance and assesses the U.S. system. Chapter 7 assesses the British system, and Chapter 8 provides a comparative assessment of the two systems and the conclusions and recommendations that flow from the entire analysis.

General Effects of Advertising Self-Regulation

"The real test of self-regulatory consumer-oriented programs is not the extent to which they purport to solve consumer problems but the way they do so in reality" (Feldman 1980, 224). There are considerable differences of opinion between sellers and consumers on this matter, because consumer problems are difficult to define and to measure, whether they will be (or are being) resolved by the numerous programs proposed or implemented.

The basic requirements for effective advertising self-regulation to emerge and achieve success are the following:

1. . . . awareness of the existence of a common problem, and the conviction that it is serious enough to warrant some attention.
2. . . . motivation . . . being willing to take the initiative in providing a solution . . . [especially] the threat of government intervention.
3. . . . the ability to exercise effective sanctions against sellers who deviate from agreed upon standards of behavior (Feldman 1980, 218–219).

The first two of these requirements were recognized long ago by the advertising business in both the United Kingdom and the United States.

Most agree that the third requirement has been met in the United Kingdom by the (ASA/CAP) Committee system. But opinion differs as to whether it has been met by the (NAD/NARB/CARU). There is also controversy as to how to define what is meant by effective sanctions and how to assess their effectiveness.

Instead of discussing only these requirements for an effective self-regulatory system, it also seems appropriate to examine whether or to what extent the British and the U.S. systems accomplish appropriate goals.

Ultimately the performance of a system of advertising self-regulation must be measured against the goals of society. As a beginning, several categories of possible effects of advertising regulation on society can be identified:

1. *Direct societal effects* (for example, consumers make fewer "purchasing errors" based on erroneous information or impressions; consumers are not offended; competitors are not injured).
2. *Spillover or third-party effects* (for example, advertisers and agencies learn from past cases and improve future messages).
3. *Market efficiency effects* (for example, free flow of accurate information in the marketplace; improved acceptance of advertising and increased effectiveness and lower cost per message effect).
4. *Political and social effects* (for example, fewer laws, less administrative agency activity, fewer court cases, all of which translate into lower costs for society, both government and business) (Italicized words are from Miller and Hutt 1983, 365. The examples have been added).

The complex task to measure these effects requires at least a two-stage evaluation: first, to measure whether the self-regulatory system causes changes in advertising practices; and second, to measure whether these changes contribute to achieving the goals of society. The measurement problems associated with such evaluations seem insurmountable at this time; needed information is too meager to achieve this "ideal." Nevertheless, it is useful to keep the goals of society in mind to guide the thinking of those who would in the future go beyond the measures of performance that have been employed in the currently available literature on this subject.

One can get a sense of the difficulty in measuring the effects and performance of an advertising self-regulatory system by noting the reasons why self-regulation does *not* work to perfection in the United States:

1. TV advertising is intrusive, and the TV medium reaches a heterogeneous audience of all ages, all educational levels, all religions, all

regional and ethnic groups, etc. It is often impossible for a commercial to speak openly and constructively to a major portion of a TV program's audience without seeming inappropriate, boring, or even offensive to another segment of this same program's audience.

2. Self-regulation by any one of the three interrelated components of the advertising industry (advertisers, agencies, media) can become regulation of one or both of the other industries. For example, if a TV network were to push its self-regulation to extremes, it could emasculate TV commercials of any interest or value for the consumer, and as a consequence, for the advertisers using these commercials. Thus, a network must pursue its concept of "acceptable" commercials with due regard for the legitimate needs of advertiser, agency, and consumer. The interplay of self-regulatory efforts, which become regulatory efforts to a second party, seeks perfect balance, but does not always find it.

3. Self-regulation, carried to a well-intentioned but misguided extreme, could become restraint of trade . . . the self-regulatory process often falls short of perfection because of the difficulty of achieving optimal results without restraining trade.

4. Self-regulation is most enthusiastically practiced by advertisers who believe that high standards of integrity benefit their businesses. Self-regulation is less enthusiastically practiced, or not practiced at all, by advertisers who do not care about the integrity of their advertising. Consumers cannot easily separate one group of advertisers from the other.

5. If the industry were to try to regulate taste in advertising, it would seriously interfere with the advertiser's rights of free speech. The public tends to be highly pragmatic, not philosophic; it believes in free speech but does not consider the trade-offs which the exercise of this great freedom may entail. Clearly, false and misleading advertising has no First Amendment protection [in the United States]. Absent that question, the values of free speech are argued in many areas and contexts. . . . While private restraints may not violate the constitution, they certainly present serious questions.

6. In our [U.S.] free economy, only very harmful products are barred from the marketplace—or allowed to be sold only under governmentally prescribed restrictions (e.g., certain drugs, products containing dangerous chemicals, etc.) But some people regard certain lawful products as undesirable and contend that they should not be advertised—or should not be advertised on television (e.g., snack foods, products which require large amounts of energy in their production or use, etc.). The NARB has no authority to pass on such disputes—and would have no basis for doing so (*Advertising Self-Regulation and its Interaction with Consumers 1979, 7–9*).

These complex conditions must cause one to have only modest expectations for the performance of advertising self-regulation. There have, however, been some attempts to assess the performance of advertising self-regulatory systems, as we also discuss. But the evidence is far from definitive.

Moreoever, one cannot assess the performance of a self-regulatory system adequately unless one also is able to assess the performance of existing government regulation of advertising. The two are interrelated in that self-regulation usually complements whatever minimum standards are set by legal controls. The greater the degree to which the legal system is concerned with advertising, the smaller the role for self-regulation and vice versa. This point is critical in understanding the differences between the U.S. and British systems; government involvement in controlling improper advertising in the United Kingdom is relatively less than in the United States, and the British self-regulatory system therefore has a larger potential mission.

We should note at this point that government regulation of advertising often is considered to be superior to self-regulation, not because government officials and legislators inherently make better decisions on what is best for society, but rather because the law and its application are *presumed* to be unbiased and to represent the interests of society; moreover, government has greater power to enforce preventive, remedial, or punitive sanctions. Little real evidence, however, supports these widely accepted presumptions.

Although a complete analysis of self-regulation cannot be made without comparing its performance to that of government regulation, we can nevertheless take our analysis to the point at which such a comparison might be made in the future.

Objectives of Advertising Self-Regulation

Self-regulation of advertising should accomplish two broad objectives:

1. To protect consumers against misleading advertising, unscrupulous advertising practices, excessive intrusion or invasion of privacy, and offensive messages, and

2. To protect the advertiser against unfair practices by competitors (Neelankavil and Stridsberg 1980).

The basic principles of the ICC take us a step further in specificity, requiring that

1. All advertising should be legal, decent, honest and truthful.

2. Every advertisement should be prepared with a due sense of social responsibility and should conform to the principles of fair competition, as generally accepted in business, and

3. No advertisement should be such as to impair public confidence in advertising (*International Code of Advertising Practice* 1982).

To these we add that one of the necessary conditions for an economy to operate efficiently and in the best interests of society is that buyers and sellers should have truthful and accurate information to make buying and selling decisions. Therefore it seems sensible to expect advertising to contribute to the ability of consumers to make informed choices under conditions of effective competition, thus facilitating the efficient allocation of resources so that needed products and services are produced. If advertising contributes to the free flow of accurate information, it contributes to the efficient matching of supply and demand. Therefore a logical test of an advertising self-regulatory system is whether it contributes to truth and accuracy in advertising.

Neelankavil and Stridsberg (1980) go beyond these objectives and identify four specific tasks that a self-regulatory system should carry out:

1. Setting standards for the advertising industry that will bear the scrutiny of outside observers, whether friendly or hostile.
2. Anticipating and resolving issues before they develop into public controversies that may erode confidence in the industry.
3. Providing an objective structure and procedures to arbitrate commercial disputes over advertising content and technique.
4. Providing prompt, swift, and objective resolution of consumer or public-interest complaints (Neelankavil and Stridsberg 1980, 4).

Neelankavil and Stridsberg then go on to refine these criteria by pointing out that public support is important to the success of a self-regulatory system, that such public support depends in large part on the reputation for independence from special interests, and that elements that contribute to the reputation for such independence include the following:

1. *Accessibility.* The staff is easily available and willing to listen and examine the merits of complaints against the provisions of its code.
2. *Objectivity.* Complaints are received and examined without bias about their source or probable impact if decisions unfavorable to advertisers are reached.
3. *Prompt action and due course.* From country to country, the pace of self-regulation differs markedly because of differences in each country's "style" of doing business. A general criticism that emerges from field reports is the excessive delays in many countries in getting self-regulatory actions initiated, processed, and settled; the same criticism is leveled at government regulation. Both complainants and

advertisers under scrutiny want assurance that the process is moving forward; they also want to have some firm idea of when it will be completed. Excessive speed can lay self-regulation open to criticism of "whitewash," but excessive and unpredictable delay—"foot dragging"—clearly undermines public and business confidence in the effectiveness of procedure. In self-regulatory bodies as well as before courts of law, "justice delayed is justice denied."

4. *Thoroughness.* Significantly, this requires not only participants who are hard working and willing to "go the extra mile" but also a high level of professional competence.

5. *Feedback.* The playback of what is happening and what is being accomplished appears essential. The IAA survey indicates great variance, from country to country, in the willingness to provide feedback, whether to the general marketing community or to the public at large. This appears to be related to cultural factors and to strong feelings at managerial levels about the right to operate in privacy.

6. *Accountability.* A self-regulatory organization must be prepared to take the consequences of its actions, whether they produce blame or praise. It must be responsible and display its responsibility by accounting for its activities to all its audiences (Neelankavil and Stridsberg 1980, 17–18).

These objectives, tasks, and criteria can be met effectively if a system has the following characteristics:

1. A clear code or set of standards, judged by all concerned to be adequate, and adhered to by the advertising industry.

2. A code or set of standards that is known to consumers, competitors, media, or any others who may wish to report infractions, with arrangements to make it cheap and easy to complain.

3. An efficient system to monitor advertising and to receive and handle complaints, and an adequate budget and staff to investigate and adjudicate breaches of the code or standards.

4. Effective sanctions (derived from the text of *Self-Regulation Codes of Practice* 1983).

In the remainder of this chapter we evaluate the U.S. system of advertising self-regulation according to these criteria.

The United States: The NAD/NARB System

Objectives of U.S. Self-Regulation of Advertising

Because we have discussed already the specific objectives and goals of the NAD/NARB/CARU, as well as those of the television networks regarding advertising control, we do not enumerate them again. It is sufficient at this point to keep in mind that the NAD/NARB system has the main objective to improve truth and accuracy in advertising. Each of the television networks has a similar objective; but in addition they desire to control advertising regarding matters of taste and decency, in accordance with their perception of prevailing social norms.

The NAD/NARB and the television networks concentrate their efforts on advertisers and advertising agencies to accomplish their "truth and accuracy" objectives. They do so by the previously mentioned activities such as publishing *NAD Case Reports*, issuing press releases on policies, making speeches to advertising industry audiences, and establishing special panels to commission research and publishing the results for use by the advertising industry. Many of the activities of the CBBB and the local BBBs are supportive of or coordinated with the NAD/NARB activities, such as publishing *Do's and Don'ts in Advertising Copy*, establishing LARPs, handling local complaints, and forwarding complaints about national advertising to the NAD when appropriate. However, the NAD/NARB has *not* had the objective to become well known to the public, and the NAD/NARB has *not* sought through direct consumer advertising and publicity to achieve high public visibility nor solicited as many complaints as possible from consumers. Likewise, little effort has been made to communicate directly and regularly with consumer groups.

However, the system routinely distributes more than 6000 of the monthly *NAD Case Reports*, including about 800 to "working media," 2500 to interested persons (for example, educators and executives with advertisers, agencies, media, or other organizations), and the remainder to corporate members of the CBBB, the ANA and the AAAA, as well as bulk mailings to AAF clubs and various institutes such as the Institute of Food Technologists and the Society of Cosmetic Chemists. The NAD does not send the *Case Reports* to individual consumers unless they have a business address.

The system also issues press releases and publishes other reports from time to time. NAD/NARB/CARU/CBBB officials make presentations regularly to industry groups and other organizations. Some of the trade press, such as *Advertising Age*, report regularly on these matters, but the public media rarely do. It appears as if those who decide what to report in the mass media must believe that consumers are not interested in the activities of the NAD/NARB/CARU. Thus, the "problem" of consumer ignorance of these matters "rests not so much in distribution of information to the media, but the failure of the media to communicate it to the public" (Feldman 1980, 227). Nevertheless, the NAD/NARB has no budget to advertise its work to consumers, nor does it seek donations of talent to prepare such advertising or time or space from the media to run such advertising.

It is necessarily difficult to assess whether the NAD/NARB broad objectives are being accomplished. As a start, it can be argued that the

NAD/NARB/CARU and the television networks are at least minimally successful in accomplishing their objectives if (1) members of society, especially consumers and business firms, are reasonably satisfied; and (2) the control systems remain sufficiently flexible to adapt to changing standards of truth, accuracy, taste, and decency so that society and government continue to be reasonably satisfied.

We first review the existing information to evaluate the self-regulatory systems; then we present our own analysis of available data to assess the performance of the systems against objectives. The main focus of this assessment must necessarily be the NAD/NARB/CARU system, because relatively less information is available on the television network systems.

In the United States the first self-regulatory line of defense against inappropriate advertising in society includes standards and codes self-imposed by advertisers, advertising agencies, individual media, advertising associations, media associations, and trade associations. All of these, of course, have a responsibility to society as well as to themselves to prepare and publish advertising that conforms to existing codes and appropriate standards. However, most of these organizations do not have extensive facilities or staff to preclear advertisements or to handle large numbers of inquiries and complaints. The major exceptions are the three television networks: ABC, CBS, and NBC. Each has a fairly comprehensive set of standards and guidelines, and each network preclears all commercials before allowing them to be aired. Their standards undergo almost constant review and adaptation according to their experience, as a means of remaining in harmony with the ever-changing norms and standards of consumers and those who represent consumer interests.

Little literature attempts to evaluate the "social" performance of individual advertisers, advertising agencies, media, and the television networks. It is clear that they have a self-interest in maintaining standards and their individual reputations such that sales of products and services are maintained at a satisfactory level. They also have a self-interest in "being seen" by consumers and by government as doing an adequate job so that government does not feel compelled to become more deeply involved in regulating advertising.

The major television network preclearance of many thousands of commercials each year seems to be effective if the small number of complaints received after commercials are run is used as a criterion. Although this criterion is imperfect, it is the only information available from networks that gives us an idea of the magnitude of consumer discontent[1] with television commercials. One might argue that even if consumers are not entirely pleased with all television advertising, at least they are rarely so unhappy that they are motivated to complain seriously about specific television commercials. We know, for example, that "of the more than

20,000 commercials given final approval last year [by ABC], less than one-half of one percent were challenged and of those challenged less than two in ten required modification or withdrawal. . . . Last year ABC received nearly a quarter million letters and phone calls. Less than two-tenths of one percent concerned commercials and of those the vast majority concerned issues of taste, mostly involving personal hygiene products, and not whether commercials were false, misleading or deceptive" (Dzodin 1986, 27). There is no reason to believe that the experiences of CBS and NBC are substantially different from that of ABC, and we may conclude that the networks are therefore at least minimally successful in that consumers and business are reasonably satisfied. Nevertheless, because the number of consumer complaints is not an adequate criterion to measure consumer dissatisfaction, more research needs to be done to determine precisely the actual level of consumer satisfaction or dissatisfaction with advertising.

Critics can argue that consumers are not able to see through some of the false, deceptive, or misleading advertising that they (the critics) can identify. Therefore one can argue that consumers need additional protection beyond these first lines of defense. Generally, major advertisers, agencies, and media agree partly with the critics—to the extent that consumers need protection from a few small (and usually local) unscrupulous advertisers and occasionally from borderline offenses of major advertisers.

The NAD/NARB/CARU system for handling complaints against national advertising is almost unknown to the U.S. consuming public. However, the great majority of consumers are aware of the existence and general purposes of the approximately 170 BBBs located throughout the United States. Nationwide, we estimate that the BBBs handle perhaps 10,000 complaints each year about advertising, although precise statistics on the operations of these "local" offices are not available. Moreover, most of the fifty state governments have a Consumer Protection Division, which works closely with the BBBs and other organizations, including the FTC and other federal agencies. If other states are similar to Michigan— which, as mentioned earlier, handles nearly 10,000 intrastate complaints about advertising each year, but has less than four percent of the nation's population—it may be that the number of advertising complaints handled by state governments through the United States is large, perhaps more than 100,000 per year. The role of self-regulatory bodies is relatively small compared with the role of government bodies.

The NAD/NARB/CARU/BBB/LARP system is the last line of defense in the self-regulatory system in the United States. Because advertising has already been deemed acceptable by those in the first lines of defense just mentioned, the BBBs and the NAD/NARB must deal with the toughest cases, which are often borderline or complex. It is not surprising that the number of these relatively difficult cases is not large, because most advertisers, agencies, and media realize that it is in their best interests to maintain at least some standards. It is also not surprising that relatively more advertisers than consumers complain. Advertisers are highly motivated to protect themselves against anything done by competitors that they perceive to be unfair to their interests, and they probably are relatively more sophisticated than consumers in identifying genuinely unacceptable advertising when they see it. The normal processes of competition involve monitoring competitor's campaigns, including identifying unacceptable advertising, especially if they believe it harms them directly.

With that background, we now examine the performance of the NAD/NARB system[2] in greater detail. The material in this section is drawn primarily from *NAD Case Reports* and other information published by the NAD/NARB. We use NAD/NARB factual data and published policy statements, but we draw our own inferences. Also, it should be kept in mind that such published data and policy information may not be complete. Therefore our performance evaluation must necessarily remain tentative.

Self-Evaluation

In 1978, the NARB created a consultative panel and asked it to determine the effectiveness of advertising's self-regulatory process. The panel commissioned a national Gallup survey, and learned that the main complaints of consumers about advertising were:

A. Advertising is not accurate or truthful.
B. Feminine hygiene products should not be advertised on TV.
C. Advertising insults the intelligence of consumers.
D. Advertisers use sex too much in advertising.
E. Potentially harmful products are advertised.
F. TV commercials are carried to excess: too many, too long, too loud, too repetitious.
G. Advertising exploits the vulnerability of children (*Advertising Self-Regulation and its Interaction with Consumers* 1979, 10).

It should be kept in mind, however that the importance of these complaints must be tempered because only a small minority of consumers believe that advertising is salient when compared with other influences on their lives, and many consumers feel positively about advertising (Bauer and Greyser 1968).

These complaints may be regarded as what the public would like to see corrected; that is, they tell us what the objectives of a self-regulatory system should be from the consumer's viewpoint. Interestingly, the Gallup survey results did not cause the NAD/NARB to change its policies in many ways that are known publicly; on the contrary, the system continued to deal only with the first and last items on the list. Although it may be argued that the NAD/NARB system does not have the power to deal adequately with some of the other matters, it may also be argued that the system should at least make some substantial effort to do so—an effort that reasonable consumers and others would regard as genuine.

Sanctions. The decisions of the NAD and the advertisers' agreements to adhere to NAD decisions are not legally enforceable.

> However, since negotiations are conducted on a voluntary basis, there is no reason an advertiser should make promises it does not intend to keep. Moreoever, failure to honor commitments could affect its credibility in any future inquiry.
> The record demonstrates the high level of commitment by companies that have participated in the process. In the event of an individual failure, the procedures require the facts be brought to the attention of a government agency with a request for corrective action. In the twelve years of operation (now fifteen], no advertiser participating in an NAD inquiry followed by an NARB appeal has declined to accept the decision (*NAD Case Report*, 15 July 1983).

Speed of Resolution of Cases

> Experience has taught there is no such thing as a standard case. Some inquiries are resolved by a simple exchange of correspondence while others may involve NAD in several meetings and require the retention of consultancy services. Competitor challenges tend to be more complex, particularly when each party provides technical data to support its position. During 1982, 64% of the reported cases were resolved within six months (*NAD Case Report*, 15 July 1983).

Cost of Cases. "On a cumulative basis, since its inception in 1971 the nominal average cost per decision has been approximately $1,500 exclusive of expenses incurred by the advertiser and complainant" (*NAD Case Report*, 15 July 1983).

Advertisers incur costs associated with cooperation with NAD/NARB/CARU, but because expensive legal counsel is kept to a minimum, advertiser costs are far less than they would be in a case adjudicated by a government agency or in the court system.

Reduced FTC Case Load. The performance of the NAD/NARB system may very well be one reason why the FTC in the late 1970s (under Chairman

Michael Pertschuk and before any shift toward deregulation) did not press as many individual complaints about advertising as it had earlier. As a former chairman of the NARB noted, the FTC "now devotes more of its resources to developing trade regulation rules as to what advertisers can and cannot do, which can be made binding on an entire industry." He added, "The Chairman and one other member of the FTC have been kind enough to commend the work of the NAD/NARB publicly in recent months. But the Commission is still there if it is needed" (Cox 1980).

It should be kept in mind, however, that the number of cases handled by the FTC is only an input measure whereas, it is more important to measure impact. "In fiscal-year 1983, the FTC acted on 98 consumer-protection matters, that is, complaints, consents, district court actions, order modifications and rule makings. Chairman Miller . . . claimed that the FTC . . . issued more advertising complaints in the past one and one-half year than in the fiscal 1977–1980 period under his predecessor" (*Advertising Compliance Service*, IV, 8 [16 April 1984], p. 8 as quoted in Boddewyn 1985, 12). The effect of FTC decisions is not limited to the parties involved in individual cases. Advertisers, agencies, and media, as well as those who administer association codes, and in particular the NAD/NARB/CARU system, are alert to the precedents set by the FTC. It is also important to keep in mind that although the NAD/NARB/CARU does not handle a large volume of consumer complaints against advertising, it is the only national organization that will accept and deal with individual consumer complaints. A consumer complaint to the FTC may become part of the record, but will not serve as the basis for regulatory action (Feldman 1980, 227).

Independent Evaluations

The first systematic attempt by an "outsider" to ascertain if the NARB was accomplishing its purpose of "sustaining high standards of truth and accuracy in national advertising" involved an analysis of the first thirty NAD decisions that had been appealed to the NARB" (Zanot and Maddox 1977). In this analysis the following became clear:

> the standard of truth and accuracy was not exclusively a literal one . . . [two cases] involved advertisements which were literally false but were not judged misleading. Conversely [in another case] advertisements were literally true but [the Panel] thought them misleading in overall impression. On the whole, the decisions have reflected a broad standard of truth and accuracy. [Also] panels have affirmed the intent of the advertiser to be irrelevant in judging whether or not deception occurred. This is consistent with court precedents set in FTC cases. . . . A criterion for judging truth and accuracy was the [impression of] the . . . target

audience at which the advertisements were aimed . . . there have been no clear precedents set as to the proportion of the audience that might be deceived before the advertising was judged misleading (Zanot and Maddox 1977, 117).

Zanot and Maddox then discussed NARB decisions relating to dangling comparatives, semantics, omission of relevant information, testimonial endorsements, puffery, the misuse of research data and surveys, and comparative advertising. They concluded that the "NARB . . . has not been especially concerned with the establishment of precedents. Their outlook is a pragmatic one and is reflected in a case-by-case approach" (Zanot and Maddox 1977, 120).

The authors also concluded that

> it is unfortunate that the NARB dismissed some cases without rendering verdicts. [They noted that] It is, of course, of the greatest importance [to accomplish the objective of sustaining truth and accuracy in advertising by causing the] misleading advertising [to] be modified or discontinued. . . . [But] the failure to render a judgment deprives all future panels, as well as those engaged in advertising on a day-to-day basis, of guidelines to direct them in their future activities (Zanot and Maddox 1977, 120). . . .
>
> the story of the NARB is one of success . . . of cooperation, not only among the trade organizations that founded and funded NARB, but among the different groups that make up the NARB membership—advertisers, advertising agency personnel, and public members . . . a large number and variety of people have become involved and have contributed to the success of NARB (Zanot and Maddox 1977, 120–121).

LaBarbera (1980a) listed several salient strengths of the NAD/NARB system.

> [It] has aided and assisted [the FTC] by reducing the number of complaints it receives. . . . If the NAD did not exist many of [the cases handled] . . . might still be in process at the FTC. [The NAD system is] able to react much more quickly to advertising abuses than is the FTC, and [the NAD/NARB system] prevents overregulation. . . . While the government has passed additional rules regulating advertising, it appears that the NAD/NARB system has prevented even greater involvement.

She also discussed weaknesses in the system, notably lack of objectivity because of inadequate public representation, and lack of public awareness of the system.

Armstrong and Ozanne (1983) examined NAD/NARB purposes from two standpoints: a consumer advocacy and an advertiser advocacy perspective. They concluded that the "NAD/NARB is heavily oriented toward the 'advertiser advocacy' model, and that it is moving further in that direction." They offer the following arguments to support this conclusion:

> NAD/NARB is not now, and never really was, intended as a clearing-house for large numbers of consumer advertising complaints. It has a small staff and a smaller annual budget (less than the cost of sixty seconds of Super Bowl advertising time). . . .
> NAD/NARB is receiving less consumer and more competitor input. . . . Few consumers are even aware of NAD/NARB's existence. . . . NAD/NARB seems to be avoiding rather than generating controversy. . . . Top 100 advertisers . . . account for about 54% of national advertising expenditures but constitute only about 30% of NAD cases, and this percentage is dropping. . . . More advertisers appear to be escaping judgement through 'previously discontinued' response . . . it maintains a low profile with respect to its major sanction, public reporting. . . . NAD/NARB has also largely avoided controversial issues of taste, morality and social responsibility. . . . NAD/NARB uses considerable amounts of judgement in selecting and evaluating cases. While NAD/NARB's charter states that NARB should develop standards, it decided early that an exhaustive code would be 'impractical, needlessly restrictive, and self-defeating' . . . no NAD standards have been developed. Such standards have been developed for CARU, however . . . this absence has left NAD/NARB open to charges of subjectivity and favoritism. . . . Under such a subjective and flexible system, NAD/NARB is more likely to address issues of concern to the advertising industry (Armstrong and Ozanne 1983, 23–24).

The evaluation by Armstrong and Ozanne depends largely on unstated assumptions and the use of the straw man technique. For example, some would argue that the distinction between a consumer advocacy and advertiser advocacy model is irrelevant, because the NAD/NARB system has from the beginning attempted to find common ground between these extremes. NAD officials add that

> such a distinction between consumer and advertiser advocacy is exaggerated if not misplaced. While it is true that NAD relies mainly on competitor complaints, only those that raise an issue of *public interest* are pursued. It does not act as the advocate for the complaining competitor or as an intervenor between advertisers but assumes them as its own (with possible additional charges, following NAD investigation) if it appears that the incriminated advertisement raises questions about the proper substantiation of its claims (Boddewyn 1985, 6–7).

Also, the size of the staff and budget is an input variable, and an evaluation should instead focus on output, or the impact of the system. (See also chapter 5 regarding the NAD/NARB/CARU budget.) Moreover, the facts and speculations illustrated in the second paragraph of this quote require the reader to make subjective inferences about the unstated evaluations of the impact or effects of the NAD/NARB system. For example, is the system working in the interests of society when the NAD/NARB receives more complaints from competitors than from consumers, when it seems to avoid rather than generate controversy, or when it avoids the controversial issues of taste, morality, and social responsibility?

To their credit, however, Armstrong and Ozanne eventually admit that consumer interests have to some extent been served by NAD/NARB:

> it has been effective in improving national advertising. . . . It has processed cases quickly and inexpensively. . . . Though competitors and NAD staffers seem to be selecting most of the cases and issues addressed, they may be more qualified to identify and evaluate poor advertising practice. . . . They have strong motivations for pointing out deceptions by competitors. . . . The low profile, behind-the-scenes nature of NAD/NARB activity has fostered a level of cooperation beyond that of previous regulators . . . [and] NAD/NARB has been effective in stopping a large number of questionable ads, even when advertisers disagreed. . . . Thus, despite NAD/NARB's strong industry orientation (or perhaps because of it) consumers have benefited substantially. Had NAD/NARB positioned itself as a strong consumer advocate, it might never have survived (Armstrong and Ozanne 1983, 25).

Looking at the business from the inside, long-time observer Stanley Cohen, former Washington editor of *Advertising Age,* pointed out that

> it is fair to say that honesty in advertising is today accepted and respected by the industry in a sense that was never true in the past. The principles are understood and the procedures for enforcing these principles are sufficiently mature that it is no longer an exaggeration to say that false and misleading advertising involving respectable companies is very rare (Cohen 1980, 162).

He goes on to give major credit for this state of affairs to the

> rejuvenated [Federal Trade] Commission [which had] put advertising at the top of its hit list. It singled out the biggest and most respected advertisers it could find, and it threw the book at them. . . . The advertisers got the message. They set up effective copy clearance procedures in their own companies and ad agencies. The TV networks became serious about screening commercials. . . . But best of all, the advertising industry created the NARB. Self-regulation by NARB is one of the reasons the FTC's staff finds so little to challenge. NARB . . . is the regulator of choice

for businessmen who are looking for a fast way to make their competitors stop cheating. . . . It confines itself to the hard core issues and does not get tangled in the theoretical unprovables. It eliminates big legal fees. It has a remarkable record of sending everyone away happy, including, incidentally the FTC (Cohen 1980, 162–163).

This observer then goes on to note that the "NARB confines itself to the legal concepts of false and deceptive already established in law by the FTC" and expresses disappointment that NARB has not "pioneered on its own to discover new concepts that deal with evolving practice in the industry." He mentions especially the currently unregulated area of misleading advertising on public issue matters and the missed opportunity to play a "conscience raising role" regarding advertising to and about products for women and the elderly.

He notes also that although the NAD/NARB system is well known to business, it "is still a well kept secret, so far as much of the public is concerned." He asks:

Who knows how much work there would be [for the NAD/NARB staff] if that vast TV audience was regularly reminded that there is an industry self regulation system sitting there, ready to swing into action if you report an ad you consider deceptive? Who knows how many undetected practices would surface to broaden our knowledge of the new forms of deception confronting consumers . . . (Cohen 1980, 163).

Cohen also observed:

It is no exaggeration to say that there is hardly a working day when NARB or its staff at NAD does not resolve some issue for a couple hundred bucks which would have cost more than the entire ad agency contribution to the system if it had gone to the FTC for investigation (Cohen 1980, 163).

Another "measure" of the performance of the NAD/NARB system is that consumerists no longer criticize the system frequently. There seems to be general recognition that the system has performed well, even with its limited resources. The NAD staff is respected, and it appears as if one "public" member on each NARB panel is enough to keep the industry experts diligent. ". . . It only takes one whistleblower to destroy the credibility of the self-regulation verdict" (Cohen 1980).

Finally, not only have FTC commissioners praised the performance of the NAD/NARB, but so have representatives of other federal agencies. For example, in 1984 the CBBB and FDA launched a program of cooperation to halt misleading advertising for fraudulent medical products. The CBBB and FDA jointly contacted 9,500 advertising managers to provide guidance to prevent misleading advertising of medical products and information on how to cooperate in the effort with the 150 FDA offices nationwide as well as the numerous BBBs. Dr. Frank Young, an FDA commissioner, commented:

> Probably the greatest cooperative effort against health fraud to date involves the splendid cooperation between the Council of Better Business Bureaus and the FDA to combat fraudulent advertising of medical products. . . . This is precisely the kind of cooperation we need between the public and private sectors (*CBBB Annual Report* 1984, 6).

The next section of this chapter contains some additional analyses to update previously published evaluations of the performance of the NAD/ NARB. This material was derived in large part from a content analysis of *NAD Case Reports*. Such information is integrated with prior published analyses to extend them when possible, and some new information is presented separately.

NAD/NARB Workload

The workload of a self-regulatory body may be taken as a crude indicator as to whether it is performing effectively, although it should be remembered that this may not reflect the number of complaints received (tables 6–1 and 6–2).

Table 6–1
Sources of Complaints Leading to Formal Cases Handled by the NAD
(in percentages)

Sources	7/1971 to 6/1983	1981	1982	1983	1984	1985
NAD monitoring	37	45	39	37	31	37
Competitors	23	31	39	42	45	41
Referrals from BBBs	16	13	10	11	10	10
Consumers	13	8	9	5	9	11
Others, including consumer organizations, consumer reporters, and industry organizations	11	3	3	5	5	1
Total percent	100	100	100	100	100	100
Total NAD cases	1741	148	140	110	105	103

Sources: 1. *Better Business News and Views* 8, 4 (August 1983), 1.
        2. *NAD Case Report* 12, 12 (January 17, 1983), 45.
        3. *NAD Case Report* 14, 12 (January 15, 1985), 43.
        4. *NAD Case Report* 15, 12 (January 20, 1986), 44.

Table 6–2
NAD/CARU Services, 1984[a]
(additional to formal cases)

| | Telephone and Written Contacts | | | |
| | NAD | | CARU | |
Requesting Organization and Action Taken	Number	Percentage	Number	Percentage
Sources				
Advertiser	128	16.5	16	9.0
Advertising agency	26	3.3	11	6.2
Professional or trade organization	45	5.8	12	6.8
Consumer organization	8	1.0	5	2.8
Government (state or federal)	20	2.6	5	2.8
Academic (faculty and students)	105	13.5	95	53.7
Consumer	255	32.8	20	11.3
CBBB/NARB	4	0.5	—	—
Local BBB	59	7.6	1	0.6
Press	95	12.2	5	2.8
Other	33	4.2	7	4.0
Total	778	100.0	177	100.0
Subject				
Request literature	145	18.6	153	86.4
Request information	296	38.0	15	8.5
Complaint				
Advertising	168	21.6	8	4.5
Business practice	155	19.9	—	—
Other	14	1.8	1	0.6
Total	778	100.0	177	100.0
Action				
Sent literature	157	20.2	156	88.2
Sent information	293	37.7	15	8.5
Referred complaint to				
Advertiser or agency	39	5.0	5	2.8
Government	8	1.0	—	—
Professional or trade organization	7	0.9	—	—
CBBB/NARB	17	2.2	—	—
Local BBB	139	17.9	—	—
Other	3	0.3	—	—
Resolved	13	1.7	—	—
Declined with explanation	102	13.1	1	0.6
Total	778	100.0	177	100.0

Source: Personal correspondence from Ronald H. Smithies, vice president, NAD, 4 February 1985.

[a]Because the performance of these services was recorded systematically for the first time in 1984, Smithies observed that the information must be treated as tentative, since the NAD is "still working to achieve consistent record keeping by the staff."

Zanot (1979) reports the total number of complaints handled by the NAD in the first seven years of operation, noting that

> . . . any evaluation of the performance and effectiveness of the entire mechanism must pay considerable attention to this initial tier in the self-regulatory effort. Also, since NARB actions and appeals are instigated as a result of NAD investigations, much of the performance of the NARB is contingent upon the effectiveness of NAD (Zanot 1979a, 41).

The number of complaints per year investigated by the NAD grew rapidly in 1971, peaking at 319 in 1972, and stabilizing at about 175 per year through 1977. The number has declined in the last few years (see table 6-1) to a total of only 103 in 1985.

Of the approximately 2,000 NAD "decisions" from 1971 through 1985, only forty-one have been appealed to the NARB. The interested parties (advertisers, complainants, and the NAD) have accepted all forty-one of the NARB decisions. From this record it may be inferred that the NAD is conducting its investigations and rendering its judgments in a responsible manner, usually acceptable to complainants as well as to defendants. Also, the reduction in such appeals in recent years (thirty-three in the first seven years from 1971 to 1978, but only eight in the last seven years from 1979 to 1985) suggests increasing acceptance of NAD decisions. Zanot (1979a) concluded that "The figures do not support . . . early critics who charged the mechanism would wear 'business blinders' and [that members of the advertising industry would] be incapable of judging their peers guilty. Likewise, the figures lend little support to any who might accuse the mechanism of a pro-consumerist bias."

It should also be noted that across the United States the approximately 170 local BBBs and their branches handle a large number of competitor and consumer complaints of all types. In 1982 the BBBs received more than 1.6 million complaints, of which about 374,000 were settled. But of these, only about 2.6 percent (or approximatley 9,700) had to do with advertising practices (*CBBB Annual Report* 1983). Virtually all of these complaints were handled by local BBBs; only a handful were forwarded to the NAD for investigation (see table 6-1).

Evidence indicates that complaint behavior is not a good indicator of consumer problems in the marketplace. One U.S. study showed that "complainers were more highly educated and had higher occupational status than the general population. Also, one fourth of the respondents accounted for nearly 50 percent of the cases. Studies have confirmed that the overwhelming majority of consumers first seek recourse from the seller" (Bernhardt, Robinson, and Semens 1983). However, most consumer complaints are concerned with matters other than advertising, and it is not known how many advertising complaints are first directed at sellers before complaints to other agencies are made.

One must also be cautious about using the volume of consumer complaints as an indication of consumer satisfaction or dissatisfaction. Experience in both the United Kingdom and the United States suggests that publicity for a self-regulatory organization will increase the number of complaints, regardless of the "quality" of the advertising.

Also, a formal complaint is only one possible response to dissatisfaction, and it is employed relatively infrequently for a variety of reasons. First, consumers rarely have good information as to where and how to complain; and even if they have such information, it often may be considered to be more trouble than it is worth, especially for low-unit price convenience goods; moreover, complaining behavior may have negative connotations, and dissatisfaction normally seems to be manifested in brand switching on the next purchase, as one study of U.S. and Mexican consumers reported. The author added that many variables other than dissatisfaction influence complaining behavior, for example, affiliative values, personality characteristics, internal motivation, and external approval differences in complaining behavior; these are partly a function of cultural differences (Villarreal-Camacho 1983).

Process-oriented consumers who shop as a social and enjoyable activity tend to associate complaining with poor consumer purchasing skills; they tend to switch brands rather than complain. Outcome-oriented consumers, in contrast, return the product when they are dissatisfied and believe that complainers are individuals who know what they want; to them complaining is acceptable (Villarreal-Camacho 1983).

NAD monitoring is one of the most important sources of "complaints" leading to NAD investigations and formal cases (see table 6–1). It is an extensive but informal process, and the main workload of identifying potential problems and investigating them is handled by knowledgeable NAD specialists, although there are instances when groups of students have been used to review advertising and to write down the principal claims in it for later review by NAD staff.

The CARU is particularly dependent on monitoring as the major source of its investigations. The assistant to the director of the CARU monitors children's advertising on network and cable television, children's syndicated programs, and programs with children's audiences such as those aired on Nickelodeon. The CARU also maintains a list of children's magazines and comic books that are used to select issues to review. Selection is based on judgment, which in turn is based on information from a variety of sources that suggests potential problems and issues that should receive priority. The assistant to the director keeps a log of broadcast programs and magazines reviewed (Weisskoff, letters to and discussions with the authors, 1986).

The CARU guidelines are used to identify questionable advertisements. They are then reviewed by the director and the assistant to the director together. If there is a clear issue a case is opened. Sometimes informal discussions with the advertiser resolve the issue, whereas other cases require further investigation and negotiation (Weisskoff, letters to and discussions with the authors, 1986).

Additionally, the workload of the NAD, including its CARU, includes informal advisories in response to advertiser inquiries, but they stop short of preclearance (Weisskoff, letters to and discussions with the authors, 1986).

The number of cases investigated is an imperfect measure of work load, because work load also includes information provided by letter or on the telephone in response to those who complain or inquire about advertising. Sometimes exceedingly helpful information can be provided in a few minutes, far out of proportion to the time it takes. In 1984 NAD received 778 incoming letters and telephone calls to complain or inquire about advertising (see table 6–2).

Table 6–2 shows the breakdown of contacts—by source, subject, and action. Many of these requests were handled easily and quickly by NAD's staff. Many also were handled by referring them to another agency, or when trivial or not actionable they were declined with polite explanation.

Although exact information is not available for earlier years, the number of competitor challenges and consumer complaints in 1984 is not greatly different from earlier estimates (letters to the author from NAD staff 1985).

From tables 6–1 and 6–2, the total number of inquiries, complaints, and cases generated from advertisers is 181, of which 47 (or 26 percent) led to investigations. Likewise, 275 inquiries, complaints, and cases were generated from consumers, of which 9 (or 3 percent) led to investigations. Because both advertisers and consumers made inquiries that were not complaints, the percentage of complaints that led to investigations is somewhat higher than can be calculated from these tables. The NAD estimates that in the past about 40 to 50 percent of competitor challenges, but less than 10 percent of consumer complaints, led to formal cases (letters to the author from NAD staff 1985).

These estimates suggest that competitor challenges, along with NAD monitoring (see table 6–1), are more likely to turn up actionable complaints than consumer inquiries and complaints, at least as far as national advertising is concerned. Although some would argue that the system ought to be responsive primarily or especially to consumer needs, these estimates suggest that improvement in truthful and accurate advertising in the full sense of these words is not likely to occur by relying solely on consumers. Perhaps those who understand advertising best (for example, NAD staff and business competitors) may be more skillful at identifying advertising "abuses."

These lines of reasoning are in harmony with past trends. For example, the volume of actionable complaints from consumers has been between eight and fifteen percent almost from the beginning, except for 1972 (the first full year of operation) when seventy-nine cases (twenty-five percent of the total), came from individual consumers. The volume of cases from consumer complaints since 1976 seems to have stabilized at less than ten percent of the total per year.

The volume of cases from complaints of consumer groups was also high in the early period of operation of the NAD, reaching a peak of 111 cases or thirty-five percent of the total in 1972 (Zanot 1979a). This source of cases quickly declined in importance, with less than five formal cases per year from such complaints since 1976.

Over the years NAD's monitoring of national broadcast and print advertising has been the largest single source of cases for investigation, although well over half of the cases are initiated from external sources. It appears as if NAD's monitoring will continue as a major source of cases, continuing to account for more than thirty percent of the cases. However, competitive challenges have become increasingly important, accounting for more than forty percent of the cases in 1983 and 1984.

During the first few years of operation local BBBs were a major source of referral complaints. The volume per year declined, however, and seems to have stabilized at about ten percent or less of the total per year.

One might argue that the NAD is accomplishing its mission by identifying a substantial proportion of its formal cases through monitoring, and that such activities benefit consumers and society to the extent that such cases lead to advertising that is more truthful and more accurate. One might also argue that competitor challenges are accepted only if there is a clear public interest in the issue. Therefore, they play a positive role in helping provide truthful and accurate information that improves consumer decision making, thereby preserving the conditions of competition that lead to efficient allocation of resources in the market economy, as well as leading directly to increased consumer satisfactions and welfare.

On the other hand, one might be concerned because consumers and especially consumer groups are relatively unimportant as a source of actionable complaints. However, there are a number of alternative explanations for the relative unimportance of consumers: (1) consumer apathy, as well as ignorance of the NAD/NARB system as a means to improve advertising; (2) consumer perception that the NAD/NARB system does not provide an appropriate or useful means to pursue consumer interests; (3) the increasing difficulty to identify clear cases of advertising that is untruthful, inaccurate, deceptive, or misleading; and (4) a decline in the fervor of consumer groups to take action, especially because they lack consumer support. Available evidence does not permit a judgment as to which explanation or explanations are most likely to be correct.

NAD/NARB Decisions

Another crude but also useful means to evaluate NAD/NARB activities is to examine the outcomes of NAD/NARB case investigations. The decision data for the left side of table 6-3 are from private correspondence with the NAD staff. The data for the right side of the table are from a content analysis of NAD cases done by one of the authors of this book. The first lines of entries in table 6-3 on both sides of the table are equivalent concepts (that is, the percentage of "advertising substantiated" and the percentage of "complaint not upheld, no change required"). However, the remaining lines in the table on the right side provide a different breakdown of details than the NAD information on the left side. It is the NAD's position that the breakdown between "total withdrawal" or "modification" of claims is not a significant distinction; thus the left side of the table shows only these "consolidated" data on line two.

However, a complaint that is upheld in part and which only requires modification usually indicates only a relatively minor "abuse," and it seems useful to know whether the advertising industry is engaging in practices that require minor modifications, as well as to know whether the NAD/NARB system is spending its time on cases leading to total withdrawal of the advertising. The breakdown on the right side of the table also shows the number of "no decisions" by the NAD, when the advertising was withdrawn voluntarily. It is the current practice of the NAD to keep the "no decision" cases to a minimum because they are inconclusive and do not provide guidance to advertisers. Indeed, this practice appears to be already reflected in the declining number of such cases from 1980 to 1984.

Examination of the first line in table 6-3, on both sides of the table, indicates that in about forty percent of the cases the complaint had no substantial merit, with the exception of 1984, in which the proportion of such cases was halved. Correspondingly, in 1984, the proportion of cases in which the complaint was valid increased dramatically, primarily those requiring modification of the advertising, but also to some extent because of an increase in decisions that the advertising should be discontinued. The decreasing number and proportion of companies choosing to withdraw voluntarily suggests that more of them preferred to fight. It would

Table 6–3
Decisions in Formal NAD Cases

Decision[a]	1971–1981%	1981%	1982%	1983%	1984%
Advertising substantiated	40	45	44	42	21
Claims modified or Withdrawn	42	53	56	58	79
Other[c]	18	2	0	0	0
	100	100	100	100	100
Total NAD cases	1891	150	140	110	105

Decision[b]	1980%	1981%	1982%	1983%	1984%
Complaint not upheld, no change required	41	43	41	42	21
Complaint upheld in full, advertising must be discontinued	4	7	3	5	13
Complaint upheld in part, advertising must be modified	8	20	27	23	45
No NAD decision because advertising was withdrawn voluntarily	41	25	28	29	20
Other[c]	7	5	1	1	1
	101	100	100	100	100
Total NAD cases	132	148	140	110	105

[a]Source of the data is letters to the authors from NAD staff and *NAD Case Reports.*

[b]Source of these data is a content analysis of 1980–1984 *NAD Case Reports.*

[c]"Other" includes cases appealed to the NARB suspended while investigation is completed by another agency, as well as cases terminated or suspended for reasons that are not known to this writer.

therefore seem that the NAD, to maintain its standards, must have been obliged to pursue cases that in earlier years would have been withdrawn voluntarily, doing so with no increase in resources. This would help explain why the total number of formal investigations has declined, while the number of cases in which the NAD reports the advertising was modified or withdrawn has increased (figure 6–1). Preliminary data for 1985 suggest that these trends are continuing.

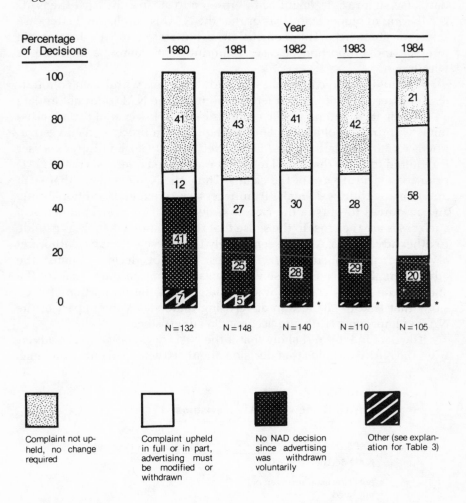

* One Per Cent

Source: Letters to the author from NAD staff and content analysis of *NAD Case Reports*.

Figure 6–1. Outcomes of Formal NAD Cases

One might conclude from tables 6–1 and 6–3 that because the number of cases investigated is declining, the NAD is performing a diminished function. However, the number of reported cases may not be an adequate measure of performance, unless it indicates that offending advertising is not being challenged; there is, however, no evidence to this effect.

On the other hand, although inconclusive, the declining number and proportion of decisions in 1984 in which the advertising was substantiated (see figure 6–1), might be interpreted to mean either that the NAD is adhering to higher standards or that the NAD is employing better case selection standards. This conclusion is buttressed by the increase in number and proportion of cases requiring that claims be modified or withdrawn.

It should be noted also that when advertising is withdrawn voluntarily prior to receipt of the first letter of inquiry, the NAD does not initiate an investigation and no public report is issued. However, if the advertising is withdrawn voluntarily after an inquiry is in process, the investigation is terminated but the case is reported (Reid 1986), and the advertiser is required to agree that it will refer any unresolved questions to the NAD prior to any future use of the claims. Thus, the NAD believes that such voluntary withdrawals make it unnecessary to expend additional time and resources to pursue the case to a decision. However, the merits of such cases are then lost in the sense that they are not available as a guide to other advertisers. Also, it seems likely that these voluntary withdrawals would, if pursued as official cases, often be decided against the advertisers. But because these withdrawals do not become a part of the statistics on NAD decisions, it seems likely that the proportion of decisions that lead to changes in advertising understates the impact of the NAD in improving truth and accuracy in advertising.

The data in table 6–4 show that if the NAD decides against an advertiser, the NARB upholds that decision about sixty-six percent of the time.

Table 6–4
NARB Review of NAD Decisions

NARB Decision	1971–1986 Number	Percentage
NAD decision upheld	27	66
NAD decision reversed or modified	8	20
Case dismissed or advertiser withdrew prior to NARB judgment	6	15
Total	41	100

Source: Letter to the authors from NAD staff and various *NAD Case Reports* and *Better Business News and Views* 8 (4):1.

One might conclude that because the NAD professional staff is overruled in about twenty percent of the cases, the NARB panel members may tend to be a little more lenient with advertisers than the staff of the NAD. One might look to the composition of NARB panels for an explanation and note that with the exception of the one public (nonadvertising industry) member, they are a "jury of one's peers" in advertising.

Two facts indicate that the NAD/NARB system is functioning well: (1) advertisers usually cooperate, because appeals from NAD decisions are rare, and (2) when appealed, the NARB usually upholds the NAD decision. Additionally a positive indication of the success of the system is that no advertiser has ever refused to abide by an NARB decision. Also the fact that no case has had to be referred to a government agency after an NARB decision indicates that NAD/NARB standards are at least as high as the standards of federal regulatory agencies. As a practical matter, a large number of NAD/NARB cases deal with matters that are not actionable by federal agencies. As such the NAD/NARB activities represent a "net contribution" to truth and accuracy in advertising.

Complaints about Advertising in Major Media

Examination of table 6–5 suggests that the pattern of complaints about advertising carried in the major media has not changed very much over the years. Because the total number of formal cases per year has declined somewhat, the number of complaints per year in each of the major media categories has also declined modestly. But the proporation of complaints stemming from the major media categories has remained remarkably stable.

Looking at table 6–5 and taking the data from tables 6–2 and 6–3 into account, it appears as if the NAD is maintaining about the same intensity of activity, shifting only slightly perhaps in spending a little less time on monitoring than in earlier years and more time on cases that would have been dropped voluntarily in prior years.

Broadly, it may also be concluded from the data in table 6–5 that the NAD/NARB system continues to give approximately the same balance of attention to complaints about advertising in each of the major media. Because the same criteria for accepting complaints have been followed for a number of years, it also seems reasonable to conclude that neither advertisers nor the media have made progress in disciplining themselves to improve truth and accuracy in advertising to the point that the number of complaints in any one major medium has declined drastically. It should also be remembered that the television networks prescreen many thousands of commercials per year, and it is not surprising that the NAD needs to handle only so few television cases.

Table 6–5
Complaints about Avertising in the Major Media Leading to Formal NAD Cases

Type of Medium in Which the Advertising Appeared	1 July 1971–30 April 1982			Complaints Handled									
	Number		Percentage	1980		1981		1982		1983		1984	
		Average (11 yr)		Number	Percentage	Number	Percentage	Number	Percentage	Number	Percentage	Number	Percentage
Magazines	757	69	38	48	36	56	38	45	32	48	43	41	39
Newspapers and supplements	552	50	28	20	15	24	16	25	18	25	23	22	21
Print, but medium not identifiable	—	—		18	14	11	7	20	14	11	9	9	9
Television	792	72	40	62	47	61	41	62	44	55	50	45	43
Radio	84	8	4	3	2	4	3	8	6	2	2	10	9
Other[a]	422	38	21	16	12	18	12	15	11	11	11	15	15
Total complaints	2,607[b]	237	131	167[b]	126	174[b]	117	175[b]	125	152[b]	138	142[b]	136
Total NAD cases	1,968	180		132		148		140		110		105	

Source: Data for 1971–1982 are from letters to the authors from NAD staff; data for 1980–1984 are from content analysis of *NAD Case Reports*.

[a]Other includes nonmeasured media such as outdoor, transportation, direct mail, point-of-purchase materials, catalogues, and comic books.

[b]Some cases involved advertising in more than one medium.

Complaints by Product Categories

Table 6-6 contains information on the top seven product classes that generate formal advertising complaint cases handled by the NAD/NARB system. Over the entire period of operation of the system, about a half dozen additional product categories have, on occasion, generated up to three or four percent of advertising complaints. But, in general, those in the category of "other" not only generate fewer advertising complaints in total, but also are spread more thinly over a broad range of other products. Examination of table 6-6 reveals that six of the seven product categories also show recent signs of some decline compared with the number of advertising complaint cases handled by the NAD in the first ten years of operation. Only one category, food and beverages, seems to be at or above the average of the first ten years. In addition the number of complaints in the "other" category has declined somewhat. But perhaps the most significant finding in the "other" category is that the complaints seem to be more evenly dispersed over a larger number of products; from 1980 to 1983 no category beyond the top seven accounted for more than 2 percent of complaints. These findings suggest that the NAD/NARB system is making progress in its preventative function. Although such change cannot be attributed solely to the NAD/NARB system, it appears as if at the very minimum the system is at least a positive force assisting in this progress.

The apparent exception to the indicated progress is "food and beverages." From 1980 to 1984 the number of cases in this category seems to be about the same as the average of the first ten years, although the number is a little more important as a percent of the total. About all one can conclude from these data is that the NAD has continued to pursue food and beverage cases vigorously, but no apparent progress has been made in reducing the number of complaints.

At this point it would be well to keep in mind the criteria the NAD uses to accept complaints formally for investigation. The essential requirement is that a complaint raise an issue of public interest. This "public interest criterion" should serve to increase the credibility of the NAD in the minds of those who believe that the NAD/NARB system should focus on the interests of society rather than on the interests of the advertising business.

Moreover, more public interest issues are at stake with some products because some product categories generate more cases than others. Such NAD "acceptance" decisions are an indicator that the NAD is engaging in conduct that is likely to benefit consumers in society by improving truth and accuracy via substantiation in important product categories. Presumably, if the NAD mission is being accomplished, the number of complaints

Table 6-6
Complaints Leading to Formal NAD Cases, by Product Categories

Product Category	Complaints Handled											
	Number						Percentage					
	1971–1981[a] (Total Yearly Avg.)	1980[b]	1981[b]	1982[b]	1983[b]	1984[b]	1971–1981[a] (Yearly Avg.)	1980[b]	1981[b]	1982[b]	1983[b]	1984[b]
Food and beverages	274/27	22	31	29	20	28	14	17	21	21	18	27
Cosmetics, personal care	231/23	14	22	17	10	11	12	11	15	12	9	10
Household cleaning and related	195/19	11	17	11	8	5	10	8	11	8	7	5
Autos and accessories	225/22	7	15	9	9	7	12	5	10	7	8	7
Medical, health, drug	169/17	13	9	14	12	9	9	10	6	10	11	9
Leisure, toy, sporting	169/17	18	7	15	16	11	9	14	5	11	15	10
Appliances, consumer electronics	115/11	5	4	7	5	6	6	4	3	5	5	6
Others	570/57	42	43	38	30	28	29	32	29	27	28	27
Total	1,948	132	148	140	110	105	101[c]	101[c]	100	101[c]	101[c]	101[c]

[a]Source: Tabulation received from letters to the authors from NAD staff.

[b]Source: Tabulation from content analysis of 1980–1984 monthly NAD case reports.

[c]Adds to more than 100 percent owing to rounding.

in the relevant product categories would tend to decline; likewise the number of complaints leading to discontinuance or modification of the advertising should decline. And indeed the data do indicate that this expectation is being achieved very slowly in most product categories. It is difficult to ascertain if the volume of such cases continues because advertisers continue to make the same "violations" or if the NAD continues to increase its standards by identifying and pursuing additional "violations" that in previous years would not have been as high priority as other earlier cases.

The skeptical outsider might suspect that the NAD uses the public interest criterion to provide a way of avoiding difficult cases. However, no available evidence indicates that the NAD acts in this way. NAD published statements indicate that the public interest criterion is a way to avoid becoming involved in battles between competitors that they should handle by themselves in a market system.

Table 6–7 shows the proportion of NAD decisions in selected product categories that (1) required no change and (2) led to change—either required or voluntary. The product categories requiring the lowest proportion of changes for the period 1980 to 1984 were (1) cosmetics and personal care, and (2) household cleaning and related. It could be inferred that in the future these categories are the least likely to be productive for the NAD, or that greater care should be exercised by selecting fewer of them to become formal cases compared with the other categories. One could also infer that the remaining product categories are the most likely to lead to needed change as a result of NAD actions, especially (1) food and beverages, (2) leisure, toy, and sporting, (3) appliances, consumer electronics, and (4) other.

The data in table 6–7 also suggest that in 1983 and 1984 the NAD may have improved its selection of cases, because the number of cases for which no change eventuated dropped dramatically. Correspondingly, the number of cases leading to change continued its upward trend. The inference is that the NAD has been able to increase its relative effectiveness in improving truth and accuracy in advertising in the last three years.

The only other discernible trend in table 6–7 seems to be for the category of "foods and beverages." There is an apparent increase in the number of cases in which changes in the advertising were required or made "voluntarily." Other product categories do not show similar patterns.

Basis of Complaints

In general the NAD evaluates complaints on the basis of the previously described concepts of truth and accuracy, with particular emphasis on

Table 6-7
Formal NAD Decisions on Complaints by Product Category, 1980–1984

Product Categories	NAD Decision											
	No Change Required						Change Required or Advertising Voluntarily Discontinued Prior to NAD Decision[a]					
	Number of Complaints[b]					Five-Year Percentage	Number of Complaints[b]					Five-Year Percentage
	1980	1981	1982	1983	1984		1980	1981	1982	1983	1984	
Food and beverages	12	16	13	4	7	40	10	13	17	16	21	60
Cosmetics, personal care	8	13	6	5	4	52	3	6	12	5	7	48
Household cleaning and related	5	8	7	5	2	70	1	6	4	3	3	30
Autos and accessories	1	10	3	4	1	41	8	3	6	5	6	59
Medical, health, drug	6	2	8	7	0	46	4	6	3	5	9	54
Leisure, toy, sporting	5	2	3	4	2	26	11	5	10	11	9	74
Appliances, consumer electronics	4	1	4	2	0	34	6	5	3	1	6	66
Other	12	11	16	14	6	34	25	24	24	16	21	65
Total	53	63	60	45	22	40	68	68	79	62	82	60

Source: Content analysis of 1980–1984 NAD Case Reports.

[a]These columns include the number of cases in which the NAD requested that advertising be discontinued or modified, plus those cases in which the advertising was voluntarily discontinued, making a NAD decision unnecessary.

[b]The total number of complaints does not add exactly to the total number of cases mentioned in earlier tables because a few complaints were handled in some other manner, such as acceptance of a decision by another agency which will or had investigated the same case.

whether consumers are misled. Therefore a detailed basis for examining the nature of complaints was developed, and the content analysis yielded the data in tables 6-8 and 6-9.

The first two categories in table 6-8 account for the great majority of cases. The other categories overlap sometimes (that is, an ambiguous price claim might also be misleading or a testimonial might also be unacceptable as a claim substantiation). However, some of the complaints in these other categories, such as a safety issue in advertising to children, also stand alone. Whenever it was possible to do so, specific issues outside of the first two categories were specified so as to be able to infer the priorities of the NAD from the relative frequency of certain types of complaints.

It appears as if complaints about comparisons continue to be an important matter, although the complaints about "price comparisons and worth and value claims" seem to be declining.

Complaints about "acts of omission" seem to have peaked in 1982 and 1983, and one might infer that some advertisers may have learned how to avoid such "offenses"; if so, one may wish to give the NAD/NARB system some credit for playing a role in making advertising more truthful and accurate in this respect. The cases in other categories do not seem to indicate any other apparent trends.

Table 6-9 relates the bases of complaints to NAD decisions. From 1980 to 1983 nearly half of the substantiation cases yielded adequate evidence to support the advertiser (see table 6-9). But in 1984 the ratio dropped to about twenty-five percent. It appears that the preventative purpose of advertising substantiation has not yet been accomplished adequately. On the other hand, it also appears as if advertisers fare better in substantiation cases than with other issues, all of which require an even higher proportion of advertising to be discontinued or modified (line one of table 6-9). Therefore, one might infer that the NAD/NARB system has made more progress on substantiation than on other issues, and that increasing priority ought to be given to some of the other issues. NAD advertising cases that deal with misleading statements, visuals, or semantics are not only frequent, but the proportion that are judged unacceptable is a very high seventy percent. Clearly, further improvement is possible, and it might be argued that the NAD should do more to make advertisers aware of the kinds of issues that are unacceptable.

Direct comparison advertising in which a competitor is identified, including both price and nonprice claims, was a major issue or basis for complaint in nearly twenty-five percent of the cases from 1980 to 1984 (calculated from line items three and four in table 6-8). The majority of these complaints probably stem from competitors, because "competitor challenges usually, though not always, involve comparative claims" (*NAD Case Report* 1983). With regard to the NAD/NARB goals and purposes,

Table 6-8
Basis of Complaints Handled in Formal Cases by the NAD, 1980-1984

Basis of Complaint	Complaints Handled									
	1980		1981		1982		1983		1984	
	Number	Percentage	Number	Percentage	Number	Percentage	Number	Percentage	Number	Percentage
Unacceptable evidence to substantiate claims	87	66	108	73	105	75	93	85	84	80
Misleading statement: visual or semantics	60	45	75	51	119	85	73	66	87	83
Comparisons other than price	22	17	28	19	29	21	21	19	25	24
Price comparisons and worth and value claims	7	5	10	7	6	4	4	4	1	1
Acts of omission	6	5	9	6	15	11	17	15	8	8
Protection of children	5	4	9	6	9	6	8	7	9	9
Use of the words *free, up to*, and *from*	3	2	9	6	4	3	3	3	8	8
Ambiguous price claim or quote	5	4	6	4	4	3	6	5	4	4
Puffery and obvious exaggerations	7	5	0	0	8	6	4	4	1	1
Misuse of guarantees and warranties	1	1	4	3	8	6	2	2	1	1
Misuse of testimonials or endorsements	2	2	2	1	1	1	4	4	1	1
Safety	1	1	3	2	2	1	0	0	2	2
Nonavailability of advertised products and bait and switch	0	0	2	1	3	2	1	1	1	1
All others	7	5	4	3	10	7	5	4	6	6
Total complaints	213[a]	162[a]	269[a]	182[a]	324[a]	231[a]	241[a]	219[a]	238[a]	229[a]
Total NAD cases	132		148		140		110		105	

Source: Content analysis of 1980-1984 *NAD Case Reports*.
[a]Many complaints were based on more than one issue.

Table 6–9
Formal NAD Decisions on Complaints by Basis of Complaint, 1980–1984

	NAD Decision											
	No Change Required						Change Required or Advertising Voluntarily Discontinued Prior to NAD Decision[a]					
	Number of Complaints					Five-Year	Number of Complaints					Five-Year
Basis Complaint	1980	1981	1982	1983	1984	Percentage	1980	1981	1982	1983	1984	Percentage
Unacceptable evidence to substantiate claims	29	42	51	44	21	43	27	51	59	49	61	57
Misleading statement, visual or semantics, or use of research or product tests	6	20	51	23	17	30	49	51	67	41	67	70
Comparisons other than price	7	13	12	6	5	35	10	13	16	14	19	65
Price comparisons and worth and value claims	1	5	2	1	0	35	6	5	4	1	1	65
Acts of omission	0	1	1	3	0	10	5	7	14	13	7	90
Protection of children	0	3	1	1	0	13	5	6	8	7	9	87
Use of the words *free, up to,* and *from*	0	2	0	1	0	12	2	7	4	2	8	88
Ambiguous price claim or quote	1	3	2	2	1	39	4	3	2	2	3	61
Puffery or obvious exaggerations	2	0	5	1	0	42	5	0	3	2	1	58
Misuse of guarantees or warranties	0	1	2	1	0	27	0	3	6	1	1	73
Misuse of testimonials or endorsements	2	0	1	1	0	36	1	2	0	3	1	64
Safety	1	0	0	0	0	14	0	3	2	0	1	86
Nonavailability of advertised products or bait and switch	0	0	0	1	0	12	0	2	3	1	1	88
All others	9	2	0	0	0	19	25	11	4	2	5	81

[a]These columns include the number of cases in which the NAD requested that advertising be discontinued or modified, plus those cases in which the advertising was voluntarily discontinued.

however, it is important to note that comparative misrepresentations are more likely to be subject to correction by competitors than are noncomparative claims (*NAD Case Report* 1983). Although table 6–9 shows that sixty-five percent of comparison advertising cases lead to discontinuance or modification of the advertising, an even higher percentage of many other noncomparative claims leads to such resolution. Therefore, the NAD/NARB system should, as it does, concentrate its efforts in a balanced way with special emphasis on noncomparative claims.

Some of the additional categories that seem to merit special attention from the NAD are protection of children and the use of the words *free, up to,* and *from* regarding price information. Most of the remaining issues not only occur less frequently, but do not seem to be as frequent of sources of "offenses." Therefore they do not seem to require particular emphasis.

Literature on advertising regulation in former years indicates that such issues as puffery, misuse of testimonials, or bait and switch were especially important. Although historical statistics on the number and importance of complaints about such issues are not available, they were given considerable space in the literature. For example, Alexander (1967) gave almost as much space to criticisms of testimonial advertising as he did to criticisms of advertising containing price information. But, from 1980 to 1984, the NAD handled eight times as many advertising complaints relating to price information as it handled regarding testimonial advertising. Apparently some progress has been made in reducing the number of testimonial "abuses."

Puffing received relatively little attention in the literature before 1975, and as judged by the number of complaints handled by the NAD, it continues to be a relatively unimportant issue, in spite of the increasing volume of literature on the subject in scholarly journals in recent years.

Finally, it is instructive to note that from 1980 to 1984, partly because of the focus on truth and accuracy, certain traditional criticisms of advertising did not result in any valid complaints at all to the NAD, for example, identification as an advertisement, superstition, violence, protection of privacy, imitation, name exploitation, unsolicited home visits, and inertia selling; and there was only one example of an advertisement with a fear appeal that required modification. These practices seem to have become less frequent or, at least, less important to the NAD/NARB in recent years. It is also possible that some of these matters are handled informally and do not lead to a formal case.

Conclusions

To the extent the evidence indicates that the NAD/NARB is making a contribution to increased truth and accuracy in advertising, the system arguably helps consumers in two ways: (1) directly, in making decisions based on better information, and (2) indirectly, by making the competitive market system function more effectively.

Much remains to be done to investigate the NAD/NARB system's objectives, activities, and performance. But the evidence permits some inferences on these matters.

The NAD/NARB accomplishes its mission largely through negotiation with and cooperation from advertisers and advertising agencies. The system does not have sanctions available that permit it to coerce recalcitrant advertisers to comply with its decisions. Nevertheless it has made substantial progress in achieving its objectives.

Regarding objectives or purposes, it should be recognized not only that the industry acts in its own self-interests, which of course is to be expected, but the NAD/NARB system has deliberately chosen to pursue objectives that serve consumers in society—a form of enlightened self-interest.

With regard to its activities the NAD/NARB has chosen to be selective in the cases it handles formally. The public interest or important issue criterion is of greatest importance, so that the system does not deal only with issues important to particular competitors. The system handles complaints that stem from advertising in all of the major media. Although a great deal of information exists to guide advertisers on probable NAD/NARB standards to evaluate advertising, there is no formal code or set of standards (except for children's advertising) that national advertisers can consult. *Do's and Don'ts in Advertising Copy* (undated) is a voluminous reference for this purpose, but not especially easy to use as a day-to-day guide for the advertising practitioner. It seems to be desirable for the NAD/NARB system to use its experience and to prepare a formal code of standards. Not only would advertisers gain, but the discipline of doing the task may help the NAD/NARB crystalize more clearly its own detailed objectives, operations, priorities, and standards—and therefore its efficiency and performance.

In general, the success of the NAD/NARB system seems to have been greatest (1) in preventing future advertising without adequate substantiation from being run and (2) in preventing certain kinds of unacceptable claims. In this respect it is worth noting that every year the system not only distributes routinely *NAD Case Reports* and other information to the media and to other parties, but also handles numerous telephone and mail requests for literature and information from advertisers, agencies, professional and trade organizations, consumer organizations, government, educators, students, consumers, the press, and others. The internal clearance systems of advertisers, agencies, and media use this readily available information to help them avoid producing advertising that might later turn out to be unacceptable. Virtually all advertising by major companies and agencies undergoes scrutiny with these internal clearance systems, albeit with varying degrees of rigor.

On the other hand, the remedial or corrective function is relatively minor in terms of the number of cases that the system is able to handle. Also the NAD cannot correct harm done, nor can it assess penalties or fines. And, because the NAD/NARB system does not comprise members who might fear expulsion if they contravened the code, the system does not have this kind of leverage.

The effectiveness of the NAD/NARB system is enhanced by the fact that most formal cases stem from the division's own monitoring activities or from the advertising industry. The cases they identify are much more likely to lead to meaningful action than complaints from consumers, which often are relatively unsophisticated. The NAD/NARB system, it must be remembered, must function to benefit consumers and society, even though consumers may not be the best source of the most meaningful "violations."

Complaints from competitors that lead to formal cases are particularly important, because the NAD/NARB system is then in a position to enhance the normal competitive process and the efficiency of the market economy. Valid complaints lead to a reduction in deceptive or misleading advertising and therefore improve the flow of truthful and accurate information, helping the economy to function, preserving competition, and working to the best interests of consumers in society.

The NAD seems to have improved its efficiency in selecting cases recently, because both the number and proportion that lead to changes in advertising have increased, despite the decline in the total number of formal cases by about twenty-five or thirty percent in recent years.

The effectiveness of the NAD is also evident from the high rate of cooperation and compliance by the advertising industry. This cooperation does not seem to stem from low NAD/NARB standards. Rather, it stems from industry acceptance of the need to maintain the integrity of the system. It also seems likely that a system that leads to such industry cooperation and compliance is superior to a system that leads to confrontation or to industry resistance against what they would see as an infringement on the legitimate rights of sellers in a market economy.

The NAD has rightly focused much of its attention on frequently advertised products with big budgets. The number of successful "prosecutions" in certain product categories demonstrates the need for continued high priority on food and beverage advertising and other major consumer product categories. The data also indicate, however, that the NAD needs to cast its net to encompass an increasing number of other product categories in which the successful "prosecution" rate is even higher.

The main bases for complaints continue to be inadequately substantiated claims, misleading messages, or misuse of information; comparison advertising, advertising directed to children, and the use of various words relating to price information. Thus, these categories should continue to receive high priority over the large number of other issues that with the help of the NAD/NARB system already seem to have declined in frequency and importance.

Finally, at this time there appears to be no evidence that the climate of federal government deregulation has influenced adversely the operations of the NAD/NARB systems. The superficial analyst might look only at the reduced number of formal cases handled. But it is more useful to look at performance on the basis of objectives accomplished, namely, to improve truth and accuracy in advertising. Although the evidence presented here is not definitive, it suggests strongly that the NAD/NARB system is continuing to do at least as much as in the past to accomplish objectives important not only to the advertising industry but also to consumers and society. This conclusion is supported by the evidence on efficiency in case selection, changes in "unsatisfactory" advertising, and the focus on important issues that affect future truth and accuracy in advertising.

Additional anecdotal evidence supports this view. For example, when the FTC proposed changes in the advertising substantiation program, the advertising industry protested (*AAAA response* 1983). Recently it was reported that "when the FTC failed to act on a complaint challenging deceptive nutrition claims in Campbell's 'Soup is good food' campaign, the Center for Science in the Public Interest turned to the New York state attorney general's office and to the National Advertising Division (NAD). . . . The NAD struck first, recommending that certain nutrition claims be dropped. . . . In another case, the National Broadcasting Co.'s office of broadcast standards required changes in Del Monte's 'As nutritious as fresh cooked' ad campaign after the FTC failed to act on a complaint. . . . Later the NAD investigated . . . and found the entire campaign to be unsubstantiated . . . NAD . . . [has] also acted on . . . complaints challenging advertising by the National Coffee Assn. [and] Coca-Cola . . . in each case . . . after the FTC had failed to respond."(Silverglade 1985, 20, 24).

Notes

1. Of course, consumer groups have general complaints about television advertising, or advertising of certain products such as alcoholic beverages, or advertising to certain groups such as children.

2. We ignore the activities of the BBBs and LARPs regarding local advertising only because little information is available.

References

Advertising Evaluation and Policy Statement (1972) (New York: National Advertising Review Board, 20 January 1972).

Advertising Self-Regulation and its Interaction with Consumers (1979) (New York: National Advertising Review Board).

Alexander, George J. (1967), *Honesty and Competition* (Syracuse, New York: Syracuse University Press).

The American Association of Advertising Agencies Response to the Federal Trade Commission's Inquiry on the Advertising Substantiation Program (1983) (New York and Washington: Board of Directors of the AAAA, 13 July 1983).

Armstrong, Gary M. (1984), "An Evaluation of the Children's Advertising Review Unit," *Journal of Public Policy and Marketing* 3:38–55.

Armstrong, Gary M., and Ozanne, Julie L. (1983), "An Evaluation of NAD/NARB Purpose and Performance," *Journal of Advertising* 12(3):15–26, 52.

Bauer, R.A., and Greyser, S.A. (1968), *Advertising in America: The Consumer View* (Boston: Harvard University, Graduate School of Business Administration, Division of Research).

Beatson, Ronald (1984), "The Image of Advertising in Europe," *International Journal of Advertising* 3:361–367.

Bernhardt, Kenneth L., Robinson, Larry M., and Semans, Debra (1983), "Consumer Complaint Handling," in Patrick E. Murphy et al. (eds.), *AMA Educators' Proceedings* (Chicago: American Marketing Association, Series No. 49:369–373).

Better Business News and Views, various issues.

Boddewyn, J.J. (1985), "US Advertising Self-Regulation: The FTC as Outside Partner of the NAD/NARB," mimeographed draft, March 1985.

Buell, Victor P. (1977), *The British Approach to Improving Advertising Standards and Practice: A Comparison with the US Experience* (Amherst: University of Massachusetts, School of Business Administration).

CBBB Annual Reports, various years.

Cohen, Stanley (1980), "Self-Regulation in Advertising through the NAD and NARB," *Proceedings of the Annual Conference of the American Academy of Advertising/1980,* James E. Haefner (ed.) (Urbana-Champaign: University of Illinois), 162–164.

Cox, Kenneth (1980), "Self-Regulation of Advertising Through the NAD and NARB," *Proceedings of the Annual Conference of the American Academy of Advertising/1980,* James E. Haefner (ed.) (Urbana-Champaign: University of Illinois), 157–159.

Diamond, Steven L., Ward, Scott, and Faber, Ronald (1975), "Consumer Problems and Consumerism: Analysis of Calls to a Consumer Hotline," Working Paper 74–5, (Cambridge, Mass.: Marketing Science Institute).

Do's and Don'ts in Advertising Copy (undated) (Washington: Council of Better Business Bureaus, various dates [a looseleaf service for advertisers, advertising agencies, broadcasters, and printed media]).

Dzodin, Harvey C. (1986), "The ABCs of American Television Advertising Review and Clearance," Remarks before the International Bar Association, New York, 19 September 1986 (mimeographed).

Ewen, William H. (1975), *The National Advertising Review Board 1971–1975* (Washington, D.C.: Council of Better Business Bureaus).

Feldman, Laurence P. (1980), *Consumer Protection: Problems and Prospects,* 2nd ed. (St. Paul: West Publishing Company).

Inquiries and Complaints: Statistical Summary of 1982 Data (1983) (Arlington, Va.: Council of Better Business Bureaus).

International Code of Advertising Practice (1982) (Paris: International Chamber of Commerce).

LaBarbera, Priscilla A. (1980a), "Advertising Self-Regulation: An Evaluation," *MSU Business Topics* (Summer 1980), 55–63.

LaBarbera, Priscilla A. (1980b), "Analyzing and Advancing the State of the Art of Advertising Self-Regulation," *Journal of Advertising* 9(4):27–38.

Miller, Joseph C., and Hutt, Michael D. (1983), "Assessing Societal Effects of Product Regulations: Toward an Analytic Framework," in Patrick E. Murphy et al. (eds.), *1983 AMA Educators' Proceedings,* Series No. 49 (Chicago: American Marketing Association), 364–368.

Miracle, Gordon E. (1985a), "A Brief History of US Advertising Self-Regulation to 1970," in Nancy Stephens (ed.), *Proceedings of the 1985 Conference of the American Academy of Advertising* (Tempe., Ar: College of Business, Arizona State University, R2–R7).

Miracle, Gordon E. (1985b), "Advertising Regulation in Japan and the USA: An Introductory Comparison," *Waseda Business and Economic Studies,* No. 21, 35–69.

NAD Case Report, various issues.

NAD Case Report (1983), 15 July 1983, 13(6):20–23.

NARB (various dates), *Reports of the NARB Panels.*

Neelankavil, James P., and Stridsberg, Albert B. (1980), *Advertising Self-Regulation* (New York: Hastings House).

Purdon, Roger A. (1972), "Advertising Self-Regulation—A New Reality," presented to the 1972 Annual Meeting of the American Association of Advertising Agencies, Boca Raton, Fl., 16 March 1972.

Robinson, Larry M. (1979), "Consumer Complaint Behavior: A Bibliography of Research Findings," in Ralph L. Day and Keith Hunt (eds.), *New Dimensions of Consumer Satisfaction and Complaining Behavior* (Bloomington, Ind.: Division of Research, School of Business, Indiana University), 196–201.

Scherer, F.M. (1970), *Industrial Market Structure and Economic Performance* (Chicago: Rand McNally and Company), Chap. 1.

Self-Regulation Codes of Practice (1983) (Brussels: European Advertising Tripartite, April 1983).

Silverglade, Bruce A. (1985), "FTC Oversight Still Needed," *Advertising Age,* 3 June 1985, 20, 24.

Statement of Organization and Procedure of the National Advertising Review Board (1980) (New York: NARB, 19 June 1980).

Swartz, James E., and Neman, Thomas E. (1983), "NAD and NARB Reviews as a Reflection of Societal Trends: The Case for Natural Foods," in Donald W. Jugenheimer (ed.), *Proceedings of the 1983 Convention of the American Academy of Advertising,* 70–73.

Villarreal-Camacho, Angelina (1983), "Consumer Complaining Behavior: A Cross-Cultural Comparison," in Patrick E. Murphy et al., (eds.), *1983 AMA Educators' Proceedings* (Chicago: American Marketing Association), 68–73.

Zanot, Eric J., and Maddox, Lynda (1977), "National Advertising Review Board Decisions Involving Common 'Problem' Areas of Deception in Advertising," in Gordon E. Miracle (ed.), *Proceedings of the Annual Conference of the American Academy of Advertising* (East Lansing: Department of Advertising, Michigan State University), 117–121.

Zanot, Eric J. (1979a), "The National Advertising Division: The Hidden Backbone of the National Advertising Review Board," in Steven E. Permut (ed.), *Proceedings of the Annual Conference of the American Academy of Advertising* (New Haven: School of Organization and Management, Yale University), 39–45.

Zanot, Eric J. (1979b), "The National Advertising Review Board, 1971–76," *Journalism Monographs* 59 (February 1979).

Zanot, Eric J. (1980a), "A Review of Eight Years of NARB Casework: Guidelines and Parameters of Deceptive Advertising," *Journal of Advertising* 9(4):20–26, 42.

Zanot, Eric J. (1980b), "Foundation of Self-Regulation," in James E. Haefner (ed.), *Proceedings of the Annual Conference of the American Academy of Advertising* (Urbana: Department of Advertising, University of Illinois), 155–156.

7

An Assessment of Performance: The United Kingdom

Introduction

The introductory section of chapter 6 provided the framework for our assessment of performance in that chapter as well as for this one; that framework therefore will not be repeated here. In this chapter we discuss the system of self-regulation in the United Kingdom.

The United Kingdom: The ASA/CAP System

Objectives of British Self-Regulation of Advertising

Because we have discussed already the specific objectives and goals of the ASA/CAP Committee system of self-regulation for print, cinema, and poster advertising, we will not enumerate them again. It is sufficient to keep in mind at this point that the ASA/CAP Committee system has as its main objectives to ensure that (1) advertising within its remit is legal, decent, honest, and truthful; (2) such advertising should be prepared with a sense of responsibility both to the consumer and to society; (3) all advertisements should conform to the principles of fair competition as generally accepted in business; and (4) the ASA/CAP Committee should be seen as the body that has responsibility to accomplish these objectives.

From its inception in 1962 the system adhered to the first three of these general principles. The fourth item regarding public visibility evolved later. Lord Tweedsmuir, chairman of the ASA in 1972, wrote in his annual report for 1972–1973 that "the Authority is clear that only by a policy of greater openness can it meet, as it should, the growing demand in all spheres for greater accountability" (*ASA Annual Report* 1983–1984, 5).

As stated in the previous chapter it can be argued that the ASA/CAP Committee system, the IBA Code of Advertising Standards, and the several industries that have fair competition codes relating to advertising are at least minimally successful if (1) members of society, especially consumers and business firms, are reasonably satisfied; and (2) the control systems remain sufficiently flexible to adapt to changing standards in accomplishing these general objectives to the satisfaction of society and government. To evaluate the system against these criteria, we review information from the ASA/CAP Committee system as well as information from independent sources.

There are several lines of defense against advertising that do not meet the provisions of *BCAP*. The Code makes it plain that the ultimate responsibility for an advertisement is with the advertiser. Most major national advertisers in any case belong to ISBA, one of the organizations represented on the CAP Committee, whose members are thereby bound to uphold and enforce the Code's provisions. Advertising agencies are bound by the terms of their media recognition agreements, which state that all the advertising they supply to the media must conform with the provisions of the Code. In addition, most large agencies belong to the IPA, another body represented on the CAP Committee. The last defense between the industry and the consumer is the media. Again, most media belong to organizations that are members of the CAP Committee, but they have an additional incentive to scrutinize material they receive in that a publisher has a legal liability for anything appearing in his publication.

Some media and organizations have codes of their own that affect advertising. In every case, however, these are intended to supplement *BCAP*, and in no sense aim to replace or circumvent it. Because government regulation also plays a relatively minor role in the United Kingdom, it may be assumed that the influence of the Code is considerable on all sides of the advertising industry—far greater than the influence of the NAD/NARB system in the United States.

Self-Evaluation

The *BCAP* is fairly well known among the general public, with unprompted public awareness of the ASA increasing from from eleven percent to twenty-three percent from 1980 to 1982 (*ASA Annual Report* 1982–1983, 13). Perhaps public response to the ASA's advertising campaign creates additional pressures on the advertising business. In any event, the ASA feels that it is important to be widely known as the institution that safeguards high standards of advertising by enforcing *BCAP*. The Authority uses two main methods for disseminating knowledge of its work:

1. Advertisements prepared by a professional advertising agency, and run with space donated by advertising media.

2. Direct personal relations with, and presentations to, those in the advertising industry and members of other interested organizations (such as consumer groups and educational institutions) (*ASA Annual Report* 1980, 4).

The ASA also publishes "editorials" on issues of interest in its monthly case reports (*ASA Annual Report,* 1980, 5) and issues news releases in certain cases.

The objectives of the ASA's campaign to the public are to inform would-be complainants of the existence of the ASA and to tell them how to use it. The campaign in 1980 consisted of a series of advertisements in the national and regional press and magazines, and also on posters. ... Launched in February, 1980, the number of complaints in 1980 increased 94% over 1979, and the quality of complaints showed remarkable improvement" (*ASA Annual Report* 1980).

The maturity of the ASA/CAP Committee system was evident also in that in December 1980 the CAP published its first report on the outcome of intraindustry complaints (that is, complaints made by one advertiser about another) (*ASA Annual Report* 1980, 13).

The ASA/CAP Committee has not evaluated itself in a separate published report devoted to that purpose. However, one can find self-evaluative statements throughout published ASA literature, especially in ASA annual reports, monthly case reports, and in the reprints of speeches by ASA staff. In general, the ASA believes that it is doing a good job of being visible to consumers and government officials; and that it is serving business and society well by handling a substantial volume of inquiries, consumer complaints, and advertising industry complaints and especially by monitoring advertising in the media. Additionally, in presentations to industry professional and educational organizations and other groups, the ASA believes that it is doing important work by informing others about important issues and sensitizing them to be alert to avoid problems and deal with problems when they arise. To these ends, films, slide presentations, and literature are available for widespread use by interested groups.

Sanctions. Critics often point out that self-regulatory organizations lack legal authority and power to impose penalties to enforce compliance. The ASA has been characterized not only "as a toothless beast, lacking legal sanctions, but also a mere dependency of the advertising industry which set it up and finances it" (*ASA Annual Report* 1981, 5). The chairman of the ASA, Lord McGregor of Durris, who has no advertising connections, responds:

Toothless we are not. The sanction of the willingness of newspapers and periodicals to withhold their space from recalcitrant advertisers at our request is a complete sanction, to say nothing of the undesirable effects for advertisers of the publicity which inevitably accompanies some of the Authority's adjudications. [Moreover, the ASA has] the advantages of a regular income . . . without leading strings upon [its] independence. (*ASA Annual Report* 1981, 5).

If the ASA finds a breach of the Code, it asks the advertiser for assurance that the offense will not be repeated. Usually the advertiser agrees. When not, the ASA

issues notices to media organizations . . . advising them of the advertiser's failure to comply with the Code. Such notices . . . usually take the form of notifying the media that the Authority cannot recommend acceptance of advertisements containing claims which were the subject of the complaint—spelling out claims where necessary—since these contravened the Code, which media organizations are pledged to support. Alternatively, media may be informed that the advertiser is no longer trading or is in liquidation (*ASA Annual Report* 1981, 25).

The ASA seems to believe that its sanctions are not only adequate, but probably as effective as is possible under the conditions that exist in the United Kingdom. Chairman Lord McGregor states, "In my view, the self-imposed sanctions which the ASA uses would not be strengthened in practice by substituting a legal for a voluntary process" (*ASA Annual Report* 1981, 5).

Reduced Government Workload. Numerous laws affect advertising, as discussed elsewhere in this book, and the OFT is very much interested in seeing that advertising is regulated in accordance with the law and in the best interests of society. However, the ASA/CAP Committee system handles the regulations of advertising in print, poster, cinema, and other nonbroadcast media so comprehensively and satisfactorily that it is rare to find an unlawful advertisement, thus leaving little for government action. And, while exact statistics are not available on costs, the relative informality and absence of attorney fees surely means that costs are much less than if government legal action were needed. Likewise, the speed of resolution of cases is generally far greater than if a government agency or courts (or both) were required to resolve them. Morever, the great bulk of the ASA/CAP Committee workload so far comprises issues that do not constitute infringements of the law, and are adjudicated according to stricter standards than the law imposes.

ASA/CAP Committee's Scope of Activities

In addition to commercial advertising in print, poster, and cinema media, the ASA/CAP Committee has broadened its scope in a number of ways in recent years.

First, it has looked into specialized or controversial topics to determine if it should function in additional ways. A study was conducted and published in 1982 entitled *Herself Appraised: The Treatment of Women in Advertising,* which did not reveal widespread dissatisfaction among women about advertisements. Concerns about nudity or explicit references to sexuality, menstruation, and related matters were not sufficiently widely shared for advertisements containing such material to be declared offensive in terms of the *BCAP.* The reaction of respondents did not suggest that additional rules related to the depiction of women in advertisements were needed. The ASA concluded that it is not its function "to use the enforcement of the Code as a means of promoting social change, however desirable; though common sense suggests, and observation confirms, that advertisers, no doubt moved by an awareness of where their commercial interest lies, will always be ready to adjust their appeals as the sensitivities of their audiences change" (*ASA Annual Report* 1983–1984, 7).

The seventh edition of the *BCAP* preserves the principle that an advertisement expressing the advertiser's position on a matter of political controversy is outside the scope of the Code. The Authority therefore will not concern itself with opinions expressed in such advertisements or with evidence used to support or explain them. There are, however, certain requirements that political advertisers must follow: their advertisements must be readily recognizable for what they are, they must leave no doubt as to the advertiser's identity, and they must include the advertiser's address or telephone number when these are not otherwise readily available.

A distinction is drawn between political advertisements that express an opinion and those that appeal for funds. In advertisements that express an opinion, assertions of fact are treated as they would be in commercial advertisements, particularly in terms of being backed by adequate substantiation (*BCAP* 1985, B.6).

In 1982 the post office established the Direct Mail Services Standards Board, which requires direct mail sales materials to adhere to the *BCAP* and *BCSPP.* The Board remits any relevant issues to the Authority for adjudication (*ASA Annual Report* 1982–1983, 6).

In 1984 the ASA broadened its scope and versatility by adding as members the Direct Mail Services Standards Board and the Videotex Industry Association, Ltd. "Their enrollment emphasizes that the provisions of the Code are equally appropriate to advertising in a variety of new and diverse media" (*ASA Annual Report* 1984–1985, 8).

Independent Evaluations

In addition to requiring that advertising be legal, *BCAP* extends to areas untouched by the law. These areas are described generally by the words *decent, honest,* and *truthful,* and are carried out in spirit and in principle to reflect changing conditions and public attitudes (*Review of the UK Self-Regulatory System of Advertising Self-Control* 1978, i).

The ASA/CAP Committee system was sufficiently successful by 1981 that the debate concerned refinements in the efficiency of the system rather than whether it should be supplanted by government or made a part of government. One criticism of the ASA/CAP system is that it has a "tendency to triviality . . . [that] a small but vocal minority in the British Advertising industry . . . would rather have a legal system of control, for it feels, with much justification, that the law would be kinder to the industry than its own system of control tends to be" (Painter 1981, 29). This type of criticism underscores the effectiveness of the system.

However, other critics in the 1970s argued that the ASA/CAP Committee system required substantial improvements, which to a large extent, as we discuss later, have since been implemented. It is worthwhile here to review the events of the late 1970s as a preface to the changes that the ASA/CAP Committee system underwent in the early 1980s.

After pressures from the Secretary of State and the DGFT in 1974, the ASA undertook in April 1975 an advertising campaign with two main purposes: (1) to inform the public of the existence of the self-regulatory control system and (2) to tell the public how to make complaints to the ASA. In the first year of the campaign the ASA spent £158,000 and received the equivalent of £228,000 of free space from the media. During 1976 and 1977 the advertising was continued at a comparable level. During 1978 the ASA committed £275,000 to advertising and received the equivalent of about £500,000 in free space (*Review of the UK Self-Regulatory System of Advertising Control* 1978, 10).

As a result the number of complaints received by the ASA rose rapidly, from 516 in the twelve months between April 1974 and March 1975, to 3,850 during 1976 and 1977, and to 4,269 in 1977 and 1978. Of the approximately 4,000 complaints, somewhat less than 2,000 were pursued (*Review of UK Self-Regulatory System of Advertising Control* 1978, 9).

In November 1977 the OFT, the Consumers Association (CA), and the AA formed a working party to devise research into the current standard of press and magazine advertising (*Review of the UK Self-Regulatory System of Advertising Control* 1978).

This review of the system reported that the vast majority (ninety-three percent) of advertisements in newspapers conform to the Code, although the equivalent figure for national publications is only eighty-seven percent, the working party believed that this thirteen percent failure rate was high, although few infringements seemed to amount to gross deception likely to cause consumers significant harm (*Review of the UK Self-Regulatory System of Advertising Control* 1978, i).

Regarding the work of the ASA/CAP Committee system, the *Review* (1978, i–ii) indicated that there was no reason to question the quality of decisions on cases, but that such decisions took too long to reach. The *Review* also recommended that more efforts should be devoted to prepublication vetting and to postpublication monitoring.

Regarding sanctions the *Review* noted that the ASA's prime sanction was the power of the media to deny advertising space to offending advertisers or agencies. Although effective in theory, the report concluded, this sanction was applied too slowly.

The *Review* concluded that although the situation was *not* "of crisis dimensions crying out for drastic action," there was some need for legislative reinforcement of the ASA's position.

> We have concluded that the best legislative measure would be one of giving the Director General of Fair Trading a power to proceed to the court for an injunction to restrain an advertiser or a medium in a situation where, in his opinion, an advertisement was likely to deceive, mislead or confuse, where speedy and effective action was necessary and where action by the ASA had not been or would not be likely to be, sufficiently quick and effective to prevent the continued use of the advertisement . . . a power of this kind would be infrequently used . . . [it] would not duplicate the work of the ASA, only supplement it . . . the power would [not] extend to the area of taste and decency (*Review of the UK Self-Regulatory System of Advertising Control* 1978, iii).

The *Review* also made a number of other recommendations, one of which was to extend the scope of the Code (1) to cover nonmedia and foreign language advertisements as well as editorial offers; (2) to improve the internal workings of the council, secretariat, and panels; and (3) to consider the possibility of additional sanctions.

The recommended extensions of the work of the ASA regarding prevetting and monitoring would "gradually enable the ASA to take initiatives with individual advertisers where failures of the Code have occurred, instead of merely responding to complaints; and to spot undesirable trends developing in particular markets and areas" (*Review of the UK Self-Regulatory System of Advertising Control* 1978, ii).

"[I]n 1974 a Consumers' Association Study found that fourteen percent of advertisements in national newspapers and magazines breached the Code . . . the equivalent figure for 1978 was still as high as thirteen percent . . . however minor may seem some of the breaches . . . they in fact portray a disturbing disregard of the Code" (*Review of the UK Self-Regulatory System of Advertising Control* 1978, 43). The report also noted elsewhere: "we believe that the importance of the *BCAP* is such as to necessitate statutory intervention to ensure its observance" (*Review of the UK Self-Regulatory System of Advertising Control* 1978, 44).

Although the DGFT concluded that a wider system of statutory advertising control was not needed, the OFT review suggested that the self-regulatory system consider using additional sanctions: (1) corrective advertising and (2) fines (levied by the sponsoring associations on the CAP Committee or their members. The associations would be expected to expel members who refused to pay the fine). Neither suggestion has been adopted, nor does it appear likely that they will be adopted in the future.

The results of the research to identify failures in the Code must be interpreted in light of the validity of the methods used to achieve the results. The AA, in a review of the research on which the OFT Review was made, pointed out that the "amateur" assessors identifying advertisements that contravened the Code made many questionable decisions. The AA report detailed examples of assessor misunderstanding of what contravenes the Code and definitions of terms (*OFT Research* 1978, 13–14). The AA report added that in the ASA's view there were "a large number of advertisements wrongly failed by the assessors in consequence of their misinterpretation of the facts relating to a given advertisement" (*OFT Research* 1978, 14–15). The AA report went on to identify numerous examples of incomprehensible, indefensible, and trivial objections, acceptance of adviser's opinions without opportunity for the advertiser to comment, failure to check further on inadequate substantiation, basing judgment on unsupported subjective opinions, and inconsistencies in the approach of assessors (*OFT Research* 1978, 15–17). The AA also criticized the sample and lack of weighting procedures, pointing out that the OFT "failure" rate is not only too high, but that most "fails" were trivial (*OFT Research* 1978, 18). Moreover, the AA assessment concluded that consumers for whom the advertising was salient might view advertisements differently from the assessors, and "take information from them in different ways from the assessors who were specifically checking them against the Code" (*OFT Research* 1978, 19). The AA conducted an additional analysis of the data that indicated that with few exceptions there was "no difference in the general pattern of responses [of consumers] between advertisements which passed or failed the Code (*OFT Research* 1978, 22). The AA concluded: "The report is so inconclusive that it is unlikely that the OFT or anyone else will be able to use it to prove anything. The main "helpful" finding to emerge is that no particular groups of people appear vulnerable to advertising as is often suggested" (*OFT Research* 1978, 24).

In February 1979 it was announced to Parliament that a working party had been established to assess "the scale of any problem posed by weaknesses in the self-regulatory control operated by the [advertising] industry. . . . Membership was drawn from the Advertising Association (AA), the Advertising Standards Authority (ASA), the National Consumer Council (NCC), the Office of Fair Trading (OFT), the Home Office, the

Lord Chancellor's Department and the . . . [subsequently renamed] Department of Trade. The Working Party's remit . . . and . . . Terms of Reference were adopted on 23 July 1979: to consider whether, and if so to what extent, the existing self-regulatory system of advertising control in the United Kingdom requires reinforcement; to make any necessary recommendations and to report" (*The Self-Regulatory System of Advertising Control—Report of the Working Party* 1980, 2).

The Working Party considered the 1978 DGFT's recommendations. Against the background and findings of this report, the Working Party considered the possible weaknesses in the coverage of the present arrangements, the effectiveness of sanctions, the implications of EEC activities on misleading and unfair advertising, and the principal options for strengthening the self-regulatory arrangements. The main recommendation of the Working Party was that the DGFT should be given power to seek an injunction to stop publication of "an advertisement likely to deceive or mislead with regard to any material facts" (*The Self-Regulatory System of Advertising Control—Report of the Working Party* 1980, 14).

Another independent evaluation of the ASA/CAP Committee system, with some additional useful perspectives, comes from Professor J.J. Boddewyn of the City University of New York. He pointed out that the credibility and legitimacy of the ASA and its reputation for objectivity depend on the independence of the ASA from the advertising industry. Although funding comes from the advertising industry, it is a fixed percentage, collected automatically, and not subject to influence by advertisers or agencies. But, although financial independence is assured, the *BCAP* is drawn up exclusively by industry representatives; however, the ASA Council with a majority of nonadvertising members "checks in any case if the Code meets public expectations, and it puts pressure on the CAP Committee to make the necessary revisions" (Boddewyn 1983). The ASA Council has the power to overrule CAP Committee decisions.

The Council also exercises control over the handling of complaints by the secretariat, which has to report to the Council on every case, whether it thought an investigation was necessary. The secretariat has the power to ask an advertiser for interim action when it believes this to be necessary, but the Council has the final decision as to whether a complaint should be pursued and how it should be resolved (*BCAP* 1985, Introduction, 30). "If even *one* Council member requests pursuit, the matter is investigated" (Boddewyn 1983–86).

Thus it seems likely that "outside representation of the ASA Council has contributed to the acceptance and effectiveness of the ASA self-regulatory system. The major contribution . . . is that they grant a 'seal of quality' . . . to the ASA by vouching for its independence and greater objectivity in code development and application. This, in turn, generates credibility and legitimacy. . . . The fact that the ASA can find and retain such otherwise busy prominent outsiders provides the basis for such credibility" (Boddewyn 1983, 90). Moreover, retaining a number of industry members probably leads to decisions that are more sophisticated and accurate than outsiders could make because they provide professional knowledge of advertising to augment the objectivity of nonindustry members.

In appraising the system, it is also useful to examine the opinion of leaders of consumer organizations. The "private and prestigious Consumers' Association," as quoted by Boddewyn (1983, 88), attests to the effectiveness of the system. He notes, "Self-regulatory codes are seldom effective. . . . The one obvious success has been the *British Code of Advertising Practice* but it operates under conditions favouring success." Boddewyn adds:

> This last quote refers to the "effective sanctions" applicable by the ASA. These include: (a) media agreeing to stop the publication of an ad found to be in violation of the ASA Code; (b) media denying access to the incriminated advertiser; (c) withdrawing the professional privileges of the implicated advertising agencies; (d) publicizing the name and offense of violators; and (e) advising complainants to draw the matter to the attention of the relevant enforcement authority if a law appears to have been broken. The Council, in deciding to uphold a complaint, mandates its staff to take steps to obtain compliance with its adjudications.
>
> Such sanctions are relatively frequently used and are routinely accepted by the participating media. Even though the application of such sanctions would still take place if no outsiders sat on the ASA Council, their presence adds credibility and weight to the sanctioning process (Boddewyn 1983, 88).

Recently R.W. Lawson (1985) investigated complaint behavior with respect to advertising in the United Kingdom, examining the responses of the ASA toward advertising complaints. Some of the ASA's responses reveal its performance. For example, in the case of complaints alleging untruthful statements in advertisements, the ASA decisions (in the sample selected) upheld the complainant 85.7 percent of the time. On other serious issues such as false impression, exaggeration, and omission of relevant information, the ASA has supported the complainant in the great majority of the cases. On relatively infrequent and unimportant issues such as puffery and irrelevance, the ASA decisions rarely favor the complainant. Although Lawson does not draw conclusions that evaluate the ASA/CAP Committee system, the evidence he presents suggests that the system rightly focuses its efforts on the information aspects of advertising, which are the most frequent sources of consumer complaints, while at the same time remains sensitive to the relatively infrequent but emotionally laden complaints of puffery, irrelevance, sex, violence, safety, children, and fear (Lawson 1985, 287).

> In a recent study Jones and Pickering (1985) concluded that generally it seems there is quite a high level of desire to adhere to the terms of the codes, though it is claimed that some advertisers deliberately "sail close to the wind. . . ."
>
> In general, however, the UK system of advertising self-regulation has a high level of acceptance on the part of key interest groups and, as we have noted, it has received strong support from public bodies in the face of EEC attempts to enforce a legal form of advertising control. Where there are concerns these point to the desirability of paying greater attention to the need to control persistent offenders, to increase the emphasis on substantiation (perhaps including a "truth mark" where substantiation has been provided) and to provide for corrective advertising where a misleading claim has been made. Perhaps, given the nature of advertising, it would be appropriate to look for greater efforts to ensure that all advertisers know more clearly the standards that are being sought and have their print advertisements also prevetted, since ex ante control could be easier to achieve in advertising than with most other codes of practice (Jones and Pickering 1985, 67–68).

We return to these recommendations in our final chapter.

Functions and Workload of the CAP Committee

"The principal function of the committee is to coordinate the actions of member associations so as to achieve the highest degree of compliance with the Codes" (*CAP Committee* 1985). The committee handles only intratrade matters and does not accept complaints or inquiries from nonindustry sources, as described earlier. It has four standing subcommittees that handle much of the detailed work, particularly prepublication advice, and operate in the areas of mail order and direct response, health and nutrition, sales promotion, and financial advertising. The Committee is assisted by the Copy Panel in matters relating to interpretation of the Code. It is also represented on the SFD Viewing Committee, which undertakes prepublication scrutiny of all press advertisements for posters and front-of-house photographs for films in the "18" category.

Table 7–1 indicates the volume of work undertaken by the Committee in terms of the number of complaints and their investigation, requests for information, and the preclearance of cigarette advertisements.

The Copy Panel met on ten occasions in 1984 to give advice on forty-eight complaints. This panel was established several years earlier to

Table 7–1
Intraindustry Complaints Handled by the
CAP Committee

	1982	1983	1984
Complaints received	1,058	1,132	1,055
Complaints requiring investigation	424	307	368
Complaints upheld, in whole or in part	306	247	169
Complaints that did not contravene the Code	118	60	56
Complaints not pursued[a]	396	592	542
Complaints withdrawn by complainant	238	161	145
Requests for copy advice on interpretation of the code			
Written	922	888	794
Telephone	n.a.	n.a.	2,271
Clearance certificates for cigarette advertisements	360	274	227

Source: *ASA Annual Reports*, various years.

[a]Not pursued because the complaint was: (1) about television, (2) outside remit (for example, unlawful), (3) not justified, (4) already investigated, or (5) more details needed.

provide advice on particularly "contentious areas such as comparative claims, denigration of competitors, and allegations of omission of information or misleading statements in advertisements" (*ASA Annual Report* 1984–1985, 10).

"The Society of Film Distributors (SFD) Viewing Committee is responsible for the scrutiny before publication of all press advertisements, posters and front of house photographs of films. . . . The CAP Committee and the British Board of Film Censors have advisers on this committee. In 1984, 80 press and poster advertisements and 670 front of house photographs were submitted for approval. Most were approved with only minor changes" (*ASA Annual Report* 1984–1985,11).

Functions and Workload of the ASA

Complaints Handled. From the mid-1960s through 1972 the volume of complaints submitted to the ASA averaged approximately 200 per year. In 1973 and 1974 the volume increased to 446 and 516, respectively, and then rose rapidly in the next years to 3,367 in 1979 and 6,533 in 1980. Thereafter the growth was relatively modest, to a total of 7,733 in 1984, as shown in table 7–2. Tables 7–3 and 7–4 provide additional details on the ASA workload, distinguishing between mail order delays and advertising copy complaints.

Table 7–2
Complaints Received by the ASA from Consumers

	1980		1981		1982		1983		1984	
	Number	Percentage	Number	Percentage	Number	Percentage	Number	Percentage	Number	Percentage
Total received	6,533	100	6,145	100	7,690	100	7,548	100	7,733	100
Not pursued[a]	4,324	66	4,367	71	4,576	60	4,637	61	4,790	62
Pursued cases investigated	2,209	34	1,778	29	3,114	40	2,911	39	2,943	38
Of those cases pursued: Mail order delay										
Number of complaints	1,054	16	673	11	893	12	549	7	629	8
Number of investigations	936	14	665	11	681	9	599	8	586	8
Copy[b]										
Number of complaints	n.a.		n.a.		2,221	29	2,362	31	2,314	30
Number of different advertisements involved	1,155	18	1,105	18	1,485	19	1,248	17	1,170	15
Number of investigations	1,033	16	1,281	21	1,331	17	1,473	20	1,420	18

Source: *ASA Annual Reports,* 1980 to 1984–1985.

[a]Not pursued because the complaint was (1) about television, (2) outside remit (that is, unlawful), (3) not justified, (4) already investigated, or (5) more details needed.

[b]The number of complaints is larger than the number of different advertisments because of duplication in complaints. The number of investigations is larger than the number of different advertisements because some advertisements required investigation on more than one issue.

Table 7-3
Resolution of Mail Order Delay Complaints

	1980		1981		1982		1983		1984	
	Number	*Percentage*	*Number*	*Percentage*	*Number*	*Percentage*	*Number*	*Percentage*	*Number*	*Percentage*
Number of mail order investigations	936	100%	665	100%	681	100%	599	100%	586	100%
Number resolved by receipt of goods or refund	636	68	505	76	566	83	433	72	414	71
Not resolved[a]	300	32	160	24	115	17	166	28	172	29
Number referred to media	142	15	73	11	37	5	54	9	73	12

[a]If the seller refuses to respond or to cooperate with the ASA, the case may be referred to the media—if it is appropriate to do so. However, some mail order delays do not involve advertising media that are members of the associations that support the Code; some cases do not involve media at all. Also, some companies have gone into liquidation.

Table 7–4
Resolution of Copy Complaints

	1980		1981		1982		1983		1984	
	Number	Percentage	Number	Percentage	Number	Percentage	Number	Percentage	Number	Percentage
Number of copy investigations	1,033	100	1,281	100	1,331	100	1,473	100	1,420	100
Complaints *not* upheld, advertising was substantiated, no breach of the Code	506	49	455	36	477	36	428	29	318	22
Complaint upheld wholly or in part	527	51	826	64	854	64	1,045	71	1,102	78
Advertisers agreed to stop or correct the offence	514	50	795	62	833	63	1,014	69	1,071	75
Advertising referred to media[a]	13	1	31	2	21	2	31	2	31	2

[a]The advertising is referred to the media only if the advertiser fails to answer the ASA's inquiries, or if the advertiser fails to provide adequate substantiation and is unwilling to provide adequate assurances that the offending advertisement will not be repeated.

The ASA recognizes, as we discuss previously, that the number of "complaints from the public is not a valid index of the extent to which the Code is observed by advertisers" (*ASA Annual Report* 1982–1983,4). Complaining is only one of a number of alternatives available to a dissatisfied or offended consumer. Perhaps the most frequent behavior is to change purchasing and consumption to avoid the product or service. Thus, complaining behavior may be relatively infrequent compared with the frequency of dissatisfaction, but additional research needs to be done to test the validity of this possibility, along with measures of the nature and intensity of consumer satisfactions and dissatisfactions.

However, the volume of complaints received, investigated, and settled provides at least an indication of ASA workload, thus permitting some inferences as to whether the complaint-handling body is performing its mission.

It may be useful at this point to remind the reader that a large proportion of consumer complaints are not pursued for a variety of reasons, in addition to those reasons mentioned in the footnote to table 7–2. Often complaints are "based not on the advertisement but on imaginative reinterpretations of what the advertiser has said. Nor should complainants expect advertisers to share their attitudes and values—and complain if they do not. . . . Value judgments can only be contested if they imply something about the product which can be objectively measured—and which turns out not to be as stated" (*ASA Case Report 92* 1982, 1–2). Quality and beauty often lie in the eye of the beholder. Thus the ASA staff may conclude that a complainant has not made out a prima facie case for a breach of the Code that would warrant investigation.

Table 7–5 indicates the major "offenses" against the Code, according to consumer complaints that led to discovery of Code breaches. These complaints continue at a fairly stable level for the major categories: (1) misleading advertising and (2) advertising claims that are not substantiated. The steady level of breaches of the code in recent years in these major categories suggests that little change for the better is occurring in British advertising. However, as noted elsewhere, complaint data are not entirely adequate to draw this inference. The recently improved sampling frame for monitoring advertising should provide a better basis for judgment in future years.

Although the "other" category in table 7–5 is quite large in total, each component is small. For example, the complaints that deal with decency comprise only one or two percent, depending on the year; unfair comparisons have been about two percent in recent years. Others that seem to have been important some years ago, such as complaints about slimming, also account for only one or two percent of complaints.

Table 7–5
Breaches[a] of the *BACP* Uncovered by ASA Copy Investigations

Type of Breach	1982		1983		1984	
	Number	Percentage	Number	Percentage	Number	Percentage
Misleading advertising (*BCAP*)	273	32	350	33	374	34
Claim not substantiated (*BCAP*)	128	15	168	16	183	17
Prices not as advertised (*BCAP*)	65	8	77	7	62	6
Nonavailability of goods (*BCAP*)	46	5	54	5	45	4
Other	342	40	396	38	438	40
Total	854	100	1,045	99[b]	1,102	101[b]
Sales promotion (BCSPP)	n.a.	n.a.	72		84	

Source: *ASA Annual Reports*, 1982–1983, 1983–1984, 1984–1985
[a]A breach of the Code means the complaint was upheld wholly or in part.
[b]Does not add to 100 percent owing to rounding.

In sum, "in the vast majority of cases the breach of the Code resulted from carelessness on the part of the advertiser in preparation of the advertisement rather than any deliberate attempt to mislead" (*ASA Annual Report* 1981, 26).

The ASA continues to be concerned with claims and comparisons of objectively ascertainable facts that should be capable of substantiation. Advertisers are required to have substantiation ready when requested. They should compile a statement outlining substantiation before submitting the advertisement to a medium.

Monitoring of Advertising. Although the ASA in the 1970s had conducted a small amount of monitoring, a new program was developed in 1978 and 1979. Following the suggestions offered in outside studies and reports, the ASA developed a comprehensive program to monitor nonbroadcast advertising and sales promotion programs. Sales promotion monitoring involved all categories of promotional activity, especially within stores, as well as packaging and advertising connected with sales promotion, especially price discounting.

In the *Review of the UK Self-Regulatory System of Advertising Control* in 1978, the DGFT observed that "the processing of complaints . . . is no substitute for a properly planned programme of monitoring work. . . . Systematic monitoring can alone provide an accurate measure of the incidences of breaches of the Code and of the success or failure of the control system, and thus compensate for the misleading appearances of figures showing variations in the number of complaints over time. These may increase sharply for a product group and result in extensive criticism in the press or by broadcasters, although the actual incidences of breaches of the Code within that group may not have changed or may have fallen" (*ASA Annual Report* 1981, 5).

If appropriate probability sampling techniques are employed, along with systematic collection and interpretation of information and communication techniques utilized in advertising, it is possible to ascertain over a period of time whether advertising is changing in ways that can be attributed in part to a regulatory Code and its enforcement. Analysis and interpretation of such data can indicate whether advertising practices are changing in ways that are consonant with advertising regulatory objectives and regulatory programs to achieve such objectives. Such studies have not yet been done, but the ASA does report information on its monitoring activities that can yield preliminary insights into the effectiveness of its regulatory activities.

In 1979 the new extended monitoring program fell into three parts:

1. *Across-the-board scanning* of national daily newspapers, national Sunday newspapers and supplements, national weekly and monthly magazines, and regional and weekly newspapers. These publications were scanned for prima facie breaches of the Code and, when necessary, investigations were made and followed through in the same way as is done with consumer complaints.

2. *Special studies* of selected product categories.

3. *A quota monitoring system* based on the sample employed in the OFT's "Review" of 1978. This monitoring system aimed to ascertain the ability of advertisers in general to substantiate their claims (*ASA Annual Report* 1980, 12).

In 1980 the ASA completed the second year of its extended monitoring:

1. It completed 278 advertising investigations, most of which involved prima facie breaches of the Code. Additionally many advertisers were asked to substantiate claims that were considered potentially misleading (*ASA Annual Report* 1980, 12).

2. It examined 906 sales promotion programs and included purchasing trips to provincial centers as well as in London (*ASA Annual Report* 1980, 14).

Statistics for the *across-the-board monitoring* program for 1981 through 1984 are shown in table 7–6. In 1980 advertising was monitored by using

Table 7-6
Issues of Publications Monitored and Advertising Investigations Initiated

| | Issues of Publications Monitored | | | | | | | | Investigations Initiated | | | | | | | |
| | 1981 | | 1982 | | 1983 | | 1984 | | 1981 | | 1982 | | 1983 | | 1984 | |
	Number	Percentage	Number	Percentage	Number	Percentage	Number	Percentage	Number	Percentage	Number	Percentage	Number	Percentage	Number	Percentage
Magazines	776	36	918	38	1,101	41	743	31	109	37	90	41	112	47	64	35
National newspapers and supplements	1,018	48	1,322	54	1,452	53	1,480	62	102	35	55	25	81	34	48	26
Regional and local newspapers	332	16	192	8	164	6	165	7	71	24	70	32	36	15	64	35
Posters, leaflets, catalogues, and comics	10	0	0	0	0	0	0	0	10	3	3	1	8	3	7	4
Total	2,136	100	2,432	100	2,717	100	2,388	100	292	99[a]	218	99[a]	237	99[a]	183	100

Source: *ASA Annual Reports, 1980 to 1984–1985.*
[a]Percentage does not add to 100 owing to rounding.

sampling intervals recommended by the OFT, and publications (newspapers and magazines) were checked on a rotating basis to give a balanced sample over a four-week period.

In 1981 the range and frequency of scanning followed the same pattern.

> Relating the 282 cases initiated for prima facie breaches of the Code against the number of advertisements scanned, the following figures emerge:
>
> Magazine and Sunday Supplements (average 80 display and semi-display advertisements per publication)
>
> 76,160 advertisements—145 cases—0.19%. Newspapers of all types (average 300 display and semi-display advertisements per publication)
>
> 352,000 advertisements—137 cases—0.03% (*ASA Annual Report* 1981, 21).

Subsequently the ASA reported that the sample design did not satisfy formal statistical requirements (*ASA Annual Report* 1982–1983, 5). Thus the above percentages should not be taken as a valid estimate of breaches of the Code nationally.

When requested, thirty-nine percent of advertisers were able to substantiate their claims, and seventy-seven percent agreed to amend or withdraw the advertising in question. Eight percent were called to the attention of media members of the CAP.

In 1983 the ASA improved its monitoring sampling procedures by the following: (1) it provided a sampling frame that gave more effective coverage of publications at significantly lower staff time, (2) it set a firm statistical criterion against which the Authority could check the efficiency of monitoring, (3) it suggested improvements in the existing classification of data, and (4) it enabled the Authority to respond flexibly to the changing needs of the public and advertisers for information (*ASA Annual Report* 1983–1984, 5).

From the standpoint of evaluating the performance of the ASA (and other forces in society that influence the number of breaches of the Code), the most significant of the previously mentioned improvements was the new sampling frame:

> [It] covers all publications that fall within the Authority's jurisdiction. The sample . . . reflects the number of readers who see an advertisement, measured by the circulation of the publication in which it appears" (*ASA Annual Report* 1984–1985, 4).

This statement may not be entirely accurate, because readership is not identical to circulation, but the new sampling frame was certainly an improvement.

In 1983, the *ASA Case Report* (1982–1983) stated that the 237 cases initiated by across-the-board scanning related to the following categories (some advertisements fall into more than one category):

Substantiation	88
Potentially misleading	29
Mail order	30
Health, treatment advice	39
Slimming	23
Investment	16
Other (each 10 or less)	38
Total	263

In May 1983 the ASA took a census of about 2,200 publications from which it selected a stratified sample of 250. The preliminary findings of the study of advertisements from these publications indicated that between one and two percent were in breach of the Code. But analysis indicated that only about one in ten of these breaches was sufficiently significant to be pursued (*ASA Annual Report* 1983–1984, 5).

As part of its monitoring program, the ASA in 1980 conducted special studies of nonbroadcast advertisements for eleven different product categories, ranging from film processing to cosmetics (*ASA Annual Report* 1980, 12).

ASA monitoring accounts for a relatively small proportion of cases investigated. During the twelve-month period ending 31 March 1985, the ASA calculated that the 183 cases initiated from its monitoring activity amounted to about four percent of the 4,605 identifiable offenses against the *BCAP* and *BCSPP* (Boddewyn 1986). Further details are not available, but it is clear that monitoring is the source of a relatively small proportion of ASA investigations. Perhaps the reason is that the ASA attempts to obtain a statistically proper random sample, and does not focus its monitoring activity on particular media, products, or problem areas that might be considered particularly "fertile" to discover breaches of the codes.

In 1981 the ASA examined twelve selected product categories. Altogether, 4,727 advertisements were scanned and fifty cases were initiated for prima facie breaches of the Code. This gives a percentage of 1.05 percent of cases to advertisements examined. Although this figure is much larger than the standard monitoring figures of 0.03 percent for newspapers and 0.19 percent for magazines and Sunday supplements, it is explained by the fact that the twelve product categories came under scrutiny because of a number of product complaints about them. The most troublesome product categories were the "royal wedding" and "MPG and small print (cars)." Other product categories were cosmetic surgery, lithographic prints, exercise cycles, marriage bureaus, ready made curtains, charities, stamps, slimming, fuel costs, and toys (*ASA Annual Report* 1981, 22).

In 1982 the single most troublesome product area was that of slimming aids and slimming clubs, accounting for twenty-two percent of the total number of monitoring cases initiated, up from seven percent in 1981. The good record of the alcoholic drink industry was maintained; just less than 500 advertisements were scrutinized and only one gave rise to concern in terms of the Code (*ASA Annual Report* 1982–1983, 25).

With regard to *product categories*, in 1983, 358 advertisements were monitored, of which fifteen required detailed investigation. In 1984 the ASA expanded its product advertising monitoring into mail order; 501 were examined for possible breaches of the Code. As a result twenty-six advertisers were contacted about apparent breaches of the Code.

During 1984 the ASA carried out a survey of advertisements in additional categories to assess the level of compliance with the Code. In the category of banks and building societies, ninety-four different advertisements were studied, and of these, thirty-one failed to meet Code standards for information on interest rates; the advertisers were advised to comply. Regarding women in advertising, a survey of 114 trade and technical publications did not reveal that any action was required by the ASA under the Code. Regarding hearing aid advertisements, a study of fifty-five advertisements led to twelve investigations and eight advertisers being asked to amend their advertisements.

In April 1981 the *quota monitoring* project was initiated to make random checks on advertisers to determine if they are able to substantiate their claims (Code, Section 11.4.1). In the first eight months of the project 300 publications were studied, yielding 750 advertisements, of which ten percent gave rise to requests for substantiation. Of these seventy-five, only four failed to respond, and only one was asked to amend copy claims in the light of substantiation received. This particular task required thirty-two working days of one case officer.

During 1982, 400 publications were scanned, yielding a total advertisement sample of 2,132. Of these, requests to ninety-nine advertisers to substantiate their copy claims were made: fifty-five were substantiated in full, six in part, two were referred to the CAP, nine were unsubstantiated, seventeen failed to respond to the ASA's request, and ten were ongoing at year's end. Of the number pursued, slimming accounted for more than half (*ASA Annual Report* 1982–1983, 25–26).

In 1983 350 publications were studied, yielding an advertisement sample of 1,745. After examination, substantiation was requested from advertisers in sixty-three cases. Of these, forty-three claims were substantiated and seven were not substantiated, and in eight cases the advertiser failed to respond. The remaining five cases were not concluded by 31 December 1983.

It is impossible to interpret these figures without knowing the basis on which advertisements were selected for substantiation. Taking the

1983 returns, for example, it could be argued that standards must be high because of 1,745 advertisements that were scrutinized, in only seven cases (0.4 percent) claims could not be substantiated and in eight (0.45 percent) advertisers failed to reply. This assumes, however, that the remainder (that is, those scrutinized but not investigated) were without fault. On the other hand, they represent 10.5 percent and 12.5 percent, respectively, of the advertisements that actually were investigated, so that if these were in any way representative of the mass of advertising published in the United Kingdom, then almost one-fourth would be unacceptable for these two reasons alone.

The ASA is fully aware of the problem. A recent case report carried the following comment on the fact that there had been thirty-nine complaints about substantiation that month of which twenty-nine were upheld:

> That seems to us at best regrettable and at worst deplorable. It does advertisers no good to be found out in false claims; it is no more praiseworthy that they should prove either so idle or so incompetent as to be unable to demonstrate the truth of defensible claims (*ASA Case Report 133* 1986).

Sales Promotion Monitoring. In 1980 the examination of 906 promotions led to detailed enquiries into 172 of them. There were five promotions that involved two categories, so the total investigations into sales promotion practices was 177. Of these, 63 (thirty-six percent) were found acceptable and 114 (sixty-four percent) proved to be breaches of the *BCSPP*. The main breaches concerned (1) clarity of presentation of the offer, (2) the availability of the full rules, and (3) results of prize promotions (*ASA Annual Report* 1980, 14).

Also in 1980 advertisements relating to sales promotion in print media were monitored. Of a total of 1,588 cuttings received, only ten disclosed any prima facie cause for inquiry, and five of these eventually disclosed breaches of the Code. Thus it appears as if the vast bulk of such advertising in 1980 was acceptable (*ASA Annual Report* 1980, 14).

The ASA continued to monitor sales promotions in subsequent years. In 1980 the monitoring staff made 100 store visits. In 1981, 109 store visits led to examination of 2,274 items representing 1,160 individual promotions. The 109 enquiries raised on these items led to discovery of seventy-three breaches of the Code. During 1983, ninety-seven store visits led the staff to examine 1,023 promotions and to investigate 191 of them. The staff found breaches of the Code in

1. Fifty-five cf seventy-eight cases involving prize or competition promotions.
2. Twenty-nine of fifty-one cases involving premium offers.

3. Thirty-seven of fifty-four cases involving free offers.
4. Six of six cases involving savings and refund schemes.

In 1984 members of the ASA staff made fifty-seven visits to locations throughout the country to gather 1,229 promotional items. Of these 867 were examined and eighty-eight were investigated in detail. Ninety enquiries were made, and seventy-two breaches of the Code were discovered.

Complaints about Advertising in Major Nonbroadcast Media

As shown in table 7–7, advertising in national and local newspapers accounts for a majority of consumer complaints, with the specialist press and leaflets, brochures, and catalogues providing a significant volume. Magazines account for a surprisingly low proportion of complaints, perhaps because the national press attracts advertising that in the United States (with a far less important national press) would be spent in magazines. The volume of complaints about advertising in cinema and on posters is low no doubt because it is precleared in a similar manner to television.

However, these data indicate only that consumers are dissatisfied with such advertising to the point that they complain. They do not give

Table 7–7
ASA Investigations of Consumer Complaints Against Advertising Copy Appearing in Mass Media

Medium	1983		1984	
	Number	Percentage	Number	Percentage
Magazines	123	8	78	5
National press	460	31	420	29
Local press	424	29	383	27
Specialist press	161	11	202	14
Trade press	23	2	16	1
Leaflets, brochures, and catalogues	249	17	291	20
Directories	10	1	20	1
Posters	21	1	15	1
Cinema	1	0	0	0
Total	1,472	100	1,425	98[a]

Source: *ASA Annual Reports,* 1982–1983 and 1984–1985.
[a]Does not add to 100 percent owing to rounding.

us a measure of how many dissatisfied consumers are in the population, though surveys conducted by the AA show no evidence of widespread concern (Beatson 1984, 362, 366). Nevertheless, it would be useful if the ASA were to report the frequency with which such complaints are upheld, and compare such information with that achieved by monitoring. Then it will be clearer whether the ASA should attempt to improve advertising in certain media, or should try to educate complainers to reduce the number of unjustified complaints.

Table 7-8 shows the number and proportion of consumer complaint investigations about advertising copy in selected product groups. The top "complaint-causing product categories" have changed little from 1980 to 1984 except for the emergence of computers and related items as one of the major categories. The lack of change suggests only that the ASA should continue efforts to achieve improved advertising in these categories.

It should be noted that complaints about tobacco advertising are rare, probably because of the ASA's preclearance program. Since 1975 tobacco advertising has been required to receive a CAP certificate before the media will publish it. Also, complaints about alcohol beverage advertising are rare, because brewers, distillers, and wine merchants have observed carefully the section of the code dealing with alcoholic beverages, which was incorporated on *their* initiative in 1975 (*ASA Case Report 100*).

Complaints about Children's Advertising

The ASA has for a number of years been sensitive to the effects of advertising on children and to the special responsibilities of advertising aimed at or seen by children. In general the *BCAP* requires that such advertising should not contain anything that might result in physical, mental, or moral harm to children, or which exploits their credibility, their lack of experience, or their sense of loyalty. Section C.X lays down specific guidelines regarding advertising directed to children or to which they might be exposed.

During 1979 the Authority invited a research agency to conduct research to find out how children react to and feel about advertisements, especially whether selected advertisements communicated to children in a way that contravened the Code (*ASA Annual Report* 1980, 8). The findings of this research have been used as a guide to evaluate complaints and to make judgments on such cases, thereby improving the ASA's performance in identifying and correcting unsatisfactory advertising, as well as providing advice to guide advertisers. No direct evidence is available to assess the degree of improvement in such advertising, but it seems likely that the ASA efforts have had a positive influence.

Table 7-8
Consumer Complaint Investigations About Advertising Copy by Selected Product Groups

Product Group	Complaints Investigated 1980 Number	1980 Percentage	1981 Number	1981 Percentage	1982 Number	1982 Percentage	1983 Number	1983 Percentage	1984 Number	1984 Percentage
Car, car accessories, and garages	118	11	137	11	130	10	151	10	151	11
Computers	0	0	0	0	27	2	69	5	92	6
Financial: banks and building societies, insurance, investments	26	3	51	4	58	4	72	5	89	6
Holidays	58	6	92	7	85	6	81	5	86	6
Furniture, furnishings, and household linens	44	4	35	3	n.a.	n.a.	49	3	64	5
Travel	52	5	67	5	64	5	82	6	60	4
Property and real estate agents	23	2	n.a.	n.a.	n.a.	n.a.	57	4	58	4
Services (including car rental)	30	3	88	7	54	4	55	4	37	3
Recruitment	n.a.	n.a.	22	2	34	3	38	3	36	3
Photography	47	5	48	4	51	4	46	3	35	2
Others	635	61	741	58	828	62	773	52	712	50
Total	1,033	100	1,281	101[a]	1,331	100	1,473	100	1,420	100

Source: *ASA Annual Reports,* 1980 to 1984–1985.
[a]Does not add to 100 percent owing to rounding.

Conclusions

The evidence indicates that the ASA/CAP Committee system is making a positive contribution to ensuring that advertising is legal, decent, honest, and truthful and that advertisers increasingly have a sense of responsibility to consumers, to society, and to the principles of fair competition in business. These contributions help consumers directly, so that they can make purchasing decisions based on better information; and indirectly by making the market work effectively to reward honest and efficient advertisers while penalizing those who do not adhere to high standards of decency, honesty, and truth. Moreover, because the ASA is seen as an effective control body, consumers probably believe that they are able to rely with some confidence on advertising. This consumer confidence increases the effectiveness of advertising and contributes to the efficiency of the market economy.

The ASA/CAP Committee system has not only chosen to work through its members so that they continue to improve advertising and maintain high standards, but the ASA also goes into the marketplace to monitor advertising systematically to determine if indeed progress is being made. To date the available statistics do not provide direct evidence of changes in advertising, perhaps because the proportion of offending advertisements is so small compared with the vast bulk of advertising that is in accordance with the *BCAP*. With the passage of time this monitoring seems likely to provide specific evidence to evaluate the performance of the ASA/CAP Committee system. In general, the success of the system seems to have been greatest in preventing advertising from being indecent, dishonest, or untruthful—including preventing advertising without adequate substantiation from being run.

The great bulk of advertising control for nonbroadcast media is handled by voluntary rather than government regulation. Moreover, the requirements of the *BCAP* extend far beyond the minimum base of legal standards, especially with regard to matters of taste and decency. The system also handles borderline cases of advertising that might be considered misleading to consumers or unfair to competitors, but which might go uninvestigated if only government agencies were available to do such work. Because the main responsibility for advertising control in the United Kingdom rests with the ASA/CAP Committee system rather than with government agencies, it is important that advertising and other means should be employed to inform consumers about the system and how to use it. Also, there are in the United Kingdom no local equivalents of the well-known BBBs in the United States; the central system handles both local and national advertising control. Thus the workload of the ASA nationwide is substantial; including not only the handling of several thousand cases per year but also numerous instances of providing advice, making speeches, and disseminating literature to various "publics."

The keys to ASA/CAP Committee sanctions and enforcement are (1) the independence of the system's source of financing and (2) the cooperation of media members who will refuse to carry advertising that contravenes the *BCAP*. The possibility of unfavorable publicity is also important, especially as an incentive for advertisers to avoid using unacceptable practices, thereby serving as a preventive measure. The remedial or corrective function is relatively minor, because the system can only stop unacceptable practices. It cannot correct harm done nor can it assess penalties or fines. Media associations are able to expel their members, but there are no known cases of such action.

The ASA in handling so many complaints necessarily must deal with a relatively high proportion of what might be considered frivolous or trivial complaints, thereby expending resources on matters that make relatively minor contributions to improving or maintaining appropriate standards for advertising. However, these circumstances lead to certain desirable outcomes. Consumers have increased confidence in advertising. Also complaints put pressure on advertisers to improve their advertising. Thus, on balance the system's activities may be entirely justifiable, although this issue cannot be decided on the basis of existing evidence.

One of the major indicators of the effectiveness of the performance of the ASA/CAP Committee system is that consumer associations and government—not to mention those in the advertising industry—seem to be in agreement that the system functions more effectively than government regulation of advertising could function. Moreover, the evidence indicates that the system costs society far less than a government system and it is likely that government would function more legalistically and slowly.

Finally, it appears as if the system has the necessary flexibility to adapt to changing circumstances, to expand its mission and scope of activities by dealing with advertising in new media as they evolve, and to maintain an adequate level of activities by virtue of the independence of its funding and the influence of public members on the system's policies.

> Increasingly it is not a question of self-regulation versus Government regulation but a mixture of both. In this context it is worth noting the increasing interest in the United Kingdom in the statutory reinforcement of self-regulatory codes. This has found expression in the statutory reinforcement of the advertising self-regulatory system and is now being considered on a wider scale in relation to the concept of a general statutory duty to trade fairly, which could be used to underpin all sorts of industry codes of practice that are currently lacking in effectiveness (Philip Circus, letter to the author, 13 August 1986).

References

ASA Annual Reports, various years.

Beatson, Ronald (1984), "The Image of Advertising in Europe," *International Journal of Advertising* 3:361–367.

Boddewyn, J.J. (1983), "Outside Participation in Advertising Self-Regulation: The Case of the Advertising Standards Authority (UK)," *Journal of Consumer Policy* 6:77–93.

Boddewyn, J.J. (1986), *Advertising Self-Regulation: Sixteen Advanced Systems* (New York: International Advertising Association).

Chairman's Report for 1985 (London: Code of Advertising Practice Committee).

Children and Advertising: An Investigation by the Advertising Standards Authority (1980) (London: Advertising Standards Authority).

Diamond, Steven L., Ward, Scott, and Faber, Ronald (1975), "Consumer Problems and Consumerism: Analysis of Calls to a Consumer Hotline," Working Paper 74–5 (Cambridge, Mass.: Marketing Science Institute).

Jones, T.T., and Pickering, J.F. (1985), *Self Regulation in Advertising: A Review* (London: The Advertising Association).

Lawson, R.W. (1985), "An Analysis of Complaints about Advertising," *International Journal of Advertising* 4:279–295.

Nevett, Terence R., and Miracle, Gordon E. (1987) "The British System of Advertising Self-Regulation: An Historical Perspective," Ernest F. Larkin (ed.) *Proceedings of the 1986 Conference of the American Academy of Advertising* (Norman: School of Journalism, University of Oklahoma), R2–R6).

OFT Research; A Summary of Stage One and Two of the original BMRB Reports (dated September, 1978) (undated) London: The Advertising Association (mimeographed).

OFT Review: ASA's Analysis of "failed" Ads (1978) (London: The Advertising Standards Authority [mimeographed]).

Review of the UK Self-Regulatory System of Advertising Control (1978), A Report by the Director-General of Fair Trading (London: Office of Fair Trading, November 1978 [mimeographed]).

The Self-Regulatory System of Advertising Control—Report of the Working Party (1980) (London: Department of Trade).

8
Conclusions and Recommendations

Introduction

In the early part of this book it was observed that there are both similarities and differences in the cultural, economic, legal, political, and social milieu for advertising in the United Kingdom and the United States. The detailed material in this book on the two systems of advertising regulation and self-regulation reflects the similarities and differences of the two environments.

Because the evolution and current nature of each system is a product of each environment, one cannot say that one system is necessarily better than the other. But there are sufficient similarities in the respective advertising milieus to suggest lessons that each system can learn from the other. This chapter contains recommendations that derive from these lessons.

This final chapter depends directly on the material in the body of the book, and is most meaningful to those readers who take a few extra minutes at this point to review briefly the comparisons and conclusions at the end of each preceding chapter, and contemplate them in their entirety.

We do not repeat the specific comparisons and conclusions already presented. But with an understanding of them in mind, we can draw a few lessons from them before we proceed further. These lessons fall into three categories: (1) lessons learned by government regulators, but that also are useful to those who are in the self-regulatory field; (2) lessons learned from consumerism; and (3) the generally accepted advantages and disadvantages of advertising self-regulation compared with government regulation. We draw on many sources to compile such information, but the detailed information in chapters 1 through 7 leads up to and illustrates these "general truths."

The last major section of this chapter compares the performance of the British and U.S. systems of advertising self-regulation, building directly on the subject matter of chapters 6 and 7. Throughout this chapter, as appropriate, we offer recommendations for future action.

Lessons from Governmental Regulation

The substantial efforts of the U.S. government to protect consumers in the late 1960s and 1970s have provided useful experience to guide future control of business not only by government, but also by industry self-regulation. Reactions to government regulation have led to pressures for deregulation, which in turn have reduced the pressures on industries to regulate themselves.

This process has occurred in both the United Kingdom and the United States, although differently, depending on the degree and levels of government control in various fields of business. For example, although deregulation is important in some British industries, it is relatively unimportant for advertising control because the British government has not played as important a role as self-regulation. In the United Kingdom the threat of government controls more than a decade ago led to an equilibrium between government and self-regulation of advertising. In contrast, the pendulum of regulation and deregulation in the United States seems likely to continue to swing from one direction to the other although, as we see, if the recommendations in this chapter are followed, there is an opportunity to enhance and stabilize the role of self-regulation of advertising.

The large and complex body of lessons learned by regulators is illustrated by Michael Pertschuk (1982), former chairman of the FTC in the United States. He was instrumental in shaping and carrying out regulatory policies pertaining to business in the 1960s and 1970s.

Pertschuk's views apply particularly to the United States, but are also useful to those in the United Kingdom who are interested in advertising regulation. Moreover, since the United Kingdom is a member state in the European Community, and because other Europeans will also heed Pertschuk's views, an additional reason for presenting them here is that European Community actions will influence the United Kingdom.

Pertschuk points out that some observers believe that the FTC brought many of its problems on itself "by embracing intrusive, meddlesome, inefficient, overreaching, centralized, bureaucratic regulation . . . and thereby . . . [debasing] the currency of all regulation (Pertschuk 1982, 137). Pertschuk answers:

> No. And yes. I have argued strenuously in these pages that the consumer
> movement was laid down primarily by the reaction and revolt of

business—though business was able to exploit the diffuse public dissatisfaction with government and regulation to legitimize the dismantling of consumer and other regulations that have retained undiminished popular support (Pertschuk 1982, 137–138).

Regulatory activities in the United States have been different from those in the United Kingdom. Yet, the lessons learned from the U.S. experience, as reported by Pertschuk, are also relevant to the British situation:

But there were lessons learned, sometimes painfully, in the course of transforming the consumer impulses of the sixties into the mature consumer regulation of the seventies. There were also lessons we refuse to learn.

We have learned greater respect for somber, unsentimental analysis of the effects of regulation. We, and here I believe I speak for many who view themselves as *consumer advocates, have not learned to accept that the injustice and inequity arising from inequality of bargaining power must be excluded from public policy if they cannot be measured in the economists' models* [italics ours].

We have learned to pay greater heed to the social value of the entrepreneur, to value market incentives as a creative force for productivity and growth. But *we will not learn to tolerate the force with which those very incentives sweep aside the moral and ethical constraints that mark civilized society* [italics ours].

We have learned that we must be accountable for the costs and burdens of regulation. But *we will not concede that the economist's useful, but imperfect, tool of cost-benefit analysis dictates policy judgments on what is right and what is just* [italics ours].

We have been taught respect for a fallible bureaucracy's limitations in shaping human behavior. But *we will not abandon faith in the role of government in a democratic society to redress inequity and to give appropriate expression to those non-market values people hold deeply* [italics ours] (Pertschuk 1982, 137–138).

In the last four paragraphs of this quote we have highlighted with italics the attitudes and the ideology that will continue to influence future consumerist activities. These attitudes also exist to some extent among consumerists and members of the Labour Party in the United Kingdom. But we should also highlight one of Pertschuk's main conclusions. He sums up the trend in the United States by observing: *"So the central lesson is, simply, regulatory humility"* [italics ours] (Pertschuk 1982, 139).

What the Americans seem to have learned from difficult experiences, the British seem to have evolved to in a more orderly fashion. But, although British would-be regulators probably find the U.S. experience amusing, they may also find it instructive.

But Pertschuk has more to offer. He has acquired a certain realism that is appropriate for today and the future, and for British as well as Americans. He grudgingly admits that regulators have learned from economists to

> *think through* the reality of what we believed we were achieving with our intervention in the marketplace. . . .
> They [economists] ask "what do you think you are accomplishing with this rule? Who will benefit, who will pay? What else will happen as a result of this rule; who among competitors will be the winners and the losers? In curing this marketplace failure, what others may you inadvertently cause, and what healthy market signals will you distort? Is there a less intrusive, less costly way to remedy the problem? . . . How secure are you that the world will be a better place for your intervention than if left alone?" [italics ours] (Pertschuk 1982, 139).

Pertschuk then gives consumerists, the advertising business, and government officials a useful list of specific questions and issues to keep in mind when considering new regulatory requirements. He says that "the prudent regulator should ask" the following:

1. *Is the rule consonant with market incentives to the maximum extent feasible?* Respect for the power of self-interest—of market incentives—is surely one of the salient substantive lessons learned by consumer advocates in the past two decades. . . .

2. *Will the remedy work?* In the sixties there were certain goals we pursued because they intuitively seemed self-evidently right . . . in most cases the effectiveness of a remedy will increase in direct proportion to the extent to which it seeks to utilize market incentives rather than stifle them. . . .

3. *Will the chosen remedy minimize the cost burdens of compliance, consistent with achieving the objective?* Whether it took "stagflation," the revitalization of business political action, the regulatory reform movement, or the loss of our own primitive faith in the miraculous innovative capacity of American business to convince us, let there be no doubt that the regulatory calculus must seek to minimize not only paperwork burdens but, more important, regulatory impediments to innovation, flexibility and productivity. . . .

4. *Will the benefits flowing from the rule to consumers or to competition substantially exceed the costs?* . . . One issue popular among consumer advocates—popular, in fairness, because it evokes broad grassroots support—is the effort to maintain individual price marking of supermarket items and to resist replacement of such markings by shelf markings and computer printouts. That cause has always left me insecure, because I know of no evidence to suggest that individual

price marking will benefit consumers sufficiently to offset the costs (which, of course, are passed on) of the labor-intensive price-marking process. . . .

5. *Will the rule or remedy adversely affect competition?* The economists can surely take deserved credit for alerting us to the anti-competitive dangers in direct regulation of rates or entry into a marketplace. To their alarms can be traced much of the progress made in recent years toward eliminating such regulatory burdens on competition. . . .

6. *Does the regulation preserve freedom of informed individual choice to the maximum extent consistent with consumer welfare?* The regulator must respect the manifest preference of Americans for free and informed choice over government intrusion that constrains choice. In what regulator's bosom does there not dwell a latent "nanny," solicitous of the health and well-being of his or her fellow citizens, fearful of senseless risk. . . . This regulatory itch must be resisted . . . (Pertschuk 1982, 141–148).

These points indicate newly found respect for the market system, cost-benefit analysis, the importance of competition, and free and informed consumer choice as an essential part of the market system rather than government intervention.

However, it should not be forgotten that the U.S. regulatory base is essential to the effectiveness of the NAD/NARB as a self-regulatory system. In fact the "FTC and NAD/NARB systems have developed a strong symbiosis and complementarity, and the two systems display great resemblance" in terms of (1) limited outside participation, (2) emphasis on "hard" issues and criteria; (3) choice of cases to pursue, (4) shared standards, and (5) antitrust law consensus (Boddewyn 1985b, 7–21). One may argue that the British regulatory base is complementary to the ASA/CAP Committee system, especially in view of the probable new powers to be granted to the OFT as part of the British compliance with the European Community *Council Directive on Misleading Advertising*. To be sure, however, the complementary relationship between the OFT and the ASA/CAP Committee system does not parallel the symbiotic relationship between the NAD/NARB, for reasons discussed earlier. The OFT and the ASA/CAP Committee system do not resemble each other in the previously mentioned ways.

Lessons from Consumerism

Recently, consumerist activities have declined. But because consumerism seems to rise and fall in cycles, it is likely that the spirit of deregulation will one day reverse. A generation of dedicated consumerists, led by new converts, will be ready again when or if the opportunity arises. If business fails to make constructive changes, future consumerists will lead renewed and relatively sophisticated attacks on advertising. So the question at this time is: What should business do to make it unnecessary in the minds of consumerists to return to the attack?

It is clear that the health of the market system requires broad consumer confidence in advertising as an activity that contributes to the free flow of accurate information about products and services. There is no doubt that enlightened self-interest by the entire advertising industry—advertisers, advertising agencies, the mass media, and the many other components of this industry—should take actions that continue to improve the free flow of accurate information, guided by the genuine public interest. The NAD/NARB/CARU/BBB/LARP and the ASA/CAP Committee have made excellent progress in this regard, although there are many opportunities for improvement. In particular, the ASA/CAP Committee, in addition to promoting truthful and accurate information, has shown the way to improve moral standards in advertising such as decency and honesty, since BCAP requires that advertising must be decent and honest as well as legal and truthful. Thus the ASA/CAP system has established for itself a broader mission than that of the U.S. system, one that meets at least some of the criticisms of advertising that the U.S. self-regulatory system cannot handle.

Because the pressures for advertising regulation depend in large part on consumerism and government reaction to consumer activism, it is important for the advertising industry to evaluate trends in consumerism and attempt to forecast them. Literature is substantial on this subject, for example, see Bloom (1982) for the proceedings of a conference on the future of consumerism.

Consumer organizations in the United Kingdom and the United States have not participated in major ways in the development and operation of self-regulatory systems of advertising. In the United States they preferred to work for government action; in the United Kingdom the Consumer Association and the National Consumer Council (the principal consumer bodies), accept the effectiveness of the self-regulatory system (Boddewyn 1983). On occasion members of consumer organizations have served on the ASA Council, though they did so as individuals rather than as representatives of those bodies.

One of the reasons that critics attack advertising is their perception that consumers are or should be dissatisfied with advertising. It is clear that there is considerable controversy on this point (see, for example, Jones and Pickering 1985, 5; and Rijkens and Miracle 1986, 19–33). To resolve this issue would require two broad types of research to measure (1) how consumers feel about advertising and (2) how existing advertising practices compare with some mutually agreeable objective standard. Some studies have provided information on consumer attitudes toward advertising, but it is far from clear what the precise levels of consumer satisfaction and dissatisfaction are. There is little evidence on how advertising "measures up" to objective standards, especially in the United States where no comprehensive systematic program monitors advertising, and no objective code of standards is used to evaluate advertising. This combination of circumstances requires action.

Recommendation I:
Increase Research on Consumerist Trends

The advertising industries in the United Kingdom and the United States, through their trade associations or other means, should increase their support of research on consumerist trends, for example: (1) consumer satisfaction and dissatisfaction with advertising, (2) consumer needs for information related to the purchasing process, (3) the process and effects of communication via advertising—especially measuring the accuracy or deceptiveness of advertising under varying conditions and to varying groups of consumers, and (4) effects of advertising regulatory activities on business and consumer welfare—the economic, cultural, and social effects of regulation.

Because these research topics are very broad, realistic priorities based on cost-benefit analysis must be set. To this end it is suggested that the advertising business, perhaps through its associations in the United Kingdom and the United States, should establish a working group (or groups) with comprehensive representation from inside and outside the advertising business. The already existing Advertising Educational Foundation in the United States may be useful to serve as a guide or to participate directly with British counterparts. The tasks of the working group(s) should be to define specific needs and priorities for research, identify appropriate sources of funding, publicize such information to qualified researchers, and establish procedures and responsibilities for allocating funds to prioritized projects.

Research support should be considered for qualified independent university researchers and appropriate commercial research firms to provide a balance of independent work to supplement the work done every day by industry professionals doing their jobs with advertisers, advertising agencies, and the media (see also recommendation X).

In both the United Kingdom and the United States in recent years deregulation to enhance the role of market forces and competition as a means to economic efficiency and its benefits to society has become an important part of economic policy. In the United States, with its history of relatively greater government activity to regulate advertising, deregulation has been a somewhat more significant theme than in the United

Kingdom, with its history of greater reliance on self-regulation. However, the United Kingdom is subject to influences by European Community Council Directives, which may press for greater rather than less government involvement in advertising regulation, and in addition faces the possibility of a future Labour government introducing a statutory code. Thus, although the situation has been relatively stable in the United Kingdom, the trend in the long term could be towards legislation, whereas in the United States it is likely to continue toward greater reliance on advertising self-regulation. This trend in the United States is an opportunity for the U.S. advertising industry to "put its house in order" in a way that will forestall the tendency of government to be as activist in the future as it has been in the past.

Logically, the advertising industry should take advantage of periods of relative calm to plan ahead and to improve the practice as well as the reputation of advertising. Such initiatives may help avoid or at least reduce future confrontation and conflict, as well as forestall regulatory actions that might harm rather than enhance the ability of the market system to serve business, consumers, and society as a whole.

Long-run improvement in advertising practices, as well as in the reputation of advertising, depends in part on adequate education for those who seek careers in advertising, those whose business careers bring them into contact with advertising specialists, and those who will use advertising as consumers.

Recommendation II:
Support Teaching and Research at Educational Institutions

> *The advertising industries in the United Kingdom and United States should continue their efforts to provide teaching materials, speakers, and other resources to support relevant economic education in schools at all levels. In particular, the industry should fund chairs at universities to conduct teaching and research programs that will not only serve students at those institutions, but will generate knowledge for dissemination and use at other educational institutions. Of special importance is an understanding of the economic and social consequences of the relationships between the advertising industry, consumers, and government. Appropriate research should be conducted to lead public policy and regulatory proposals, especially the balance between government and self-regulation of advertising.*

Lessons from Self-Regulation

Self-regulation of advertising has two basic objectives:

1. *To protect consumers* against false or misleading advertising and against advertising that intrudes on their privacy through its unwanted

presence or offensive content. In short, advertising must be controlled so that it is in harmony with the best interests of consumers who wish to be able to use it to guide their purchasing decisions. This objective might be called "self-enlightened," because if it is not achieved, consumers or their representatives in consumer groups or in government will likely take actions to control advertising, and such controls may not be in the best interests of all concerned.

2. *To protect legitimate advertisers* against false or misleading advertising by competitors. This objective dare not be oriented only toward the preservation of individual competitors, but must preserve the free flow of accurate information in the marketplace so that efficient competitors prevail and inefficient competitors fail. Such is the salutory effect of competition in a market economy.

Generally the advertiser view of self-regulation is that control by those who know advertising well will have two characteristics: (1) it will be effective in identifying genuine abuses (it takes a thief to catch a thief), especially in the monitoring process: and (2) it will encroach less on legitimate advertising activities.

The general consumerist view of self-regulation is that regulation by those who know advertising well will provide a weak measure of consumer protection, because those in the industry would tend to preserve their freedom to the maximum they believe is possible. The motivations of members of the British and U.S. advertising industries often are suspect because it is in their self-interest to avoid regulation by government, especially because such regulation in the United States has a history of less than full comprehension by regulators of the nature of the advertising industry and of the effects of advertising on society. Motivations of politicians also are suspect and the measures they introduce to regulate advertising may not always protect consumers.

We begin by asking whether the usual advantages and disadvantages that are claimed for self-regulation will serve society well. Therefore, we present now a list of advantages and disadvantages that have been extracted from the literature on this subject (see, for example, Rijkens and Miracle 1986, 41–43; and Boddewyn 1985b, 131–132) and from the analysis in earlier chapters of this book. We ask the reader to evaluate these advantages and disadvantages from the standpoint of the two main objectives— to protect consumers and to protect legitimate advertisers—as well as the more detailed objectives outlined in chapter 6.

1. The case for advertising self-regulation

    A. Self-discipline and cooperation lead to adherence to the spirit of the law rather than to minimal compliance because of the threat of prosecution by government. Self-interest compliance rather than coercion leads to a higher degree of commitment from advertisers than would be the case if a self-regulatory code became law. Thus, self-regulation is said to be more effective.

B. Self-regulatory systems handle matters more speedily, more simply, and with less "red tape" than governmental regulatory mechanisms or court processes.

C. A self-regulatory code is more flexible in that it can be more readily updated than new or revised government legislation can be enacted.

D. Self-regulatory systems are less costly than government regulatory measures, particularly because they avoid expensive legal fees or court costs.

E. Self-regulation creates and maintains public confidence in advertising. If advertisers are seen to behave decently and considerately—in harmony with the generally accepted standards of the community in which they operate—they will be viewed as responsible and their advertising will be credible. Public confidence in advertising is essential to its continued effectiveness and even its very existence as an important business activity.

F. Self-regulatory codes and mechanisms do not interfere with the advertising industry so that it cannot function effectively. They preserve advertising as a legitimate business activity, and minimize the negative effects of over-regulation imposed or influenced by those who do not fully understand the way advertising works and its economic and social role. Under self-regulation, marketing and advertising costs are not increased by arbitrary rules and standards that do not really aid the consumer. Correspondingly the free flow of truthful and accurate information by advertising, properly understood by buyers and sellers, helps the free market to function effectively to accomplish the appropriate intended goals of an economy.

G. Self-regulatory systems can have broader scope, to deal more easily with matters of taste and decency, especially because it can adapt to sometimes rapidly changing mores and social norms (see also C).

H. A self-regulatory system can put the *burden of proof* (substantiation or that a claim is not misleading, and so on) on the advertiser—which may not be appropriate for some legal systems.

I. Finally, and perhaps with a bit of overlap with some of these points, a self-regulatory system can help achieve better understanding and cooperation with legislators, educators, students, consumers, and officials in government bureaucracies, which in turn helps stem unwise or unwarranted regulatory activity.

2. The case against advertising self-regulation

   A. It is difficult to get 100 percent voluntary cooperation and to police the small number of unscrupulous advertisers.

   B. Enrolled members contribute different degrees of commitment in supporting the system.

   C. Open and responsive channels of communication between the self-regulatory body and consumers, and between consumer groups and agencies of the government, are difficult to maintain. As a result disenchantment may occur among advertisers or consumer groups.

   D. Self-regulatory systems do not have adequate powers, either to stop advertising quickly (as by temporary injunction) or to force compliance once an abuse has been determined.

   E. Self-regulation standards are too lax and are not strictly enforced, especially if the real objective of advertising critics is to attack or destroy the free enterprise system and to replace it with government ownership or control. Self-regulation of advertising thus perpetuates the market system.

   F. It is usually difficult to obtain adequate financing to provide a staff and resources that are able to cover more than the most egregious offenses; many complaints cannot be handled or resolved to the satisfaction of consumers, consumerists, consumer groups, and competitors.

From the standpoint of business the advantages outweigh the disadvantages. Taken collectively they suggest that self-regulation not only serves the public interest, but it also protects individual traders, especially the established members of the industry. Thus there is the danger that a self-regulatory system might exclude new forms of competition or expression in advertising that would prove beneficial to the public interest, such as the exclusion of comparison advertising when and if the time is ripe for it in a given culture. Instead of "protecting competitors," it is clear that an effective market system should "preserve conditions of effective competition," under which inefficient competitors must change their ways if they are to survive profitably and if the public interest is to be served. Normally regulatory and self-regulatory systems should also serve the consumer, directly and indirectly, which both the NAD/NARB and ASA/CAP Committee systems have as their central purpose.

On balance, the danger of "protecting competitors" as opposed to "preserving competition" seems to be somewhat greater in the British than in the U.S. system of self-regulation for two reasons: (1) stronger antitrust and restraint of trade policies in the United States, and (2) the somewhat stronger traditions in the United Kingdom of protecting against "unfair competition" (Rijkens and Miracle 1986, chapter I, especially pp. 12–18; Fulop 1977, 54–50).

Jones and Pickering (1985, 59) note: "If there is to be a general approach to this 'problem in the UK it seems that some would prefer a general prohibition on deceptive or misleading practices and on unconscionable acts or practices . . . rather than argue for a general duty to trade fairly."

In any event the NAD/NARB and the ASA/CAP Committee are well advised to continue to enhance the free flow of accurate information in the marketplace, rather than to focus on protecting individual advertisers from each other.

At this point it seems instructive to link the lessons from the experience of Pertschuk at the FTC with the lessons from our two relatively successful British and U.S. systems of self-regulation of advertising— especially the ASA/CAP Committee system.

From Pertschuk we learn of the limitations of consumer activists when allowed to pursue the "ideals" that lead to excesses, and the consequent attitude of humility that has ensued. It is clear, however, that at least the threat of government action is essential as a base for self-regulation.

The ASA/CAP Committee system, albeit less than perfect, is perhaps the leading example in the world in achieving many of the advantages of advertising self-regulation. Historically, conditions evolved in the United Kingdom that led to a level of success of the self-regulatory system that has not as yet been equaled elsewhere. The system serves as an example— in a general way as well as on specific policies and procedures—that perhaps can be adapted at least in part for use in other countries, to the extent that similar conditions suggest and different conditions permit.

Recommendation III:
Expand Self-Regulation

Although advertising conditions differ widely among nations, it is possible that some of the advantages of self-regulation may be attractive in countries where no such system currently exists, or where it is relatively undeveloped. The advertising business, consumer groups, and appropriate government agencies in such countries should therefore examine the principal features of the British and U.S. systems to evaluate the extent to which they might be appropriate in their own cases. The proposals for such cooperation by Peebles and Ryans (1978, 48–52) may be a useful guide.

This recommendation applies to (1) *business,* which must establish and administer a self-regulatory system, (2) *consumer leaders,* who must work constructively with business and government to make the self-regulatory system as effective as possible in serving the public interest, and (3) *legislators and administrators and staff members of government agencies,* who must provide not only the threat but also the cooperative attitude that successful self-regulation requires.

Comparisons of Performance

The mission and scope of the British and U.S. systems of self-regulation are broadly similar. Both have the objectives of maintaining the integrity of the market system and protecting the legitimate interests of those in the advertising industry. And both accomplish these objectives by making a genuine effort to act in the public interest, especially to promote honest and truthful advertising, which is in the best interests of consumers, individually and collectively.

But the mission and scope of the British and U.S. systems of self-regulation also are different in significant ways (see table 8–1). The ASA/CAP system deals with both local and national advertising and handles a much greater workload than the NAD/NARB system, which deals only with national advertising, while leaving local advertising control largely to the BBBs, LARPs, and local and state governments.

The U.S. federal and state governments play a far greater role in advertising control than the British government. The state governments handle many thousands of cases per year that deal with advertising. And, although the FTC handled less than one-hundred consumer protection matters in 1983, it continues to exert great influence over advertising standards by virtue of precedent-setting cases, trade regulation rules, and broadly what is known as administrative law. Other federal agencies influence advertising standards similarly in their specific areas of responsibility. Although informal and formal contacts between the NAD/NARB/CARU and government agencies are rare, in a sense the U.S. government and advertising industry are "partners" (Boddewyn 1985b).

In contrast, in the United Kingdom, the OFT (and other parts of government) play a smaller role. While the Independent Broadcasting Authority (IBA) takes care of broadcast advertising control, the government has "delegated" to the ASA/CAP Committee the primary responsibility for most of the remainder of advertising control activities. Nevertheless, the British advertising industry (including ASA) interacts frequently with the government—particularly through the AA (Boddewyn, letter to the author, 24 August 1986).

The ASA/CAP system is limited to nonbroadcast advertising; the IBA handles matters relating to radio and television advertising. In the United

Table 8–1
Comparison of Features of the NAD/NARB and the ASA/CAP Committee Systems

Feature	NAD/NARB	ASA/CAP
Scope		
Media coverage	All media, including direct mail and sales promotion	All *nonbroadcast* media, including direct mail and sales promotion
Type of advertising	National only	National and local
Functions		
Preclearance	None	Cigarette advertising
Complaint handling and investigation	From any source	From any source
Inquiries	From any source	From any source
Research	Special studies	Special studies
Monitoring	As source of complaints	As source of complaints, and systematic to identify priorities
Codes of practice	CARU, BBB, and others external to NAD/NARB; no comprehensive code	*BCAP, BCSPP*
Compliance mechanism	Negotiation and good will, publicity	Media refusal of advertisements, publicity
Case selection criteria	Public interest, avoid those involving competitor squabbles	All accepted that are within ASA/CAP remit according to *BCAP* and *BCSPP*
Funding	CBBB membership dues from advertisers and advertising agencies, and special funding by children's advertisers for CARU	0.1% of member advertising in media
Publicity	Low public profile; monthly *Case Reports*, other publications, speeches; mostly to the advertising industry, but available to the public	High public profile; monthly *Case Reports*, other publications, speeches; regular advertising to the public
Public representation	None on NAD staff; 20% on NARB review panels	None on ASA secretariat; 8 of 11 members of the council
Prior substantiation of claims	Required; subsequent evidence will also be accepted	Required to be available immediately on request

States, in contrast, the NAD/NARB/CARU system is concerned with broadcast advertising as well as advertising in other media. However, in much the same way as the IBA, the preclearance function is handled by the U.S. television networks, which also handle the small number of subsequent complaints against television advertising; but the U.S. networks are private enterprises rather than public corporations.

In contrast to the industry-oriented dependence of the NAD/NARB (to influence advertisers to accomplish its objectives), the ASA/CAP Committee system takes a broad approach. The British system does as much or more than the NAD/NARB to achieve understanding and cooperation from advertisers, agencies, media, and others in industry. But the ASA also makes a major effort to communicate directly with consumers and to maintain high visibility to generate as many legitimate consumer complaints as possible.

The ASA/CAP Committee system uses the media to enforce its decisions, whereas the NAD/NARB system relies on negotiation and voluntary compliance.

Both the NAD/NARB and the ASA/CAP Committee systems engage in extensive monitoring of media to identify inappropriate advertising. However, the ASA/CAP system has developed its monitoring activities more fully regarding sampling procedures and other methods that permit it to estimate the incidence of inappropriate advertising with known confidence intervals. These activities are useful to guide the ASA in seeking industry cooperation to minimize inappropriate advertising, as well as to provide reassurance to politicians and government officials that everything possible is being done to serve the public interest. The ASA purpose and scope are significantly broader than those of the NAD/NARB, especially in the sense that the ASA, through its monitoring, seeks to identify systematically the most urgent problem areas so that it is then more clearly in a superior position to do something about them.

A further difference in the two systems lies in their policies toward publicity to consumers. The ASA/CAP Committee system advertises extensively, trying to achieve a high public profile. In contrast, the NAD/NARB system at the national level operates with a very low public profile, depending mainly on (1) the local BBBs, which are well known to many consumers, and (2) local government, to handle local advertising control. This permits the NAD/NARB to focus its attention on national advertising that involves important issues of public interest, rather than to function primarily as a consumer complaint handling organization. The ASA/CAP Committee system, on the other hand, is concerned very much with being "seen to serve the public interest" and the advantages to society that accrue from that policy. The NAD/NARB system gets its credibility primarily because it pursues serious matters of public interest, and focuses particularly on large and important companies, hoping thereby to have a significant impact on truth and accuracy in advertising. In contrast, the ASA/CAP Committee system gets its credibility especially from its public reputation and willingness not only to handle a wide range of consumer advertising complaints, but also to assist consumers in seeking redress when appropriate. Of course, the British system also handles inquiries and complaints from the advertising industry, but monitoring and consumer complaints lead to about 80 percent of the investigations, and industry and competitor complaints account for only about 20 percent.

It is difficult to generalize about the meaning of the number and types of complaints against advertising. Although the literature is vast, views about advertising are complex. Consumer dissatisfaction may lead to complaints, or simply to brand switching; and complaints range from trivial to serious. The volume and characteristics of complaints from competitors or consumer groups seem to depend in large part on the public knowledge of the availability of a system to receive, process, and adjudicate complaints, and with the belief that sanctions lead to acceptable outcomes. Morever, the volume and nature of complaints handled by a regulatory system, as well as monitoring media to identify unacceptable advertisements, will depend in part on financial resources of the regulatory body. Thus, it is not only difficult to estimate the value of advertising complaints, but even the evidence we have is of little help in either specifying the seriousness of public dissatisfaction with advertising or evaluating the performance of the regulatory bodies.

Nevertheless, the number of inquiries and complaints handled by a self-regulatory system is an indicator of its workload and accomplishments, and consequently its need for resources. Campaigns to inform potential complainants about the system also are an indicator of both workload and the need for resources—both to advertise and to handle complaints.

Currently no information is available on the precise proportion of British consumers who are aware that the ASA exists to serve them. But ASA/CAP Committee system advertising has given the public sufficient "opportunity to see" its messages so that it can be said with some confidence that the great majority of consumers who are likely to complain about advertising are likely to know, or to be able to find out with little effort, how to do so. As a result the ASA/CAP system handles perhaps as many as 10,000 inquiries and complaints per year, and other British agencies (including the IBA and other government agencies or enforcement personnel) handle relatively few.

In contrast, the NAD/NARB/CARU system handles less than 1000 inquiries and complaints per year, and the BBBs, state governments, and several agencies of the federal government, especially the FTC, handle a relatively large but not precisely known number. The role of self-regulatory bodies is relatively small compared with the role of government bodies.

The main line of defense against unacceptable advertising in the United States is balanced between government and self-regulation, with government providing the foundation, depending in part on the NAD/NARB/CARU system and the television networks to help maintain both the legal minimums and their own more rigorous standards. Moreover, self-regulation in the United States is greatly dependent on the good will rather than the formal cooperation of the advertising business, especially the media, because antitrust considerations preclude some of the methods of enforcing formal codes and rules that might be permissible in the United Kingdom.

The ASA/CAP Committee has the mission to identify unacceptable nonbroadcast advertising and to provide the media with information so that they can refuse to carry advertising that contravenes the *BCAP*. The ASA/CAP Committee has been so successful in its work that there is widespread acceptance of the system as a superior alternative to extensive government regulation, although legislation and the OFT, as well as other government bodies capable of action, are available if needed.

On balance, it appears as if the United States, with four times the population of the United Kingdom, has methods of handling an also larger workload of inquiries, complaints, investigations, and enforcement activities, albeit with a different mix between government and self-regulation.

The mission and scope of activities of the NAD/NARB system compared with those of the ASA/CAP system are sufficiently different that a direct comparison of the budgets, personnel, and other resources of each system would be virtually meaningless. A fair comparison would require estimates of the resources that are devoted to advertising control by the U.S. BBBs, the U.S. federal and state governments, the IBA in the United Kingdom, and the advertising business in the United Kingdom and the United States.

However, it is possible to recommend changes to improve each system, and to suggest that budgets, personnel, and other resources should be adjusted to reflect such changes. Such recommendations should be based on measuring the performance of the system (or output) rather than on the basis of current resources (or input). This book therefore contains no general recommendations for changes in resources of either system, except in so far as specific recommendations would require additional resources. These "proper" amounts cannot be estimated without careful analysis of benefits and the costs needed to achieve them. In general, however, it seems as if there are a number of worthwhile activities that each system could use to justify an increase in resources.

A Formal Code for the NARB?

Up to now, a major barrier to the development of U.S. advertising self-regulatory standards and effective sanctions is "antitrust laws that frown on collusion and coercion no matter how benign their purpose" (Feldman 1980, 219). Thus any recommendation for such self-regulation must be prefaced by the observation that special care must be exercised to avoid a code that will contravene antitrust law.

However, advantages may be significant to having a formal code of advertising practices, not only from the standpoint of the advertising business, but also from a broader perspective of the welfare of the economy, the market system, and society as a whole.

First, a formal code of advertising practice can clarify the principles and practices that are appropriate to evaluate advertising. With such clarification the internal clearance systems of advertisers and agencies may be able to operate with reduced costs, increased confidence, and fewer errors requiring costly modifications or scrapped finished work. Prevention not only benefits advertisers and agencies directly. It also leads to a better general reputation for advertising, which in turn affects the credibility and effectiveness of advertising in the marketplace, and to lower costs of operating a self-regulatory system.

Flexibility in the self-regulatory system need not be sacrificed if the code is written with sufficient generality to focus primarily on principle rather than rigid prescription, allowing the continued use of the case-by-case approach, while adding clarity to the process and guidelines. The code can be treated as a living document, with provisions to make it easy to amend as conditions in society change in unexpected ways.

A formal code can give consumer organizations something concrete to reduce their fears about behind-the-scenes maneuvering to accomplish advertiser self-interests at the expense of consumers. It can also be a tool to assure consumer organizations that the advertising business is in fact maintaining a forthright program to serve consumers and society. A written code can be used by consumer organizations to assess how their concerns about advertising will be evaluated in the system. Consequently, a code probably will serve to reduce the confrontation and conflicts that spring from misunderstandings. However, experience indicates that consumer groups are likely to find a code less than fully satisfactory, because they often have their own particular agenda. But, if they are consulted adequately during the preparation of a code, and if "consumer representatives" are able to participate at some level in the administration of a code, the outcome can be positive: (1) their agendas may change, (2) they may make constructive inputs, and (3) they may take a public stance that reflects somewhat less negative or more positive attitudes toward advertising and how it should or should not be controlled by government. Because consumerist activity sometimes influences or leads to government initiatives, the development of a formal code may play an important role in the division of responsibilities for advertising control between government and the advertising business.

Knowledge that a formal code exists may also give consumers greater confidence in advertising even though experience indicates that few consumers will consult such a code.

Finally, if a code exists officials and agencies in relevant branches of government will have a more concrete understanding of the role of self-regulation, and thereby have a better basis for setting priorities for government-based initiatives to control advertising—or perhaps more acurately to see clearly what self-regulation can do and then avoid unnecessary government initiatives. Likewise, educators and students, and eventually a larger part of society, will have a better understanding of the effectiveness of self-regulation and its role vis-à-vis government regulation. Understanding of self-regulation by consumer organizations and government officials is particularly important for the long-term future.

The main objections by NAD/NARB officials to a formal code are the following:

1. The case-by-case approach—the classical common law approach to build a body of cases—works well. Each case is for a specific set of circumstances or conditions.

2. The case-by-case approach has more precision and sensitivity than a code would have.

3. For NAD cases it is usually not clear at the outset how the case will evolve; the decision evolves as the NAD follows the thought processes of the advertiser in determining whether substantiation of a claim is adequate.

4. The NAD/NARB has evolved guidelines in its cases that are specific to a given set of circumstances but are not precedents; they are only guidelines (Smithies, letters to and discussions with the author, 1986; Reid, letters to and discussions with the author, 1986).

A careful review of these objections indicates that perhaps a formal code can be written for the NAD/NARB with sufficient generality to preserve the case-by-case approach, the necessary sensitivity, the nature of the process, and the use of "guidelines" rather than "precedents." The CARU guidelines for children's advertising are written in this way. For example, the following topics are *not* mentioned in the guidelines: (1) entering strange places and conversing with strangers, (2) mail order and telephone purchasing, (3) ability to afford the product, (4) health products and safety practices, (5) manners and behavior, and (6) alcoholic beverages. Nevertheless, cases involving these issues have been handled by the CARU (*NAD Case Report,* special issue, March 1986).

Because the preparation and implementation of a formal code is not only controversial but difficult, it is recommended that the working group should commission a careful study of attitudes and opinions of advertisers and agencies toward this recommendation. Such a study should also include questions about the range of standards that should be incorporated into such a code. It may be possible, for example, that advertisers and their agencies may believe that some of the standards now included in existing specific industry codes might reasonably be included in a general code of advertising standards and practices.

The NAD/NARB system has evolved to the point that its relevant experience in defining unacceptable advertising, along with the many published guidelines for a variety of sources, should make it feasible to codify existing standards. The ASA/CAP Committee system with its long experience with *BCAP* and the *BCSPP* can also provide useful guidance. The ICC international codes of advertising and sales promotion practice (ICC 1974, 31–54), which serve as the base for self-regulatory codes in most countries that have a self-regulatory system of advertising or sales promotion controls, will also be useful. The NAD/NARB has matured so that many in advertising already have a reasonably good informal understanding of NAD/NARB standards. Although preparing a code would be complex, it is a manageable task.

Additionally, it should be remembered that the current NAD/NARB/CARU system has broad support from the advertising business. It can therefore be argued that it is sensible to retain a successful system rather than to risk upsetting the delicate balance that exists between NAD/NARB activities and industry approval and support for them. Indeed the current system and policies may maximize such approval and support. Therefore, any changes should be made with caution and should be implemented only if it is clear that adequate support for them exists. Thus a formal code probably should be based not only on current attitudes and opinions of advertisers and agencies, but also on a summary of experience from cases decided, while retaining general guidelines for flexibility in handling cases under the changing conditions of the future. The code should not be excessively legalistic and should not restrict necessary flexibility.

Recommendation IV:
Formalize a Code for the NAD/NARB

The NAD/NARB should take advantage of its relevant experience (or "case law") in defining unacceptable advertising. It should assemble a working group of knowledgeable people from the advertising industry as well as knowledgeable representatives from consumer groups, educational institutions, and government. The mission of the group should be to formalize a Code of Advertising Practices and Standards. The Code will be designed to serve as an objective and realistic base to evaluate the acceptability of major controversial types of advertising and advertising practices at the national level. It should be designed to serve as a unifying force, incorporating features of existing codes, and consolidating them to the extent practicable.

Improved Monitoring by the NAD?

The existence of a formal written code is a *sine qua non* for effective monitoring. It is virtually impossible for a monitoring staff to identify likely unacceptable advertising unless reasonably objective standards are clearly understood. The *Self-Regulatory Guidelines for Children's Advertising* serve the CARU well (Weisskoff, letters to and discussions with the author, 1986). But, it is not clear how NAD monitors are able to monitor efficiently. To be sure, NAD specialists are knowledgeable about NAD/NARB cases and standards; they look for new claims—something different; the process is quite informal, and an individual specialist will design a monitoring program for a week, selecting certain magazines and taping and reviewing commercials; the sampling and selection process is not systematic, and there is no written policy (Smithies, letter to and discussions with the author, 1986). Most CARU cases come from such monitoring (Weisskoff, letter to the author, 1986).

On the positive side, the present method of operation permits NAD specialists to focus their attention on currently important issues as they arise from consumers, consumer organizations, government, or industry sources. On the negative side, there is no way to be sure that other priorities are not overlooked, or that the system will identify other important advertising abuses that may be harming consumers in important ways.

The recent experience of the ASA in establishing guidelines for use by monitors may be useful to the NAD/NARB/CARU.

Recommendation V:
Expand Systematic Monitoring by the NAD/NARB

> *The NAD/NARB should seek additional resources and use them to establish a larger systematic program to monitor advertising across all major media, using standards in the previously recommended code as a guide. ASA experience in proper sampling to permit valid generalizations about advertising, as well as ASA experience in using a code to evaluate the advertisements in the sample, probably will serve as a useful starting point. This monitoring will have many uses, not only to identify and correct specific examples of unacceptable advertising, but also to help the U.S. system define the magnitude of the problems with "unacceptable" advertising, and thereby the appropriate mission of the NAD/NARB, and the amount of resources needed to address the problems.*

Publicity

The matter of publicity relates not only to the volume of complaints from a consumer standpoint, but also to the effectiveness of a self-regulatory body. If it is seen to be effective, consumers will have greater faith in advertising, which is in the best interests of both business and consumers, if indeed the system is effective.

NAD/NARB officials recognize that it is desirable for the self-regulatory system to be well known so that members of the public know that a system exists to protect them. But, it is argued, it is a difficult message to convey, the consumer response to such efforts is very small, and often the response has to do with matters of taste in advertising or with television programming, for example—matters with which the NAD/NARB system does not deal (Reid, letter to and discussions with the author, 1986). Nevertheless, for the same reasons that the public service activities of the Advertising Council contribute positively to the general reputation of advertising and to the reputation of the advertising business for supporting socially desirable and responsible causes, it seems likely that greater public knowledge of the activities of the NAD/NARB/CARU/LARP system would be worthwhile.

Publicity is also important because advertisers will expect that consumers will know how to make a complaint. Advertisers will know that inappropriate advertising is likely to be challenged and that action is likely to be taken by regulators who know and understand advertising.

The greatest value of publicity is not that consumers achieve satisfaction or redress, but rather the threat to advertisers that someone might complain and that unacceptable advertising will be exposed and that action will be taken—action that will be costly to the advertiser in terms of responding to the action itself as well as to the reputation of the company and its products in the consumer marketplace. Thus it seems important to have a system of adequate publicity that invites legitimate complaints and makes it easy for them to be lodged and handled, while at the same time keeping the number of uniformed or frivolous complaints to a minimum.

Recommendation VI:
Expand NAD/NARB and BBB Publicity

> *The system of self-regulation of advertising should be known and readily available to all who believe that they have a legitimate complaint. Action by competitors, consumers, consumer associations, educators, government officials, citizens who wish to seek redress, and moral and social leaders of society must serve as a deterrent to inappropriate advertising. The self-regulatory system must serve as a warning device to advertisers to adhere to acceptable standards. Therefore a self-regulatory system must publicize itself adequately. In the case of the NAD/NARB system it is suggested that two measures be taken: (1) the BBBs should publicize that they not only handle complaints about local advertising but they also will help consumers evaluate national advertising and when appropriate they will forward a complaint to the NAD, and (2) the NAD/NARB system should seek the assistance of the Advertising Council to prepare appropriate public service advertising to inform consumers and others about the existence, availability, and effectiveness of the self-regulatory system—as well as to seek donations of time and space from the media. The experience of the ASA, including examples of specific advertisements, may be useful to the NAD/NARB/ CARU.*

Financial Independence

The ASA/CAP Committee system has achieved independence from the advertising industry in four ways: (1) automatic financing, (2) a majority of nonadvertising members on the ASA Council, (3) an independent chairman, and (4) separate legal identity as a company limited by guarantee. The NAD/NARB system has achieved independence from the advertising industry in that it operates under the administration of the CBBB, which is an organization supported broadly by virtually all segments of the business world, nationally and locally, and is not dominated by advertising. Although a substantial part of funding is derived from the advertising industry, the NAD/NARB is well insulated from direct interference, although it may feel constrained to pursue general policies and practices that do not conflict with the general interests of business, particularly the advertising industry. Thus, on balance, the British system has a firmer degree of independence than the U.S. system. Because there is no readily apparent means to improve the independence of either the British or the U.S. system, no recommendation is made. However, it would seem wise for the NAD/NARB to explore alternatives that would give the NAD/NARB/CARU/LARP system greater "distance" from business influences (that is, somewhat greater autonomy to pursue the public interest). It is not only important for the NAD/NARB to be independent, but also for it to "be seen as independent." Admittedly such an approach is not without problems. The danger of "distancing" the NAD/NARB is that the further away it gets from the advertising business, the greater the danger of a withdrawal of commitment from the industry. The ASA, in this regard, has been a successful exception (Circus, letter to the author, 13 August 1986), probably because the advertising business perceives that the advantages outweigh the disadvantages.

Enforcement

The crux of voluntary control of advertising in the United Kingdom is the commitment of the media and their associations to uphold the *BCAP* and the *BCSPP*. The media depend on the ASA for an interpretation of the Codes as they apply to individual cases. Legally, the media are not bound to accept an ASA interpretation, and conceivably they could disagree with an ASA decision against an advertiser; they can, of course, also refuse an advertisement even if it has ASA approval.

The situation in the United States is substantially different in that (1) there is no written code of standards, and (2) there is the threat of potential antitrust actions against restraint of trade if the media should collude to restrict unacceptable advertising. However, if there were a generally acceptable code of standards that could be tested in court as to whether media adherence to it constitutes restraint of trade, perhaps the U.S. media could find a way to cooperate without fear of antitrust actions.

In this regard, it is important to note that the NAD/NARB system operates under the umbrella of the CBBB, which is much broader than a trade association of media such as the NAB. Therefore the experience of the NAB may not be a valid precedent to conclude that it is unlawful for the NAD/NARB to seek media adherence to an acceptable code, using NAD/NARB interpretation of the code in individual cases.

Recommendation VII:
Seek a Lawful Way for the NAD/NARB to Achieve Media Support

> *After establishing a written code of advertising standards, the CBBB/NAD should attempt to find a lawful way that the NAD/NARB system can provide media with their evaluations of the acceptability of advertising—so that the media can decide, independently of each other (to avoid contravening antitrust law) whether to accept advertising that the NAD/NARB/ CARU/LARP system decides contravenes the code.*

Another "possible solution to this problem would be the exemption of self-regulatory efforts on the part of industry groups from coverage by the antitrust laws" (Feldman 1980, 229). A possible drawback would be a "reduction in competition [that] would be detrimental both to consumers and to the larger public interest" (Feldman 1980, 230). But even if an exemption were obtained, there is no guarantee that changes in existing programs would be made. Nevertheless, the British model is worthy of further study to determine if some of its advantages can be achieved by the NAD/NARB/CARU/LARP/BBB systems.

One could argue, of course, that the NAD/NARB has achieved 100 percent cooperation from advertisers when the NAD/NARB ruled that advertising should be modified or discontinued, and therefore there is no need to have the cooperation of the media to enforce NAD/NARB decisions. However, in view of the low volume of NAD/NARB cases, and NAD selectivity in choosing cases, there is the distinct possibility that *if* the NAD/NARB had the cooperation of the media, they might pursue additional and perhaps more controversial cases. It also seems likely, from the ASA experience, that with a larger volume of investigations, a few cases would likely require force to achieve adherence. In a sense, the "perfect record" of adherence to NARB decisions reflects adversely on the system.

Media acceptance of NAD/NARB "decisions" as to whether certain examples of advertising ought to be modifed or discontinued need not be absolute. The ASA/CAP Committee functions well, although not perfectly, without an absolute commitment to compliance. To be sure, comparatively few advertisers ignore an ASA decision—in 1984 only 31 out of the 1,102 cases in which a complaint was upheld wholly or in part. In those instances the Authority was obliged to ask the CAP Committee to bring the matter to the attention of the media associations, which then informed their members. Since those media, by virtue of their membership of their trade associations, have agreed to uphold and enforce the provisions of *BCAP*, they are obliged not to accept advertisements from the advertiser in question. It should be noted, however, that an editor's decision on what to publish is final; thus a publication may well refuse an advertisement, even though it has ASA approval, as well as (theoretically) accept advertisements of which the ASA does not approve. Thus, when the ASA rules against an advertisement, the media are not absolutely bound to accept it, although in fact they always have done so (Williamson, discussion with the author, 28 July 1986).

The ASA/CAP Committee system also has occasional problems of noncompliance, within the system as well as from those who are not part of the system and who do not pledge themselves to uphold *BCAP* or the *BCSPP*. It seems likely that some form of closer cooperation between the ASA/CAP system and government agencies such as the OFT will occur from legislation pending at the time of writing.

In the United States the NAD/NARB system together with the FDA has in place a program to reduce advertising abuses concerning "rogue" sellers of foods, medicines, and medical devices (quack remedies) that have long fallen outside either government or self-regulation. This program may serve as a useful guide for similar cooperation between the ASA and British government agencies.

Recommendation VIII:
Establish Working Parties to Identify Abuses and Recommend Remedies

> *In both the United States and the United Kingdom, a commission or working party should be set up comprising the various sides of the advertising business, consumer interests, and enforcement agencies. The terms of reference should include:*
>
> 1. *Identifying any abuses not currently covered by either self regulation or legal control.*
>
> 2. *Recommending the best means of tackling them.*
>
> 3. *Recommending suitable measures for identifying any such abuses in the future as they arise.*

The latter provision would be intended to ensure that shady operators could not operate "in the margin" between the legal and voluntary systems.

It is suggested that the initiative for such action should come from the ASA in the United Kingdom, and from the NARC in the United States.

The Influence of the European Economic Community

It seems likely that the European *Council Directive on Misleading Advertising* will strengthen self-regulation in at least some of the member states, including the United Kingdom, and that any new British government powers probably will be used primarily as a backup to the self-regulatory system, supporting rather than replacing its functions—at least in the short run.

To meet the requirements of the Council Directive, as well as to maintain the integrity and performance of the ASA/CAP Committee system, it seems logical for the ASA to coordinate its activities even more closely with those of government agencies and to take an active part in assisting consumers in cases requiring legal action.

Recommendation IX:
Expand ASA / CAP Committee Support for British Legal Enforcement

The ASA/CAP Committee already has the policy to refer those matters outside its remit to the proper government agency when appropriate. And, because the ASA is already fairly well known to those who might discover unsatisfactory advertising, it is recommended that the ASA include in its publicity that it is an appropriate authority to receive complaints about unlawful practices and that it will forward such complaints to the proper government agency. The ASA, through its monitoring or from other sources, should make special efforts to discover advertising that is potentially unlawful and inform appropriate advertisers and media that it will serve as the vehicle to initiate and pursue such cases to achieve appropriate action by government agencies and the courts. The ASA should also mention in its publicity any new government powers or responsibilities that arise from meeting the requirements of the Council Directive on Misleading Advertising, or future relevant directives, and that the ASA/ CAP Committee system will support actively the government's use of such new powers.

Some might argue that the advertising business would feel betrayed if these recommendations were followed, and that it would reduce the commitment and cooperation so essential for a voluntary system to operate. However, it is difficult to see why honest advertisers will not agree to activities designed to promote compliance with the law.

Ideally, it would also seem logical to allow ASA "decisions" to be challenged in the courts, as is now possible with IBA decisions. Although such challenges probably would be extremely rare, it is important to find some way that consumers, consumer associations, and competitors can have some recourse in the case of ASA/CAP Committee decisions that they believe are not acceptable. Perhaps this matter will be handled as part of the British compliance with the Council Directive, but if not it should receive ASA/CAP Committee consideration.

Continuing Controversies

Some critics of self-regulatory systems of advertising suggest that enforcement is ineffective for a variety of reasons not yet discussed fully, pointing out that the system

1. May be used to chastise the advertiser but does not compensate consumers for loss (Jones and Pickering 1985, 67–68). To this one might reasonably respond that it is better to prevent than to provide redress, especially when appropriate redress is usually very small and difficult to measure, or when the cost would usually outweigh the benefit; in any event redress is available through the courts when sufficiently important to warrant such action.

2. Does not include the power to mandate corrective advertising (Jones and Pickering 1985, 67–68). To this one might reasonably respond that corrective advertising has been tried in some countries and subsequently abandoned for a variety of complex reasons that mostly relate to its ineffectiveness as a clearly justified tool of policy. The FTC in the United States, for example, mandated corrective advertising in a substantial number of cases over the decade of the 1970s, but has not used this action in recent years.

3. Does not provide for preclearance of print advertising, as tentatively recommended by Jones and Pickering (1985, 68, 69), when they suggest: "It would be appropriate . . . to ensure that all advertisers know more clearly the standards that are being sought and have their print advertisements also prevetted." These authors also suggest a "truth mark where substantiation has been provided." To these suggestions one can reasonably observe that of course it would be desirable for all advertisers to know the standards, but regarding prevetting and truth marks, (a) the large number of print advertisements in modern society would make such suggestions exceedingly expensive to implement; (b) they would require a staff and bureaucracy of great size; and (c) the administration of such a system would be not only complex but time consuming especially in view of geographical diversity of local and national advertisers, agencies, and the multitude of media.

These criticisms do indicate one matter of controversy that leads to a recommendation, the matter of consumer redress. While it is correct that the harm or damage done by "improper" advertising to individual consumers is undoubtedly small in most cases, not enough is known about the size and nature of the welfare loss as a result of unsatisfactory advertising, especially collectively. Class action suits are possible in the United

States, but not in the United Kingdom. Class action suits not only can provide for redress, but can also serve as a threat of possible punishment (or at least taking away ill-gotten gains) to an errant advertiser. Although such situations are rare, they are controversial and it would seem reasonable to try to resolve this controversy.

Recommendation X:
Expand Research on Benefit and Cost of Controlling
Unacceptable Advertising

> *The advertising business in the United Kingdom and the United States should support research to determine methods to measure the harm that unacceptable advertising may or may not do: (1) Who and how many people are harmed? (2) How much is each person harmed, and how much collectively? (3) What is the nature of the harm—economic loss, psychological stress, and so on? Such information could then be used by advertising regulatory or self-regulatory bodies to estimate the harm done by individual campaigns, to set priorities, and to allocate resources to particularly important types of problems—on the premise that the "harm done" is a wise criterion to make cost-benefit decisions.*
>
> *It is suggested that a working group or groups be formed, comprising comprehensive representation from inside and outside the advertising business (see also Recommendation I).*

Concluding Observations

These conclusions and recommendations are necessarily incomplete without mention of the need for further research to evaluate entire systems of advertising self-regulation comprehensively.

The ASA has endeavored to be seen to be effective by business, consumers, consumer associations, educators, government officials, members of parliament, and others. To a large extent this effort has succeeded. But there are not yet solid answers to questions about the comprehensive impact of the self-regulatory system on improving the quality of advertising. To answer such questions, programmatic research is required, consisting of a series of related projects. This book is only a beginning.

But such research requires large budgets and a concentration of researchers able to interact regularly with each other under the guidance of senior researchers. Funded chairs at universities are a step in the right direction, but additional opportunities to fund research programs, typical of those found in the physical sciences, are needed. The field of advertising has grown sufficiently in recent years, and the need for solid information on which to base public policy toward advertising is sufficiently great, to make such funding reasonable.

Although the British system of self-regulation is by no means perfect, it has a broader mission, and it appears to be more effective than the U.S. self-regulatory system. However, when considering the role of the federal and state governments in combination with the U.S. self-regulatory system, it may be that in a comprehensive sense, the U.S. system meets the needs of the U.S. economy and society as well as can be expected. However, these conjectures about the effectiveness of both systems need to be researched. In this book we have not been able to take a close look at the effectiveness of government regulation of advertising. And a comprehensive evaluation of self-regulation can be made only with a companion comprehensive evaluation of government regulation.

Nevertheless we can observe that the greater degree of advertising industry involvement in the U.S. system, together with the lack of sanctions, must cast doubt both on its objectivity and its ability to act decisively when required. As the British advertising industry discovered some years ago, justice must not only be done but must be seen to be done, though it is difficult to see how far the U.S. system could be strengthened without falling foul of antitrust legislation. It is ironic that industry measures designed to protect the consumer may in fact be hampered by legislation intended to accomplish the same end.

Moreover, during this period of deregulation, it seems likely that the U.S. system of self-regulation could and probably should establish a larger field of responsibility for itself, learning from whatever sources present themselves, including the British system.

Some broad matters of efficiency can also be addressed—even without the comprehensive research program previously suggested. Both the NAD and the ASA/CAP receive large numbers of inquiries and complaints that are not actionable and do not lead to constructive changes in advertising. Such complaints are serious from the standpoint of the complainant, but seem uninformed or frivolous to those who know the system well. In the interests of efficiency one might seek to determine how to reduce the volume of complaints that lead to wasted effort. Likewise it would be well to increase the number of informed complaints that lead to effective efforts to improve advertising.

BCAP and *BCSPP* are published, and the ASA makes substantial efforts to inform consumers, competitors, and others about these codes. From April 1979 to June 1986 the ASA distributed 60,870 copies of *BCAP* to industry and the public (Williamson, discussion with the author, 28 July 1986). Probably most major advertisers, agencies, and media have a copy, but it is not known how many advertising personnel and consumers take the time to consult it. Probably it is rare for anyone but a specialist in advertising control to have the incentive to study the Code carefully, much less remember its provisions.

Some would view this level of ignorance as deplorable. Others would accept that it is inevitable. Nevertheless, it seems desirable to ascertain just what, if anything, might be done to reduce the number of inquiries and complaints that waste the time of both the complainant and the regulatory body and to increase those that identify unacceptable advertising. To some extent we have addressed these questions earlier, pointing out that because the NAD has no formal code, it is even more difficult than in the United Kingdom for a potential complainant to decide whether it will be worthwhile to take action in a given instance. Additionally, the NAD/NARB/CARU system does not publicize itself to generate complaints, but depends more heavily on monitoring and competitor challenges. But even major advertisers have many uncertainties about the propriety of their own advertisements.

The question of publicity of a self-regulatory body's availability to receive and resolve complaints is also a double-edged sword. Past experience indicates that increased publicity leads to more actionable complaints, but also to more that are not actionable. However, because actionable complaints lead to improvements in advertising, one may conclude that increased numbers of uninformed or frivolous complaints are a necessary by-product of an effective system of self-regulation. The ASA/CAP Committee system fits this pattern.

Perhaps one can conclude that it is necessary for a system to handle large numbers of inquiries and complaints that do not merit investigation. However, such a judgment must rest in part on whether the cost of handling the increased nonactionable complaints is counterbalanced by the benefits (for example, reduced harm to consumers, increased effectiveness of competition) that accrue from the increased number of actionable cases. Such a judgment requires that we be able to measure the amount of harm, the impact on competition, and so on. Currently we can only recommend, as we have previously done, that the advertising industry support broad research programs to improve our ability to make such measurements.

At this point we can list some of the larger research questions that will need to be answered before we can suggest further improvements in the self-regulatory systems in the United States, the United Kingdom, or in other nations:

1. How do consumerism and consumerist activities influence governmental and industry self-regulation of advertising?
2. How does antitrust policy, or competition policy, influence the degree and type of advertising control by government and by the advertising industry?

3. How do a nation's cultural, economic, geographical, legal, political, and social characteristics influence the purposes and nature of advertising self-regulatory bodies as well as government regulation of advertising?

Although this book has focused on the United Kingdom and the United States, one might also seek lessons applicable to other nations. Indeed, some of our recommendations have a broader general application. Ultimately the question of what the balance should be between government and self-regulation of advertising must be answered separately for each nation. Thus our recommendations can be examined for ideas that can be adopted or modified for use elsewhere.

The cost-benefit oriented reader will by this time have many questions about the real need for the recommendations in this chapter. Currently there are relatively few pressures from consumers, consumerists, or government officials for improved regulation of advertising. Many would observe that the current system seems to be working to the satisfaction of most everyone, and might comment: "If it ain't broke, don't fix it."

One might respond that in the long term advertising will continue to be vulnerable to criticism. In the meantime it would seem wise to think about the long-term welfare of the advertising industry and to continue to use the welfare of consumers and society as a guideline for action. It is especially important to retain the credibility of advertising to consumers and its effectiveness as a marketing tool. Continuing efforts should be made to explain to the public the role of advertising in the economy and its contribution to the welfare of modern society. Such activities will help to ensure that public criticism is focused on advertising abuses rather than on a misplaced hostility toward advertising itself.

Future waves of criticism will occur, as society and the market system continue to evolve, and as consumers and government interact in increasingly complex ways. During a period of relative calm, it seems sensible for cool minds to fashion an improved system of advertising self-control—one that will meet the needs of the future. Not only is an ounce of prevention worth a pound of cure, but change and renewal are constantly with us. The long-term viability of a strong and effective self-regulatory system of advertising, one that will anticipate and be suitable for the future, is too important to be left to happen by itself. Both systems need leaders with a vision of the future.

References

Bloom, Paul N. (ed.) (1982), *Consumerism and Beyond: Research Perspectives on the Future Social Environment,* Proceedings of the Workshop Presented by the Marketing

Science Institute and the Center for Business and Public Policy, University of Maryland, 14–17 April 1982 (Cambridge: The Marketing Science Institute, April 1982, Report No. 82-102).

Boddewyn, J.J. (1983), "Outside Participation in Advertising Self-Regulation: The Case of the Advertising Standards Authority UK)," *Journal of Consumer Policy* 6(1):77–93.

Boddewyn, J.J. (1985a), "Advertising Self-Regulation: Private Government and Agent of Public Policy," *Journal of Public Policy and Marketing* 4:129–141.

Boddewyn, J.J. (1985b), "US Advertising Self-Regulation: The FTC as Outside Partner of the NAD/NARB," Mimeographed draft, March 1985.

Brandmair, Lothar (1977), *Die Freiwillige Selbstkontrolle der Werbung* (Voluntary Self-Control of Advertising) (Köln: Carl Heymanns Verlag KG).

Burleton, Eric (1982), "The Self-Regulation of Advertising in Europe," *International Journal of Advertising* 1(4):333–344.

Cohen, Ronald I. (1971) "Comparative False Advertising Regulation: A Beginning," *The Adelaide Law Review* 4(August 1971):69–112.

Dunn, S. Watson (1974) "The Changing Legal Climate for Marketing and Advertising in Europe," *Columbia Journal of World Business* 9(Summer 1974):91–98.

Fulop, Christina (1973/1974) "Restrictive Marketing Practices in the EEC," *European Journal of Marketing* 3(Winter 1973/1974).

Feldman, Laurence P. (1980), *Consumer Protection* (St. Paul: West Publishing Company).

Fulop, Christina (1977), *The Consumer Movement and the Consumer* (London: The Advertising Association).

Gupta, A.K., and Lad, L.J. (1983), "Industry Self-Regulation: An Economic, Organizational and Political Analysis," *Academy of Management Review* 8(3):416–425.

ICC (1974), *International Codes of Marketing Practices* (Paris: International Chamber of Commerce, March 1974).

Jones, T.T., and Pickering, J.F. (1985), *Self-Regulation in Advertising: A Review* (London: The Advertising Association).

Laczniak, G.R. (1983), "Framework for Analyzing Marketing Ethics" *Journal of Macromarketing* 3(1)(Spring):7–18.

Miracle, Gordon E. (1984), "An Assessment Progress in Research on International Advertising," *Current Issues and Research in Advertising,* 135–166, especially 153–156.

Miracle, Gordon E. (1985), "Advertising Regulation in Japan and the USA: An Introductory Comparison," *Waseda Business and Economic Studies,* No. 21, 35–69.

Mitnick, B.M. (1980), *The Political Economy of Regulation; Creating, Designing and Removing Regulatory Forms* (New York: Columbia University Press).

NAD Case Reports, various dates.

Peebles, Dean M., and Ryans, John K. Jr., (1978) "Advertising as a Positive Force," *Journal of Advertising* 7(2):48–52, 47.

Pertschuk, Michael (1982), *Revolt Against Regulation* (Berkeley: University of California Press).

Pickering, J.F., and Cousins, D.C. (1980), *The Economic Implications of Codes of Practice* (Manchester, Engl.: University of Manchester Institute of Science and Technology, Department of Management Sciences).

Preston, Ivan L. (1983), "A Review of the Literature on Advertising Regulation, *Current Issues and Research in Advertising,* 1–37.

Reich, Norbert, and Micklitz, Hans-W. (1980), *Consumer Legislation in the EC Countries, A Comparative Analysis* (New York: Van Nostrand Reinhold Company).

Rijkens, Rein, and Miracle, Gordon E. (1986), *European Regulation of Advertising* (Amsterdam: North Holland [Elsevier Science Publishers]).

Ryans, John K., Wills, James R., and Bell, Henry (1979), "International Advertising Regulation," *Proceedings of the Midwest Marketing Association Conference,* April 1979.

Thorelli, Hans B. (1971), "Consumer Information Policy in Sweden—What Can Be Learned?" *Journal of Marketing* 35(1):50–55.

Thorelli, Hans B., Becker, Helmut, and Engledow, J.E. (1975), *The Information Seekers: An International Study of Consumer Information and Advertising Image* (Cambridge, Mass.: Ballinger).

Thorelli, Hans B., and Thorelli, Sarah V. (1974), *Consumer Information Handbook: Europe and North America* (New York: Praeger).

Thorelli, Hans B., and Thorelli, Sarah V. (1977), *Consumer Information Systems and Consumer Policy* (Cambridge, Mass.: Ballinger).

Rosden, E.R., and Rosden, P.E. (1982), *The Law of Advertising,* Vol. 2 (New York: Matthew Bender).

Schmitter, Philippe C. (1979), "Still the Century of Corporatism?" *Review of Politics* 36(Jan.):85–131.

Thompson, Fred, and Jones, L.R. (1982), *Regulatory Policy and Practices: Regulating Better and Regulating Less* (New York: Praeger).

Appendix:
Advertising Issued
by the Advertising
Standards Authority

DO ADVERTISEMENTS SOMETIMES DISTORT THE TRUTH?

The short answer is yes, some do. Every week many hundreds of thousands of advertisements appear for the first time.

Nearly all of them play fair with the people they are addressed to.

A handful do not. They misrepresent the products they are advertising.

As the Advertising Standards Authority it is our job to make sure these ads are identified, and stopped.

WHAT MAKES AN ADVERTISEMENT MISLEADING?

If a training course had turned a 7 stone weakling into Mr Universe the fact could be advertised because it can be proved.

But a promise to build 'you' into a 15 stone he-man would have us flexing our muscles because the promise could not always be kept.

The Code covers magazines, newspapers, cinema commercials, brochures, leaflets, posters, circulars posted to you, and now commercials on video tapes.

The ASA is not responsible for TV and radio advertising. Though the

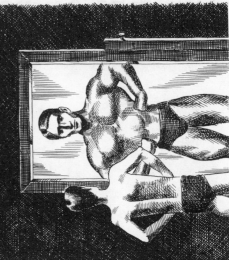

who we or the public challenge to back up their claims with solid evidence.

If they cannot, or refuse to, we ask them either to amend the ads or withdraw them completely.

Nearly all agree without further argument.

In any case we inform the publishers, who will not knowingly accept any ad which we have decided contravenes the Code.

If the advertiser refuses to withdraw the advertisement he will find it hard if not impossible to have it published.

WHOSE INTERESTS DO WE REALLY REFLECT?

The ASA was not created by law and has no legal powers.

Not unnaturally some people are sceptical about its effectiveness.

'Makes you look younger' might be a reasonable claim for a cosmetic. But pledging to 'take years off your life' would be an overclaim akin to a promise of eternal youth.

A garden centre's claim that its seedlings would produce 'a riot of colour in just a few days' might be quite contrary to the reality.

Prose so flowery would deserve to be pulled out by the roots.

If a brochure advertised a hotel as being '5 minutes walk from the beach', it must not require an Olympic athlete to do it in the time.

As for estate agents, if the phrase 'over-looking the river' translated to 'backing onto a ditch', there would be nothing for it but to show their ad the door.

HOW DO WE JUDGE THE ADS WE LOOK INTO?

Our yardstick is The British Code of Advertising Practice.

Its 500 rules give advertisers precise practical guidance on what they can and cannot say. The rules are also a gauge for media owners to assess the acceptability of any advertising they are asked to publish.

rules are very similar they are administered by the Independent Broadcasting Authority.

WHY IT'S A TWO-WAY PROCESS

Unfortunately some advertisers are unaware of the Code, and breach the rules unwittingly. Others forget, bend or deliberately ignore the rules.

That is why we keep a continuous check on advertising. But because of the sheer volume, we cannot monitor every advertiser all the time.

So we encourage the public to help by telling us about any advertisements they think ought not to have appeared. Last year over 7,500 people wrote to us.

WHAT DO WE DO TO ADVERTISERS WHO DECEIVE THE PUBLIC?

Our first step is to ask advertisers

In fact the ASA was set up by the advertising business to make sure the system of self control worked in the public interest.

For this to be credible, the ASA has to be totally independent of the business.

Neither the chairman nor the majority of ASA council members is allowed to have any involvement in advertising.

Though administrative costs are met by a levy on the business, no advertiser has any influence over ASA decisions.

Advertisers are aware it is as much in their own interests as it is in the public's that honesty should be seen to prevail.

If you would like to know more about the ASA and the rules it seeks to enforce you can write to us at the address below for an abridged copy of the Code.

The Advertising Standards Authority.

If an advertisement is wrong, we're here to put it right.

ASA Ltd, Brook House, Torrington Place, London WC1E 7HN.

DO SOME ADVERTISERS GIVE YOU TOO MANY FACTS AND TOO LITTLE INFORMATION?

It is not difficult to find yourself blinded by science.

Some advertisers are so wrapped up in their own jargon they fail to realise that to most people it's nothing more than mumbo jumbo.

But how can you be sure the facts and figures you read are accurate? And how can you tell if an over-abundance of them is not just a whitewash to conceal the truth.

SORTING OUT THE WHEAT FROM THE CHAFF.

The answers lie in a book of rules called The British Code of Advertising Practice.

It is our job as The Advertising Standards Authority to administer these rules.

Where through lack of specialist knowledge the public could be led astray the rules are detailed and specific.

Financial advertising is a good example. In essence the rules state advertisements must take into account that the complexities of finance may well be beyond the people to

interest rate can fluctuate. This must be made clear.

A hi-fi manufacturer should not merely advertise how many watts his equipment develops. Since there are several different ways of measuring sound output, he should state which method he used and give the reader a fair

But because of the sheer volume of advertising we cannot monitor every advertisement that appears.

So we encourage the public to help by telling us about inaccuracies we may not have spotted. Last year over 7,500 people wrote to us.

Every complaint is considered and if necessary submitted to our experts before we make a ruling.

WHAT WE DO TO THOSE WHO PRACTISE TO DECEIVE.

If we decide there has been a breach of any rules we ask the advertiser to amend the advertisement.

If he cannot, or refuses, we ask him to withdraw it completely. Nearly all agree without further argument.

In any case we inform the publishers, who will not knowingly accept any advertisement which we have decided contravenes the Code.

If the advertiser refuses to withdraw the advertisement he will find it hard if not impossible to have it published.

whom the offer appeals.

An investment ad inviting direct response has to include a great deal of explanatory wording.

For instance, past growth of '500% in 5 years' would have to be qualified by the exact five years to which it referred. And all investment ads have to carry wording to the effect that the value of investments and the income from them, if quoted, can go down as well as up.

WHEN ONE AND ONE MAKES SIX.

In protecting the public from being misled we are often accused of being pernickety.

We once received a complaint that a car with a 1442cc engine had been advertised as a '1.5'.

People 'in the know' apparently accept this as normal. But our complainant pointed out that his employer's mileage allowance for a '1.5' was for engines over 1451cc.

What meant little to the car trade meant a lot to him, and we were pleased that the advertiser amended the ad to include the exact engine size in the text.

READING BETWEEN THE LINES.

It's not enough for a building society to promise 'worth 13.93% to basic rate income tax payers' when the actual

basis for comparison. And as for computers it is not on to advertise what a piece of equipment will do and simply assume that the reader will know he needs several other items in order to operate it.

OUR LIMITATIONS.

The British Code of Advertising Practice covers newspapers, magazines, cinema commercials, posters, brochures, leaflets, circulars posted to you, and now commercials on video tapes.

It does not cover TV and radio advertising. Though the rules are very similar, they are administered by the Independent Broadcasting Authority.

THE VALUE OF YOUR OWN SPECIALIST KNOWLEDGE.

Unfortunately some advertisers are unaware of the Code, and breach the rules unwittingly. Others forget, bend or deliberately ignore the rules.

That is why we keep a continuous check on advertising, either by ourselves or in conjunction with experts.

The ASA was not created by law and has no legal powers.

Not unnaturally some people are sceptical about its effectiveness.

In fact the ASA was set up by the advertising business to make sure the system of self-control genuinely worked in the public interest.

For this to be credible the ASA has to be totally independent of the business.

Neither the chairman nor the majority of his council members is allowed to have any involvement in advertising.

Though administrative costs are met by a levy on the business, no advertiser has any influence over ASA decisions.

Advertisers as a whole accept it is as much in their interests as the public's to keep on the right side of the rules.

If you would like to know more about the ASA and the rules it seeks to enforce you can write to us at the address below for an abridged copy of the Code.

The Advertising Standards Authority.

If an advertisement is wrong, we're here to put it right.

ASA Ltd, Brook House, Torrington Place, London WC1E 7HN.

DO SOME ADVERTISERS GO TOO FAR TO ATTRACT YOUR ATTENTION?

Every week many hundreds of thousands of advertisements appear for the first time.

Some stand out from the multitude by virtue of their relevance, wit or charm.

Others for less creditable reasons.

It is our job as the Advertising Standards Authority to look into any serious malpractices, and make sure they don't happen again.

HOW FAR CAN AN ADVERTISER GO?

This is a vexed question because sometimes there is a very fine line between what is above board and what is below the belt.

One rule in our Code states, 'Advertisements should contain nothing which is likely, in the light of generally prevailing standards of decency and propriety, to cause grave or widespread offence.'

This could terrify an old person living alone, and we would do all we could to put a stop to it.

WHO CAN WE THROW THE BOOK AT?

The British Code of Advertising Practice covers newspapers, magazines, cinema commercials, posters, brochures, leaflets, circulars posted to you, and now commercials on video tapes.

Last year over 7,500 people wrote to us.

WHAT WE DO TO THE BULLY BOYS.

If we decide there has been a breach of any rules we ask the advertiser to amend the advertisement.

If he cannot, or refuses, we ask him to withdraw it completely.

Nearly all agree without further argument.

In any case we inform the publishers, who will not knowingly accept any ad which we have decided contravenes the Code.

If the advertiser refuses to withdraw the advertisement he will find it hard if not impossible to have it published.

CAN ADVERTISERS PUSH US AROUND.

The ASA was not created by law and has no legal powers.

Not unnaturally some

There is no doubt at all what we would do with an advertisement which depicted someone being eaten alive.

But what about a car advertisement which addressed the reader as 'Ye of little faith'?

A few people might regard it as offensive, but not, we think, the majority.

Although the phrase is of biblical origin, it has slipped into common usage as a metaphor for the sceptical.

PREVENTING UNDERHAND TACTICS.

Another rule states, 'Advertisements should not without justifiable reason play on fear.' What is 'justifiable', and what isn't?

Again we take the view we think the majority would.

We might regard an ad acceptable if it showed how a widow and her children were able to survive on the proceeds of her deceased husband's life assurance.

While offering an answer to a frightening problem it does not in itself induce fear.

But suppose a security firm sent a leaflet through the post that said 'I'm a burglar, and I can get into your house as easily as this leaflet.'

It does not cover TV and radio advertising.

Though the rules are very similar, they are administered by the Independent Broadcasting Authority.

WHY WE ASK YOU TO GRAB A PEN.

Unfortunately some advertisers are unaware of the Code, and breach the rules unwittingly.

Others forget, bend or deliberately ignore the rules.

That is why we keep a continuous check on advertising.

But because of the sheer volume we cannot monitor every advertiser all the time.

So we encourage the public to help by telling us about advertisements they think ought not to have appeared.

people are sceptical about its effectiveness.

In fact the ASA was set up by the advertising business to make sure the system of self control genuinely worked in the public interest.

For this to be credible, the ASA has to be totally independent of the business.

Neither the chairman nor the majority of ASA council members is allowed to have any involvement in advertising.

Though administrative costs are met by a levy on the business, no advertiser has any influence over ASA decisions.

Advertisers are aware it is as much in their interests as the public's to uphold advertising standards.

If you would like to know more about the ASA and the rules it seeks to enforce you can write to us at the address below for an abridged copy of the Code.

The Advertising Standards Authority.

If an advertisement is wrong, we're here to put it right.

ASA Ltd, Brook House,
Torrington Place, London WC1E 7HN.

4th Edition

The Advertising Standards Authority. Freespace Production Service.

This folder contains fifteen advertisements in various sizes to be cut out and used as artwork. The advertisements can be enlarged or reduced to fill any available space. If solid black areas are not acceptable, please lay the appropriate screen on the reversed panel.

For letterpress publications please produce blocks as required and invoice our advertising agents – Davidson Pearce Ltd., 67 Brompton Road, London SW3 1EF – quoting the publication, size of block and "ASA Freespace."

Publishers are kindly requested to restrict the reproduction of any of these advertisements to one per issue.

Issued by the ASA Freespace Production Service, c/o Davidson Pearce Limited, 67 Brompton Road, London SW3 1EF (Tel: 01-589 4595), from whom additional copies are available on request.

It's easy to complain about an advertisement. Once you know how.

One of the ways we keep a check on the advertising that appears in the press, on posters and in the cinema is by responding to consumers' complaints.

Any complaint sent to us is considered carefully and, if there's a case to answer, a full investigation is made.

If you think you've got good reason to complain about an advertisement, send off for a copy of our free leaflet.

It will tell you all you need to know to help us process your complaint as quickly as possible.

The Advertising Standards Authority. ✔
If an advertisement is wrong, we're here to put it right.

ASA Ltd, Dept 1 Brook House, Torrington Place, London WC1E 7HN

This space is donated in the interests of high standards of advertising.

It's easy to complain about advertisements. But which ones?

Every week millions of advertisements appear in print, on posters or in the cinema.

Most of them comply with the rules contained in the British Code of Advertising Practice.

But some of them break the rules and warrant your complaints.

If you're not sure about which ones they are, however, drop us a line and we'll send you an abridged copy of the Advertising Code.

Then, if an advertisement bothers you, you'll be justified in bothering us.

The Advertising Standards Authority. ✔
If an advertisement is wrong, we're here to put it right.

ASA Ltd, Dept 2 Brook House, Torrington Place, London WC1E 7HN

This space is donated in the interests of high standards of advertising.

It's easy to complain about advertisements. But which ones?

Every week millions of advertisements appear in print, on posters or in the cinema.

Most of them comply with the rules contained in the British Code of Advertising Practice.

But some of them break the rules and warrant your complaints.

If you're not sure about which ones they are, however, drop us a line and we'll send you an abridged copy of the Advertising Code.

Then, if an advertisement bothers you, you'll be justified in bothering us.

The Advertising Standards Authority. ✔
If an advertisement is wrong, we're here to put it right.

ASA Ltd, Dept 2 Brook House, Torrington Place, London WC1E 7HN

This space is donated in the interests of high standards of advertising.

It's easy to complain about an advertisement. Once you know how.

One of the ways we keep a check on the advertising that appears in the press, on posters and in the cinema is by responding to consumers' complaints.

Any complaint sent to us is considered carefully and, if there's a case to answer, a full investigation is made.

If you think you've got good reason to complain about an advertisement, send off for a copy of our free leaflet.

It will tell you all you need to know to help us process your complaint as quickly as possible.

The Advertising Standards Authority. ✔
If an advertisement is wrong, we're here to put it right.

ASA Ltd, Dept 1 Brook House, Torrington Place, London WC1E 7HN

This space is donated in the interests of high standards of advertising.

It's easy to complain about an advertisement. Once you know how.

One of the ways we keep a check on the advertising that appears in the press, on posters and in the cinema is by responding to consumers' complaints.

Any complaint sent to us is considered carefully and, if there's a case to answer, a full investigation is made.

If you think you've got good reason to complain about an advertisement, send off for a copy of our free leaflet.

It will tell you all you need to know to help us process your complaint as quickly as possible.

The Advertising Standards Authority. ✔
If an advertisement is wrong, we're here to put it right.

ASA Ltd, Dept 1 Brook House, Torrington Place, London WC1E 7HN

This space is donated in the interests of high standards of advertising.

It's easy to complain about advertisements. But which ones?

Every week millions of advertisements appear in print on posters or in the cinema.

Most of them comply with the rules contained in the British Code of Advertising Practice.

But some of them break the rules and warrant your complaints.

If you're not sure about which ones they are, however, drop us a line and we'll send you an abridged copy of the Advertising Code.

Then, if an advertisement bothers you, you'll be justified in bothering us.

The Advertising Standards Authority.
If an advertisement is wrong, we're here to put it right. ✓

ASA Ltd, Dept 2 Brook House, Torrington Place, London WC1E 7HN

This space is donated in the interests of high standards of advertising.

If an advertisement is wrong we're here to put it right.

If you see an advertisement in the press, in print, on posters or in the cinema which you find unacceptable, write to us at the address below.

The Advertising Standards Authority. ✓
ASA Ltd, Dept 3 Brook House, Torrington Place, London WC1E 7HN

If an advertisement is wrong we're here to put it right.

If you see an advertisement in the press, in print, on posters or in the cinema which you find unacceptable, write to us at the address below.

The Advertising Standards Authority. ✓
ASA Ltd, Dept 3 Brook House, Torrington Place, London WC1E 7HN

If an advertisement is wrong we're here to put it right.

If you see an advertisement in the press, in print, on posters or in the cinema which you find unacceptable, write to us at the address below.

The Advertising Standards Authority. ✓
ASA Ltd, Dept 3 Brook House, Torrington Place, London WC1E 7HN

If an advertisement is wrong we're here to put it right.

If you see an advertisement in the press, in print, on posters or in the cinema which you find unacceptable, write to us at the address below.

The Advertising Standards Authority. ✓
ASA Ltd, Dept 3 Brook House, Torrington Place, London WC1E 7HN

It's easy to complain about advertisements. But which ones?

Every week millions of advertisements appear in print, on posters or in the cinema. Most of them comply with the rules contained in the British Code of Advertising Practice.

But some of them break the rules and warrant your complaints.

If you're not sure about which ones they are, however, drop us a line and we'll send you an abridged copy of the Advertising Code. Then, if an advertisement bothers you, you'll be justified in bothering us.

The Advertising Standards Authority. ✓
If an advertisement is wrong, we're here to put it right.
ASA Ltd, Dept 2 Brook House, Torrington Place, London WC1E 7HN

This space is donated in the interests of high standards of advertising.

It's easy to complain about an advertisement. Once you know how.

One of the ways we keep a check on the advertising that appears in the press, on posters and in the cinema is by responding to consumers' complaints.

Any complaint sent to us is considered carefully and, if there's a case to answer, a full investigation is made.

If you think you've got good reason to complain about an advertisement, send off for a copy of our free leaflet.

It will tell you all you need to know to help us process your complaint as quickly as possible.

The Advertising Standards Authority. ✔
If an advertisement is wrong, we're here to put it right.

ASA Ltd. Dept 1 Brook House, Torrington Place, London WC1E 7HN

This space is donated in the interests of high standards of advertising

If an advertisement is wrong we're here to put it right.

If you see an advertisement in the press, in print, on posters or in the cinema which you find unacceptable, write to us at the address below.

The Advertising Standards Authority. ✔

ASA Ltd. Dept 1
Brook House, Torrington Place,
London WC1E 7HN

It's easy to complain about advertisements. But which ones?

Every week millions of advertisements appear in print, on posters or in the cinema.

Most of them comply with the rules contained in the British Code of Advertising Practice.

But some of them break the rules and warrant your complaints.

If you're not sure about which ones they are, however, drop us a line and we'll send you an abridged copy of the Advertising Code.

Then, if an advertisement bothers you, you'll be justified in bothering us.

The Advertising Standards Authority. ✔
If an advertisement is wrong, we're here to put it right.

ASA Ltd. Dept 2 Brook House, Torrington Place, London WC1E 7HN

This space is donated in the interests of high standards of advertising.

It's easy to complain about advertisements. But which ones?

Every week millions of advertisements appear in print on posters or in the cinema.

Most of them comply with the rules contained in the British Code of Advertising Practice.

But some of them break the rules and warrant your complaints.

If you're not sure about which ones they are, however, drop us a line and we'll send you an abridged copy of the Advertising Code.

Then, if an advertisement bothers you, you'll be justified in bothering us.

The Advertising Standards Authority. ✔
If an advertisement is wrong, we're here to put it right.

ASA Ltd. Dept 2 Brook House, Torrington Place, London WC1E 7HN

This space is donated in the interests of high standards of advertising.

Index

About the Authors

Gordon E. Miracle has been professor of Advertising at Michigan State University since 1966. He served as chairman of the Department of Advertising from 1974 to 1980 and also as chairman of the Ph.D. program in mass media in 1973–74. In addition to his earlier faculty positions at the University of Wisconsin and the University of Michigan, Dr. Miracle has been visiting professor at the North European Management Institute in Norway. In 1985 he received an Advertising Educational Foundation Fellowship that he served at McCann-Erickson Hakuhodo and was a Fulbright Research Scholar at Waseda University in Tokyo. He has been the recipient of numerous grants and fellowships, from the Marsteller Foundation, the Ford Foundation, and others. Also he has served for many years as a consultant to industry and government in the United States and abroad.

Professor Miracle is the author, coauthor, or editor of seven books, including *Management of International Advertising, International Marketing Management,* and *European Regulation of Advertising*. He has also written more than fifty shorter professional and scholarly publications. His biography has appeared in *Who's Who in America* and *Who's Who in the World* since the 1980/1981 editions.

Terence Nevett holds a Ph.D. from the University of London, and the British professional qualification M.CAM. After working in advertising and marketing in London he entered academic life, first at the College for the Distributive Trades and subsequently as principal lecturer at the Polytechnic of the South Bank. In 1984 he was named Procter and Gamble Distinguished Professor by Michigan State University, and was visiting professor there the following year. Since 1985 he has been professor of marketing at Central Michigan University, Mount Pleasant. Dr. Nevett has presented conference papers and given many advertising industry seminars on the subject of regulation, and his articles have appeared in such journals as the *International Journal of Advertising* and the *Journal of Marketing Education*. He is a contributor to the *Dictionary of Business Biography*, has a chapter on "Advertising and Editorial Integrity" in *The Press in English Society* (edited by M. Harris and Alan Lee), and is the author of *Advertising in Britain: A History*. He is also on the Board of Governors of the History of Advertising Trust.